Examining Speaking

Research and practice in assessing second language speaking

D1121161

Examining Speaking

Research and practice in assessing second language speaking

Edited by Lynda Taylor
Consultant to University of Cambridge ESOL Examinations

CAMBRIDGE UNIVERSITY PRESS
Cambridge, New York, Melbourne, Madrid, Cape Town,
Singapore, São Paulo, Delhi, Tokyo, Mexico City

Cambridge University Press
The Edinburgh Building, Cambridge CB2 8RU, UK

www.cambridge.org
Information on this title: www.cambridge.org/9780521736701

First published 2011

Printed in the United Kingdom at the University Press, Cambridge

A catalogue record for this publication is available from the British Library

Library of Congress Cataloging-in-Publication data
    Examining speaking : research and practice in assessing second
language speaking / edited by Lynda Taylor
    p. cm - (Studies in language testing ; v. 30)
Includes bibliographical references and index
ISBN 978-0-521-73670-1
1. Language and languages-Ability testing. 2. Language and
Languages-Study and teaching. I. Taylor, Lynda B.
    P53.4.E98 2011
    418.0028'7--dc23

ISBN 978-0-521-73670-1

Contents

Abbreviations

ACTFL	American Council for the Teaching of Foreign Languages
AERA	American Educational Research Association
ALTE	Association of Language Testers in Europe
AOG	Assessment & Operations Group
APA	American Psychological Association
AUA	Assessment Use Argument
AWL	Academic Word List
BC	British Council
BEC	Business English Certificates
BULATS	Business Language Testing Service
CAE	Certificate in Advanced English (Cambridge English: Advanced)
CASE	Cambridge Assessment of Spoken English
CB	Computer Based
CBT	Computer Based Testing
C–C	Candidate–Candidate
CEF	Common European Framework
CEFR	Common European Framework of Reference for Languages
CELS	Certificates in English Language Skills
CELTA	Certificate in Teaching English to speakers of other languages
CET	College English Test
CIEP	Centre International d'Etudes Pédagogiques
CIS	Candidate Information Sheet
CLA	Communicative Language Ability
CoE	Council of Europe
COPI	Computer Oral Proficiency Interview
CPE	Certificate of Proficiency in English (Cambridge English: Proficiency)
CRELLA	Centre for Research in English Language Learning and Assessment
CUP	Cambridge University Press
DELTA	Diploma in English Language Teaching to Adults
DIALANG	Diagnostic Language (Assessment)
DIF	differential item functioning
EALTA	European Association of Language Testing and Assessment
EAP	English for Academic Purposes

EAQUALS	European Association for Quality Language Services
ECD	Evidence-Centered Design
EFA	Exploratory Factor Analysis
EFL	English as a Foreign Language
ESL	English as a Second Language
ESOL	English for Speakers of Other Languages
ESP	English for Special Purposes
ETS	Educational Testing Service
FACETS	Multi-faceted Rasch Measurement analysis program
FCE	First Certificate in English (Cambridge English: First)
FSI	Foreign Service Institute
GENOVA	Generalisability theory analysis program
iBTOEFL	Internet Based Test of English as a Foreign Language
ICFE	International Certificate in Financial English
IDP	International Development Program
IELTS	International English Language Testing System
IIS	IELTS Impact Study
ILEC	International Legal English Certificate
ILTA	International Language Testing Association
IOE	Instructions to Oral Examiners
ISE	Instructions to Speaking Examiners
ISO	International Organization for Standardization
IWG	Item Writer Guidelines
JLTA	Japan Language Testing Association
KET	Key English Test (Cambridge English: Key)
L1	First Language
L2	Second Language
LCE	Lower Certificate in English
LIBS	Local Item Banking System
LMS	Lower Main Suite
MFRM	multi-faceted Rasch measurement
MPRs	Minimum Professional Requirements
NCLB	No Child Left Behind Act
NCME	National Council on Measurement in Education
OPI	Oral Proficiency Interview
PET	Preliminary English Test (Cambridge English: Preliminary)
PL2000	Progetto Lingue 2000
PRC	People's Republic of China
PSL	Professional Support Leader
PTE	Pearson Test of English
QA	Quality Assurance
Q&A	Question and answer
QPP	Question Paper Production

RITCP	Registration, Induction, Training, Certification, Performance
RTL	Regional Team Leader
SE	Speaking Examiner
SEM	Structural Equation Modelling
SETC	Speaking Examiner Trainer/Co-ordinator
SIA	Social Impact Assessment
SiLT	Studies in Language Testing
SLA	Second language acquisition
SOPI	Simulated Oral Proficiency Interview
SPEAK	Institutional version of TSE
TBL	task-based learning
TESOL	Teaching English to Speakers of Other Languages
TKT	Teaching Knowledge Test
TL	Target Language
TL	Team Leader
TLU	Target Language Use
TOEFL	Test of English as a Foreign Language
TSE	Test of Spoken English
TTCs	Test taker characteristics
TWE	Test of Written English
UCLES	University of Cambridge Local Examinations Syndicate
UMS	Upper Main Suite (i.e. FCE, CAE and CPE)
VOIP	Voice over Internet Protocol
VPA	Verbal Protocol Analysis
VRIP	Validity, Reliability, Impact, Practicality
WEAVER	A model of word-form encoding in speech production
YLE	Young Learners English Tests

Series Editors' note

Examining Speaking is the third volume in the *Studies in Language Testing* (SiLT) series that addresses the approach used by Cambridge ESOL in the assessment of language skills, the first being SiLT 26, *Examining Writing* by Shaw and Weir (2007) and the second being SiLT 29, *Examining Reading* by Khalifa and Weir (2009). This volume sets out to describe and evaluate how Cambridge ESOL tests different levels of speaking in English as a Second Language across the range of examinations it offers spanning the Reference Levels of the Common European Framework of Reference (CEFR) from A2 to C2, through focusing largely on the five General English examinations in the Cambridge ESOL Main Suite (*KET, PET, FCE, CAE, CPE*, recently rebranded as *Cambridge English: Key; Preliminary; First; Advanced;* and *Proficiency*). As with the earlier *Examining Writing* and *Examining Reading* volumes, it does so by presenting an explicit framework that structures the approach to validation according to a number of dimensions or parameters. It utilises the same theoretical framework which was originally proposed by Weir (2005a) and which seeks to take account of both the aspects of cognition, related to the mental processes the individual needs to engage in order to address a task, and the features of language use in context that affect the ways in which a task is addressed. The authors also look at the practical assessment issues related to the marking and scoring of speaking tests. As with *Examining Writing* and *Examining Reading* therefore, this volume explores the triangular relationship that emerges between three critical internal dimensions of language testing tasks – the test taker's *cognitive abilities*, the *context* in which the task is performed and the *scoring process*. Set alongside these are the twin external dimensions of consequential validity and criterion-related validity.

Testing speaking 1913–2012

Cambridge ESOL has been involved in the assessment of speaking skills ever since it launched its first English language examination in 1913. Since that time we have seen a significant development in our understanding of the Speaking construct from its early conceptualisation as an integrated skill, assessed via dictation, reading aloud tasks and conversation, through to the approaches documented in this volume.

When the Certificate of Proficiency in English (CPE) was introduced in 1913, speaking featured as a skill in its own right with a separate Oral

Paper. The history and most recent revision of CPE is well documented in SiLT 15, *Continuity and Innovation: Revising the Cambridge Proficiency in English Examination 1913–2002* (Weir and Milanovic (Eds) 2003). The volume explains how the approach to the design of CPE in 1913 was based on *The Practical Study of Languages* (Sweet 1899) and candidates spent over 12 hours on a demanding set of activities that included translation to and from English, an essay on a topic such as Elizabethan travel and discovery, an English literature paper, English phonetics, dictation, reading aloud and conversation. Reading aloud, dictation and conversation formed a separate Oral Paper in the 1913 examination and in addition there was a substantial paper in Phonetics.

1913 examination

(i) Written: (a) Translation from English into French or German 2 hours

(b) Translation from French or German into English, and questions on English Grammar 2½ hours

(c) English Essay 2 hours

(d) English Literature (The paper on English Language and Literature [Group A, Subject 1] in the Higher Local Examination) 3 hours

(e) English Phonetics 1½ hours

(ii) Oral: Dictation ½ hour

Reading Aloud and Conversation ½ hour

A century ago, therefore, language learners wishing to certificate their command of English as a foreign or second language faced 'an extremely demanding test of their abilities' (Weir 2003:2), in which the testing of spoken language ability, both directly and indirectly, was integral to assessing their overall English language proficiency. Since 1913, most new Cambridge ESOL examinations have followed the model originally set by CPE and they have included a direct Speaking test as an integral component of the language test battery, alongside tests of Reading, Writing, Grammar, Vocabulary, and later Listening. (For more details see accounts of other Cambridge tests in Hawkey 2004a, 2009, and O'Sullivan 2006.)

Despite his faith in the validity of the oral component, Jack Roach, Assistant Secretary at the University of Cambridge Local Examinations Syndicate (UCLES) 1925–45, was keenly aware of the challenges that direct speaking assessment poses for testers, and he was among the first language testers to research some of the complex issues surrounding the face-to-face format. As early as 1945 he produced a report entitled *Some Problems of Oral Examinations in Modern Languages: An Experimental Approach Based on the Cambridge Examinations in English for Foreign Students*. Roach was particularly interested in how to describe levels of L2 speaking performance, and how to standardise Oral Examiners so that they rate candidates in a fair and consistent manner – questions which continue to exercise language testers today. Roach's work can therefore justifiably be regarded as both ground-breaking and ahead of its time.

The work of the Council of Europe in its Modern Languages programme, the emergence of the Threshold level, and the rise of the communicative language teaching movement all happened in the 1970s and 1980s and impacted on the Cambridge approach to language testing. The 1975 revisions saw CPE taking a shape that in its broad outline is familiar to the candidate of today. The Listening and Speaking tests in particular represented major developments on the 1966 revision and echoed the burgeoning interest in communicative language teaching in the 1970s, with its increasing concern for language in use as against language as a system for study. The 1970s saw a change from teaching language as a system to teaching it as a means of communication as detailed in Widdowson's 1978 volume *Teaching Language as Communication.*

An important study carried out in the late 1980s was also to have quite a powerful influence on the shape of things to come. Bachman, Davidson, Ryan and Choi (1995) carried out a Cambridge-sponsored study entitled *An Investigation into the Comparability of Two Tests of English as a Foreign Language* (SiLT 1). While ostensibly looking at the comparison between Cambridge's First Certificate in English (FCE) and the Test of English as a Foreign Language (TOEFL), offered by Educational Testing Service (ETS), in order to establish an empirical link between the level systems of each examination, this study actually ended up providing an in-depth critique of the Cambridge approach with specific reference to the then well developed and documented psychometrically oriented approach as demonstrated by the TOEFL. Significant issues in relation to reliability and validity emerged for the Cambridge tests which were addressed vigorously with the 1996 release of the FCE and subsequent release of CPE in 2002.

Partly as a result of Bachman et al's study a much sharper focus on test construct definition and validation emerged. Where test construct had had to be pieced together *post hoc* from test specifications in earlier releases of FCE and CPE, there were now explicit statements on test construct. The Speaking paper in particular, underwent fairly radical revision and its construct was defined as 'Understanding the propositional, functional and sociolinguistic meanings at word, phrase, sentence or discourse levels and of Speaking outcomes relevant to FCE takers (i.e. gist, specific information, detail, main idea, deduced information).' Measures were put in place not only to develop test content with systematic reference to the underlying construct but also to validate the nature of that construct. Additionally, the resulting work on standardising the test format and the development of the interlocutor frame were of major importance and instrumental in improving the reliability of the Speaking tests across the Main Suite.

During the early 1990s, following the establishment of the Evaluation Unit (later to become the Research and Validation Group), Cambridge ESOL embarked upon an extensive and long-term research and validation agenda associated with its approach to speaking assessment. Over the past two decades outcomes from this research have informed the revision of existing examinations (e.g. PET, FCE and CPE) as well as the development of new examinations (e.g. KET and CAE). As the number of Cambridge ESOL's level-based tests grew and as a suite of coherent levels began to emerge, work also began in the 1990s to develop a Common Scale for Speaking which would help test users interpret levels of performance in the Cambridge tests from beginner to advanced, identify typical performance qualities at particular levels, and locate performance in one examination against performance in another. At around the same time, considerable resources were invested by Cambridge to develop a quality assurance and management system to support the growing cadre of examiners for its face-to-face Speaking tests worldwide. The Team Leader (TL) System, which began in 1994, was developed as a network of professionals working on Cambridge's Main Suite examinations; various levels of overlapping responsibility (speaking examiner, Team Leader, Senior Team Leader) combined with a set of procedures that laid down minimum professional requirements for examiner recruitment, induction, training, co-ordination, monitoring and evaluation. In 1999 Cambridge ESOL established the Performance Testing Unit, under the leadership of Lynda Taylor, with a specific brief to (i) further develop the Team Leader System and extend its quality assurance remit to cover all the Cambridge Speaking tests, and (ii) drive and co-ordinate research in the area of performance testing, both speaking and writing. Over the past decade much of the research undertaken by Cambridge into many different aspects of speaking and writing assessment has appeared in the public domain, often presented at academic conferences or published in peer review journals.

Since the mid-1990s we have also seen the emergence of the *Common European Framework of Reference for Languages: Learning, Teaching Assessment* (Council of Europe 2001) which encourages examination providers to map their certification to the Framework. This volume examines how Cambridge has approached this task in significant depth when exploring criterion-related validity. The approach taken by Cambridge seeks not simply to establish the relationship with the Framework through a one-off study, but, more importantly, to deploy a methodology that ensures a long-term and continually verifiable relationship which is surely in the overall best interests of test users.

Skills assessment at Cambridge is now underpinned more formally than ever by a validation framework based on Weir (2005a) and building on the work of Bachman (1990) which informed validation activities in the 1990s, as well as the VRIP (Validity, Reliability, Impact, Practicality) approach developed by Cambridge during the 1990s. The approach outlined in this volume not only allows Cambridge to determine where current examinations are performing satisfactorily in relation to a range of relevant validity parameters, it also provides the basis for improvement and the construction of an ongoing research agenda. It provides an important benchmark against which test developers can evaluate the effectiveness of their respective approaches and it offers test users a model of what to expect from responsible examination providers.

The structure of the volume

Examining Speaking follows a similar structure to that which was successfully adopted for its sister publications *Examining Writing* (Shaw and Weir 2007) and *Examining Reading* (Khalifa and Weir 2009). The outline shape closely follows their organisation with separate chapters on *test taker characteristics; cognitive validity; context validity; scoring validity; consequential validity;* and *criterion-related validity*. Apart from the opening and closing chapters, each of the other six chapters takes one component of the socio-cognitive validation framework to examine it in detail with reference to the Cambridge ESOL Speaking tests, i.e. discussion of issues arising in the *research* literature on each component part is followed by consideration of Cambridge ESOL *practice* in that area.

There is, nonetheless, a significant difference in approach between the two earlier volumes and this one. While *Examining Writing* and *Examining Reading* were primarily co-authored publications, *Examining Speaking* is an edited collection of chapters from a team of contributors. All the chapter authors are acknowledged specialists in language teaching, learning and assessment, many in the specific field of speaking testing and assessment. In addition, they have direct experience of working with the Cambridge Speaking tests from a number of different perspectives (test design and development, test writing and administration, exam preparation and materials development, oral examining, test validation and research). As a result, they are able to combine their extensive theoretical knowledge with practical application and expertise in these areas, and so provide valuable insights into the complex endeavour or ecology that constitutes the assessment of spoken language proficiency. In doing this they draw on input from other informants as explained in the opening chapter.

Chapter 1 offers an introduction that sets the scene for what follows in the rest of the volume. It explicates the audience for the volume, its intended purpose and the ground that will be covered. It also details a short historical perspective on the tradition of assessing speaking at Cambridge. The methodological appropriacy in the volume is explained and the multiple voices appearing in the volume are discussed.

In Chapter 2 on *test taker characteristics* Barry O'Sullivan and Tony Green discuss the test taker who stands at the heart of any assessment event. They review the general research literature in this area and report on research undertaken into Cambridge ESOL tests to demonstrate how the tests take account of key test taker characteristics. This covers not only general features of the candidature cohort that need to be reflected in tests at different proficiency levels, e.g. age, but also the ways in which test taker characteristics arising from special needs or disabilities on the part of individual candidates are catered for through test accommodations or modifications.

Chapter 3 on *cognitive validity*, by John Field, reviews what the theoretical and empirical research to date tells us about the nature of speaking, particularly the cognitive processing involved, both in a first and second language. He examines the processing involved in the Cambridge ESOL Speaking test tasks across different proficiency levels and evaluates the extent to which this can be claimed to replicate or reflect 'real-world' processing when speaking in the world beyond the test.

In Chapter 4 Evelina Galaczi and Angela ffrench examine in detail the many *context validity* parameters, or contextual variables, that have been recognised in the research literature to impact on spoken language performance. They go on to analyse the contextual variables that characterise content and tasks used in the Cambridge Speaking tests in order to understand how these are differentiated across proficiency levels. Administrative procedures associated with the production and delivery of Cambridge ESOL's Speaking tests are described in detail in Appendices C and D of the volume.

Chapter 5 by Lynda Taylor and Evelina Galaczi focuses on *scoring validity*, exploring the many factors associated with the rating of speaking tests, including assessment criteria, rating scales, rater training and standardisation. The available research literature in these areas is reviewed, and some of the research undertaken by Cambridge ESOL over the past 20 years is highlighted. The policy and procedures which have emerged as a result of this ongoing research and validation programme in relation to undertaking large-scale standardised speaking assessment are presented.

Chapter 6 by Roger Hawkey considers the *consequential validity* of speaking tests, exploring issues of test washback and impact to establish where and how these play out within the complex process of validating high-stakes international examinations. He surveys Cambridge ESOL's research initiatives and studies undertaken to help it understand the consequential validity of its exams, especially as it relates to testing speaking ability.

Chapter 7 by Hanan Khalifa and Angeliki Salamoura examines issues of *criterion-related validity*, in particular the need to establish comparability across different tests and between different forms of the same test, as well as with external standards. They describe and discuss how Cambridge ESOL has addressed this for its own tests, and how the board has linked, or maintained a pre-existing link, between its examinations and the reference levels of internationally accepted frameworks such as the CEFR and the ALTE frameworks.

Finally, in Chapter 8 Lynda Taylor and Cyril Weir draw together the threads of the volume, summarising the findings from applying the validity framework to a set of Cambridge Speaking tests. They reflect upon how far the tests in their current incarnation operationalise contemporary thinking and research evidence about the speaking ability construct and they consider where refinements might be appropriate in future revision projects. They also make recommendations for further research and development which would benefit not only Cambridge ESOL but also the wider testing community.

Michael Milanovic and Cyril J Weir
Cambridge – March 2011

Acknowledgements

This volume has taken much longer to reach final publication than originally hoped or anticipated, for several reasons. Though the project started at about the same time as its companion volume, *Examining Reading* (published in 2009), changes in internal staffing and the re-prioritisation of various projects within Cambridge ESOL meant that the scope and authorship of the volume had to be constantly revised in response to evolving circumstances. In addition, the sheer complexity of undertaking large-scale face-to-face-speaking assessment as it is operationalised by Cambridge ESOL meant that there was much ground to be covered and many stakeholders to be consulted in order to ensure that a comprehensive and accurate picture of both theory and practice could be compiled and presented through this volume. For all these reasons, there were times when it seemed as though the volume might never see the light of day. Indeed, assigning it a number in the *Studies in Language Testing* series proved to be premature as it turned out, and thus a mixed blessing!

Happily, *Examining Speaking* has finally reached its place on the bookshelf alongside its sister publications *Examining Writing* and *Examining Reading*. As was true for its older siblings, there exists a long list of friends and colleagues to whom I am indebted for their generous contribution in bringing this volume to fruition. At the top of the list must be the individual chapter contributors: Angela ffrench, John Field, Evelina Galaczi, Anthony Green, Roger Hawkey, Hanan Khalifa, Barry O'Sullivan, Angeliki Salamoura, and Cyril Weir. Without their professional expertise, clarity of expression, patience and perseverance this volume could never have made it into print.

Special thanks must also go to Dr Glenn Fulcher (University of Leicester) and Dr Sari Luoma (Ballard and Tighe), both of whom are acknowledged experts in the field having published their own contributions on the assessment of spoken language ability. They kindly agreed to review the complete manuscript once it had been assembled and their insightful comments and constructive criticism enabled us to revise and refine the final version in important ways before it went into production. Their long-established expertise, sound advice and willing collaboration have, I believe, contributed significantly to the quality of this volume.

I am extremely grateful to the large number of people from academic and practitioner communities both within and beyond ESOL who have provided valuable input to or feedback on individual chapters. Dr Ardeshir Geranpayeh, Dr Andrew Somers, Dr Evelina Galaczi and Roumen Marinov (of the Research and Validation Group) provided data analysis for and critically reviewed Chapter 2 on test taker characteristics. Janet Bojan, Angela ffrench, Chris Hubbard and Ruth Shuter (of the Assessment and Operations Group) also played a key role in ensuring the accuracy of data and information presented in this chapter. Further insights on Chapter 2 were provided by John Field. Chapter 3 on cognitive validity received valuable input from Kathy Gude (a long-serving and highly experienced Chair and Professional Support Leader for Cambridge's Speaking tests). For Chapter 4 on context validity, sincere thanks are due to Dr Norbert Schmitt (University of Nottingham) for his analysis of lexical resources in some of the Main Suite Speaking tests, as well as to Kathy Gude, Petrina Cliff and Nick Kenny (Chairs of the CAE, FCE and PET Main Suite Speaking papers) for their critical review of the overall chapter content. Chapter 5 benefitted greatly from the input of several longstanding and experienced Professional Support Leaders for the Cambridge Speaking tests: Sue Gilbert (Switzerland), Dr David Horner (France/Luxembourg) and Adriana Cánepa (Argentina/ Chile). Their diligent and attentive reviews of chapter sections relating to their respective areas of professional activity were invaluable. Finally, thanks must go to Chris Hubbard, Claire McCauley and Laura Mungovan (Customer Services) who significantly contributed to the compilation and checking of the organisational policy and procedures described in Appendices C and D. This volume could not have been completed without the co-operation of all those mentioned above. Their expertise and the time they have given from their busy schedules is greatly appreciated.

As ever, Professor Cyril Weir (University of Bedfordshire) has maintained a close involvement in the development of the entire volume throughout its long gestation. As one of the Series Editors for *Studies in Language Testing* and as co-author of *Examining Speaking*'s older siblings, his editorial guidance, advisory feedback and good humour have been a great source of support and encouragement, enabling me to stay on track and reach the finishing line.

Finally, I would like to acknowledge the support and encouragement of Dr Michael Milanovic (Cambridge ESOL Chief Executive). Since he first joined Cambridge ESOL in 1989, his interest in and enthusiasm for Cambridge's longstanding commitment to the assessment of second language speaking proficiency is a matter of record. Ultimately, it is his vision which has made the publication of this and of other volumes in the series a reality.

To all of the above, and to any others I have failed to mention, I extend my sincere thanks and appreciation.

Lynda Taylor
March 2011

Notes on contributors

Angela ffrench holds an MEd in Language Testing from the University of Bristol, and an MA from the University of Cambridge. Having been involved in teaching and testing English for 20 years, both in the state and private sectors, Angela joined Cambridge ESOL in 1991. She has been involved in all aspects of developing and administering tests and assessment criteria, in the training of item writers, in pretesting and analysing test material, and in the grading of examinations, but has always had a particular interest in the testing of speaking. Angela is currently Assistant Director in the Assessment and Operations department of Cambridge ESOL, with overall responsibility for IELTS and Cambridge Young Learners English Tests.

John Field taught language psychology and child language development at the University of Reading (UK); he also teaches the cognitive aspects of second language acquisition at the Faculty of Education in Cambridge. He has a long-standing interest in the processes that underlie first and second language skills. He researches and writes on second language listening in particular and his recent book *Listening in the Language Classroom* (Cambridge University Press 2008) proposes alternatives to the traditional comprehension method used for listening practice. In another life, John was an ELT materials writer, syllabus designer and teacher trainer, working especially in Belgium, Spain, Saudi Arabia and China. He wrote two series for BBC English By Radio and was an inspector of private language schools.

Evelina Galaczi is a Senior Research and Validation Manager at University of Cambridge ESOL Examinations. She holds an EdD degree in Applied Linguistics from Teachers College, Columbia University (USA) and has extensive experience as an ELT teacher, teacher-trainer and programme administrator. Her current role at Cambridge involves providing ongoing operational and quality assurance support for the Speaking component of Cambridge ESOL examinations as well as publishing research on these products. She is also involved in providing validation and research support to the Teaching Awards suite of examinations. Her research interests include performance assessement with specific reference to the testing of speaking, discourse analysis and qualitative approaches to assessment research.

Anthony Green is Reader in Language Assessment at the University of Bedfordshire (UK). He is the author of *IELTS Washback in Context* (2007) and *Language Functions Revisited* (2011) and has published widely on language assessment. He is involved in managing funded research projects, supervising research students and carrying out language testing consultancies worldwide. He has extensive experience of all stages of test development and delivery including work as a test designer, item writer and examiner for tests of speaking skills. Current research and consultancy interests include the relationship between assessment and learning, especially in relation to the Common European Framework of Reference (CEFR), the assessment of literacy skills and practical test development.

Roger Hawkey has many years of experience in English language teaching, teacher education, course design, and assessment projects in Africa, Asia and Europe. He is now a consultant on testing with Cambridge ESOL and a Visiting Professor at the Centre for Research in English Language Learning and Assessment (CRELLA), University of Bedfordshire (UK). He has published widely in applied linguistics, language teaching and assessment, including three volumes in Cambridge's *Studies in Language Testing* series – *A Modular Approach to Testing English Language Skills* (2004), *Impact Theory and Practice* (2006) and *Examining FCE and CAE* (2009).

Hanan Khalifa is an Assistant Director leading on Research at University of Cambridge ESOL Examinations. She holds an MA in Applied Linguistics and a PhD in Language Testing. Hanan is widely experienced in educational assessment and program evaluation, having given plenaries, workshops and courses on language learning, teaching and testing at international events. She has carried out consultancies for international agencies on curriculum design, test development, capacity building, measuring institutional change and school management excellence. Recent research projects include: alignment to international standards, bilingual education, and assessment impact. Her 2009 book – *Examining Reading* with Cyril Weir – is a standard text on Association of Language Testers in Europe (ALTE) training programmes and on certain MA/MPhil programmes in the UK.

Barry O'Sullivan is Professor of Applied Linguistics, Director of the Centre for Language Assessment Research (CLARe) and Assistant Dean for Academic Enterprise at Roehampton University, London (UK). He has written two books on language testing, *Issues in Testing Business English* (2006) and *Modelling Performance in Tests of Spoken Language* (2008). He has published widely in the area and has presented his work at conferences around the world. He is active in language testing globally, working with ministries, universities and examination boards. Recent projects include developing affordable tests for Mexico, CEFR-linking projects in the UK, Mexico and Turkey and a major international placement test for the British Council.

Angeliki Salamoura is a Principal Research and Validation Manager at University of Cambridge ESOL Examinations. She holds a PhD in Second

Language Processing (Psycholinguistics) from the University of Cambridge (UK), and has a number of publications in this field. She has worked as a postdoctoral researcher on English language processing in the same university where she developed a strong background in quantitative research. She also has experience as an EFL teacher overseas. Her current role at Cambridge ESOL involves working on state sector projects, on the development and validation of bespoke assessment products and on CEFR-related topics. Her research interests include methodological approaches to linking examinations and maintaining alignment to the CEFR, quantitative research methodology and bilingual/second language processing.

Lynda Taylor is a Consultant to University of Cambridge ESOL Examinations and formerly Assistant Director of the Research and Validation Group there. She holds an MPhil and PhD in Applied Linguistics and Language Assessment from the University of Cambridge (UK). She has over 25 years' experience of the theoretical and practical issues involved in L2 testing and assessment, and has provided expert assistance for test development projects worldwide. She regularly teaches, writes and presents on language testing matters and has co-edited and contributed to several of the volumes in Cambridge's *Studies in Language Testing* series, including *IELTS Collected Papers* (2007), *Multilingualism and Assessment* (2008), *Language Testing Matters* (2009) and *Aligning Tests with the CEFR* (2010).

Cyril J Weir holds the Powdrill Chair in English Language Acquisition at the University of Bedfordshire (UK) and is Guest Professor at Shanghai Jiao Tong University, PRC. He has taught short courses and carried out consultancies in language testing, evaluation and curriculum renewal in over 50 countries worldwide. He has published many books on language testing, including *Language Testing and Validation: an evidence-based approach* (2005), *Examining Writing* (2007) and *Examining Reading* (2009). He is also joint Series Editor of *Studies in Language Testing*. Current interests include academic literacy and test validation.

1 Introduction

Lynda Taylor
Consultant to Cambridge ESOL

The context for the volume

Examining Speaking stands as the third in a series of volumes designed to explore the constructs underpinning the testing of English language skills. The specific focus in this volume is on the testing of second language speaking ability. The title is a companion to two earlier construct-focused volumes in the series, *Examining Writing* by Shaw and Weir (2007) and *Examining Reading* by Khalifa and Weir (2009). A fourth volume – *Examining Listening* – is in preparation at the time of writing and its publication will complete a set of four volumes focusing on the four skills as they have been traditionally conceptualised and operationalised by the language testing and assessment community over many years.

This fourfold categorisation of language proficiency (i.e. according to the skills of reading, writing, listening and speaking) has been adopted as the organising principle behind the series because it continues to occupy a central role in the activities of examination boards and other language test providers. However, some consideration is given to integrated skills testing, for example, reading into writing in summary tasks in the reading volume, and reading as input into writing tasks in the writing volume. Some descriptive frameworks choose to compartmentalise overall language proficiency according to dimensions or skill-sets other than the traditional quartet, e.g. enabling skills (such as lexis and grammar, etc.), or they focus instead on integrated skills (listening/ speaking, reading into writing). Interestingly, the *Common European Framework of Reference for Languages: Learning, teaching, assessment* (Council of Europe 2001) proposes several different ways of categorising language proficiency: one approach subdivides overall proficiency into Speaking/ Writing/Understanding (with Understanding being used to cover Reading and Listening); an alternative approach conceptualises proficiency according to Receptive/Productive/Interactive dimensions (in this case Speaking can be either Productive or Interactive); and a third approach adds a further skill of Mediation. In light of this, the four volumes, each with their dominant focus on a single language skill, are not intended to offer the definitive or last word on approaches to describing language proficiency for assessment purposes. As the language testing profession continues to reconceptualise and expand its understanding of the complex interaction of skills making up language proficiency, it is always possible that additional construct-oriented volumes will be added to the *Studies in Language Testing* series in the future.

Given its function as part of a coherent set of skills-focused volumes, *Examining Speaking* not surprisingly covers some of the ground already mapped out by its predecessors, *Examining Writing* and *Examining Reading*. A strong family resemblance will be discernible between the volumes, in terms of both format and approach. The theoretical framework for validating language examinations first outlined in Weir (2005a) remains the springboard for reflecting upon our understanding and conceptualisation of the speaking ability construct for assessment purposes. The Cambridge ESOL examinations are once again taken as the practical context for undertaking a critical evaluation of Speaking tests ranging across different proficiency levels, enabling us to examine how the theoretical framework for validation can be operationalised in practice and with what outcomes. As in previous volumes, each chapter closely scrutinises Cambridge practice in terms of the particular component of the framework under review. Although each volume replicates the approach of its predecessors to some degree, it also seeks to build upon and extend the earlier work reported in the series, bringing fresh and novel insights into the process of construct definition and operationalisation for the particular skill of interest. It thus allows Weir's original (2005a) theoretical framework to be developed and refined in light of the experience of applying it in practice.

It is only appropriate at this point to acknowledge the existence of other important frameworks and models that are available to language testers and examination boards. These include Evidence-Centered Design (ECD) as proposed by Mislevy, Steinberg and Almond (2002, 2003; see also Mislevy, Almond and Lukas 2003), and Assessment Use Argument (AUA), as set out by Bachman (2005) and Bachman and Palmer (2010). Other test providers have found these to be an accessible and fruitful way of guiding their practical test design and validation, as demonstrated by Chapelle, Enwright and Jamieson (2008). However, Cambridge ESOL has found the socio-cognitive model, first offered by Weir in 2005 and later refined through the experience of applying it to operational tests, to match well with the kinds of tests the examination board produces, addressing the validation questions that arise and providing some of the answers that are needed. The model has proved to be both theoretically sound and practically useful over a number of years in relation to a variety of different examinations produced by Cambridge ESOL and for this reason is used as the framework for description and analysis in this and previous volumes.

The intended audience for the volume

The intended audience for the volume is primarily the constituency of professional language testers who are directly involved in the practical assessment of second language speaking ability. This growing constituency around the world typically includes staff working for examination boards and testing agencies at regional, national and/or international level, as well as those working within education ministries whose remit is to advise on the development of assessment policy or the implementation of examination reform programmes. In an age where public institutions such as examination boards and related organisations are increasingly called to account for how and why they design and administer their tests in the way they do, issues of openness and transparency are of growing importance. We believe that the approach outlined and exemplified in this volume offers one way of placing in the public domain the rationale and evidence in support of testing policy and practice. By sharing one examination board's expertise and experience in this way, we hope that other institutions and test providers will be encouraged and enabled to review and reflect upon their own testing theory and practice, and thus engage in a similar exercise in public accountability for their own assessment products.

The volume is also directly relevant to the academic language testing and assessment community, i.e. researchers, lecturers and graduate students, especially those with a specific interest in assessing spoken language ability. While the overview of the theoretical and empirical research should be of obvious and immediate value to them, members of the academic language testing community will hopefully find the detailed description and discussion of operational language testing practices just as useful. The complex practical constraints facing an examination board can sometimes mean that experimental research findings are not immediately or readily applicable to large-scale testing activities. Operational testing, as opposed to language testing research, often has to concern itself with far more than just the issues of construct definition and operationalisation, assessment criteria and rating scale development. Large-scale commercial tests conducted on an *industrial* scale, such as those offered by Cambridge ESOL and similar agencies, are usually located within a complex ecology comprising multiple, interacting factors, many of which are simply not present or relevant in more academically oriented language testing research endeavours. Such factors include sustainability issues to do with test production, delivery and processing systems; practical issues concerning test timing, security, cost, accessibility; organisational issues relating to personnel (e.g. developing and sustaining the rater cadre) or management (e.g. the revision of an existing test, or development of its replacement). This is particularly true for both the direct and the semi-direct testing of L2 speaking ability, for which practicality and sustainability are core considerations, as will become apparent later in this volume. Hopefully, the explication of theory and practice presented in this volume will contribute to a broader and deeper understanding of the issues for all of us who are involved in the assessment of speaking.

There will undoubtedly be other readers for whom certain sections, if not the whole, of this volume will be of interest and relevance, perhaps because they are involved in teaching and assessing L2 spoken ability, or because they are preparing learners to take one or more of the Cambridge ESOL examinations. Such readers include English language teachers, curriculum developers, course book writers and other materials developers. Although, for obvious reasons, the primary focus of this volume is on the testing of English as a second language, we hope that some of the theory, principles and practice that are explored and explained in the volume will prove helpful to teachers and learners of languages other than English as a second/foreign language, and especially to teachers of those less commonly taught languages for which assessment theory and testing practice are still in the early stages of development and remain relatively under-resourced.

In addition to the audiences highlighted above, we anticipate that this volume will be of direct interest to the vast community of English language professionals who, in one way or another, are personally involved with the Cambridge ESOL Speaking tests. They include the hundreds of test materials writers who draft and edit Speaking test tasks and rubrics for the multiple proficiency levels, as well as the many thousands of Speaking test personnel (speaking examiners (SEs)) around the world, working in teams alongside Team Leaders (TLs), Regional Team Leaders (RTLs) and Professional Support Leaders (PSLs) to deliver the Speaking tests and to assess test takers' performances as fairly as possible. The Cambridge ESOL examinations could not function as successfully as they do without the expertise and dedication of this professional cadre worldwide. Indeed, these specialists have made their own contribution to the development of this volume as this chapter will make clear.

Finally, in a globalised world where the testing and assessment of second, third or additional language skills are steadily moving centre stage in education and society, this volume is offered as a contribution towards the promotion of assessment literacy. Language tests and the scores they generate are increasingly used across contemporary society worldwide: within education, from primary age to higher education; in employment contexts, from the professional registration of health professionals, to health and safety issues in the catering or construction industry; and, more controversially, in migration and citizenship policy and practice around the world. These trends mean that there are not simply more people taking tests. Growing numbers of people are directly involved in selecting or developing tests and in using test scores for decision-making purposes. In practice, they often find themselves doing this without much background or training in assessment to equip them for the role. They include classroom teachers tasked with designing or delivering standardised tests to evaluate their pupils' progress, tests that are sometimes then used to hold teachers and schools accountable for that progress, or the apparent lack of it. A similar burden of expectation is laid on staff in university admissions, in professional bodies and in immigration agencies to know what tests measure and what test scores mean, and to understand how to integrate them into their complex, usually high-stakes decision-making processes. The language testing community is in a position, indeed it has a moral obligation, to encourage the sharing of the core knowledge, skills and understanding that underpin good quality assessment as widely and accessibly as possible for the benefit of all. (For a fuller discussion of the importance of assessment literacy and approaches to its development, see Taylor 2009a.)

In summary, then, this volume is offered as a rich source of information for a wide variety of audiences on multiple aspects of examining L2 speaking ability.

The purpose of the volume

As explained above, *Examining Speaking* is one of a series of *construct*-oriented volumes focusing upon the four language skills of writing, reading, speaking and listening. The genesis of the series lies partly in a close collaboration that developed in the early 2000s between, on the one hand, applied linguistics and language testing specialists at Cambridge ESOL, and, on the other, Professors Cyril J Weir and Barry O'Sullivan, both of whom were at that time working at the University of Roehampton, Surrey. There was on their part a shared interest and enthusiasm with Cambridge ESOL in finding ways to explore more systematically the nature of construct validity in language testing and assessment, and especially to bridge the gap between research and practice, between theoretical construct definition and applied construct operationalisation in relation to real-world language testing, particularly the sort of large-scale language testing undertaken by examination boards and agencies such as Cambridge ESOL. Initial discussions led to the conceptualisation of a long-term project to research and draft a series of documents (e.g. position papers, research reports, and published monographs) which would describe and reflect upon the theory and practice of assessment and how this is operationalised in the Cambridge ESOL examinations, with particular reference to the multiple proficiency levels of the General English suite of tests, traditionally referred to as the Cambridge Main Suite (MS). It was envisaged this project might include the publication of a set of academic volumes within the *Studies in Language Testing* series.

A major motivation for embarking on such a project was the growing expectation in the public domain, both nationally and globally, for examination boards and other test providers to be transparent and accountable in what they do, especially in terms of the standards to which they adhere, the quality and validity claims they make for their products, and the provision of theoretical and empirical evidence in support of these claims. This external, public expectation emerging within wider society was paralleled by a growing sense within the language testing and assessment profession itself of the need to develop its own *professional ethic*. It is in the light of this awareness that the field of language testing and assessment has undergone a process of increasing professionalisation over recent years. An abundance of quality standards, ethical codes and guidelines for good testing practice has been embraced or generated by language testers, in many cases touching upon matters that extend well beyond a test's purely technical qualities. Examples include the *Code of Fair Testing Practices in Education* (Joint Committee on Testing Practices 2004) and the AERA/APA/NCME *Standards* (1999), both of which concern assessment in general. There also exist language testing specific codes such as the ALTE *Code of Practice* (1994), the ILTA *Code of Ethics* (2000), the EALTA *Guidelines for Good Practice* (2006) and the ILTA *Guidelines for Practice* (2007). Professional associations of language testers and testing organisations were established during the 1990s at national, regional and international level, including the Japan Language Testing Association (JLTA), the Association of Language Testers in Europe (ALTE), the International Language Testing Association (ILTA), and the European Association of Language Testing and Assessment (EALTA). Kunnan (2004, 2008) reflects on the ethical milieu that emerged for language testers, prompted by various factors in the professional field such as: demands for accountability and responsiveness to clients; increased use of language tests and types of delivery methods; use of new measurement and other analytical techniques; and expanded concepts of validity (i.e. Messick 1989, 1996). Kunnan suggests the language testing community responded to these factors by developing explicit standards and codes for its community and practice, and that its professional ethic continues to evolve informed by the wider literature in ethics and moral philosophy.

An ethic that embraces openness, transparency and accountability is essential given that examination boards and other testing institutions offer assessment tools whose use has both direct and indirect consequences for education and wider society. Such consequences may be high stakes, influencing an individual's life chances, the formulation of public policy or the shaping of attitudes in society. Messick's re-conceptualisation of validity, which brought together traditional validity concerns but also added value implications and social consequences as essential facets, undoubtedly contributed to growing awareness of the consequences of testing, intended and unintended, positive and negative; and this trend is clearly illustrated in the wealth of research literature published over recent years on the theory and practice of language testing washback and impact (see, among others, Alderson and Wall 1996, Cheng 2005, Cheng, Watanabe and Curtis 2004, Green 2007, Hawkey 2006, Kunnan 2000, Wall 2005, Wall and Horak 2006, 2008), as well as other publications discussing the role of testing in education and society (see, for example, McNamara and Roever 2006, Shohamy 2001, 2008, Spolsky 2008).

Transparency and accountability are particularly important for testing organisations that offer multiple tests targeted at different proficiency levels, domains of language use or groups of language users. In this context, examination providers need recourse to an explicit and appropriate methodology for describing, analysing and comparing their tests in a systematic and comprehensive manner so that test users can clearly understand the features of each testing option available to them and can decide appropriately on their selection and use.

Cambridge ESOL has never subscribed to a philosophy of 'one size fits all' where English language assessment is concerned. Over time, in response to changing trends in language learning and to evolving market demands and opportunities, the examination board has developed a wide range of assessment products that include: tests at *different proficiency levels* (e.g. KET, PET, FCE, CAE, CPE); tests involving a *multi-skills package* (e.g. IELTS) and tests which are *modular* (e.g. ESOL Skills for Life); tests across *different language domains* (e.g. General English, Academic English, Business English); tests for *teachers* of English (e.g. CELTA, DELTA) and tests for *young learners* of English (e.g. YLE); tests in *pencil and paper mode* (e.g. Standard BULATS) and tests in *computer mode* (e.g. BULATS Online Courses); tests for *certificated* use and tests for *institutional* use.

The development and promotion of a variety of testing instruments places an obligation upon the test producer to be able to clearly demonstrate how they are seeking to meet the demands of validity in each product and, more specifically, how they actually operationalise criterial distinctions, not only between tests offered at different *levels*, i.e. on the *vertical* proficiency continuum, but also between alternative testing *domains*, *formats* and *modes*, i.e. along a *horizontal* axis.

To be able to do this requires some sort of methodology for analysing and describing the component validity features of any test, as well as for constructing an interpretative framework of reference within which multiple tests and their respective validity features can be explicitly presented and co-located. The use of such a methodology has the potential to achieve two significant and beneficial outcomes for the language testing world. First, it should enable test *producers* to assemble and present, with some degree of transparency and coherence, the validation evidence and arguments in support of quality claims made for each of their tests so that these can be scrutinised and evaluated. Secondly, it should serve as a means of communication, assisting test *users* to understand better the nature of the testing tools available to them and aiding them in decisions about which test or tests best suit a given purpose and context of use. Transparency and coherence are stated aims underpinning the development of the Common European Framework of Reference (CEFR), first released by the Council of Europe in draft form for consultation in 1996, and formally published in 2001, as explained by one of its original authors Brian North (2008:21). North also expressed the hope that the CEFR would 'establish a metalanguage common across educational sectors, national and linguistic boundaries that could be used to talk about objectives and language levels', as well as 'providing encouragement to practitioners in the language field to reflect on their current practice' (2008:22). Cambridge ESOL's construct volumes embody similar aspirations and can thus be seen within a broader historical frame, especially, though not exclusively, within the European language education context, in which there has been an increasing focus on the need to analyse and describe language proficiency for the purposes of learning, teaching, and assessment.

The theoretical framework for validating language examinations first outlined in Weir's *Language Testing and Validation: An evidence-based approach* (2005a) offered Cambridge ESOL a potential approach and methodology for undertaking such an enterprise in relation to its own examinations. Drawing upon theoretical and empirical research in the field, it provided a useful conceptual heuristic for identifying core features in the process of improved construct definition for the tests. More importantly, perhaps, it also offered the hope that it could be proactively applied to operational tests, i.e. to the *test-in-practice* rather than just the *test-in-theory*. It was anticipated that a socio-cognitive framework for validating examinations, as expounded by Weir (2005a), would permit a systematic and comprehensive critical evaluation of construct definition *and* operationalisation, and ideally furnish explicit evidence, both theoretical and empirical, to support claims about the usefulness of the Cambridge ESOL tests. The socio-cognitive approach to test validation resonated strongly with the thinking and practice on test development and validation which had been emerging in Cambridge ESOL during the 1990s, namely the VRIP approach where the concern is with Validity (the conventional sources of validity evidence: construct, content, criterion), Reliability, Impact and Practicality. The early work of Bachman (1990) and Bachman and Palmer (1996) underpinned the adoption of the VRIP approach, as set out in Weir and Milanovic (2003) and found in various Cambridge ESOL internal documents on validity (e.g. Milanovic and Saville 1992a, 1996a). Weir's approach covers much of the same ground as VRIP but it attempts to reconfigure validity to show how its constituent parts (context, cognitive processing and scoring) might interact with each other. Speaking, the construct of interest in this volume, is viewed as not just the underlying latent trait of speaking ability but as the result of the constructed triangle of trait, context and score (including its interpretation). The approach adopted in this volume is therefore effectively an *interactionalist* position, which sees the speaking construct as residing in the interactions between the underlying cognitive ability, the context of use and the process of scoring, as discussed by Weir (2005a), as well as in an earlier internal paper by O'Sullivan and Weir (2002), originally commissioned by Cambridge ESOL to explore some of the research issues involved in L2 speaking assessment.

Like its predecessors *Examining Writing* and *Examining Reading*, therefore, this volume develops a theoretical framework for validating tests of second language speaking ability, a framework which then informs an attempt to articulate and evaluate the Cambridge ESOL approach to assessing L2 speaking skills. The perceived benefits of a clearly articulated theoretical and practical position for assessing speaking skills in the context of the Cambridge ESOL examinations are essentially twofold:

- *Within Cambridge ESOL* – this articulated position will deepen understanding of the current theoretical basis upon which Cambridge ESOL assesses different levels of language proficiency across its range of products, and will inform current and future test development projects in the light of this analysis. It will thereby enhance the development of equivalent test forms and tasks.

- *Beyond Cambridge ESOL* – it will communicate in the public domain the theoretical basis for the tests and hopefully provide a more clearly understood rationale for the way in which Cambridge ESOL operationalises this in its tests. In addition, it may provide a suitable framework for others interested in validating their own examinations, offering a principled basis and a practical methodology for comparing language examinations across the proficiency range. It therefore adds to the range of frameworks and models now available to test developers for analysing and describing the qualities of their tests and for guiding their research and validation activity.

The focus of the volume

The intention, then, in this volume is to apply a theoretical framework for validating tests of second language speaking ability in order to examine, articulate and evaluate the approach to assessing L2 speaking skills adopted by Cambridge ESOL. The board's suite of examinations in General English (the Main Suite) offers a useful picture of how speaking ability is measured across a broad language proficiency continuum, i.e. from beginner to advanced. Its five levels correspond to equivalent levels of ALTE and of the Common European Framework of Reference (CEFR). The levels reflect the levels of language ability familiar to English language teachers around the world, that have been described as 'natural levels' (North 2006:8), not in the sense that they are themselves naturally occurring phenomena in either language acquisition or learning, but rather in the sense that language teachers and educators, especially in ELT, gradually came to perceive them as *useful* curriculum and examination levels. The relationship between Cambridge ESOL levels, ALTE levels and the CEFR levels is discussed in detail in Chapter 7. However, for initial orientation the reader is referred to Table 1.1 for an overview of

ALTE Can Do statements for Listening/Speaking and to Table 1.2 which provides CEFR A1 to C2 performance level descriptors for Speaking. In their development, the ALTE Can Do statements were originally organised into three general areas: Social and Tourist; Work; and Study. Each of these areas

Table 1.1 ALTE Can Do statements for Listening/Speaking

CEFR Levels (ALTE Levels)	Listening/Speaking Can Do Statement			
	Overall General Ability	Social and Tourist typical abilities	Work typical abilities	Study typical abilities
C2: Mastery (ALTE Level 5: Good User)	CAN advise on or talk about complex or sensitive issues, understanding colloquial references and dealing confidently with hostile questions.	CAN talk about complex or sensitive issues without awkwardness.	CAN advise on/handle complex delicate or contentious issues, such as legal or financial matters, to the extent that he/she has the necessary specialist knowledge.	CAN understand jokes, colloquial asides and cultural allusions.
C1: Effective Operational Proficiency (ALTE Level 4: Competent User)	CAN contribute effectively to meetings and seminars within own area of work or keep up a casual conversation with a good degree of fluency, coping with abstract expressions.	CAN keep up conversations of a casual nature for an extended period of time and discuss abstract/ cultural topics with a good degree of fluency and range of expression.	CAN contribute effectively to meetings and seminars within own area of work and argue for or against a case.	CAN follow abstract argumentation, for example the balancing of alternatives and the drawing of a conclusion.
B2: Vantage (ALTE Level 3: Independent User)	CAN follow or give a talk on a familiar topic or keep up a conversation on a fairly wide range of topics.	CAN keep up a conversation on a fairly wide range of topics, such as personal and professional experiences, events currently in the news.	CAN take and pass on most messages that are likely to require attention during a normal working day.	CAN give a clear presentation on a familiar topic, and answer predictable or factual questions.

Table 1.1 Continued

CEFR Levels (ALTE Levels)	Listening/Speaking Can Do statement			
	Overall General Ability	Social and Tourist typical abilities	Work typical abilities	Study typical abilities
B1: Threshold (ALTE Level 2: Threshold User)	CAN express opinions on abstract/ cultural matters in a limited way or offer advice within a known area, and understand instructions or public announcements.	CAN express opinions on abstract/cultural matters in a limited way and pick up nuances of meaning/ opinion.	CAN offer advice to clients within own job area on simple matters.	CAN understand instructions on classes and assignments given by a teacher or lecturer.
A2: Waystage (ALTE Level 1: Waystage User)	CAN express simple opinions or requirements in a familiar context.	CAN express likes and dislikes in familiar contexts using simple language such as 'I (don't) like. . .'	CAN state simple requirements within own job area, such as 'I want to order 25 of. . .'	CAN express simple opinions using expressions such as 'I don't agree'.
A1: Breakthrough (ALTE Break-through Level)	CAN understand basic instructions or take part in a basic factual conversation on a predictable topic.	CAN ask simple questions of a factual nature and understand answers expressed in simple language.	CAN take and pass on simple messages of a routine kind, such as 'Friday meeting 10am'.	CAN understand basic instructions on class times, dates and room numbers, and on assignments to be carried out.

Source: Council of Europe (2001:249–257).

included up to three scales, for the skills of Reading, Writing and Interaction; hence in Table 1.1 Listening/Speaking are combined into a single scale for Interaction. (For more details of this project see Appendix D in Council of Europe 2001:244–257.)

In relation to Speaking, the CEFR (Council of Europe 2001) draws a distinction between Spoken *Interaction* and Spoken *Production*; illustrative scales for the six framework levels are provided in the Framework – nine separate scales for Spoken Interaction (overall, conversation, information exchange, etc.), and five for Spoken Production (e.g. overall, sustained monologue, public announcement, etc.). Given the complex nature of these

Table 1.2 CEFR Common Reference Levels: Self-assessment grid for Speaking

	A1	A2	B1	B2	C1	C2
Spoken Interaction	I can interact in a simple way provided the other person is prepared to repeat or rephrase things at a slower rate of speech and help me formulate what I'm trying to say. I can ask and answer simple questions in areas of immediate need or on very familiar topics.	I can communicate in simple and routine tasks requiring a simple and direct exchange of information on familiar topics and activities. I can handle very short social exchanges, even though I can't usually understand enough to keep the conversation going myself.	I can deal with most situations likely to arise whilst travelling in an area where the language is spoken. I can enter unprepared into conversation on topics that are familiar, of personal interest or pertinent to everyday life (e.g. families, hobbies, work, travel and current events).	I can interact with a degree of fluency and spontaneity that makes regular interaction with native speakers quite possible. I can take an active part in discussion in familiar contexts, accounting for and sustaining my views.	I can express myself fluently and spontaneously without much obvious searching for expressions. I can use language flexibly and effectively for social and professional purposes. I can formulate ideas and opinions with precision and relate my contribution skilfully to those of other speakers.	I can take part effortlessly in any conversation or discussion and have a good familiarity with idiomatic expressions and colloquialisms. I can express myself fluently and convey finer shades of meaning precisely. If I do have a problem I can backtrack and restructure around the difficulty so smoothly that other people are hardly aware of it.

S
P
E
A
K
I
N
G

Spoken Production					
I can use simple phrases and sentences to describe where I live and people I know.	I can use a series of phrases and sentences to describe in simple terms my family and other people, living conditions, my educational background and my present or most recent job.	I can connect phrases in a simple way to describe experiences and events, my dreams, hopes and ambitions. I can briefly give reasons and explanations for opinions and plans. I can narrate a story or relate the plot of a book or film and describe my reactions.	I can present clear, detailed descriptions on a wide range of subjects related to my field of interest. I can explain a viewpoint on a topical issue giving the advantages and disadvantages of various opinions.	I can present detailed descriptions of complex subjects integrating sub-themes, developing particular points and rounding off with an appropriate conclusion.	I can present a clear, smoothly flowing description or argument in a style appropriate to the context and with an effective logical structure which helps the recipient to notice and remember significant points.

Source: Common European Framework of Reference (Council of Europe 2001:26–27).

13 illustrative scales, including the fact that descriptors for the A1 and C2 levels are often left underspecified (or even entirely unspecified), the composite descriptors used in the CEFR self-assessment grid have been included instead in Table 1.2 to help orientate the reader to the levels. (See Jones 2002 and Chapter 7 for further information on a Cambridge ESOL project that linked the ALTE levels to the CEFR.)

When considering the ALTE table (1.1) and the CEFR table (1.2), the reader may feel that the distinctions between adjacent levels are not always clear and the characterisations on occasion imprecise. A key aim of this volume is to try and improve on these descriptions by clarifying the underlying theoretical construct of Speaking at CEFR Levels A2 to C2 combined with a close examination of Cambridge ESOL practice to specify more precisely, where possible, differences between adjacent levels in terms of a range of contextual and cognitive parameters.

Although the Main Suite of General English examinations forms a major source of reference in this volume for illustrating how the speaking construct differs from level to level in Cambridge ESOL examinations (see Table 1.3), the volume will also make reference to other Speaking tests from examinations in the Cambridge ESOL family such as the Business English Certificates (BEC) and the International English Language Testing System (IELTS) examinations which cater for more specific ESP and EAP populations. This is intended to provide further clarification of how various performance parameters help establish distinctions between different levels of speaking proficiency on the vertical axis, and may begin to provide some insights into the criterial features across domains and modes on the horizontal axis too. It will also demonstrate how research conducted in relation to these examinations has had wider effects throughout the range of examinations offered, for example in helping improve aspects of scoring validity. These more specialist English examinations are well documented in their own right in other volumes in the *Studies in Language Testing* series (Davies 2008, O'Sullivan 2006), and the reader is referred to these for comprehensive coverage of their history, operationalisation and quality assurance. BEC examinations are taken by those wishing to gain a qualification in Business English as a result of the growing internationalisation of commerce and the need for employees to interact in more than just a single language (see O'Sullivan 2006 for full details of this test). IELTS is principally used for admissions purposes into tertiary level academic institutions throughout the world (see Davies 2008 for a detailed history of the developments in EAP testing leading up to the current IELTS). Overviews of the Speaking elements of these examinations are shown in Tables 1.4 and 1.5 below for information and comparative purposes.

Table 1.3 A description of Cambridge ESOL's General English (Main Suite) levels in terms of what materials candidates can handle and what they are expected to be able to do in Speaking

CPE (C2)	CPE candidates are expected to answer questions giving general information about themselves and answer more open questions requiring speculation or an opinion. They are expected to carry out a peer–peer collaborative task, in response to oral prompts and supported by visual stimuli that provide them with the opportunity to interact and co-operate with each other. They are also expected to deliver a short piece of extended discourse in response to written prompts. Candidates at this level should be able to use social and general interactional language, exchange ideas on concrete and abstract topics, reach a decision through negotiation, express and justify opinions, agree/disagree, suggest, speculate and evaluate.
CAE (C1)	CAE candidates are expected to give information of a factual, personal kind, responding to questions about their interests, experiences, e.g. work, study, travel. They are expected to deliver a brief piece of extended discourse in response to visual stimuli and written prompts. They are expected to carry out a peer–peer collaborative task, in response to written prompts and supported by visual stimuli that provide them with the opportunity to interact and co-operate with each other. Candidates at this level should be able to use social and general interactional language, exchange ideas on concrete and abstract topics, reach a decision through negotiation, express and justify opinions, agree/disagree, suggest, speculate and evaluate.
FCE (B2)	FCE candidates are expected to be able to give information of a factual, personal kind, responding to questions about their work, leisure time and future plans. The are expected to deliver a short piece of extended discourse in response to visual stimuli and written prompts. They are also expected to carry out a collaborative peer–peer task, in response to written prompts and supported by visual stimuli that provide them with the opportunity to interact and co-operate with each other. Candidates at this level are expected to use social and general interactional language, exchange ideas on mostly concrete topics, reach a decision through negotiation, express and justify opinions, agree/disagree, suggest, speculate and evaluate.
PET (B1)	PET candidates are expected to be able to give information of a factual, personal kind, responding to questions about present circumstances, past experiences and future plans. They are expected to use functional language to make and respond to suggestions, discuss alternatives, make recommendations and negotiate agreement in response to a visual prompt in a collaborative peer–peer task. They are expected to be able to describe photographs and manage discourse, using appropriate vocabulary in a longer turn. Finally, they should talk about their opinions, likes/dislikes, preferences, experiences and habits in a follow-up conversation on the same topic as the photographs.
KET (A2)	KET candidates are expected to be able to use language associated with meeting people for the first time, giving information of a factual personal kind. They should also be able to ask and answer questions about factual information on a prompt card (e.g. times, prices, etc.). Candidates should be able to demonstrate strategies for dealing with communication difficulties, e.g. paraphrasing or asking for clarification.

Source: Personal communication with Main Suite Assessment Managers and University of Cambridge ESOL Examinations: Handbooks for Teachers (2005, 2007, 2008).

Table 1.4 A description of BEC levels in terms of what materials candidates are expected to be able to handle and what they are expected to be able to do in Speaking

BEC Higher (C1)	BEC Higher candidates are expected to respond to questions and expand on responses, talk briefly about themselves, provide concise information on where they come from and their job/studies, and use functional language related to agreeing, disagreeing, expressing opinions and preferences. They are also expected to be able to prepare and deliver a short piece of extended speech on a business-related topic, using a prompt which contains a general statement. They should be able to sustain a peer–peer discussion based on a business-related situation and an abstract discussion topic, using relevant functional language and strategies to express opinions and justify decisions.
BEC Vantage (B2)	BEC Vantage candidates are expected to respond to questions and expand on responses, talk briefly about themselves, provide concise information on where they come from and their job/studies, and use functional language related to agreeing, disagreeing, expressing opinions and preferences. They are also expected to be able to prepare and deliver a short piece of extended speech on a business-related topic, using a prompt which contains a question and a couple of supporting ideas. They should be able to sustain a peer–peer discussion based on a business-related situation, using relevant functional language and strategies to express opinions and justify decisions.
BEC Preliminary (B1)	BEC Preliminary candidates are expected to be able to talk briefly about themselves, to provide concise information on subjects such as their home, hobbies and jobs, and to perform simple functions such as agreeing, disagreeing and expressing preferences. They are also expected to be able to prepare and deliver a short piece of extended speech on a business-related topic, based on a prompt which contains a question and a range of supporting ideas. They should be able to sustain a peer–peer discussion based on a business-related situation, using relevant functional language and strategies.

Source: Personal communication with BEC Subject Manager and University of Cambridge ESOL Examinations: BEC Handbook for Teachers (2008).

Further comment may be helpful here on the twin issues of test purpose and test specificity and how these issues relate to the Speaking tests which are scrutinised or referred to in this volume. Test purpose is sometimes defined in terms of type of test and its function, i.e. whether it is designed for selection, certification or diagnostic purposes (Davies, Brown, Elder, Hill, Lumley and McNamara 1999). McNamara (1996:92) writes of the 'rationale' for a test in terms of '*who* wants to know *what* about *whom* and for what *purpose*?' Definition of test purpose or rationale will naturally guide decisions about test content and format, approaches to scoring and test administration procedures. The 1999 *Standards for Educational and Psychological Testing* stress the importance of defining 'the purposes of the test and the domain represented by the test', so that it is clear 'what dimensions of knowledge, skill,

Table 1.5 A description of IELTS in terms of what materials candidates are expected to be able to handle and what they are expected to be able to do in Speaking

Candidates for IELTS Speaking, which is a multi-level test, are expected to engage with three tasks which require them to answer short questions, speak at length on a familiar topic, and discuss more abstract questions. The candidates will deal with functions including providing personal information, expressing and justifying opinions, explaining, suggesting, speculating, expressing preferences, comparing, summarising, narrating, etc. Part 1 of the test consists of questions based on familiar or personal context; Part 2 elicits an independent long turn from the candidate on an accessible topic relating to candidates' experience; in Part 3 the Examiner invites the candidate to participate in discussion of a more abstract nature, based on verbal prompts thematically linked to the Part 2 topic.

Source: Personal communication with IELTS Subject Manager and University of Cambridge ESOL Examinations, British Council, IDP Australia: IELTS Handbook (2005, 2007).

processes, attitude, values, emotions, or behavior are included and excluded' (AERA/APA/NCME 1999:43–44; see also Fulcher and Davidson 2007). This last reference touches upon the complex inter-relationship between the test (and the scores it generates) and the world beyond the test (in which the test scores are used to achieve some practical purpose). In the world beyond the test, scores from the test need to be interpretable in a valid and meaningful way since they are likely to be used for decision-making purposes for individuals and institutions, sometimes with significant or high-stakes consequences. Kane (1992) explains how inferences can be used to construct an interpretive argument in support of test validity claims, building on notions of 'generalisation' and 'extrapolation' from the test and its scores to the world beyond the test. (See also the Assessment Use Argument proposed by Bachman and Palmer (2010), which is based on Toulmin's (2003) approach to practical reasoning, using inferential links to build an argument structure.)

Questions of test purpose and of the validity of inferences that can be drawn from scores on a test lead us on to questions of specific purpose testing and the nature of test specificity. Both Douglas (2000) and O'Sullivan (2006) provide a comprehensive discussion of this area and its challenges, including the difficulty of determining exactly how far a test can be considered general or specific in its focus and purpose. This volume, like the previous construct volumes, focuses primarily on the General English examinations offered by Cambridge ESOL (KET–CPE). These tests were primarily developed to meet the educational needs of particular age groups and ability levels, for the most part within school or college-based language learning contexts worldwide. Their purpose or function can therefore be seen as supporting English language teaching and learning in such contexts, whether that teaching and learning takes place formally (e.g. in a classroom) or more informally (e.g. through a home-stay or self-study programme). The Cambridge Main Suite tests (KET–CPE) are 'general' tests in the sense that, unlike IELTS, BEC or BULATS (the Business Language Testing Service), they are not intentionally linked to a specified domain of language use (other than perhaps the broad pedagogic domain) but rather to a general-purpose context. Unlike specific-purpose tests, they are therefore not designed to reflect domain-specific language in terms of its 'precise' or 'context-appropriate' characteristics (e.g. its vocabulary, syntax, rhetorical organisation).

Despite the *Standards'* emphasis on defining test purpose and domain (i.e. the dimensions of knowledge, skill, processes, attitude, values, emotions or behaviour to be included or excluded), a definition of general language proficiency is understandably difficult to pin down since it represents such a broad, unboundaried construct. Specific purpose domains and language may appear easier to define, though some suggest that defining the boundaries of specific context areas can be equally problematic (Davies 2001, Elder 2001). O'Sullivan appears to treat this traditional 'general versus specific' distinction more lightly, suggesting that all language tests are to some degree 'specific' and can be 'placed somewhere on a continuum of specificity from the broad general purpose test . . . to the highly specific test . . .' (2006:14). He further proposes that specific purpose language may actually sit within general language, located at its core: 'Business language, like scientific or medical language, is situated within and interacts with the *general language domain*, a domain that cannot, by its very nature be rigidly defined' (2006:7). For language test developers, therefore, the general–specific purpose distinction may not be as straightforward as we might hope.

This has interesting implications regarding the take-up and use of language tests for purposes or in contexts for which they may not have been originally or explicitly designed. The *Standards* readily acknowledge that tests can be designed or used to serve multiple purposes, but they also caution that such tests are unlikely to serve all purposes equally well (AERA/APA/NCME 1999:145). It is sometimes argued that 'General English' tests cannot be suitable for workplace recruitment because they were not originally designed for specific occupational purposes. In some cases this is undoubtedly true. A general purpose test is highly unlikely to be adequate for certificating the specialised, often technical language skills required in certain professional contexts, e.g. the occupation-specific language of oil rig workers, air traffic controllers or radiographers. It is clear that examinations should not be used for purposes for which they are clearly not intended and no claim is made in this volume that Cambridge ESOL's General English tests, such as FCE or CAE, are suitable for certificating the sort of occupation-specific language described above. Certification of this type of linguistic ability is likely to demand a different and highly specific test, and such a test may need to be developed internally by the profession or employer, with expert assistance from testing specialists. Such a test is also likely to involve the assessment of occupation-specific knowledge and skills beyond the purely linguistic (e.g. the technical legal knowledge needed for a courtroom exchange, or the clinical skills needed for doctor–patient interaction). However, it is not unreasonable to assume that General English tests, such as FCE or CAE, can serve a useful function in evaluating a language user's proficiency level for some employment or educational contexts, perhaps acting as an initial filter before they embark on more specialised language training and assessment that is specific to the occupational context. In both employment and educational contexts, not all language use lies at the 'highly specific' end of the specificity continuum; much of it is more general in nature, e.g. in the everyday exchanges of the office environment or in the social interaction that takes place on the university campus. This is consistent with O'Sullivan's notions of 'core and general language use domains' (O'Sullivan 2006:177). It is possible, therefore, to see how a General English test *may* be perceived as useful by a range of test users because it fulfils a necessary function, while not being sufficient in itself to meet every aspect of the assessment need.

Test developers and providers bear the primary responsibility for ensuring that all test users fully understand the intended design purposes of any tests and test users need to be made fully aware of any likely limitations that should be placed upon generalisation and extrapolation from test scores. Responsible test providers aim to achieve this through their publicly available documentation and their ongoing interaction with their stakeholder constituencies. Nonetheless, the ALTE *Code of Practice* (1994), the *Standards* (AERA/APA/NCME 1999) and most other recent professional guidelines for language testing also stress that the appropriate and ethical use of tests must be a *shared* responsibility between test providers and test users.

The tradition of speaking assessment at Cambridge

In this introductory chapter it may be helpful to provide readers with a brief historical background on the tradition and experience of Cambridge ESOL in relation to assessing L2 speaking ability. This will hopefully explain the examination board's historical legacy as far as performance assessment is concerned, as well as contextualise the strong emphasis the reader will note in the volume on the direct, face-to-face method for oral assessment, and the relatively limited focus on other approaches to testing speaking, such as semi-direct and indirect methods.

While some writers have suggested that the origins of oral performance testing date back to the middle of the 20th century (Lowe 1988, McNamara 1996), others point to a much longer and richer history, citing Imperial China's civil service examination system, the 'palace test', in the 10th century (Miyazaki 1976:74), or the ancient 'shibboleth test' recorded in the biblical

Hebrew Book of Judges (Spolsky 1995:15). Early examples of oral tests of language ability can also be found in the classical approach to education offered by universities in Western Europe, and later in the USA (Spolsky 1995:9–10, 17–18, 21). Despite these early examples, it is fair to suggest that modern oral proficiency exams date from more recent times, though still rather earlier than the mid-20th century as Lowe (1988) and McNamara (1996) appear to claim.

It was the examination traditions of the British university education system that shaped the overall approach to testing and assessment which developed during the second half of the 19th century within the University of Cambridge's Local Examinations Syndicate (UCLES), a department of the University of Cambridge. Founded in 1858, UCLES (now known as Cambridge Assessment) provided British secondary school students with access to public examinations in 'local' test centres in provincial towns and cities rather than requiring them to undertake costly rail journeys to Cambridge (Watts 2008:37). In the mid-19th century the development of localised, university-administered public examinations systems, such as those offered by UCLES, brought educational and employment opportunities to a much larger sector of the British population than hitherto and was a critical factor in enabling the development of mass public education. During the second half of the 19th century, UCLES extended its examination provision overseas to 'local' centres in countries as diverse as Trinidad, South Africa, Mauritius, New Zealand and Malaya – all British colonies at that time (Spolsky 1995:63, Watts 2008:45).

In 1913, 50 years after it was founded, UCLES introduced its first English language proficiency examination. The Certificate of Proficiency in English (CPE) was a high-level test designed for 'foreign students who sought proof of their practical knowledge of the language with a view to teaching it in foreign schools' (Roach 1945:34). The CPE was a 12-hour examination consisting of several Written papers, including a Translation paper into/from English, an Essay paper and an English Literature paper. It also included a compulsory Oral component that adopted a *direct, face-to-face* approach to assessing spoken language ability. Test takers faced half an hour of reading aloud and spontaneous conversation with an examiner, plus half an hour of oral dictation. The result was a Speaking (and Listening) test lasting a full hour. Interestingly, the examination also included a 90-minute written paper on English Phonetics, suggesting that theoretical and applied knowledge of what words sounded like and how they should be produced were also considered important components of language proficiency at that time. Spolsky suggests the new CPE test in 1913 reflected 'the growing interest in direct method teaching', which 'required of teachers "reliable command of the language for active classroom use" rather than academic or descriptive ability' (Spolsky 1995:63); this may explain the prominence given to assessing aspects of spoken language ability within the test battery. A century ago, therefore, language learners wishing to certificate their command of English as a foreign or second language faced 'an extremely demanding test of their abilities' (Weir 2003:2), in which the testing of spoken language ability, both directly and indirectly, was integral to assessing their overall English language proficiency.

Interestingly, the original design and development of CPE highlights for us the challenge discussed in the previous section of determining how far a language test is actually 'general' or 'specific' in terms of its 'test purpose'. From one perspective, the new CPE in 1913 could be regarded as a 'General English' test of overall language proficiency, since it covered both receptive and productive skills quite comprehensively, though apparently with no particular emphasis on relating these to a specific domain. From another perspective, and according to both Roach (1945) and Spolsky (1995), CPE was a high-level test designed to provide proof of a knowledge of the English language needed for the specific purpose of being able to teach it in the classroom in schools overseas. McNamara (1996:28) suggests it was the early 1960s that saw *test purpose* as beginning to determine the form of tests as much as any linguistic theory of the knowledge or skills being tested. The comments of both Roach and Spolsky, however, suggest that test purpose and test specificity may have been a significant consideration in test development long before that.

Was CPE in 1913 a general purpose test or a domain-specific test? Or was it a blend of the two? Did the inclusion of Translation and English Literature papers make the test more specific, or were these components simply considered an integral part of the overall language proficiency construct as it was understood at that time? After all, the content and structure of CPE mirrored Certificates in Proficiency in other modern European languages at that time, such as French and German. We cannot be definitive about what was in the minds of the original CPE test developers and it is probably unlikely that the test developers of a century ago worked with the terms and concepts that are familiar to language testers today. Nevertheless, the example of the original CPE illustrates quite well the dilemma and questions that language testers continue to face when designing and developing a new test, or when re-engineering an existing test. What does it mean in theory for a test to be 'general' or 'specific'? Is the distinction always as clear-cut as we believe or wish it to be? How is the theory operationalised in practice? And what happens when a test takes on something of a life of its own in the world beyond the constraints and controls of the original test developers?

The history of CPE also helpfully illustrates for us how examinations evolve over time, sometimes changing their purpose in the process. In 1913 CPE was introduced 'to meet the needs of foreign students who wished to furnish evidence of their knowledge of English with a view to teaching it in foreign schools' (Wyatt and Roach 1947:126). This purpose is made explicit in the examination board's 1913 Regulations. By 1933, however, this purpose had disappeared from the printed Regulations, and by 1947 Wyatt and Roach state that CPE was 'open to all candidates whose mother tongue is not English and it is designed not only for prospective teachers but also for other students with a wide range of interest within the field of English studies'. It would seem that while the test purpose and the test taker constituency of CPE 'generalised' over this period, the test still retained its relevance for L2 teachers of English presumably because it was perceived to be relevant and useful to broader pedagogical needs. (See Weir 2003, in Weir and Milanovic 2003, for a full account of CPE's evolution throughout the 20th century.)

Fulcher and Davidson (2009) offer us an interesting conceptual analysis of changes in test use over time, drawing upon the field of architecture as a metaphor for language test development. Their discussion of 'test retrofit' provides the language testing community with a valuable framework for exploring this important area of the changing use of tests, though their analysis may risk oversimplifying what is in fact a more complex reality. For example, the theoretical distinction they draw between 'upgrade retrofit' and 'change retrofit' may not always be clear-cut in practice. The development of CPE and its legacy with regard to subsequent Cambridge tests testify to the complexities surrounding rigid notions of test purpose and specificity and how these can evolve over time within a wider and changing ecology. It is essential that the take-up and use of a language test, along with the nature of its test taker constituency, are carefully monitored over time, and that the test itself is adapted accordingly to take account of changing purposes or trends, some of which may be beyond the control of the test provider. For example, if test candidates become younger because more English language teaching and learning worldwide takes place lower down the age-range in the primary as opposed to the secondary curriculum (Graddol 2006), then test topics may need to change, as in the case of the recently developed PET and KET for Schools examinations. Similarly, if CAE is to be widely adopted as an English language proficiency requirement for university entry, then the test may need to become more academically oriented with regard to features of cognitive and context validity.

Since 1913, most new Cambridge ESOL examinations have followed the model originally set by CPE and they have included a direct Speaking test as an integral component of the language test battery, alongside tests of Reading, Writing, Grammar, Vocabulary, and later Listening. (For more details see accounts of other Cambridge tests in Hawkey 2004a, 2009, and O'Sullivan 2006.) Cambridge ESOL has thus accumulated considerable experience of the theory and practice of oral language proficiency assessment over many decades and across a wide variety of proficiency levels and domains, ranging from beginner to highly proficient, and from young learner English to using English for study or work. It is important to note, however, that Cambridge was not alone in adopting the direct approach to oral proficiency assessment. In the USA in the 1950s, for example, the Foreign Service Institute developed its FSI Oral Interview – a direct test in which the test taker interacts in the target language of interest. (See Fulcher 2003, McNamara 1996 and Spolsky 1995 for more on the FSI Oral Interview.)

Typically, Cambridge Speaking tests adopt a direct, face-to-face format in one of several variants (e.g. singleton, paired, group). The direct, face-to-face format is of course not the only test method available to exam developers for assessing aspects of spoken language proficiency. Semi-direct methods, such as a tape-mediated test, and even indirect methods, such as a written paper (cf the English Phonetics paper in the original CPE), may be seen as having an important role to play within a language proficiency assessment battery, though these have never been the dominant paradigms for the Cambridge exams. Interestingly, the indirect approach embodied in the CPE Phonetics paper from 1913 to 1932 was relatively shortlived. In an internal memo dated 1931, Jack Roach, Assistant Secretary to UCLES from 1925 to 1945, explained the rationale for eliminating this paper, together with any requirement of knowledge of phonetics, on grounds that: (1) school and university exams no longer required knowledge of phonetics; (2) pronunciation could be adequately tested in the Oral exam; (3) CPE was not a test of aptitude for teaching English, and thus proficiency in phonetics was not needed, and even if it was required in some contexts the CPE test might not provide adequate evidence (an interesting argument given the earlier discussion in this chapter on test purpose and specificity); (4) the phonetics component was off-putting for many candidates, deterring them from entering for the exam, or making it difficult to find suitable tuition if they did enter. The removal of the phonetics paper in 1932 was seen as making the syllabus more accessible to a wider public (Weir 2003:3).

Despite his faith in the oral component, Roach was keenly aware of the challenges that direct speaking assessment poses for testers, and he was among the first language testers to research some of the complex issues surrounding the face-to-face format. As early as 1945 he produced a report entitled *Some Problems of Oral Examinations in Modern Languages: An Experimental Approach Based on the Cambridge Examinations in English for Foreign Students*. Roach was particularly interested in how to *describe* levels of L2 speaking performance, and how to *standardise* Oral Examiners so that they rate candidates in a fair and consistent manner – questions which still continue to exercise language testers today. Roach's work can therefore justifiably be regarded as both ground-breaking and ahead of its time. Spolsky (1990) provides a full description of this work noting that it:

> ... appears to have been one of the first discussions in print of the problems of reliability and validity in the testing of oral proficiency in a second language ... pride of place for a direct measure of oral language proficiency is usually granted to the oral interview created by the Foreign Service Institute (FSI) of the US State Department developed originally between 1952–56 ... It turns out to be the case, however, that many of the important issues the FSI linguists had to struggle with, especially those concerning reliability, had been anticipated and intelligently ventilated in a paper written some years before the FSI activity started, printed and circulated internally among examiners of the University of Cambridge Local Examinations Syndicate (UCLES) (Spolsky 1990:158).

Roach laid the foundation for the research agenda which slowly began to emerge within Cambridge ESOL over subsequent decades and which started to bear significant fruit following the establishment of the Evaluation Unit in 1989 (see Taylor 2003). Not surprisingly, much of the research into speaking assessment that has been conducted by Cambridge ESOL since the early 1990s is cited or summarised in this volume to show how it has informed and shaped the evolution of the Cambridge Speaking tests to this point in time, and will undoubtedly continue to do so.

Commitment over nearly a century to the direct approach to speaking assessment, and to undertaking research, reflects Cambridge ESOL's long-standing concern for *authenticity* in testing, i.e. the attempt to develop tests that approximate to the 'reality' of language use beyond the test (sometimes called 'real-life performance'). This concern was taken up more vigorously during the communicative testing movement of the 1970s and 1980s (see Alderson 2000, Carroll 1980, Hawkey 2004a, Morrow 1979, Weir 1983, 1990, 1993 and 2005a). During the 1990s, Cambridge ESOL found it helpful to conceptualise authenticity according to Bachman and Palmer's (1996) two-way categorisation: *interactional authenticity*, which is a feature of the cognitive activities of the test taker in performing the test task (see Chapter 3 on cognitive validity below), and *situational authenticity,* which attempts to take into account the contextual requirements of the tasks (see Chapter 4 on context validity). The Cambridge ESOL approach to speaking assessment acknowledges the importance of both these perspectives, and though full authenticity may be unattainable in the testing situation, it recognises that, as far as is possible, attempts should be made to use situations and tasks which are likely to be familiar and relevant to the intended test taker.

An examination board's choice of oral proficiency test method will invariably depend on a variety of complex factors, including practicalities such as the heavy administrative demands and the significant costs that can be incurred in delivering speaking tests, as well as factors relating to validity, and, within that, reliability. Changing assessment needs in education and society, together with the advent of new and innovative technologies, mean that test producers, including Cambridge ESOL, are likely to keep a range of testing methods under review and to investigate these as appropriate. In recent years, for example, this has included exploring the opportunities afforded by computer-mediated and internet-based options.

During the early 1990s, following the establishment of the Evaluation Unit (later to become the Research and Validation Group), Cambridge ESOL embarked upon an extensive and long-term research and validation agenda associated with its approach to speaking assessment. Over the past two decades outcomes from this research have informed the revision of existing examinations (e.g. PET, FCE and CPE) as well as the development of new examinations (e.g. KET and CAE). As the number of Cambridge ESOL's level-based tests grew and as a suite of coherent levels began to emerge, work also began in the 1990s to develop a Common Scale for Speaking which would help test users interpret levels of performance in the Cambridge tests from beginner to advanced, identify typical performance qualities at particular levels, and locate performance in one examination against performance in another. This was in part a response to Alderson's (1991) call for more 'user-oriented scales' which also found later expression in the development of both the ALTE Can Do statements and the CEFR. The Cambridge ESOL Common Scale for Speaking (Table 1.6 on page 26) is designed to be useful to test takers and other test users (e.g. admissions officers or employers). The description at each level of the Common Scale aims to provide a brief, general description of the nature of spoken language ability in real-world contexts. In this way the wording offers an easily understandable description of performance, informed by empirical evidence, which can be used, for example, in specifying requirements to language trainers, in formulating job descriptions and in articulating language requirements for new posts.

The methodological approach in the volume

The methodological approach adopted in this volume builds directly upon that originally laid out in Weir (2005a), and subsequently applied and refined in Shaw and Weir (2007) and in Khalifa and Weir (2009).

The validation process is conceptualised in a *temporal frame* to identify the various types of validity evidence that need to be collected at each stage in the test development, monitoring and evaluation cycle. It is represented graphically in Figure 1.1 on page 28.

The framework is described as *socio-cognitive* in that the abilities to be tested are demonstrated by the *mental* processing of the candidate (the cognitive dimension); equally, the use of language in performing tasks is viewed as a *social* rather than a purely linguistic phenomenon, resonating with the CEFR's perspective on language for a social purpose which sees the learner (and presumably the test taker) as 'a social agent who needs to be able to

Table 1.6 The Cambridge ESOL Common Scale for Speaking

LEVEL MASTERY
C2 CERTIFICATE OF PROFICIENCY IN ENGLISH:
Fully operational command of the spoken language
- Able to handle communication in most situations, including unfamiliar or unexpected ones.
- Able to use accurate and appropriate linguistic resources to express complex ideas and concepts and produce extended discourse that is coherent and always easy to follow.
- Rarely produces inaccuracies and inappropriacies.
- Pronunciation is easily understood and prosodic features are used effectively; many features, including pausing and hesitation, are 'native-like'.

LEVEL EFFECTIVE OPERATIONAL PROFICIENCY
C1 CERTIFICATE IN ADVANCED ENGLISH:
Good operational command of the spoken language
- Able to handle communication in most situations.
- Able to use accurate and appropriate linguistic resources to express ideas and produce discourse that is generally coherent.
- Occasionally produces inaccuracies and inappropriacies.
- Maintains a flow of language with only natural hesitation resulting from consideration of appropriacy or expression.
- L1 accent may be evident but does not affect the clarity of the message.

LEVEL VANTAGE
B2 FIRST CERTIFICATE IN ENGLISH:
Generally effective command of the spoken language
- Able to handle communication in familiar situations.
- Able to organise extended discourse but occasionally produces utterances that lack coherence and some inaccuracies and inappropriate usage occur.
- Maintains a flow of language, although hesitation may occur whilst searching for language resources.
- Although pronunciation is easily understood, L1 features may be intrusive.
- Does not require major assistance or prompting by an interlocutor.

LEVEL THRESHOLD
B1 PRELIMINARY ENGLISH TEST:
Limited but effective command of the spoken language
- Able to handle communication in most familiar situations.
- Able to construct longer utterances but is not able to use complex language except in well-rehearsed utterances.
- Has problems searching for language resources to express ideas and concepts resulting in pauses and hesitation.
- Pronunciation is generally intelligible, but L1 features may put a strain on the listener.
- Has some ability to compensate for communication difficulties using repair strategies but may require prompting and assistance by an interlocutor.

LEVEL WAYSTAGE
A2 KEY ENGLISH TEST:
Basic command of the spoken language
- Able to convey basic meaning in very familiar or highly predictable situations.
- Produces utterances which tend to be very short – words or phrases – with frequent hesitations and pauses.
- Dependent on rehearsed or formulaic phrases with limited generative capacity.
- Only able to produce limited extended discourse.
- Pronunciation is heavily influenced by L1 features and may at times be difficult to understand.
- Requires prompting and assistance by an interlocutor to prevent communication from breaking down.

Source: Examinations Handbooks (2008).

perform certain actions in the language' (North 2009:359). The framework represents a unified approach to gathering validation evidence for a test. Figure 1.1 is intended to depict how the various validity components (the different types of validity evidence) fit together both temporally and conceptually. Weir explains that 'the arrows indicate the principal direction(s) of any hypothesised relationships: what has an effect on what, and the timeline runs from top to bottom: before the test is finalised, then administered and finally what happens after the test event' (2005a:43). Conceptualising validity in terms of temporal sequencing is of value as it offers test developers a plan of what should be happening in relation to validation and when it should be happening. The model represented in Figure 1.1 comprises both *a priori* (before-the-test event) validation components of *context* and *cognitive validity* and *a posteriori* (after-the-test event) components of *scoring validity*, *consequential validity* and *criterion-related validity*.

A number of critical questions will be addressed in applying this socio-cognitive validation framework to Cambridge ESOL Speaking tests across the proficiency spectrum:

- How are the physical/physiological, psychological and experiential characteristics of candidates catered for by this test? (Focus on the *test taker* in Chapter 2.)
- Are the cognitive processes required to complete the test tasks appropriate? (Focus on *cognitive validity* in Chapter 3.)
- Are the characteristics of the test tasks and their administration appropriate and fair to the candidates who are taking them? (Focus on *context validity* in Chapter 4.)
- How far can we depend on the scores which result from the test? (Focus on *scoring validity* in Chapter 5.)
- What effects do the test and test scores have on various stakeholders? (Focus on *consequential validity* in Chapter 6.)
- What external evidence is there that the test is measuring the construct of interest? (Focus on *criterion-related validity* in Chapter 7.)

These are the types of critical questions that anyone intending to take a particular test or to use scores from that test would be advised to ask of the test developers in order to be confident that the nature and quality of the test matches their requirements.

The *Test taker characteristics* box in Figure 1.1 connects directly to the *Cognitive* and *Context validity* boxes because, as Weir points out 'these individual characteristics will directly impact on the way the individuals process the test task set up by the *Context validity* box. Obviously, the tasks themselves will also be constructed with the overall test population and the target use situation clearly in mind as well as with concern for their cognitive

Figure 1.1 A framework for conceptualising Speaking test validity
(adapted from Weir 2005a:46)

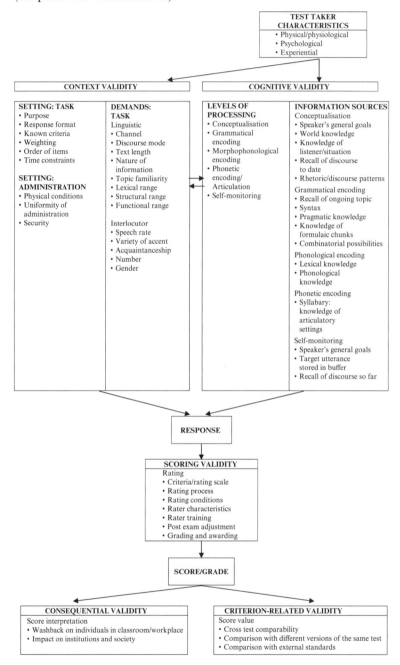

validity' (2005a:51). Individual test taker characteristics can be sub-divided into three main categories:

- *physical/physiological characteristics* – e.g. individuals may have special needs that must be accommodated such as visual impairment or a speech impediment
- *psychological characteristics* – e.g. a test taker's interest or motivation may affect the way a task is managed, or other factors such as preferred learning styles or personality type may have an influence on performance
- *experiential characteristics* – e.g. a test taker's educational and cultural background, experience in preparing and taking examinations as well as familiarity with a particular test may affect the way the task is managed.

All three types of characteristics have the potential to affect test performance (see Chapter 2 for more detail on this).

Cognitive validity is established by *a priori* evidence on the cognitive processing activated by the test task before the live test event (e.g. through verbal reports from test takers), as well as through the more traditional *a posteriori* evidence on constructs measured involving statistical analysis of scores following test administration. Language test constructors need to be aware of the established theory relating to the cognitive processing that underpins equivalent operations in real-life language use (see Chapter 3 for detail).

The term *content validity* was traditionally used to refer to the content coverage of the task. *Context validity* is preferred here as the more inclusive superordinate which signals the need to consider not just linguistic content parameters, but also the social and cultural contexts in which the task is performed (see Chapter 4 for detail). Context validity for a speaking task thus addresses the particular performance conditions, the setting under which it is to be performed (such as response method, time available, order of tasks as well as the linguistic demands inherent in the successful performance of the task) together with the actual examination conditions resulting from the administrative setting (Weir 2005a).

Scoring validity is linked directly to both context and cognitive validity and is employed as a superordinate term for all aspects of reliability (see Weir 2005a, Chapter 9, and Chapter 5 in this volume). Scoring validity accounts for the extent to which test scores are arrived at through the application of appropriate criteria and rating scales by human judges, as well as the extent to which they exhibit agreement, are as free as possible from measurement error, stable over time, appropriate in terms of their content sampling and engender confidence as reliable decision-making indicators.

Messick (1989) argued the case for also considering *consequential validity* in judging the validity of scores on a test. From this point of view it is necessary in validity studies to ascertain whether the social consequences of test interpretation support the intended testing purpose(s) and are consistent with other social values (see Chapter 6 for detail). There is also a concern here with the washback of the test on the learning and teaching that precedes it as well as with its impact on institutions and society more broadly. Weir's (2005a) framework included a third element within the *Consequential validity* component relating to *avoidance of test bias*. The issue of test bias, however, really takes us back to the *Test taker characteristics* box. The evidence collected on the test taker should be used to check that no unfair bias has occurred for individuals as a result of decisions taken earlier with regard to contextual features of the test. In light of this, we have chosen in this volume to locate discussion of bias and measures to check for and avoid bias within Chapter 2 on the test taker rather than in Chapter 6 (which is where it was dealt with in the previous construct volumes). This allows Chapter 6 to restrict its focus to matters of impact and washback; more importantly, it also reflects the evolution of Weir's own thinking in this area since 2005.

Criterion-related validity is a predominantly quantitative and *a posteriori* concept, concerned with the extent to which test scores correlate with a suitable external criterion of performance with established properties (see Anastasi 1988:145, Messick 1989:16, and Chapter 7 for detail). Evidence of criterion-related validity can come in three forms.

Firstly, if a relationship can be demonstrated between test scores and an external criterion which is believed to be a measure of the same ability. This type of criterion-related validity is typically subdivided into two forms: *concurrent* and *predictive*. *Concurrent validity* seeks an external indicator that has a proven track record of measuring the ability being tested (Bachman 1990:248). It involves the comparison of the test scores with this external measure for the same candidates taken at roughly the same time as the test. The external measure may consist of scores from some other Speaking tests, or ratings of the candidate by teachers, subject specialists, or other informants (Alderson, Clapham and Wall 1995). *Predictive validity* entails the comparison of test scores with another measure of the ability of interest for the same candidates taken some time after the test has been given (Alderson et al 1995).

A second source of evidence is demonstration of the qualitative and quantitative equivalence of different forms of the same test, by means of validation studies involving verbal protocol analysis with test takers as they complete speaking tasks or generalisability analyses comparing performance across speaking tasks.

A third source of evidence results from linking a test to an established external standard, or to an interpretative framework of reference such as the Common European Framework of Reference (CEFR) through the comprehensive and rigorous procedures of familiarisation, specification, standardisation and empirical validation (Council of Europe 2003a). Linking tests to an external standard or framework is not straightforward, however, and the use of the CEFR in this way remains somewhat contentious. Even if the recommended linking procedures have been followed, claims about CEFR alignment for any given test may need to be considered with some caution and careful attention paid to other essential quality aspects of the test in question. For a fuller discussion of the challenges and risks of CEFR linking, see Milanovic and Weir (2010).

Although for descriptive purposes the various elements of the model in Figure 1.1 are presented as being separate from each other, a close relationship undoubtedly exists between these elements, for example between context validity and cognitive validity. Decisions taken with regard to parameters in terms of task context will impact on the processing that takes place in task completion. Within the specific context of practical language testing/assessment, there exists a third dimension that cannot be ignored: the process of scoring. In other words, at the heart of any language testing activity we can conceive of a triangular relationship between three critical components:

- the test taker's cognitive abilities
- the task and context
- the scoring process.

These three dimensions, which are reflected in the *Cognitive validity*, *Context validity* and *Scoring validity* boxes of Figure 1.1 offer a perspective on the notion of construct validity which has both sound theoretical and direct practical relevance for test developers and producers. By maintaining a strong focus on these three components and by undertaking a careful analysis of their tests in relation to these three dimensions, test providers should be able to provide theoretical, logical and empirical evidence to support validity claims and arguments about the quality and usefulness of their exams. In addition, the interactions between, and especially within, these aspects of validity may well eventually offer further insights into a closer definition of different levels of task difficulty. For the purposes of the present volume, however, the separability of the various aspects of validity will be maintained since they offer the reader a helpful descriptive route through the socio-cognitive validation framework and, more importantly, a clear and systematic perspective on the literature that informs it.

The structure of the volume

Examining Speaking follows a similar underlying structure to that which was successfully adopted for its sister publications *Examining Writing* (Shaw and Weir 2007) and *Examining Reading* (Khalifa and Weir 2009). The outline shape closely follows the organisation of the framework described in Figure 1.1 with its six component parts explained above. Apart from the opening and closing chapters, each of the other six chapters takes one component of the socio-cognitive validation framework to examine it in detail with reference to the Cambridge ESOL Speaking tests, i.e. discussion of issues arising in the *research* literature on each component part is followed by consideration of Cambridge ESOL *practice* in the area.

There is, nonetheless, a significant difference in approach between the two earlier volumes and this one. While *Examining Writing* and *Examining Reading* were primarily co-authored publications, *Examining Speaking* is an edited collection of chapters from a team of contributors. All the chapter authors are acknowledged specialists in language teaching, learning and assessment, many in the specific field of speaking testing and assessment. They have direct experience of working with the Cambridge Speaking tests from a number of different perspectives (test design and development, test writing and administration, exam preparation and materials development, oral examining, test validation and research). As a result, they are able to combine their extensive theoretical knowledge with practical application and expertise in these areas, and so provide valuable insights into the complex endeavour or ecology that constitutes the assessment of spoken language proficiency. In doing this they draw on input from other informants as explained below.

This opening chapter sets the scene for what follows in the rest of the volume. In Chapter 2 on test taker characteristics Barry O'Sullivan and Tony Green discuss the test taker, who stands at the heart of any assessment event. Chapter 3 on cognitive validity, by John Field, reviews what the theoretical and empirical research to date tells us about the nature of speaking, particularly the cognitive processing involved, both in a first and second language. In Chapter 4 Evelina Galaczi and Angela ffrench examine in detail the many context validity parameters, or contextual variables, that impact on spoken language performance. Chapter 5 by Lynda Taylor and Evelina Galaczi focuses on scoring validity, exploring the diverse factors associated with the rating of speaking tests, including assessment criteria, rating scales, rater training and standardisation. Chapter 6 by Roger Hawkey considers the consequential validity of speaking tests, exploring issues of test washback and impact to establish where and how these play out within the complex process of validating international examinations. Chapter 7 by Hanan Khalifa and Angeliki Salamoura examines issues of criterion-related validity, in particular the need to establish comparability across different tests and between different forms of the same test, as well as with external standards. In the final chapter, Lynda Taylor and Cyril Weir draw together the threads of the volume, summarising the findings from applying the validity framework to a set of Cambridge Speaking tests and making recommendations for further research and development.

The multiple 'voices' in the volume

In the two previous construct volumes, the authors drew attention in their opening chapter to the fact that, as the volume progresses, readers will become aware of different *voices* in the book, together with varying styles of expression. This notion of multiple voices will be even more apparent in *Examining Speaking*, given that this is an edited volume, with chapter contributions from a variety of authors each of whom writes in their own style and, to some degree, from their own perspective. Beyond this, however, the voices of a range of other contributors will hopefully be detected and appreciated, all of whom make a unique and lasting contribution to our understanding of the issues under discussion.

The presence of multiple voices can be regarded as a strength of the volumes since it allows the many and varied participants in the language testing enterprise to be brought together so that their perspectives can be shared and their contributions duly acknowledged. Amongst them are voices from the wider academic community of theorists and researchers in the fields of Applied Linguistics and Language Testing (including those from competitor examination boards), who provide us with the essential theoretical foundations and guiding principles, and thus help to shape our current thinking and practice. Other voices, offering key insights on Cambridge ESOL policy and practice in speaking assessment, come from the community of language testing practitioners within Cambridge ESOL, i.e. Assessment and Operations staff, Research and Validation staff, Systems and Production personnel, and many other internal Cambridge ESOL staff who are directly responsible for developing, administering and validating the board's examinations. In addition to this internal practitioner community, there exists a vast cadre of external professionals upon whom the Cambridge ESOL examinations depend. They include item writers, test centre administrators, speaking examiners, trainers and seminar presenters, and their voices can be detected in the extensive use of quotations from or references to examination handbooks, item writer guidelines, examination reports, test centre documentation, examiner training materials, etc.

As was the case for *Examining Writing* and *Examining Reading*, this volume places into the public domain a wealth of information relating to the operational activities of ESOL examinations. Some of this updates material which has previously been available. Other documentation has up to now been internal and confidential, usually for proprietary reasons, and is appearing in the public domain for the first time. Some reference will also be made to internal working reports and other documentation which are not currently available in the public domain. Like any large institution, Cambridge ESOL undertakes a large number of investigations and routine analyses relating to its examinations on a day-by-day basis. These typically take the form of internal working papers and reports which cannot easily be released into the public domain without extra attention to write them up for external publication, e.g. on the board's website or in print media. Occasionally, documents include proprietary or commercial information which makes them unsuitable for release. In recent years Cambridge ESOL has sought to channel much more of its research into the public domain via peer-review journals and other academic publications in the field of language assessment and educational measurement. While this strategy has proved fairly successful, the editorial resources available in-house to achieve this remain limited when set alongside daily operational demands. References in this volume to internal reports and working documents that are not in the public domain are included because they are relevant to the discussion in hand and because they help to illuminate the workings of a large examination board.

Conclusion

Chapter 1 of *Examining Speaking* has argued that the credibility of language tests depends to a large extent upon a coherent understanding and articulation of the underlying latent abilities or construct(s) that they seek to represent. If these construct(s) are not well defined or understood, then it becomes difficult to support claims test producers may wish to make about the usefulness of their tests, including claims that a test does not suffer from factors such as construct under-representation or construct-irrelevant variance. Examination providers need to be able to demonstrate transparently and coherently, to both internal and external audiences, how they conceptualise language ability and how they operationalise it for assessment purposes, especially with regard to satisfactory differentiation of levels across the proficiency continuum.

The characterisation of overall language proficiency, and of its component skills, remains an ongoing process among applied linguists and language testers even though some progress has been made since the late 1980s when Spolsky commented as follows: 'Communicative competence theories have not yet clarified the relationship between function and structure, nor provided a theoretical basis for exhaustively describing the components of language proficiency or delimiting the boundaries between them' (Spolsky 1989:144). Applied linguists and language testers (Bachman 1990, Bachman and Palmer 1996, McNamara 1996, and others) sought to address this through their theoretical work during the 1990s, offering the wider language testing community valuable frameworks for our thinking and our practice concerning the nature of language ability and its assessment. More recently, work by Mislevy, Steinberg and Almond (2002, 2003), Weir (2005a) and Bachman and Palmer (2010) has helped to move forward our understanding of the complex nature of language test design, development and validation in theory and practice.

This volume aims to demonstrate how Cambridge ESOL has found the Weir framework to fit particularly well with its way of thinking about the validation questions that arise for the kinds of tests that the board offers. The socio-cognitive framework for test validation outlined in this chapter offers us a promising methodology for attempting such an enterprise. It seeks a sound foundation in underlying theory and conceptualises validity as a unitary concept, while at the same time allowing a systematic analysis of six core components that reflect the practical nature and quality of an actual testing event. Drawing upon multiple professional perspectives, combined with a wide variety of documentary and other sources, the following chapters now address each of these six components in greater detail, beginning with test taker characteristics in Chapter 2.

2

Test taker characteristics

Barry O'Sullivan
Roehampton University

Anthony Green
University of Bedfordshire

Introduction

Chapter 1 argued that, to be considered valid, test tasks must engage test takers in the cognitive processes that are required for effective communication in the target language use (TLU) domain. From this point of view, it is imperative that in designing tests for a population of language users, we should take account of any characteristics of the people being tested that may affect the nature of these processes. This requires a clear and unambiguous descriptive framework incorporating key variables relating to the test taker that need to be considered in test development because of the effects they may have on processing. Without an understanding of the test taker, we cannot be confident that our tasks or items will elicit from the test takers concerned a performance which reflects, as far as is possible, the particular language ability being tested. If, as we will suggest in this chapter, language test performance is affected by predictable variation between test takers in their cognitive processing, any failure to take account of the population for which the test is intended can result in tests (and therefore inferences informed by test scores) that are either biased towards or against particular groups or individuals.

From a different perspective, if we are to create test instruments that reflect the needs and interests of test takers, we need to place them at the centre of our testing cycle, involving them in test development and revision. This chapter suggests a framework for describing test taker characteristics and uses this as a basis for a discussion of how characteristics of the test taker are incorporated in the Cambridge ESOL approach to the testing of speaking and the test development cycle.

While this volume has dedicated separate chapters to test taker characteristics, cognitive validity and context validity, we do not take this to imply that the three are independent of each other. On the contrary, the characteristics of the test taker that most interest us here are of course those aspects of their cognitive and other resources that affect language use in specific social contexts. In this chapter we are concerned with identifying those characteristics which influence or relate to the resources that the test taker brings with them to the test event; later chapters focus on the cognitive processes that test takers engage in during language use and test performance (Chapter 3) and the impact of contextual variables on performance (Chapter 4).

Test taker characteristics

When discussing what he calls the 'elements of uncertainty' which may contribute to measurement error in examinations, Edgeworth (1890:615) makes reference to factors 'too subtle for the Calculus and Probabilities to handle: such as the variation of the candidate's spirits'. This early realisation of the potential effect on test performance of a range of factors associated with the test taker has, over the last century, perhaps because of the challenging 'subtlety' to which Edgeworth alludes, received little attention from test writers or researchers. Current concerns with test fairness, which emphasise the social responsibility of language testers, have highlighted the need to avoid bias against certain test takers where this can be operationalised.

Though the test taker is central to the validation process, the literature relating to characteristics of the test taker is surprisingly small. Those studies that exist have tended to consist of efforts to establish a framework for describing the test taker (a pre-theoretical approach) or efforts to identify particular characteristics of the test taker which affect performance (an empirical approach).

Pre-theoretical classifications

The personal attributes of test takers, referred to as *test taker characteristics* (TTCs) by Bachman (1990) may be divided into those which are *systematic*, in that they will consistently affect an individual's test performance, and those which are *unsystematic* or *random*. The systematic attributes referred to by Bachman (1990:164) include 'individual characteristics such as cognitive style and knowledge of particular content areas, and group characteristics such as gender, race and ethnic background'. These characteristics are systematic in that they tend to affect performance, though the precise nature of the effect will of course vary from person to person, and, we would suggest, from context to context.

Other descriptions of TTCs include Alderson, Clapham and Wall (1995), Bachman and Palmer (1996), Brown (1995) and Cohen (1994). As in the framework offered by Bachman (1990), these descriptions focus on the threat to test validity caused by the introduction of bias towards test takers displaying the characteristics described. It is interesting to note the diversity of the elements in these lists, particularly when we consider that they were all published within a very short time of each other. The only similarities to be seen are the inclusion by Alderson et al (1995), Cohen (1994) and Bachman and Palmer (1996) of *age* as a characteristic, the references to test taker *background* (*first language* and *educational background*) in Alderson et al (1995) and Bachman and Palmer (1996), and finally the inclusion of *motivation* in the work of Alderson et al (1995) and Brown (1995). We can therefore say that these descriptions demonstrate a lack of consensus regarding what should be incorporated in a typology of test taker characteristics (see O'Sullivan 2000b:19–23 for a fuller comparison of these typologies).

Theoretical classifications

Brown (1995) offers the most inclusive of the four frameworks. He takes into account a series of characteristics under the headings physical, psychological and individual. While Brown's framework does not comprehensively encompass the elements included in the other three descriptions listed above, it goes further by categorising test taker characteristics according to these three dimensions. He sees *physical characteristics* as encompassing the physical and physiological attributes of the test taker; *psychological characteristics* include such features as motivation, memory and concentration; finally, *individual characteristics* include test wiseness, test taking strategy use and a variety of other features that do not readily fall into the other categories such as speed of response.

Based on the above research and on his own earlier work, O'Sullivan (2000b) develops Brown's (1996) framework to propose a more comprehensive model of the test taker; see Table 2.1.

Table 2.1 Test taker characteristics (adapted from O'Sullivan 2000b:71–72)

Physical/Physiological	Psychological	Experiential
Age	Personality	Education
Gender	Memory	Examination preparedness
Short-term ailments	Cognitive style	Examination experience
Longer-term disabilities	Affective schemata	Communication experience
	Concentration	TL–country residence
	Motivation	Topic knowledge/
	Emotional state	Knowledge of the world

In this table, *physical/physiological characteristics* can be seen in terms of obvious fixed biological features:

- age
- gender

as well as other physical and physiological characteristics:

- short-term ailments, such as a toothache or earache, a cold or flu etc.
  – by their nature these illnesses are unpredictable and are not usually relevant to the construct, and

- long(er)-term illnesses or disabilities, such as problems with hearing, vision or speaking – either speech defects such as a stammer or lisp, or a deformity of the mouth or throat which affects production; or speech difficulties associated with other physical attributes such as age.

Table 2.1 lists *psychological characteristics* as those relating to:

- Personality – we know from research such as that carried out by Berry (2004) and Nakatsuhara (2009) that personality plays a significant role in task performance, particularly where different formats are used (solo, paired or group).
- Memory – it is important to ensure that performance is not affected by a test taker's ability to memorise information from the task input.
- Cognitive style – this is most likely to impact on performance where a particular task favours an individual with a particular style or approach to problem solving. It is important to remember that in most tests the task is there to elicit a sample of language so actually solving a problem is rarely likely to be relevant.
- Affective schemata – according to Bachman and Palmer (1996:68) these 'provide the basis on which language users assess, consciously or unconsciously, the characteristics of the language use task and its settings in terms of past emotional experiences in similar contexts'. It is therefore critical that we limit the potential for negative affect by steering clear of topics that are likely to cause upset to some test takers (e.g. death, illness etc.).
- Concentration – particularly relevant when we take into consideration the age of the test takers. It would be unfair to ask your learners to concentrate for long periods on test task performance without some deterioration in that performance.
- Motivation – while it is not easy for test developers to take into account the different levels and types of motivation present in the test population, we must try to ensure that the contents of our tests do not negatively affect this motivation. We therefore attempt to include, for example, tasks that are both realistic and likely to evoke the interest of the test takers. This also highlights the need to take into account the physical and experiential characteristics of the test population.
- Emotional state – this refers to the more transient emotions of the test taker during the test event. Proper training of examiners in ways to deal with these emotions can help each test taker to come to terms with whatever is happening within the event and achieve the best performance they are capable of.

Experiential characteristics encompass influences that are external to the test taker, and include:

- Educational experience including, but not restricted to experience of learning the target language.

  Specific experience of the examination in question is likely to be an important factor – preparation through a course of study for example, or having taken the examination before. This might include experience of the types of topic typically included in the test as well as of the actual task and item types used.

- Experience in communicating with others, particularly in the target language (but this may also refer to L1 communication – young learners, for example, might have little experience of interacting with previously unknown interlocutors).

  Related to this, previous experience of life in the target culture may also affect performance. A learner is likely to experience less anxiety after living for some period of time in a TL country or among TL speakers.

  General or world knowledge is also likely to play an important part in test performance and needs to be taken into account when designing a task for a particular population. Adult learners and young learners or groups from different cultural backgrounds can be expected to have different kinds of knowledge about the world.

In Table 2.1, the characteristics are listed separately, but are not seen as mutually independent. There is likely to be constant interaction between features during test performance. Take, for example, the notion of 'strategy use', seen as an aspect of *strategic competence* by Bachman (1990). It is likely that the successful (or unsuccessful) use of a particular strategy is a reflection of either a learner's underlying strategic competence (a psychological characteristic), or of strategic knowledge, for example some experience they may have had of observing successful, or unsuccessful, use of that strategy (an experiential characteristic), or a combination of both. In the same way we cannot always tell why a learner uses a strategy at a particular juncture; it may be that they find it difficult or impossible to produce a particular phoneme which is present in another known response (a physiological characteristic) or that they are too shy or withdrawn to commit themselves to a particular response (a psychological characteristic), or a combination of the two. It is therefore appropriate to consider each of these characteristics both separately and in terms of their possible interaction.

Test taker characteristics: Cambridge ESOL practice

In the section that follows, we will look at how Cambridge ESOL responds to the test taker in its Main Suite examinations of General English proficiency. By using the framework suggested in Table 2.1, we offer a systematic and comprehensive procedure that can act as a guide for all test developers to ensure that they take the test taker more fully into account when designing and administering their tests.

Knowing the candidature

A first step in understanding the impact of test taker characteristics is to collect data on relevant features. Cambridge ESOL asks all test takers to complete a Candidate Information Sheet (CIS) (see Appendix B) when they sit for any of their examinations. Included in the CIS is information related to the level of *education* of the candidature, of their degree of *examination preparedness* and *examination experience,* in addition to other information such as *age*, *gender*, *nationality* and *first language*.

Gathering this data serves two key purposes:

- The examination board is able to build up a clear picture of the profile of the population sitting for each test. This information is invaluable when it comes to test revision as changes in the intended population mean possible changes to the test. Table 2.2 (see pages 42–44) describes the typical test population based on data from the CIS completed by test takers in 2009.
- The CIS is also of real value when it comes to exploring the psychometric qualities of the tests, e.g. when exploring for task or item bias, as we shall see later in this chapter.

More detailed variants of the CIS have been developed for research purposes (see, for example, Kunnan 1995), but these are typically not practicable for routine operational use.

Physical/physiological characteristics: Cambridge ESOL practice

Age and gender

An example of how the routine collection of test taker data can assist in understanding a large test candidature is given in Figures 2.1, 2.2 and 2.3 (pages 45–46). In Figures 2.1 and 2.2 we can see that the typical age of the population for each of the Cambridge ESOL Main Suite examinations rises with the level of the examination itself. This has direct consequences for task format and content at each level as the test production process incorporates the age profile of the candidature and materials are piloted with representative groups of learners with opportunities for qualitative feedback on the appropriateness of the topics (see Chapter 4 on context validity). Similarly, it can be seen from Figure 2.3 that there is a balance of male and female test

Table 2.2 Test takers' profile for Main Suite examinations in 2009

L1 Top 10	%	Age	%	Gender	%	Educational level	%	Test preparation by attending classes	%	Reasons for taking Main Suite examination	%	Examination experience	%
CPE (C2)													
Greek	30	15 or under	6	Females	58	College/University	31	Attended	72	Further study of English/other subjects	14	Same exam	1
Spanish	16	16–18	30	Males	36	Secondary school	22	Didn't attend	27	Help career advancement	22	Other exams	30
German	9	19–22	22	Blank response	6	Primary school	0	Blank response	1	Personal interest	10	Blank response	69
Portuguese	7	23–30	24			Blank response	46			University recognition	3		
Polish	5	31 or above	17							Blank response	51		
Dutch	3	Blank response	1										
French	3												
Italian	3												
Romanian	2												
Catalan	2												
Blank response	8												
Other L1s	11												
CAE (C1)													
Spanish	19	15 or under	4	Females	60	College/University	34	Attended	82	Further study of English/other subjects	21	Same exam	1
German	16	16–18	40	Males	37	Secondary school	38	Didn't attend	17	Help career advancement	33	Other exams	23
Polish	8	19–22	24	Blank response	3	Primary school	0	Blank response	1	Personal interest	13	Blank response	76
Romanian	6	23–30	21			Blank response	28			University recognition	5		
Portuguese	6	31 or above	11							Blank response	27		
French	4	Blank response	1										
Italian	4												
Swedish	4												
Dutch	3												
Greek	3												
Blank response	10												
Other L1s	10												

FCE (B2)

First language	%
Spanish	26
Italian	11
Greek	10
German	9
French	6
Portuguese	5
Polish	4
Catalan	3
Czech	2
Russian	2
Blank response	10
Other L1s	11

Age	%
15 or under	18
16–18	44
19–22	15
23–30	15
31 or above	7
Blank response	1

Gender	%
Females	57
Males	39
Blank response	4

	%
College/University	27
Secondary school	48
Primary school	1
Blank response	23

	%
Attended	87
Didn't attend	12
Blank response	1

	%
Further study of English/other subjects	23
Help career advancement	34
Personal interest	12
University recognition	7
Blank response	24

	%
Same exam	2
Other exams	14
Blank response	84

PET (B1)

First language	%
Italian	28
Spanish	22
German	7
Greek	5
Arabic	4
Chinese	4
French	3
Portuguese	3
Catalan	2
Turkish	2
Blank response	11
Other L1s	9

Age	%
12 or under	8
13–14	23
15–18	52
19–22	8
23 or above	8
Blank response	1

Gender	%
Females	55
Males	42
Blank response	3

	%
College/University	13
Secondary school	70
Primary school	8
Blank response	9

	%
Attended	87
Didn't attend	11
Blank response	2

	%
Further study of English/other subjects	26
Help career advancement	28
Personal interest	11
University recognition	8
Blank response	26

	%
Same exam	3
Other exams	19
Blank response	77

Table 2.2 Continued

	L1 Top 10	%	Age	%	Gender	%	Educational level	%	Test preparation by attending classes	%	Reasons for taking Main Suite examination	%	Examination experience	%
KET (A2)	Italian	24	12 or under	30	Females	53	College/University	5	Attended	86	Further study of English/other subjects	33	Same exam	10
	Spanish	22	13–14	47	Males	43	Secondary school	63	Didn't-attend	11	Help career advancement	19	Other exams	16
	Chinese	10	15–18	14	Blank response	4	Primary school	24	Blank response	2	Personal interest	11	Blank response	74
	Greek	6	19–22	2			Blank response	8			University recognition	4		
	Turkish	4	23 or above	5							Blank response	31		
	Portuguese	3	Blank response	1										
	French	3												
	Russian	2												
	Arabic	2												
	Catalan	2												
	Blank response	10												
	Other L1s	3												

Source: Output data generated using CIS data from 2009 administration sessions.

Figure 2.1 Age profile of test takers taking KET and PET examinations in 2009

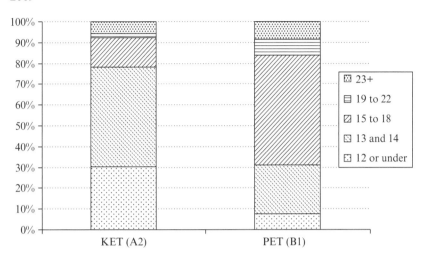

Figure 2.2 Age profile of test takers taking FCE, CAE and CPE examinations in 2009

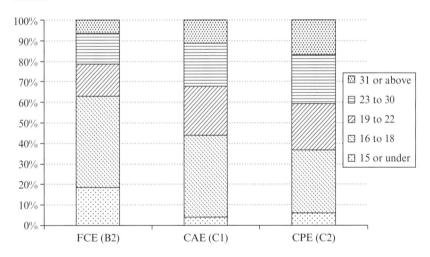

takers at each level, although as we progress through the test levels the percentage of male test takers decreases. Given this balance, the types of topic included must not reflect the interests of one gender group – see Chapter 4 for examples. The collection of data related to these two characteristics allows the test writers to take into account the actual population and any changes that occur, rather than relying on assumptions or approximations based on anecdotal evidence that may be inaccurate or outdated.

Figure 2.3 Gender profile of test takers taking Main Suite examinations 2009

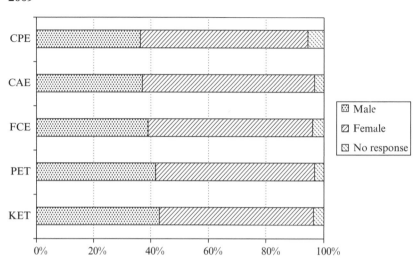

Research into the impact of age and gender on performance has most often been carried out in conjunction with exploration of the psychological and experiential characteristics and will be addressed further in discussion of these features in the relevant sections below.

Short-term ailments

In the case of short-term difficulties, such as minor illnesses or injuries, test centres are encouraged to take a supportive attitude, for example by bringing forward or delaying the Speaking test paper where possible. If this occurs, as the test format calls for two or three test takers to be examined during a single test event, the centre may need to apply for the test taker to take the test with a partner who is not doing the examination.

Where test takers are temporarily indisposed during a Speaking test and this is felt to have affected their performance, a Special Consideration form is completed and submitted to Cambridge ESOL immediately following the test (see also Appendix D). Reports of this nature are scrutinised by a panel of senior examiners who estimate the extent of the disadvantage and may award additional marks accordingly.

Longer-term disabilities

The most obvious impact on test development is made by the physical characteristics of the test takers. A quick search through the web pages of any serious national or international test will outline the special arrangements, or *accommodations* (as they are usually known in the USA), set in place to ensure that all test takers are given an equal opportunity to demonstrate their language skills to the best of their ability.

Cambridge ESOL encourages test takers to apply for special arrangements through their local test centre when they feel they qualify for such measures and sets out the disabilities for which special arrangements are typically made. Where a disability has not been declared in advance, but is felt to affect performance, an application for special consideration (see above under *short-term ailments*) may be made. The major categories of special arrangements that are common across most Cambridge ESOL tests are as follows:

Those involving modified material

- Braille forms
- enlarged print forms
- hearing-impaired (lip-reading) forms of a Listening test
- single format Speaking tests
- question papers/answer sheets produced on coloured paper.

Administrative arrangements

- exemption from Listening and/or Speaking components
- additional time
- provision of a Reader and/or amanuensis
- use of a copier to produce a transcript
- use of a word processor
- use of a coloured overlay, e.g. for dyslexic test takers
- use of a partner who is not doing the examination in the Speaking test
- separate facilities for taking the test or test battery
- use of headphones for the Listening test
- supervised breaks (where a test taker can have a break which does not count towards the standard examination time), e.g. for a test taker with concentration difficulties, or repetitive strain injury.

The area of special arrangements is highly complex and an application from a single test taker for special arrangements does not lead in programmatic fashion to a single measure being put in place. Instead, a whole series of special arrangements may be needed. Taylor (2003) cites the example of a visually impaired test taker who may require:

- a specially modified test paper – Braille or enlarged print
- separate facilities for taking the test or test battery

- an individual invigilator as well as a Reader and/or amanuensis or the use of a word processor or Braille typewriter on the day
- permission for extra time to complete their papers.

In the case of Speaking tests there is a series of special arrangements that apply to students with hearing, visual, speaking or other difficulties, such as Asperger's Syndrome. In every case, the exact combination of special arrangements that is most appropriate will need to be determined individually in consultation with the test taker through the local test centre.

Special arrangements for test takers with speech or hearing difficulties

In the case of Cambridge ESOL Main Suite examinations (KET, PET, FCE, CAE, and CPE) as well as for the BEC suite, test takers normally take the Speaking test with a partner – and in some cases with two partners. This can cause some problems with the provision of special arrangements, as the welfare of all test takers must be taken into account if the test is to be fair to all participants. Notwithstanding these potential problems, test takers with speech or hearing difficulties may apply (through their local test centre) for any of the following conditions to be applied to their Speaking test:

- *extra time*: This might apply to test takers who take longer than usual to assimilate prompt material such as text, to understand what people are saying or to articulate responses
- *to take the test with a partner who is not a test taker* (e.g. a friend who is not taking the examination): This may help the test taker to lip-read what their partner is saying more easily, or it might apply in cases where the test taker could potentially disadvantage a partner, e.g. a test taker with a speech impediment
- *to take the test without a partner* (i.e. in those parts of the test which usually ask both test takers to talk to each other, the test taker may talk to the examiner instead): This would, for example, be an appropriate provision for a hearing impaired test taker who relies on lip-reading, as it is more straightforward for someone in this position only to have to lip-read one person.

Test takers are encouraged to communicate their requests through their language teacher (where they are attending a course of study designed to prepare them for the test) and the local test centre well before the actual test date so that arrangements can be made in good time. No requests will be considered after the test has been taken, and a minimum period of notice is required in order to be able to ensure that test takers can be provided with the most appropriate special arrangements. All requests that are supported by the centre are then forwarded to Cambridge ESOL where they are evaluated and a final decision made, sometimes following extensive communication with the centre in order to ensure that, as far as possible, the special arrangements agreed are appropriate.

While the emphasis is clearly on providing the test taker with the maximum of support in terms of these special arrangements, it is a fundamental principle that the assessment objectives of the test must not be compromised (the test must still test what it purports to test, and the test taker's final result must not give a misleading impression of their attainment). Visually or hearing impaired test takers must not be given an unfair advantage over other test takers. In line with this approach, Cambridge ESOL does not allow the use of signing in the Speaking test as it is believed that the essential nature of the construct of speaking would be so radically changed by its use as to render the results of the test meaningless.

Unfortunately, there will be cases where test takers have severe hearing difficulties and the special arrangements described above will not be sufficient. A test taker, for example, who cannot lip-read, can apply for exemption from *either* the Listening test *or* the Speaking test in certain exams. If the test taker then passes the examination, they receive a certificate which is endorsed (i.e. it has the following statement printed on it): 'The test taker was exempt from satisfying the full range of assessment objectives in the examination.'

Special arrangements for test takers with visual difficulties

In addition to the special arrangements available to students with speech or hearing difficulties, there is a similar set of arrangements for those with visual difficulties. The request for these special arrangements is again made through the local test centre before the test event – often in consultation with a teacher and/or the centre.

The arrangements are in many ways similar to those for students with speech or hearing difficulties, i.e.:

- *Extra time* (where a test taker takes longer than usual to read any exam material or decide what they want to say).
- *Taking the test with a partner who is not doing the examination* (an arrangement designed to eliminate any bias towards or against the partner of a test taker qualifying for special arrangements).
- *Taking the test without a partner* (like the arrangement for test takers with hearing difficulties, this applies to those parts of the test which usually ask both test takers to talk to each other. Again, the test taker may talk to the examiner instead).
- *Adapted visual material*, e.g. the use of 'verbal' rather than visual material.

Since parts of the Cambridge ESOL Speaking test for the Main Suite examinations use pictures taken from newspapers or magazines, there is a possibility that test takers with visual difficulties may experience negative construct-irrelevant impact on their test performance. By this we mean their performance may be poor due to their inability to actually see the materials rather than to their spoken language ability. In order to deal with this, the visual materials used in the Speaking tests can be adapted or modified. This is typically done either by enlarging the image, or by offering Braille or enlarged print forms of written descriptions of the pictures.

On the Cambridge ESOL website, there is an example given of the Braille form of the FCE Speaking test. In this form the test consists of the following parts:

- A brief personal information exchange with the examiner.
- The test taker is given short written descriptions of two photographs in Braille. They then have about one minute to compare and contrast the situations in the descriptions and give opinions about them.
- The test taker takes part in 'various conversational activities' using Braille notes or information.

Other special arrangements

In addition to speech, hearing or visually impaired test takers, there may occasionally be other grounds for applications for special arrangements. Test takers with learning difficulties, e.g. Asperger's Syndrome, or those in closed institutions, e.g. prisons, usually apply for single rather than paired test taker versions of Speaking tests. *Speaking Examiner Support Files* are supplied to speaking examiners both in the UK and internationally, with detailed instructions on administering the special forms of Speaking tests.

Applications for special arrangements

Taylor (2003:2) reports that the total number of test takers seeking special arrangements for the Upper Main Suite (UMS) Speaking and Listening papers in 2001 was just 11. When we consider that she reports in the same paper the total number of test takers for the Cambridge ESOL examinations was then 'well over one million' this figure is negligible, as is the figure for test takers seeking exemption from these same papers in 2001 (a total of seven). The number of visually or hearing impaired test takers who were granted special arrangements in the Cambridge Speaking tests between 2005 and 2009 is summarised in Table 2.3.

As we can see from Table 2.3, hearing and visual difficulties account for the majority of applications for special arrangements in the Speaking

Table 2.3   The number and nature of special arrangements requests for Cambridge ESOL Speaking tests from 2005 to 2009

Special arrangements*		2005	2006	2007	2008	2009
Hearing Difficulties	Total cases	73	72	65	61	47
Visual Difficulties	Total cases	72	78	70	58	68
Exemptions	Total cases	1	3	0	1	6

* *Note that some test takers may receive more than one form of special arrangement on the same paper (e.g. adapted materials and extra time).*

test. Test takers with hearing difficulties most often request arrangements for extra time and/or taking the test using the single format, i.e. without a partner. Those with visual difficulties typically request extra time and/or adapted test materials, i.e. Braille or enlarged print forms. Even though modified Speaking test materials are available to test takers, the number of applications for these remains small, e.g. in 2007 there were only nine cases requesting special Braille and enlarged print forms of the FCE, CAE and CPE Speaking tests. Only a very small number of test takers seek exemption from the Speaking test; applications for exemption from the Listening test tend to be more common. Although the number of requests both for special arrangements and for exemption has risen since 2001, these remain a tiny proportion of the overall test candidature. In 2007, for example, the proportion of special arrangements specifically associated with the Speaking test was fewer than 10% of the total number of 1,888 test takers who requested special arrangements across the different papers of the Cambridge examinations that year. The majority of cases dealt with concern FCE, CAE and CPE (i.e. the Upper Main Suite examinations in the Cambridge ESOL product range).

Cambridge ESOL routinely monitors the take-up of its Special Circumstances provision on an annual basis and presents a general report each year on its website. The report reviews statistics on the cases dealt with during the previous year and updates stakeholders on new projects and developments in the field of special arrangements. The range of provisions in the Cambridge ESOL examinations continues to expand across the product range, perhaps in part because technology increasingly enables test takers with disabilities to access educational opportunities, including assessment opportunities.

In addition to these special arrangements, a range of specialist equipment designed to enable those with disabilities to read, write, speak or listen, or to access standard technology (e.g. a computer) has become available. The term *access technology* is now used to refer to this equipment which includes video magnifiers, Braille note-takers and screen-reading software. For an examination board, the use of access technology raises some important policy and practice issues relating to technological support and test security, as well as equity. Following a review of policy on the use of access technology by test takers, in 2007 Cambridge ESOL released a Guide to Access Technology for candidates, parents and teachers. Although only a small number of applications has been received to date, it is likely that in the future an increasing number of test takers will consider preparing for and entering Cambridge ESOL examinations using access technology.

While both access technology and special arrangements are designed to remove barriers to success for test takers with hearing and/or visual difficulties, there remains relatively little empirical evidence from the language testing literature to show how they benefit (or fail to benefit) particular students or how the arrangements affect the nature of the test itself. What research has been done is almost entirely in the areas of the testing of reading and mathematics. Much of this research predated the introduction in the USA of the 'No Child Left Behind' act in 2001, though since that time there has been an upsurge in interest in the area. In the two major reviews of the literature into special arrangements there are no studies in which the focus of attention is language testing, let alone the testing of speaking (Sireci, Li and Scarpati 2003, Thompson, Blount and Thurlow 2002). Twist and Lewis (2005) confirm what they refer to as the 'dearth of evidence' from the UK in their review of the literature on the impact of special arrangements in large scale testing.

The lack of empirical basis for special arrangements when combined with the apparently subjective nature of the whole process – it is unclear what evidence the test taker needs to produce in order to gain the support of the test centre in order that they might support any application for a special arrangement, or even multiple arrangements – means that we are essentially ignorant of the actual need for, or effect of such changes to test performance conditions. Though considerable research has been conducted with English Language Learners (ELLs) in the USA (see, for example, Abedi 2008 and Abedi, Hofstetter and Lord 2004), much of this has been undertaken with immigrants and indigenous groups needing accommodation in school-based learning and assessment contexts, rather than with international EFL learners with disabilities. Evidence from general education studies in the USA suggests that the interaction hypothesis, the current theoretical basis of these special arrangements, 'needs qualification' (Sireci et al 2003:60). This is because while the assumption has been that any special arrangements will only benefit test takers with disabilities and will result in no significant benefit for other test takers, evidence from the literature strongly suggests that all test takers might benefit from the types of special arrangements typically used. It is likely, for example, that many test takers would like to be offered additional time to complete their papers.

Again here we would remind the reader of the fundamental lack of research in the area of testing speaking in particular, a situation which exacerbates the problem. We simply do not know what effect the special arrangements have on test takers whose spoken language is tested under the different conditions implied by the special arrangements listed above. The very small numbers of test takers and the diversity of the disabilities involved mean that conducting research into the effects of special arrangements is extremely challenging. However, it is clearly essential that the questions are investigated in the interests of ensuring fair access to opportunities: the fundamental principle underlying their provision.

Before leaving this section it would be wise to consider one aspect of test special arrangements generally missed in the literature. Were all cultures to have similar attitudes towards disability, both in terms of definitions of what constitutes a disability, and of how disabilities should be dealt with, the whole area of special arrangements would be complex but manageable. The fact that there are broad differences across cultures means that solutions that are appropriate in one country may be seen as wholly inappropriate in another. It may be that the only way we can be sure of complete fairness is for the test developer in the international market to design their tests with the co-operation of stakeholders regarding the kind of special arrangements demanded in different contexts. This, in itself, is likely to have an impact on the comparability of the test results from all of these different contexts.

Psychological characteristics

The potential impact of psychological characteristics is even more difficult to quantify than that of the physical/physiological characteristics discussed above, although there has been some research into the effect on test taker performance in this area. While these characteristics are relevant to all test formats, they are of particular importance where test takers interact with each other. In a speaking test involving two or more individuals there will be interactions between the psychological characteristics of the participants. Furthermore, the affective reactions of test takers to these variables, or to groups of these variables, is likely to be different when the encounter with an interlocutor is live, rather than with a disembodied voice from a machine, or a presentation to an imagined audience (as is often the case for individual monologic tasks in speaking tests).

Personality

Berry (2004) reports on a series of studies designed to investigate how the degree of introversion and extraversion of test takers (established using the Eysenck Personality Questionnaire) impact on their oral test performance. In the first of her studies, which focused on the group oral format with four to six members in each group, Berry (2004:104) reports that introverts are affected by the degree of extraversion present in the group while extraverts do not appear to be affected. Where the task format is changed to a paired task there are no significant differences and Berry (2004:183) concludes that 'personality pairing alone is not a sufficient condition to predict the occurrence of systematic differences in performance'. In a follow-up analysis of her data, Berry (2004:186–7) found that there were differences between her male and female participants, though the small number of females suggests that these differences should be treated with some caution.

Summarising her studies, Berry (2004:222) questions the validity of the group oral since the degree of extraversion or introversion of the participants appears to represent a significant source of construct irrelevant variance. Her findings also imply that using a single language elicitation task format in an interaction-based speaking test is potentially problematic.

Personality: Cambridge ESOL practice

In order to counter any negative effect on test taker performance in its Speaking tests, Cambridge ESOL includes a number of language elicitation tasks and a range of formats to engage test takers in different discourse modes, see Table 2.4. This approach has the effect of ensuring that all test takers have an opportunity to perform at their best during the test event, thus controlling for any 'personality' effect. Interlocutors are also instructed to control the interaction to redress possible imbalances in test taker output during certain parts of the test, if required.

Table 2.4 Cambridge ESOL Speaking test format

Task format	Discourse type
One to one interview	Interview (examiner directed)
Individual long turn	Monologue
Interaction with other test taker	Dialogue
Discussion (test takers and examiner)	Interview (again examiner directed)*

* see O'Sullivan, Weir and Saville (2002) for a discussion of the language functions elicited by each test part as well as Chapter 4.

Affective schemata

There have been a number of studies looking at the effect on speaking test performance of affective reactions of test takers to variations in performance conditions. The first of these studies was Locke (1984), an exploratory study of a small group of students who tended to achieve higher scores when interviewed by male examiners. This study was followed by Porter (1991a), who again reported a significant effect with test takers again scoring higher when interviewed by men, a result replicated in his follow-on study (Porter 1991b), though here there was evidence that the perceived status of the interviewer was also a significant factor.

While all of these early studies focused on Arab students (predominantly male), a later study by Porter and Shen (1991) explored the affective reactions of a group of students of mixed background to the gender, perceived status, and interaction style of their examiners. The results of the research showed no significant difference in the results for the 'status' variable, while finding that the 'gender' variable was again significant, though this time subjects achieved higher scores when interviewed by a woman. In addition, it was observed that those interactions in which the interviewers employed a more supportive or 'female' interaction style (Fishman 1978a, 1978b, Leet-Pellegrini 1980, Zimmerman and West 1975) generated significantly higher scores.

O'Sullivan (1995) looked at the performance of a group of students from different language and cultural backgrounds on a pair of tasks (a one-to-one structured oral interview and a pair-work activity) each performed under two conditions – once with an interlocutor of similar age and a second time with an interlocutor who was either significantly older or younger. The results of this study indicated that there was a significant age effect (p<.05) for the older Arab students (who tended to achieve superior scores when working with an older peer). However, no further significant differences were found with either group, suggesting that the impact of the variable *relative age* is of limited importance, at least for these two groups of learners.

In the most wide ranging body of work to date on the impact of affect, O'Sullivan conducted a series of studies in which variables were first isolated and the effects noted, and subsequently groups of variables were explored in interaction. In the initial studies, significant effects were found for two of the three variables explored: gender of interlocutor (O'Sullivan 2000a) and degree of acquaintanceship (O'Sullivan 2002). No effect was found for the relative age of test taker and interlocutor (O'Sullivan 1995, 2000b).

In O'Sullivan's later studies (see O'Sullivan 2000b) there was a series of mixed findings. In one of these, a group of over 300 Turkish students were randomly assigned partners in a speaking test that involved interaction with another student. Analysis of the results indicated that there were significant effects for acquaintanceship (both male and female students achieved higher scores when interacting with people they regarded as strangers) and for interlocutor gender, but not for perceived relative personality. The final study, of over 500 test takers' performance on the FCE Speaking test, found that there were a series of highly complex interactions among the variables explored, though interestingly enough, all were found to have some effect. O'Sullivan concluded that there was clear evidence that test takers have affective reactions to variables associated with their interlocutor, and that these reactions could result in significant and systematic differences in their test scores. This might be used as an argument against including face-to-face interaction in a speaking test of the kind typically employed by Cambridge ESOL. However, the benefits of using this task format can be seen as outweighing the limitations if the purpose of the test requires that it elicits a broad range of informational, interactional and discourse management functions relevant to a variety of TLU tasks (see O'Sullivan et al 2002).

Affective schemata: Cambridge ESOL practice

In the Cambridge ESOL Speaking tests, test takers are engaged in a series of tasks (see Table 2.4 above) in which they are expected to perform both interactively (with the examiner and with another test taker) and solo. Fairness is enhanced by providing variety: test takers have opportunities to interact with different people, as well as having an opportunity to perform an extended monologue.

Affect can also be reflected in test taker reactions to both task format (see O'Sullivan 2000b) and task topic (see for example Lumley and O'Sullivan 2005, Smith 1989, Zuengler 1993). These aspects of affect demand particular sensitivity in the Cambridge ESOL Speaking tests given the international diversity of the candidature. They are taken into account by varying the task format (see above) and by careful monitoring of task topics. In the case of the latter, this is done using a list of 'taboo' topics which are considered to be potentially upsetting to test takers, either because they are perceived as being culturally or morally offensive (e.g. stereotypical representations of individuals or groups; political or religious topics), or because they may cause negative emotive reactions (topics such as death, serious illness etc.). (See Chapter 4 for more discussion of task characteristics.)

Motivation

The level of motivation of a test taker is likely to affect performance in a speaking test in a number of ways. Because of the nature of the speaking test, motivation is an even more complex issue than with tests of other language abilities. This is because in the speaking test event there are variables that can potentially impact on motivation which are either not present with the testing of other skills or at least are less likely to affect performance. Specifically, we are referring here to the interlocutor, though the nature of spoken interaction means that the test setting might also have a greater effect on performance than it might with other skill areas (see Figure 2.4).

Figure 2.4 Motivation in speaking tests

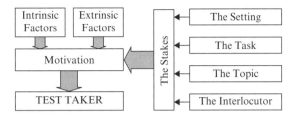

Motivation: Cambridge ESOL practice

The format of the Cambridge ESOL Speaking tests takes motivation into account by:

- systematically gathering information on the test takers' reasons for sitting the test
- setting clear and unambiguous guidelines for test centres, so that the settings of the tests are as similar as possible across the test population – though clearly practical differences across a global population mean that there will always have to be some degree of flexibility in these arrangements
- ensuring through test development and design that task formats and topics are likely to result in a clear purpose for speaking
- ensuring that all test events are delivered as planned by the test writers – this is done through a systematic monitoring of test events by Team Leaders and/or Professional Support Leaders (see Chapter 5 and Appendix D).

Experiential characteristics

The earliest systematic research into the impact on test performances of variables associated with the background of particular test takers was begun over 30 years ago, with what we will refer to here as the TOEFL studies. In this series, researchers identified a series of variables associated with test takers that represented potential sources of construct irrelevant variance. In brief, the most relevant studies in terms of this review focused on areas such as native language/country/region (Alderman and Holland 1981, Angoff and Sharon 1974, Hosley 1978, Swinton and Powers 1980 – all of whom found significant variation among the groups examined), gender of the test taker (Blanchard and Reedy 1970, Odunze 1982, Wilson 1982 – only Wilson found significant differences) and student major and text context in the reading paper (Hale 1988 – again a significant interaction between the variables was found). While it should be noted that these studies represent just a small proportion of the over 70 studies carried out over a period of about a decade, they are the only studies to focus primarily on what we see as characteristics of the test taker.

In addition to the TOEFL studies, there have been a small number of works that have looked at the effects of test taker characteristics on aspects of speaking. In the earliest of these, Suter (1976) examined how a set of 20 predictor variables were related to the pronunciation accuracy of his 61 subjects from four language backgrounds (Japanese, Thai, Persian and Arabic). The results suggest that care must be exercised when attempting to define demographic variables such as 'residency in the target language country', as, in this case, the effect of such a variable may well depend on the age at which that residency started. Suter's results suggest that this is quite a complex area, with certain aspects falling into each of the three categories (significant and positive, significant and negative and non-significant).

In a later study, Kunnan (1995) used SEM to explore the effect of variables associated with the test taker on performance in a range of tests (TOEFL, SPEAK, TWE – institutional forms of the Educational Testing Service's *Test of Spoken English* and *Test of Written English* respectively – and all five papers of the FCE). The categories used were: subject background; exposure to TL; monitoring; and motivation, though this final category was not used because of the unreliability of the data from the questionnaire (Kunnan 1995:38). Results suggested that of the four variables associated with participant background (formal instruction and informal exposure to English either in the subject's own country or in an English speaking country) only one proved to have a substantial effect on test performance – formal instruction in an English speaking country. On the other hand, participants' monitoring of their linguistic performance was found to have a substantial effect on test performance. Kunnan concluded that 'influences on EFL test performance are dependent on many factors working in concert, not a few factors working in isolated ways' (1995:78). In fact, it is one of the advantages to the SEM approach that these interactions are highlighted in the graphic output of the results. However, O'Sullivan (2000b) points to some limitations associated with the way the speaking and listening papers were analysed, thus calling these findings into question.

Experiential characteristics: Cambridge ESOL practice

Analysis of data gathered via the Candidate Information Sheet (CIS) (see Appendix B), which is completed by all test takers taking Cambridge ESOL examinations, helps to provide a clear picture of the experiential profile of the test taker population in terms of *educational level*, *preparedness*, *reasons for* and *experience of taking examinations*, as well as *L1*, *age*, and *gender* and *nationality*. It allows the examination board to monitor how well Speaking test topics and tasks used in the test are matched to the test takers. This is done both qualitatively through review processes during the test production cycle and quantitatively through analysis of the test's psychometric and other qualities via task bias studies (see below). They are also important in informing test revision projects since changing trends in the intended population are likely to lead to changes to the test's format and content.

Table 2.2 describes the typical test population based on data from the CIS completed by Main Suite test takers in 2009 and it reveals some interesting trends in the test taker population across the proficiency levels:

- **First Language (L1).** Main Suite examinations are taken by test takers throughout the world with the majority of test takers in European and South American countries. Table 2.2 lists the top 10 L1s featuring in the 2009 administration (on an annual basis speakers of at least 100 different L1s take these tests).

- **Age.** Test takers' age increases steadily across the levels from KET to CPE with younger test takers taking KET/PET and more mature or older test takers sitting for CAE/CPE.

- **Gender.** In general, more females than males take an examination. The proportion of female test takers increases steadily up the proficiency continuum from CEFR A2 level to C2 level (i.e. from KET to CPE).

- **Educational level.** The majority of test takers are in full-time education whether in schools or higher education. KET has the highest percentage (26%) of primary school test takers in the Suite. This may reflect the downward shift of English language teaching and learning into the primary school curriculum around the world, a growing trend noted by Graddol (2006). The proportion of secondary school test takers taking Main Suite examinations decreases as the proficiency level of the examination increases. As for test takers attending college or university, they represent at least one third of the candidature taking CAE or CPE. Their number is highest in CAE followed by CPE.

- **Preparation for an examination.** A large proportion of test takers undertake a preparatory course before taking an examination. This proportion slightly decreases from CAE upwards.

- **Reasons for taking an examination.** Test takers enter an examination for a variety of reasons: out of personal interest, to improve employment prospects, for further study or to fulfil an employer/university admission requirement. The most popular reasons are career advancement and further study.

- **Experience in taking examinations.** Test takers who responded to this question have previous test taking experience, i.e. they are familiar with test taking conditions, with similar test tasks, or with completion of similar answer sheets. Test takers at the lower levels, i.e. KET and PET tend to sit for the same exam more than once. This percentage decreases as the level of proficiency increases.

At the Speaking test development stage steps are taken to reduce as far as possible the extent to which any test taker is disadvantaged in relation to other test takers by the content of the test. The information gathered on the candidature profile as exemplified in Table 2.2 is used for this purpose. Characteristics such as first language, age, gender, educational level, and reasons for taking an examination are considered when putting together new test specifications and when selecting topics and tasks for existing examinations. For example, Table 2.2 above, together with Figures 2.1 and 2.2, show that KET and PET test takers are different from FCE, CAE and CPE test takers at least in terms of age group and primary purpose for taking an examination. Thus, a topic on lifestyles and living conditions is typically more appropriate to the latter groups while a topic on hobbies and leisure is better suited to the former. Being appropriate to a particular age group, not favouring one gender over the other, and not privileging a particular L1 or a specific culture are essential criteria to guide text selection and task construction. Specific guidelines are provided to test writers to ensure a balance is struck among these characteristics as far as possible and practical. To ensure sample representation at the trialling stage, the use of CIS information is critical and Chapter 4 provides further discussion of these issues in relation to decisions on the contextual parameters of tasks and topics.

It is clearly important that all test takers and those instructing them should be as familiar as possible with both the test itself and with relevant details pertaining to the administration of the test. This is of particular concern with a speaking test, where learners often report anxiety at having to speak in a public setting and to a stranger, often for the first time in their lives. In order to deal with this, Cambridge ESOL makes a variety of materials for all their examinations freely available in the public domain. Exam-related handbooks, teacher seminars, examination reports and teaching resources are downloadable from the Cambridge ESOL website (www.CambridgeESOL. org). These offer detailed descriptions of the test, the intended uses of the test, hints to test takers and their teachers on how to prepare for the test papers, and clear specification with realistic sample test papers. Video/DVD recordings of Speaking tests designed to help to familiarise test takers with the test format are also available to teachers and test takers. In addition, staff from Cambridge ESOL regularly conduct training seminars for teachers involved in preparing test takers for the examinations. Public access to information about a test and the provision of exemplars of a test are in line with the Association of Language Testers in Europe (ALTE) *Code of Practice* (1994) which states that producers of language examinations must provide 'representative samples or complete copies of examination tasks, instructions, answer sheets, manuals and reports of results to users of language examinations' (<http://www.alte.org/cop/index.php>). In fact any member of ALTE guarantees to provide examination users and takers with information 'to help them judge whether a particular examination should be taken or if an available examination at a higher or lower level should be used'. ALTE members also commit to providing test takers with the information they need in order 'to be familiar with the coverage of the examination, the types of task formats, the rubrics and other instructions and appropriate examination-taking strategies'.

The routine monitoring of the demographic make-up of the candidature of a given examination enables any changes in the test taking population to be observed so that these can inform later review and revision of the test in question. Broadening the cultural context of Main Suite examinations in recent years has indeed been led by an awareness of the diversity of its candidature (Murray 2007). Similarly, changes over the years in the average age of test takers are reflected in the choice of the source material and in the provision of examinations more suited to the target age group, e.g. the newly developed KET for Schools and PET for Schools. Data which is gathered on test takers' experience in taking examinations and whether they have attended preparation classes helps shape the support and information provided to test takers through such channels as the Cambridge ESOL website.

Test bias and differential item functioning (DIF) research

Avoiding test bias favouring or penalising any group of test takers must be a priority for the test provider, particularly when important decisions concerning the test taker are going to be based on the scores. Hambleton and Rodgers (1995:1) define bias as 'the presence of some characteristic of an item that results in differential performance for individuals of the same ability but from different ethnic, sex, cultural, or religious groups'. An item or task is considered potentially biased if it contains content or language that is differentially familiar to subgroups of test takers, or if the item structure or format is differentially difficult for subgroups of test takers.

As we have seen above, in the field of language testing individual test taker characteristics such as cultural background, background knowledge, cognitive characteristics, native language, ethnicity, age and gender have typically been identified as potential sources of bias; these have all been discussed together with the ways in which Cambridge ESOL seeks to mitigate the potential effect of bias arising from such factors. It is worth remembering Bachman's (1990:278) caveat that group differences must be treated with some caution as they may be an indication of differences in actual language ability rather than an indication of bias. For example, extraversion or socia-bility may well be an advantage to a test taker in a direct speaking test but we might argue that a test designed to eliminate this advantage as a source of possible bias would almost certainly lose key aspects of its construct. This touches upon the complex issue of whether the construct of speak-ing is defined in more purely linguistic terms, or whether it also embraces communication skills (Taylor and Wigglesworth 2009).

Zumbo (2007) refers to 'the introduction of the term *differential item func-tioning* (to replace *item bias*)', thus enabling a distinction to be made between item impact and item bias. For Zumbo, 'Item impact described the situation in which DIF exists, because there were true differences between the groups in the underlying ability of interest being measured by the item. Item bias described the situations in which there is DIF because of some character-istic of the test item that is not relevant to the underlying ability of interest (and hence the test purpose)' (2007:224). Geranpayeh and Kunnan (2007:1) draw on this conceptual distinction when they comment that it is 'essential for test developers to continuously monitor their tests in terms of whether all test takers are receiving a fair test . . . One approach to this problem has been to examine test scores from a pilot group or, if the test has already been launched, to examine test scores from a large sample of test takers and detect items that function differently for different test taking groups and to inves-tigate the source of this difference. This approach is called *differential item functioning* (DIF).' Examples of DIF studies undertaken by Cambridge ESOL include Banks (1999) and Geranpayeh (2001). These studies examined the country and age bias in the First Certificate in English and Preliminary English Test and recommended further investigation into the DIF of *listening item* types.

Following an observation of DIF, an interpretive investigation of its probable source is needed so that an informed, context-based judgement decision can be made on whether there is bias in the test. Geranpayeh and Kunnan (2007:1) describe how they investigated whether the test items on the Listening section of the CAE examination functioned differently for test takers from three different age groups. Although statistical and content anal-ysis procedures detected DIF in a few items, expert judges were not able to identify the sources of DIF for these items. This neatly illustrates the point made above that the presence of DIF does not necessarily imply that an item or test is biased.

Item-based tests for assessing reading and/or listening ability clearly lend themselves readily to the sorts of DIF studies referred to above. However, the more task-based approach typically used in speaking assessment is less amenable to these types of statistical investigation. In light of this, although *post-hoc* analyses undoubtedly have a role to play, the ongoing enterprise of reducing bias to a minimum in speaking tests in the Cambridge validity context depends heavily on the development and systematic application of test production and delivery systems. As Khalifa and Weir remind us, the avoidance of bias is 'not simply about checking whether or not you can identify it after the event (through research-oriented investigations and studies)' (2009:188). They conclude that 'if due care and attention is paid to the test taker at the design and development stage the chance of serious bias is in all likelihood reduced' (2009:187). Cambridge ESOL systems designed to reduce the danger of test bias include careful item writing and materials production processes, through strict item writer recruitment, induction, training, co-ordination, moderation and e aluation (see Saville 2003:78–96), as well as the whole item/test developm nt process, through various stages of writing, editing, trialling, pretestii g, monitoring, evaluation and revision (see Appendix C). As will be cl. ir, the focus in this chapter has been firmly upon test taker characteristics and in this regard we have discussed the role the Cambridge ESOL Candid i Information Sheet (CIS) can play when it comes to exploring the qualitie of the tests and the potential for differential task functioning. However speaking assessment involves interactions between tasks, raters and rating criteria (as well as test takers) and these too can be sources of potential bias, requiring systematic investigation through various types of analysis. Since such analyses also relate directly to matters of test reliability they will be dealt with in Chapter 5 on scoring validity.

Finally, in relation to test taker characteristics, Weir and Milanovic (2003:103) describe the key role for CIS data analyses at Cambridge ESOL Grade Review and Awards meetings:

> The performance of large groups of candidates (or cohorts) is compared with cohorts from previous years, and performance is also compared by country, by first language, by age and a number of other factors, to ensure that the standards being applied are consistently fair to all candidates, and that a particular grade 'means' the same thing from year to year and throughout the world.

Conclusion

For a successful testing programme it is important both that test developers understand the nature of the test takers and that test takers have a good appreciation of the content and purpose of the test. This chapter has outlined some of the ways in which test takers can be informed about test content and how this can be shaped to reflect their level of maturity and knowledge of the world. The chapter has also suggested ways in which an examination board can build and maintain its knowledge of test takers and how it can seek to use this knowledge to enhance fairness, whether by taking account of demographic trends in the candidature or by responding to individual circumstances. We have argued that a good deal of research remains to be done to explore how such efforts may impact on test validity, but such concerns do not detract from the ongoing need to ensure equality of access to the opportunities that tests of this nature can open up.

3 Cognitive validity

John Field
University of Reading

This chapter considers the cognitive validity of the Speaking tasks which feature in the Cambridge ESOL suite. By 'cognitive validity' is to be understood the extent to which the tasks in question succeed in eliciting from candidates a set of processes which resemble those employed in a real-world speaking event. A second consideration is how finely the relevant processes are graded across the levels of the suite in terms of the cognitive demands that they impose upon the candidate.

Previous volumes in this series have considered the cognitive validity of Cambridge ESOL tests of writing and reading. This chapter can therefore draw upon the format and approach already established in Chapters 3 of Shaw and Weir (2007) and Khalifa and Weir (2009). As with the earlier analyses, a major goal is to propose a cognitive model of the construct in question, which can serve as a framework for judging the cognitive validity of any test of skilled performance. The model is not drawn from testing theory but from independent insights afforded by empirical research into the psychology of language use.

It needs to be borne in mind that this is the first volume of the series to tackle the spoken modality. While there are certain parallels in the processing model presented here – especially with the model of writing proposed by Shaw and Weir (2007) – there are also marked differences. Perhaps the most important distinguishing characteristic of the oral skills is that they typically operate under tight time constraints that are not usually present in writing and reading. An interactional speaker self-evidently does not have time for planning and revising in the way that a writer does. Due account will be taken of this important difference in the discussion that follows.

The chapter falls into three parts. Firstly, there is an explanation of the general notion of cognitive validity, which retraces some of the points made in earlier volumes but does so with specific reference to the present exercise. Next, some background is provided to research findings on the nature of L1 speaking; and a process account of the skill is proposed, drawing chiefly upon the model devised by Levelt (1989). The Levelt model is adapted to provide a five-part framework for an examination of the cognitive validity of the tests in the Cambridge ESOL suite. The discussion then goes on to consider two important characteristics of the types of speech elicited by the tasks in the text. Clearly, this entails some consideration of task design, leading us into a grey area at the interface between cognitive and context validity. But the goal here is to consider these particular features strictly in terms of any likely additional cognitive demands which they impose upon the candidate.

The cognitive validation exercise

Cognitive validity: a rationale

An important consideration in establishing the validity of tests that aim to measure performance is the extent to which the task, test content and prevailing conditions require the taker to replicate the *cognitive processes* which would prevail in a natural (i.e. non-test) context. This aspect of validity is especially critical in the case of tests that assess general competence in any type of skill across a proficiency continuum – a category into which the Cambridge ESOL Main Suite of General English tests (KET–CPE) clearly falls. The concern of these exams is with the test taker's ability to apply the four language skills at varying levels of proficiency, rather than with the simple measurement of linguistic knowledge. Furthermore, their value to a user of the test scores lies in their predictive power: their ability to indicate how competently a candidate might be expected to perform in actual L2 contexts. Thus it becomes important for test producers to know, and to be able to demonstrate, how far what happens in the testing situation replicates cognitive processing in the world beyond the test, so that test users can have confidence in the meaningfulness and usefulness of the score outcomes from the test.

Interest in the psychological processes underlying language test performance has a long history, dating back at least as far as Carroll (1968); but it received new impetus recently from the work of Cyril Weir. Weir (2005a) expresses concerns over traditional *post hoc* approaches to investigating construct validity, where statistical methods such as factor analysis are applied to test results in order to establish the nature of the construct that has been tested. He raises the issue of whether the data derived might to some extent be compromised by the form and content of the test and by the assumptions underlying its design. To put it in simple cognitive terms, he identifies the dangers of relying exclusively on an approach that attempts to track back from a product or outcome to the process that gave rise to it. Instead, he argues for what he terms *theory-based validity* (or more recently *cognitive validity*): a complementary approach to test validation which takes account, at an initial stage, of empirical evidence as to the nature of the construct that the test aims to assess. Weir (2005a:18) makes his point powerfully:

> There is a need for validation at the *a priori* stage of test development. The more fully we are able to describe the construct we are attempting to measure at the *a priori* stage, the more meaningful might be the statistical procedures contributing to construct validation that can subsequently be applied to the results of the test. Statistical data do not in themselves generate conceptual labels. We can never escape from the need to define what is being measured, just as we are obliged to investigate how adequate a test is in operation.

This additional strand of construct validation attempts to ensure that, besides benefiting from feedback from piloting and past administrations, test design also draws in a principled way upon external evidence concerning the nature of the expertise which is to be targeted. For a more detailed account of the arguments, see Chapter 3 of *Examining Reading* (Khalifa and Weir 2009).

This is not a simple matter of ecological validity. The goal is to establish whether the tasks proposed by a test designer elicit mental processes resembling those which a language user would actually employ when undertaking similar tasks in the world beyond the test. The processes in question might relate to the way in which the user assembles or interprets input; or they might reflect the cognitive demands imposed upon the user by facets of the task.

The cognitive perspective

The focus in this chapter is thus upon *process* rather than product, the application of the skill rather than the linguistic knowledge that underpins it. Consequently, the framework that is to be outlined will rely chiefly upon theory and evidence taken not from testing studies or from general linguistics but from psycholinguistics and speech science. Within those fields, two areas of enquiry are particularly relevant to the present exercise. The first consists of *research on language production*: specifically, on how speech is stored and assembled by the user. The second concerns *the nature of expertise*; the assumption here being that the ability to produce speech fluently and with a high degree of automaticity is a type of *expert* behaviour which has certain elements in common with playing chess or driving a car.

Because second language acquisition (SLA) commentators occasionally misunderstand what cognitive approaches to language skills entail, it may be helpful to provide a brief explanation of the thinking that underlies them. It is mistaken to suggest that, in examining language processing, cognitive scientists ignore issues of context or deny their relevance. On the contrary, they concern themselves quite closely with the types of decision-making which occur when an utterance is adjusted to take account of listener-relevant factors, such as illocutionary intent or shared knowledge

(Levelt 1989: Chapter 1). They also take into account the possible impact upon a speaker's attentional resources of affective factors such as tiredness or anxiety. But their principal focus is on the mental operations which are engaged by language users under normal circumstances and the way in which situation-specific information of various kinds can be integrated into those operations.

It is also incorrect to assert that cognitive psychologists rely upon the assumption that all language users behave identically. While certain processing routines may provide the easiest and most efficient routes to language production and reception, some users (including L2 learners) achieve the same goals by less direct means. It is evident that individuals, whether speaking in L1 or L2, vary enormously in the range of vocabulary they command and in their powers of expression. It is also evident that L2 speakers respond in very individual ways to the challenges posed by an inadequate lexical or grammatical repertoire. Similarly, there is no suggestion that test designers can afford to ignore the influence of factors arising from individual speaker differences of age, gender, ethnicity, first language background, etc., as discussed in the previous chapter on test taker characteristics.

Nevertheless, the premise is adopted that underlying the four language skills are certain established and shared routines which can be traced by examining and comparing the performance of expert language users. This assumption is supported by two lines of argument:

a) *The universal argument.* All human brains are similarly configured. They can be assumed, at some level of generality, to share processing routines which are broadly similar in that they reflect the strengths and limitations of the organ and the means it adopts for transmitting information. These routines might be deemed to contribute not simply to the forms that language takes but also to the ways in which it is processed in performance.

b) *The expertise argument.* A marked difference between an adult L1 speaker and an L2 learner lies in the fact that the former has had many years of experience during which to develop the most rapid and most effective processing routines for dealing with the vagaries of the target language – and to develop them without competition from deeply ingrained routines associated with another language. An understanding of how such expert users perform should thus assist us in directing the development of novice users. The novice/expert distinction is not, of course, an all-or-nothing one. There exists a continuum of expertise stretching from novice to expert user, which is highly relevant in the context of language proficiency assessment, where gradations of ability need to be distinguished and accredited for teaching and learning, employment or other social purposes. As Chapter 1 explained, a fundamental aim of this volume (and of the companion volumes in the series) is to improve our understanding of the key criterial parameters that differentiate one proficiency level from another, and to provide empirical (as well as intuitive and experiential) evidence in support of claims that a test or a test taker is or is not at a particular level.

In line with the notion of 'cognition' that has just been outlined, it will be assumed in considering the speaking skill that variation between tasks due to situation or genre falls outside the remit of cognitive validity (see Chapter 4 on context validity). Similarly, the discussion will in the main exclude consideration of social-affective factors which might influence the content or delivery of the speaker's utterances; these features are the concern of social rather than cognitive psychology and fall under the speaker-specific aspects covered in Chapter 2. To the extent that the present chapter considers linguistic difficulty at all, it does so purely in terms of the cognitive effort which the assembly of a syntactic structure or the retrieval of a piece of vocabulary might require. More general issues of linguistic accuracy, fluency and complexity are covered in Chapter 4.

The scope of the chapter

The direction taken in this study conforms closely to Weir's original (2005a) concept of theory-based or cognitive validity. Broadly, the approach to validation as it has been operationalised (Shaw and Weir 2007, Khalifa and Weir 2009) entails constructing an empirically attested model of the target skill as employed by expert users under non-test conditions; then relating the processes which feature in the model to the specifications of the test under examination. The models presented in the previous accounts of writing and reading were based upon information-processing principles, thus enabling the researcher to identify specific phases through which a language user normally proceeds (though the point is well made by Shaw and Weir that the phases are not necessarily sequential and that not all of them are obligatory). These phases provide a framework for determining in a systematic way how the various processes which make up performance in a skill are represented, explicitly or implicitly, in the test criteria.

While adhering closely to this line of attack, Khalifa and Weir (2009) extended the scope of cognitive validation by considering not simply the standard processes involved in employing the language skill in question, but also the varying cognitive demands placed upon the candidate by the range of tasks that are specified in the test format. This is especially apposite in the case of reading, since it enables consideration of the different types of reading elicited by the tasks and their relative complexity.

Tests of L2 speaking afford parallels in the form of two important task variables which determine the cognitive demands placed upon the candidate and the extent to which a task can be said to replicate a real-life speaking process. They are:

- the nature of the interaction between speaker and interlocutor
- the extent to which planning is permitted.

Following the presentation of the processing model and its application to the specifications of the Cambridge ESOL suite, there will therefore be a brief consideration of the ways in which the suite handles these two aspects of speaking in its task design. The discussion will adopt a strictly cognitive perspective, to avoid overlap with the more extensive examination of task design in Chapter 4.

In sum, the purpose of this chapter is:

i)   To consider the nature of cognitive processing involved in first and second language speaking by reviewing the relevant academic literature, both theoretical and empirical.

ii) To propose a model or framework against which speaking tests, including those produced by Cambridge ESOL, could be analysed, described and evaluated for the purposes of cognitive validation.

iii) To apply the model to a specific set of Cambridge ESOL Speaking tests at the different Main Suite proficiency levels in order to generate an *a priori* descriptive analysis of the cognitive processes underlying the test takers' performance.

iv) To consider other cognitive factors which might determine the relative difficulty of tests at different levels in the Cambridge ESOL suite. These relate to task variables which can be seen as adding to or alleviating the cognitive demands made upon the candidate.

Psycholinguistic accounts of speech production

Speaking is one of the most complex and demanding of all human mental operations. Levelt (1989:199) points out that an expert speaker of English produces utterances at a typical rate of about 150 words per minute, or 2.5 per second. Under pressure, the rate can rise to five per second. A normal educated adult L1 speaker might have an active vocabulary of about 30,000 words. This means that a fluent speaker makes the right choice from these 30,000 alternatives between two and five times per second, and maintains this rate of performance without any clear time limit, other than the need to cede the turn at some point to an interlocutor. Levelt comments: 'There is probably no other cognitive process shared by all normal adults whose decision rate is so high.' All the more reason, then, for those who design tests of speaking to have a detailed understanding of the nature of the skill and of the processes that contribute to it.

Extensive empirical research (psychological, neurological and phonetic) into all aspects of the skill of speaking has enabled commentators to achieve a fair degree of consensus as to the processes engaged when individuals assemble a spoken utterance in their first language. Early psycholinguistic research in the 1960s into producing and analysing spoken language concerned itself greatly with syntactic structure and with the extent to which the rules of grammar (particularly Chomskyan grammar) might have *psychological reality* (i.e. represent the processes in which a speaker engages when producing an utterance). These enquiries indicated that the clause was an important unit of speech assembly; but proved otherwise generally inconclusive. (See Aitchison 2008 for an accessible extended discussion.) It was at this point that many psycholinguists turned to an evidence-driven approach to speech production in preference to one that was largely shaped by established linguistic theory. One line of enquiry built upon emerging evidence from phonetics in respect of phenomena such as pausing. It became clear that brief pauses (generally of 0.2 to 1.0 seconds) were necessary for the forward planning of speech; and the location of these planning pauses was found to correspond quite consistently with syntactic boundaries, again implicating the clause as a unit of assembly. One theory (Beattie 1983) suggested that the length of planning pauses varied according to whether the planning in question related solely to the form of the next utterance or whether it additionally anticipated the conceptual content of later utterances.

A second line of enquiry focused especially on the errors made by naturally performing speakers, known as *slips of the tongue.* The notion was that by examining failures of the speech assembly system, one might gain insights into the cues that speakers were using in aiming for their targets. Slips of the tongue provided evidence suggesting that a syntactic frame was prepared by a speaker in advance of lexical items being slotted into it (*He found a wife for his job,* substituted for the target *He found a job for his wife.*) and that morphological markings were added at quite a late stage (*She come backs tomorrow*)[1]. These findings provided the basis for an early model of speech production by Garrett (1980, 1988), which drew also upon research into the speech impairments associated with aphasia. Important in Garrett's model were the assumptions a) that a preliminary structural frame is established into which the outcomes of a parallel lexical search are inserted; and b) that there is an initial planning phase where the syntactic framework and the links to lexis are abstract, followed by a phase where they are realised concretely in terms of word order and phonological word form.

A problem to which Garrett and others gave much thought was the extent to which syntactic assembly was so closely intertwined with semantic considerations that it could not be treated as a distinct operation. The advent of brain imaging has shed new light on this vexed question; neuroscientists (Kutas, Federmeier and Serreno 1999: 366–368) have succeeded in identifying an event-related potential (a pattern of electrical activity in the brain) that is distinctively associated with syntax and a separate one that is associated with semantic processing. This suggests that the two processes may also be distinct in psychological terms.

Slips of the tongue also provided valuable insights into the process of *lexical retrieval* – i.e. the way in which a speaker uses a target meaning in order to locate a particular word in their mental lexicon. Examples such as *white Anglo Saxon prostitute* (= Protestant) or *I've been continuously distressed* (= impressed) *by her* (Fromkin 1973) indicate that language users employ more than meaning in their word search; they also draw upon certain intimations about the form of the word they are seeking (its length, stress patterns, initial syllable etc.). See Aitchison 2003 (16–23, Chapter 12) for a discussion.

On the basis of this and other evidence, a number of researchers since Garrett have proposed models of speech production, the most widely cited being that of Levelt (1989). Some of the models relate specifically to the way words are accessed and articulated, including WEAVER (Roelofs 1997) and the framework proposed by Bock and Griffin (2000), which incorporates the many variables that determine the speed and ease of lexical retrieval.

Models of speech production, like many others in cognitive psychology, resemble flow charts. They represent speaking in terms of a series of stages through which a speaker needs to proceed when assembling an utterance. Their point of departure is an idea in the mind, and the end-product is a disturbance of the air caused by the operation of the speaker's articulators (tongue, teeth, lips etc.). For the sake of convenience, the stages are often represented as sequential; but the point should be made at the outset that one stage does not necessarily wait upon another. On a principle sometimes referred to as *incremental production* (Kempen and Hoenkamp 1987, Levelt 1999:88), it is widely accepted that material can be passed on to the next stage of processing, even though it is incomplete. Let us say that so far only the first words of a sentence have been encoded phonologically; if they form a unit (e.g a Noun Phrase such as *The man I met* . . .) they can be submitted to the next level for phonetic encoding as a cluster or even an intonation group.

In addition, current thinking is that language skills such as speaking are based upon highly interactive processes, in which information flows in a top-down direction as well as a bottom-up one. To give a simple example, in assembling a sentence such as *'Any idea of the time?'*, a speaker would not have to proceed word by word and phoneme by phoneme, but could draw upon stored memories of the way in which the sentence as a whole had been achieved the last time it was uttered and the time before.

Levelt (1989, 1999) makes clear that any model of speech production, whether in L1 or in L2, needs to incorporate a number of stages. Field (2004:284) identifies them as:

a) a *conceptual stage*, where the proposition that is to be expressed first enters the mind of the speaker

b) a *syntactic stage*, where the speaker chooses an appropriate frame into which words are to be inserted, and marks parts of it for plural, verb agreement etc.

c) a *lexical stage*, where a meaning-driven search of the speaker's lexicon or vocabulary store takes place, supported by cues as to the form of the word (e.g. its first syllable)

d) a *phonological stage*, where the abstract information assembled so far is converted into a speech-like form

e) a *phonetic stage*, where features such as assimilation are introduced, which reduce articulatory effort; and where the target utterance is converted into a set of instructions to the articulators

f) an *articulatory stage*, in which the message is uttered.

It is important to note that the first three of these stages are abstract and not in verbal form. It is only at stage (d) that linguistic forms become involved. A model of speaking also needs to allow for:

- a *forward planning mechanism* at discourse level, which (for example) marks out in advance which syllable is to carry sentence stress

- a *buffer,* in which an articulatory plan for the current utterance can be held while the utterance is actually being produced

- a *monitoring mechanism,* which enables a speaker to check an utterance for accuracy, clarity and appropriacy immediately before it is uttered and almost immediately afterwards.

A cognitive processing framework for speaking

Levels of analysis

As already mentioned, the most comprehensive account of L1 speech production to date is the one provided by Levelt (1989), drawing upon some 15 years of empirical research. There are a number of reasons for proposing this model as the basis for the cognitive validation of L2 speaking tests. Firstly, among psycholinguists and speech scientists, it is by far the most widely cited, and has informed many recent research studies. Secondly, it is a staged model, with various levels of processing specified in a way that provides a means of analysing test specifications in a systematic manner.

Importantly from the point of view of the present exercise, it contributed to Weir's initial socio-cognitive framework for validating speaking tests. Weir's set of constituent processes (2005a:46) employs a number of Leveltian terms (*conceptualisation, formulation* and *articulation*), as well as the notion of a target message being transformed from pre-verbal form to phonetic plan and then to overt speech. The Levelt model also quite closely resembles the process model for writing outlined earlier in this series by Shaw and Weir (2007). There is a good reason for this. The Shaw and Weir model was based upon Kellogg (1996), with additions proposed by Field (2004); and both Kellogg's categories and Field's modifications were strongly influenced by Levelt's model of speaking. Consequently, the reader familiar with the Shaw and Weir volume will note close parallels between the processes for assembling written texts identified there and those that are discussed here in relation to speaking, though there are some important differences in the terms used.

Levelt's original 1989 model features four major stages (*conceptualisation, formulation, articulation* and *self-monitoring*). However, an updated version (1999) divides 'formulation' into two, distinguishing between an operation that provides a general framework for the utterance and one that converts this abstract plan into phonological form. It also recognises two aspects of 'articulation': creating a set of instructions to the articulators (lips, tongue, larynx etc.) and then carrying out those instructions. The stages that we will consider here are thus as follows:

- *Conceptualisation*: generating an idea or set of ideas for expression
- *Grammatical encoding*: constructing a syntactic frame and locating the lexical items that will be needed (similar to *micro-planning* as conceptualised by Shaw and Weir 2007 in respect of writing)
- *Phonological encoding* (Levelt's 1999 term is *morpho-phonological encoding*): converting the abstract output of the previous stage into a string of words which are realised phonologically (the equivalent of *translation* in Shaw and Weir 2007)
- *Phonetic encoding:* adjusting the phonological sequence to make articulation easier; linking each of the syllables to a set of neural instructions to the articulators; storing the instructions in a buffer while the clause is being articulated
- *Articulation:* producing the utterance (the equivalent of *execution* in Shaw and Weir 2007)
- *Self-monitoring*: focusing attention on the message immediately before and shortly after it is uttered in order to check for accuracy, clarity and appropriacy (a rough equivalent to *editing* in a writing context).

Figure 3.1 presents a version of Levelt's model of speech assembly, which has been modified considerably to meet the needs of the present enquiry. It is

Figure 3.1 Adapted version of the Levelt model (1989:9), separating levels of processing from outputs of processing

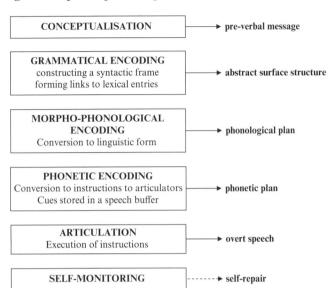

important to recognise that the model (1989:9, 1999:87) represents two distinct types of phenomenon: a) the set of processes employed by the speaker in assembling an utterance; and b) the different forms taken by the message as it is reshaped by the intending speaker. In the interests of clarity, the two are displayed here in separate columns. The reader should bear in mind that what is shown as the output of a given stage also forms the input to the following one.

The model shown here lacks an important component of the reading model proposed by Khalifa and Weir (2009), in that it does not show an executive mechanism or 'goal setter' which controls and directs the attention of the speaker, takes account of context and prevailing circumstances and supports decision making. Levelt himself (1989:20–22) acknowledges the role of such a mechanism in conceptualisation and in self-monitoring but stresses the fact that elsewhere speaking is heavily dependent upon processes that are highly automatic and thus not subject to central control.

Nevertheless, to bring the model into line with the Khalifa and Weir account, it is useful to make clear the information sources upon which the speaker draws (whether automatically or with a degree of intentionality) when assembling an utterance. The relative richness or poverty of those sources is clearly an important factor in shaping the performance of a second language listener. Describing L1 speech assembly, Levelt (1999) identifies three main information sources: a *mental lexicon*, in which the speaker's vocabulary repertoire is stored; a *syllabary* which stores an experiential record of the articulatory gestures which enable the speaker to utter all the syllables of the language; and the individual's store of *world knowledge*. To this, a more detailed account would add some kind of *syntactic store*, though one can remain neutral as to whether it consists of the type of grammar rule favoured by linguists, of a set of stored examples or of procedural rules which enable the rapid assembly of phrases. It also seems important to clearly separate conceptual knowledge of the world, the situation and the addressee from the speaker's *discourse representation*, or record of what has been said so far in the conversation.

Clearly, the quality and availability of all these information sources affect the individual's ability to construct accurate and appropriate L2 utterances. A performance deficit in a test of L2 speaking might arise from:

- *linguistic sources:* gaps in the mental lexicon, imprecise or incomplete representations in the syllabary, inability to encode a syntactic pattern into a form of words
- *knowledge sources*: cultural gaps in world knowledge or pragmatic knowledge
- *failures of comprehension or recall* which leave gaps in the discourse representation.

A relatively detailed model of speaker information sources is shown in Figure 3.2. Those that can be considered part of linguistic knowledge are marked with a grey tone; those not so marked relate broadly to world knowledge, experience or recall of the conversation so far. The distinction in the figure between *current topic* and *discourse representation* merits a brief comment. Levelt (1999) refers to the role of current topic in generating a new utterance in interactional speech or in licensing a new topic that is thematically linked. It also plays a part in the decision to employ an anaphor (for example a pro-form such as *she, it, this* or *did so*) to refer to an entity or idea currently foregrounded in the minds of both speaker and listener. The discourse representation carried forward by both speaker and listener has an altogether wider role. It constitutes a record of all that has been said so far in the conversation, enabling either party to refer back or to check a new comment for consistency with what has already been said or for general relevance.

The validation framework in an L2 context

The stages of the adapted Levelt model will now be explained in some detail, with particular attention given to the factors which may shape the performance of L2 speakers under task conditions like those in the Speaking tests of

Figure 3.2 Information sources feeding into the phases of the processing system

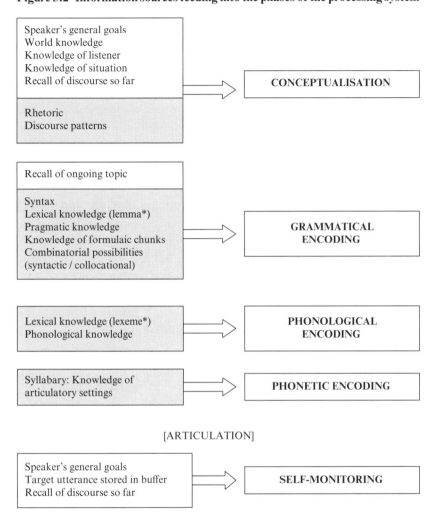

* *In the 1999 update of his model, Levelt distinguishes between three components in a lexical entry in the mind storing information about a word. There is a semantic component which enables a match to be made between a meaning and the target word; a lemma containing syntactic information about the word (its word class and combinatorial possibilities); and a lexeme containing information about the word's phonological form and morphology.*

the Cambridge ESOL suite. Throughout the discussion, we need to bear in mind that, though language users assemble speech with astonishing facility given the complexity of the skill, certain limits still apply to their performance. Most obviously, there are physiological constraints which make it impossible for the articulators to achieve a speech rate of more than about eight syllables per second (Miller 1951). But there are also psychological constraints: the human processor (responsible not just for language production and reception but for handling all kinds of mental task) is characterised by its *limited capacity*. What this entails is that an increase in the demands created by one aspect of a task will limit the performer's ability to deliver in other areas. Thus, it is very difficult for a language user to speak and write at the same time or for an individual to memorise a set of facts while repeating nonsense words.

The limitations upon what can be held in the mind short-term have two important implications for any discussion of the role of the second language speaker:

a) For a low-proficiency L2 speaker, the process of retrieving words and syntactic patterns is much more effortful than it is with a native speaker – potentially limiting performance in other areas of the speaking process, such as the ability to hold long-term plans in the mind.

b) The complexity of the task that is set can affect performance. The more difficult the task, the more attention the speaker gives to handling it and the less will be available for the delivery of speech.

So, in any consideration of the processes in which test takers engage, full account needs to be taken of these *cognitive demands* upon them.

Conceptualisation

Levelt (1989:107) envisages conceptualisation as entailing two types of operation:

- *macro-planning*, in which a set of speech acts is anticipated
- *micro-planning*, at a more local level relating to the role and form of the upcoming utterance.

These resemble the subdivisions proposed by Shaw and Weir (2007) in their framework for the cognitive validation of L2 writing. However, macro-planning in speaking is much more constrained than it is in writing. The speaker is under pressure to respond promptly in most speaking contexts, thus limiting the time available for planning and structuring content. In addition, there are working memory constraints on how much longer-term material the L2 speaker can store while at the same time dealing with current production demands (unless, of course, the speaker has the support of pen and paper to record their intentions). Micro-planning is much more localised. It positions the intended utterance in relation to the discourse as a whole by taking account of knowledge shared with listener and current topic. It also adds indications of language-specific features such as tense or interrogation to the proposition that is to be expressed.

Levelt's account of how the message is generated (1989: Chapter 4) views spoken interaction as a process of joint construction, in which a speaker has to relate each new utterance to a shared discourse framework. Amongst the factors which Levelt identifies as affecting both macro- and micro-planning are: awareness of the ongoing topic, thematisation of new information, recognition of information shared and not shared with the listener, accommodation to the point-of-view and even the form of words of the interlocutor and certain basic principles which determine how information is ordered.

Grammatical encoding

As already suggested, Levelt's original *formulation* phase can be treated as falling into two parts. The first entails the construction of a *surface structure*, an abstract framework for the sentence to be uttered, based upon a syntactic pattern. The second converts the framework and the associated lexis to phonological form; this involves *retrieving* the appropriate forms from memory.

Levelt views surface structure as built around the major components of the idea that the speaker wishes to express. Thus, the proposition *I put two pounds in the meter* would, in an English speaker, trigger the valency pattern associated with the word PUT:

[Agent + PUT + thing put + destination].

Syntactic complexity is clearly a factor in the cognitive difficulty of producing an utterance. Raters readily assume that inability on the part of an L2 speaker to form a particular structure derives from a lack of linguistic knowledge; but it may equally well derive from the demands of assembling the structure and of retaining it in the mind while the utterance is being produced.

In tests of speaking, however, linguistic content is often expressed not in terms of syntactic complexity of form but in terms of the language functions which test takers are required to perform. This makes it simpler to envisage the transition from the test taker's initial idea to a template for an utterance. It can be treated as a matter of *mapping* from the function that the test taker wishes to perform to the pattern that best expresses that function. Discussion of pragmatic language falls mainly within Chapter 4, which concerns itself with linguistic criteria; but it is important to recognise that any staging of the functions to be performed is also a staging of cognitive demands. The issue at stake is not primarily the difficulty of the language that has to be retrieved, but how easy it is for the test taker to perform the mapping exercise. Contributory factors might include the frequency and transparency of the function and the complexity of the form of words that expresses it.

Phonological encoding

For the second language speaker, the most critical phase of forming an utterance is the one at which they retrieve phonological forms from memory in order to give concrete form to what has been planned. Whereas the process of retrieval in one's first language is generally rapid, automatic and accurate, it is likely to be much slower in a second language, especially at lower levels of proficiency. The search is likely to be more effortful, requiring higher levels of attention; and the speaker is likely to be less confident of the outcome.

A widely favoured view of second language acquisition represents it as the acquisition of a type of *expertise*, and traces parallels, sometimes sustainable, sometimes not, with the acquisition of the ability to drive or to play chess (Anderson 1983). According to this analysis, a speaker's ability to retrieve L2 word forms from memory develops as a result of increasing familiarity with the operation. The speaker begins with a retrieval process which is laboured and heavily *controlled* in terms of the attention it demands (compare the careful step-by-step way in which a driver first learns to change gear). By dint of continued use of the process, what were once separate steps become combined, and the move from stimulus to output becomes increasingly *automatised* (Schneider and Schiffrin 1977) until the speaker can achieve it without the conscious allocation of attention. The development is known as *proceduralisation*. Motivated learners often find a means of assisting it by *rehearsing* forms of the spoken language in their minds in anticipation of speech encounters that may occur. For an application of the notions of automaticity and control to second language performance see DeKeyser (2001), Robinson (2003) and Kormos (2006:38–51)[2].

Evidence of increasing proceduralisation in L2 speakers is often marked by a shift towards producing language in chunks (Wray 2002). What begins as an utterance assembled piece by piece (*I + do + not + know + why*) later becomes articulated as a single unit (*dunnowhy*). It also appears to be stored in the mind in this form, enabling more rapid retrieval. By taking this path, L2 speakers align their behaviour with a native speaker's (and indeed with their own behaviour in L1). The speed with which native speakers assemble grammatically correct sentences can only be explained if we recognise that the operation relies heavily upon stitching together well-established and often-used combinations of words. Strong evidence for this comes from the productions of sports commentators, forced to plan their utterances under extreme time pressures (Kuiper 1996, quoted in Wray 2002):

> *They're off and racing now + threading its way through + round the turn they come*

and from the productions of sound-bite politicians (Frost interview with Tony Blair, quoted in Fairclough 2000:112):

. . . I think it's sensible + if for example in areas like erm + the constitution or indeed in respect of erm education it may be + or any of the issues which matter to the country + you can work with another political party because there are lots of things we have in common with the Liberal Democrats why not do it.

It should also be noted that the chunking process promotes grammatical and lexical accuracy. Rather than having to make a series of decisions, any one of which could misfire, the speaker produces a single unit, ready made and internally accurate and consistent. In the case of the L2 speaker, we should thus expect increased chunking to be accompanied by an increase in syntactic and collocational accuracy.

There is a small problem with this analysis so far as the designers of international tests are concerned, which should not pass unnoticed. The development of speaking skills, as described here, assumes an *EFL* (English as a Foreign Language) context, by far the most common situation worldwide. The learner is taken to begin with word-level information (plus a few standard and highly conventionalised formulae such as *How do you do?*) which then becomes integrated into larger structures. However, learners acquiring a language naturalistically in an *ESL* (English as a Second Language) situation often proceed in the opposite direction: first acquiring chunks and then deconstructing them. Raters may thus need to be more wary of treating chunking as evidence of increasing oral proficiency in the case of an ESL population. See Fillmore (1979) for data relating to naturalistically acquired L2.

The phenomenon of chunking forms part of a larger theory of second language acquisition which is gaining wide acceptance and which has particular relevance to the speaking skill. There is evidence that the human mind is capable of storing far more information than we previously supposed. It has been suggested that our ability to use a language may be the product of multiple stored traces of utterances that we have heard over the years (for an introduction, see Dąbrowska 2005: Chapter 2). The principle can be applied at all levels: explaining our ability to distinguish variant forms of phonemes and words (Bybee 2000) as well as the reductions to which syntactic patterns are sometimes subject in the mouths of speakers. On the basis of this analysis, our stored linguistic knowledge is serendipitous, a product of any exposure we may have had to the language in question. The communicative competence underlying the ability to express oneself orally in L2 is an *emergentist* phenomenon (N. Ellis 2003), i.e. the result of an accumulation of individual encounters, both receptive and productive. The issue of frequency (whether of lexical items or syntactic patterns) comes very much to the fore (Bybee and Hopper 2001), since the more often a learner comes across a particular feature, the more detailed is the representation of it that is stored.

Whether one accepts the emergentist argument or not, it is reasonable to expect a graded suite of tests of L2 speaking to take account of the speaker's move from slow and intentional retrieval at lower levels to a high degree of automatisation at higher levels, and from individually assembled strings of words to the production of formulaic sequences. These developments make an important contribution towards a listener's impression of *fluency*.

Fluency is a notoriously slippery concept, and attempts to define it have caused much controversy over the years. As Luoma (2004:88) points out, the term can be given a wide range of definitions, from narrow specifications relating to hesitation and speech rate to broader ones that are 'virtually synonymous with "speaking proficiency". Furthermore, it is not a simple question of identifying features that are physically present in a speaker's productions; there is also the issue of how those features are *perceived* by a listener. With this in mind, Lennon (1990) suggests that ratings of fluency in speaking tests differ from scores based upon quantifiable facets such as accuracy and appropriacy because they draw purely upon performance phenomena.

However, the assertion perhaps misses the point. Judgements of fluency are heavily influenced by the ease with which a speaker retrieves and assembles word forms. Lennon himself describes fluency as 'an impression on the listener's part that the psycholinguistic processes of speech planning and speech production are functioning easily and effectively' (1990:391). Schmidt (1992) goes further and explicitly links fluency with automaticity. It is certainly possible to identify a number of surface features in the speech of a test candidate which provide indicators of proceduralisation and thus of the speaker's progress towards more automatic retrieval processes. They include the chunking of words, the distribution of pausing and the average length of stretches of uninterrupted speech.

Increased chunking of word strings by L2 learners manifests itself in a number of ways. Firstly, as already noted, there are likely to be gains in accuracy because a chunk is produced in a way that is pre-constituted. There are also likely to be improvements in aspects of delivery such as rhythm because the chunks are stored as phonological wholes; this leads to the impression of a more native-like command of the mechanics of producing the L2.

Chunking enables several words to be produced as a unit, almost as if they were a single lexical item. Its effects are thus observable in the speaker's *length of run* – often taken to be the mean number of syllables uttered between pauses. Raupach (1987, cited in Towell and Hawkins 1994:222) compared French-acquiring German schoolchildren before and after a period of residence in France and found increases of up to four syllables in their mean length of run.

One cannot detach consideration of length of run from consideration of how frequently the speaker pauses. The more pauses there are, the shorter the runs are and the more fragmented the discourse is likely to appear, whether in L1 or L2. But the issue here is not just how often a speaker pauses but also *how long* and *where*. All speakers, however fluent, need to pause at syntactic boundaries – often clause boundaries (Levelt 1989:256–60) – for the purposes of planning what comes next. In the case of a less fluent speaker (e.g. an L2 learner of low proficiency), the process of constructing an utterance will be slow and effortful in terms of retrieval (locating the phonological form of a lexical item), of morphological marking (adding the correct inflections) and of assembly. One can thus anticipate longer pauses at planning boundaries. But such a speaker may also:

a) plan the forthcoming syntactic unit only partially because of the heavy cognitive demands which the process entails, and therefore have to resume planning while actually producing it

b) revise the phonetic plan while in the process of uttering because of limited linguistic resources or because of the perception that it has misfired.

The results are seen in breaks in connected speech which occur not at syntactic boundaries but *within* syntactic units, and which might best be termed *hesitations* (Cruttenden 1986:37–38) rather than pauses. The more frequently this kind of interruption occurs, the less likely a speaker is to be rated as fluent, whether in L1 or L2. Laver (1994:537) comments as follows:

> When the speaking turn is broken into individual utterances by the insertion of silent or filled pauses at the junctures between the phonemic clauses, it can be regarded as non-continuous but fluent, in that the linguistic material of the phonemic clauses is uninterrupted. When the silent or filled pause falls internally within a phonemic clause, breaking its coherent intonational structure, then the speaking turn can be regarded as non-continuous and interrupted or hesitant. If the clause internal pause is silent, the effect of inserting the pause into the speaking turn will be to multiply the number of separate utterances making up the speaking turn.

Once again, chunking assists the speaker – here because it simplifies the planning process and reduces the need to revise plans while speaking. The results are seen in shorter planning pauses and a much lower incidence of hesitation.

To summarise, discussion of 'retrieval' (i.e. converting the abstract output of the previous stage into linguistic form) has led us to identify a number of physical characteristics which are associated with progress in the acquisition of L2 speaking skills and which together form possible indicators of fluency. They are:

• use of pre-assembled chunks – leading to syntactic accuracy and native-like rhythmic properties

• length of run

• duration of planning pauses at syntactic boundaries

• frequency of hesitation pauses.

For a more extensive specification, see Fulcher's checklist of phenomena contributing to dysfluency (1996), which draws upon empirical evidence; see also work by Hasselgreen (2005).

Phonetic encoding, articulation

Levelt points out (1989:413) that: 'fluent articulation is probably man's most complex motor skill. It involves the co-ordinated use of approximately 100 muscles, such that speech sounds are produced at a rate of about 15 per second.' In the case of the second language speaker, there are further complications in the pre-existence of:

a) a set of phonological representations in the mind which serve to define the phoneme values of L1, plus

b) a set of highly automatic processes, attuned to the articulatory settings of L1 and the movements which link one to another.

The accommodation of these two elements to the unfamiliar values of the target language forms the basis of any cognitive account of how L2 articulation is acquired. One should not lose sight of the fact that poor L2 pronunciation does not result solely from an inability to form the target sounds but also from an inadequate representation of those sounds in the mind and/or the inability to communicate the appropriate signals to the articulators.

It is also relevant that the need to focus upon adjusting the articulators to unfamiliar settings imposes additional cognitive demands upon the speaker. Such demands can potentially detract from the speaker's ability to store and hold in the mind a detailed phonetic plan for the utterance being produced (Levelt 1989:414–422), the result being short and dislocated productions. This is particularly to be expected in circumstances where the speaker feels that 'correct' pronunciation is a requirement and that considerable resources of attention need to be directed towards ensuring that articulation is precise.

There is thus considerable pressure upon test designers to ensure that, while account is taken of pronunciation in tests of speaking, it does not feature so prominently that it inhibits the candidates from producing longer and phonologically cohesive pieces of discourse. Test specifications need to strike a fine balance, focusing upon *intelligibility* (Smith and Nelson 1985) rather than upon narrow considerations of *accuracy*. Gradation of difficulty can be positive – reflecting an increasing approximation to L2 segmental and suprasegmental norms – or it can be negative, representing the gradual elimination of traces of L1 phonology.

The reliance upon the rather subjective notion of intelligibility might be questioned in some quarters, not least on the grounds that the criterion typically entails *intelligibility to a native speaker*. However, this dependence is significantly reduced in speaking tests that involve peer interaction (such as the paired Cambridge ESOL Speaking tests), where the intelligibility of the test taker to another non-native speaker is also put to the test.

A different concern about the assessment of intelligibility focuses on the unrepresentative nature of the assessor, usually somebody whose own phonological representations are finely honed by dint of long exposure to a wide variety of L2 accents (see Kenworthy 1987: Chapter 2 for an interesting discussion of this issue). It can be suggested that this very expertise potentially diminishes the predictive power of the tests since intelligibility to the assessor does not guarantee intelligibility to the wider L1 public. However, practical considerations have to prevail here: the alternative, of using 'lay' assessors, is not a viable solution, given the potential implications for reliability. The alternative is to raise awareness of the issue among examiners of speaking so that they are encouraged to imagine themselves in the position of a listener with less experience of L2 varieties, as is the case with Cambridge ESOL examiners (see Chapters 4 and 5).

Self-monitoring

In the final stage of the speaking process, a speaker assesses how precisely and effectively each utterance realises the plans that were laid down during its assembly. *Self-monitoring* might compare the rhetorical impact of what was said against the goals of the speaker at the conceptualisation stage. It might compare the syntactic structure that was actually produced against the frame selected during formulation. Or it might compare the realisation of a particular word against the correct form of the word that is stored in memory. For a skilled speaker, a major concern is whether the utterance is unambiguous and whether it conveys clearly to the listener the speaker's pragmatic intentions.

Self-monitoring thus potentially takes place at many different levels of a message. However, Levelt (1989:463) concludes that it is extremely unlikely that an L1 speaker can attend to all the levels in the brief time span available – especially given that the speaker is also intent on completing the utterance under delivery and on planning the next one. Certain levels might be prioritised (in much the same way that teachers of writing sometimes choose to focus only on errors of spelling or of sentence construction). Levelt suggests that the exact levels that are monitored may reflect the demands of the prevailing context and that the degree of monitoring may fluctuate during the course of an extended utterance.

These comments are illuminating when considering the self-monitoring of L2 speakers. As noted several times in this account, the effort of assembling speech in a second language makes additional cognitive demands, which limit the speaker's performance compared to that in L1. From this, it seems reasonable to conclude that second language speakers are even more prone to limit their self-monitoring to specific target areas. A number of researchers (e.g. Lennon 1984, Poulisse 1993, van Hest 1996) have suggested that they pay more attention to errors of lexical appropriacy than to errors of grammatical accuracy, though Kormos (2006:131) remains unconvinced on the basis of her research with Hungarian learners. It is clearly dangerous to generalise because factors such as task type and instructional tradition may lead to variations in the amount of attention allocated to monitoring and in the importance attributed to accuracy. But it would seem likely that lower proficiency learners focus attention on linguistic features rather than pragmatic ones, comparing one or more of their syntax, lexis and pronunciation with what they perceive to be L2 norms. A mark of increased competence as an L2 speaker would thus be a gradual increment in the extent to which the speaker heeds the effectiveness with which the message has been conveyed.

A further consideration in both L1 and L2 is the way in which the speaker handles the recognition that problems of transmission have occurred. A competent speaker needs to be able to *self-repair* efficiently and promptly following certain implicitly recognised norms (Levelt 1989:478–499), which may or may not be language-specific.

A note on timing

Psycholinguistic accounts of speaking do not always make it clear that the processes which contribute to planning[3] an utterance can occur at three different points:

a) before the speech event

b) while an interlocutor is speaking

c) immediately before or during the speaker's turn.

This has consequences for the way one interprets the model of speaking just outlined. It also serves to distinguish two types of speech event: one where extensive pre-planning is not possible and one where it is.

The ability to plan at point (a) is restricted in most genres of speech event. An exception can be found in pre-planned monologues such as lectures, where the speaker has the opportunity not only of choosing the propositions to be addressed but also of ordering them and making the connections between them plain. There is even a possibility of encoding the ideas phonologically and rehearsing the form of words to be used by turning them over in the mind. It is only in this type of speech event that speaking comes close to the degree of planning that is possible in skilled writing (Shaw and Weir 2007).

Most genres of speech event are dialogic, and call for immediate responses to points made by an interlocutor. Planning therefore has to be reactive and to take place while the event is ongoing. Ample evidence that a degree of active planning is undertaken while an interlocutor is speaking (point (b)) can be found in the way that a new turn in natural speech often overlaps with the preceding one. But much planning also takes place at point (c), while the speaker is actually engaged in their own turn. As already noted, it occurs during short planning pauses, usually located at the end of a syntactic structure such as a clause. During these pauses, speakers face a complex task. They have to assemble the next utterance by means of grammatical, phonological and phonetic encoding. But they also have to plan ahead conceptually, taking adequate account of where the present turn is leading or how the listener has reacted. An early study of planning pauses (Beattie 1983) identified what appears to be a regular pattern in which a phase of short pauses for linguistic planning gives way regularly to a phase of longer pauses where a degree of forward conceptual planning also takes place. More recent research by Roberts and Kirsner (2000) appears to confirm the existence of this *temporal cycle*.

Cognitive processing: Cambridge ESOL practice

We have represented speech production, whether in L1 or L2, in terms of an adapted and simplified Levelt (1989, 1999) model that falls into six major phases of processing: *conceptualisation, grammatical encoding, phonological encoding, phonetic encoding, articulation* and *self-monitoring*. This cognitive model has the potential to provide us with a validation framework for analysing and describing the operations that take place in tests of speaking, and will now be applied specifically to a set of Cambridge ESOL tests at different proficiency levels.

The evidence presented here is drawn from multiple sources, including: the set of sample speaking tests for KET, PET, FCE, CAE and CPE, which appear in Appendix A of this book; the Cambridge ESOL *Instructions to Speaking Examiners 2011* (referred to throughout as ISE); the specifications in the relevant Handbooks for Teachers; the Main Suite Speaking Test Assessment Scales; and the Cambridge Common Scale for Speaking (see page 26 in Chapter 1). The review thus attempts to link construct specifications with the other two points of the test-content triangle in the form of task specifications and assessment specifications.

Conceptualisation

As already noted, Levelt (1989:107) envisages conceptualisation as entailing two types of operation:

- *macro-planning*, in which a set of speech acts is anticipated
- *micro-planning* at a more local level relating to the role and form of the upcoming utterance.

In terms of L2 testing criteria, one might consider 'conceptualisation' under two main headings:

a) *Provision of ideas* – the complexity of the ideas which test takers have to express and the extent to which the ideas are supplied to them

b) *Integrating utterances into a discourse framework* – the extent to which test takers are assessed on their ability to relate utterances to the wider discourse (including their awareness of information shared with the interlocutor).

A further factor which plays an important part in assisting conceptualisation is whether the speaker is given time to pre-plan what to say (in terms of general ideas, of the links between those ideas or of the actual form of words to be used) or not. The question of pre-planning is partly a matter of task design and is therefore discussed later when considering task demands.

Provision of ideas

Retrieving information and generating ideas impose heavy cognitive demands upon a speaker. If the need for conceptualisation is reduced, then the task becomes less onerous, allowing more working memory to be allocated to retrieving the relevant linguistic forms. This is one means by which a designer can adjust test requirements to make allowance for the more effortful processing demands faced by an L2 speaker with limited knowledge and experience of the target language. Another important consideration in deciding how much support to provide is the need to ensure that a test does not too heavily reward the candidate's imagination rather than their language proficiency.

In the Cambridge ESOL specifications, one can identify two broad determinants of cognitive difficulty. The first lies in the *availability* of the information demanded of the test taker. An emphasis in the early stages upon personal and everyday information assists test takers because it asks for the retrieval of information that is conceptually simple and easily accessed. (This is an interesting side benefit of what would appear to be the testers' main concern: namely, to grade the difficulty of the language that is needed to achieve the task.)

The task content gradually moves towards more abstract discussion at CAE and CPE level. The relevant specifications from the Cambridge ESOL Common Scale for Speaking are as follows:

KET: 'able to convey basic meaning in very familiar or highly predictable situations'
PET: 'able to handle communication in most familiar situations'
FCE: 'able to handle communication in familiar situations'
CAE: 'able to handle communication in most situations'
CPE: 'able to handle communication in most situations, including unfamiliar or unexpected ones'

These availability criteria are (like some others in the Common Scale and Can Do statements) not very sharply differentiated. But the way in which they are operationalised in actual Cambridge ESOL tests is well illustrated in the interview stage of the sample material at the end of this volume. The questions in PET Part 1 (p. 315) relate to candidates' names, occupations and home towns – familiar terrain indeed, and material that is quite easily pre-rehearsed. At FCE level, the questioning in Part 1 (p. 318) still features familiar topics (home, local town, school, jobs) but is considerably more open-ended. In Part 1 of the CAE sample (p. 321), some standard questions are retained; but there are also wider topics such as future plans, travel and holidays and personal tastes and habits. The specifications 'unfamiliar' and 'unexpected' contribute to a substantial hike in cognitive difficulty in Part 1 of the CPE materials (p. 324) where wide-ranging questions cover housing, the importance of study routines and sports facilities and elicit personal views on social change, communications, internet shopping and space tourism. (For a more detailed discussion of the gradation of topic content across the proficiency levels, see Chapter 4.)

A second consideration is how much *support* is provided by the test rubric in the form of ideas that the candidates might wish to express. An obvious way of grading difficulty in a suite of speaking tests is to gradually reduce this support as the level of the exam increases. However, that seems not to have been the policy adopted in the Speaking tests of the Cambridge ESOL suite: quite detailed written or visual support for conceptualisation is provided in all five Speaking tests from KET to CPE.

The benefit of this is that it ensures comparability between the performances of candidates at a given level since the concepts and the areas of lexis upon which they draw are similar. Importantly, it also avoids the danger of weighting assessment at the higher levels too heavily in favour of the test takers' imagination rather than their language.

Nevertheless, the support given is carefully calibrated in terms of *how specific it is* and *how complex the cues are*. The cognitive demands are ratcheted up gradually by moving:

- from set questions for interlocutors to looser and more open ones
- from the precise demands of prompt cards to visual cues that require description and then on to visual cues which need to be compared and evaluated
- from a single prompt (usually in visual form) to multiple ones
- from single-modality prompts to multi-modality ones which combine oral rubrics with both visual and written stimuli.

There is thus a cline which begins with simple written prompts which serve to constrain the form and content of the productions in KET (in the sample materials, posters advertise an air museum and a bookshop). It moves on to visual prompts of gradually increasing number and complexity; and the role of spoken rubrics is expanded from FCE onwards (in the sample FCE materials, candidates are asked not to describe what they see but to bring an interpretation to bear). Written cues in the form of questions continue to be used in FCE and CAE to support visuals. For example, in the CAE sample materials on p. 322, candidates are asked orally why a group of people in a photo have come together and how important their relationships might be; but these open-ended questions also appear in written form above the photos. In CPE, the written support is minimal (in the sample, it consists of only four words *Poster campaign – insurance protection*) and the candidate has to rely heavily on their listening proficiency.

Table 3.1 provides a more detailed outline of the types of information required of the test taker at each level of the suite, set against the type of support assisting conceptualisation.

Integrating utterances into a discourse framework

Amongst the factors which Levelt identifies as affecting both macro- and micro-planning are: awareness of the ongoing topic, thematisation of new information, recognition of information shared and not shared with the listener, accommodation to the point-of-view and even form of words of the interlocutor and certain basic principles which determine how information is ordered. The Cambridge ESOL specifications take indirect account of factors such as these in the advice to interlocutors on how to handle highly formulaic and pre-rehearsed language that does not sufficiently recognise the interlocutor as a participant in a dialogue (ISE:15, 26, 32, 38). More importantly, the ability to relate utterances to a wider discourse representation is explicitly taken to be a determinant of successful performance. A 'discourse management' criterion is included in the assessment scales for all levels except for KET.

Grammatical encoding

As noted earlier, the linguistic content of speaking tests is often specified not in terms of grammatical structure but in terms of the language functions which test takers are required to perform. This makes it easier to describe the transition from the test taker's initial idea to a rough template for an utterance. It can be treated as a question of *mapping* from the function that the test taker wishes to perform to the pattern that best expresses that function.

The issue under discussion when considering cognitive validity is not the complexity of the language that has to be retrieved (discussed in Chapter 4) but how easily the test taker is able to perform the mapping exercise. There are two ways in which the demands of mapping can be reduced in order to lighten the cognitive load upon lower level test takers with limited linguistic resources. One lies in restricting the number of functions that a test taker is

Table 3.1 Cambridge ESOL suite: information elicited and information provided

Test	Elicited	Provided
KET	'factual personal' information	Oral. Interviewer questions.
	everyday non-personal information	Visual. Prompts with cue words 'to stimulate questions and answers . . . related to daily life' *[See Part 2 of sample KET material, p. 314]*
PET	'factual, personal' information	Oral. Interviewer questions. *[See Part 1 of sample PET materials, p.315]*
	'own views and opinions about an imaginary situation'	Visual. Prompts 'designed to generate ideas' *[See Part 2 of sample PET materials, p. 316]*
	describing photo	Visual. Prompt: one colour photo. *[See Part 3 of sample PET materials, p. 317]*
	discussion on topic	Oral. Prompts by interlocutor. *[See Part 4 of sample PET materials, p. 317]*
FCE	give 'basic personal' information	Oral. Interviewer questions. *[See Part 1 of sample FCE materials, p.318]*
	compare a pair of photos	Visual. Photos with a written question. *[See Part 2 of sample FCE materials, p.319]*
	decision-making task (no correct ans.)	Visual. Photos / pictures with two questions. *[See Part 3 of sample FCE materials, p.320]*
	discussion on topic	Oral. Interlocutor led questions. *[See Part 4 of sample FCE materials, p.320]*
CAE	personal information, opinions	Oral. Interviewer questions. *[See Part 1 of sample CAE materials, p.321]*
	comment on / react to visuals	Visual. Photos / pictures plus two written questions. *[See Part 2 of sample CAE materials, p.322]*
	decision-making task	Visual. Photos / pictures plus two written questions. *[See Part 3 of sample CAE materials, p.323]*
	express, exchange and justify opinions	Oral. Interlocutor led questions. *[See Part 4 of sample CAE materials, p.323]*
CPE	personal information, opinions	Oral. Interviewer questions. *[See Part 1 of sample CPE materials, p.324]*
	react to visuals/decision-making task	Visual. One or more photos. *[See Part 2 of sample CPE materials, p.324/5]*
	impart information; express, exchange and justify opinions	Visual. Written question Oral. Interlocutor led questions. Oral. Interlocutor prompts. *[See Part 3 of sample CPE materials, p.326]*

Source: Instructions to Speaking Examiners, 2011

expected to perform (particularly in relation to a single task). The need to employ a multiplicity of functions is self-evidently more demanding upon the processor than the need to employ only one or two. The other takes account of how accessible a given function is likely to be. Functions that are familiar, frequent and concrete will clearly be mapped more rapidly and reliably than those which are not.

Table 3.2 indicates which new functions are added to the repertoire at each level of the suite. Rather than following the specifications in the Speaking Test Features, which indicate a wide range of *possible* functions at each level, it is based upon a close reading of the interactive task types with a view to establishing what are the *necessary* functional demands which they impose.

Table 3.2 Incremental functional requirements of Cambridge Speaking tests (based on demands of tasks)

Exam	Functional demands
KET	factual presentation
	requesting facts
PET	referring to past – present – future
	suggesting
	agreeing and disagreeing
	giving cause – reason – example
FCE	comparing and contrasting
	giving an opinion
	negotiating
	speculating
	decision making
	expressing modality
CAE	expressing and justifying opinions
	hypothesising
	summarisation
CPE	evaluation

Clearly, assessors take adequate account of the language resources available to a test taker at each level for expressing these functions. There is also a well-designed gradient in terms of the demands imposed upon the test taker: moving from the presentation of simple facts to the expression of functions which are increasingly multiple and abstract. Examining a sample of the visually stimulated tasks (some long-turn, some candidate–candidate) in the materials at the end of this volume, there is a clear progression:

- KET Part 2: reporting factual information from posters relating to prices, times, numbers, size etc. on p. 314
- PET Part 3: describing what is happening in a photo on p. 316
- FCE Part 2: speculating about what is happening in a photo; then expressing a personal viewpoint connected to the photo (in the materials on p. 319, making a choice and expressing a personal interest)
- CAE Part 3: on p. 323: discussing the difficulties of different types of fund raising
- CPE Part 2: speculating on why photos might have been taken, then exploring their usefulness to a poster campaign on p. 324–5.

It is noticeable that there is a hike in cognitive difficulty at FCE level: in particular, it is here that the test taker is required to handle issues of modality and to give reasons for choices, which can prove both conceptually and linguistically difficult. It represents a considerable advance on what is required of a candidate at PET level.

Phonological encoding

The discussion of the cognitive framework on pages 80–84 identified a number of characteristics which are associated with proceduralisation in the acquisition of L2 speaking skills and which together form indicators of fluency. They are:

- use of pre-assembled chunks – leading to syntactic accuracy and native-like rhythmic properties
- length of run
- duration of planning pauses at syntactic boundaries
- frequency of hesitation pauses.

Of these characteristics, the one most consistently represented in the specifications and instructions to assessors for the Cambridge ESOL Speaking tests is *hesitation*. At the lowest level of the suite, an attempt is made to allow for the greater cognitive demands of planning when one's linguistic and phonological resources are limited. KET examiners are advised: 'Candidates at this level may need some thinking time before they respond. Be sensitive to this and do not rush candidates, but do not allow pauses to extend unnaturally' (ISE:15). In the Common Scale for Speaking, there is an attempt to define hesitation according to the factors that might be responsible for it:

KET: 'Responses are limited to short phrases or isolated words with frequent hesitation and pauses.'

PET: 'Produces utterances which tend to be very short – words or phrases – with frequent hesitations and pauses.'

FCE: 'Has problems searching for language resources to express ideas and concepts resulting in pauses and hesitation.'

CAE: 'Maintains a flow of language with only natural hesitation resulting from considerations of appropriacy or expression.'

CPE: 'Pronunciation is easily understood and prosodic features are used effectively; many features, including pausing and hesitation, are "native-like".'

The descriptors could perhaps be more specific, with a sharper distinction made between extended pausing due to planning difficulties, hesitation due to delayed planning or restructuring during the utterance, and hesitation associated with lexical retrieval.

Hesitation as a factor is also mentioned consistently at levels above KET in the assessment criteria for Discourse Management Here, interestingly, a recent revision of the criteria has resulted in thi indicator of fluency being closely linked to another – namely, length of un The panel below shows the performance descriptors at the middle of the m irks range for each test.

PET: 'Produces responses which are extended beyond short phrases, despite hesitation.' (ISE:48)

FCE: 'Produces extended stretches of language despite some hesitation.' (ISE:52)

CAE: 'Produces extended stretches of language with very little hesitation.' (ISE:56)

CPE: 'Produces extended stretches of language with ease and with very little hesitation.' (ISE:50)

Chunking does not feature prominently as a criterion. The problem is perhaps partly that formulaic language can be both a negative and a positive indicator so far as an assessor is concerned. On the one hand, it can indicate dependence upon a limited range of highly conventionalised formulae, some of them rote learned; on the other (as previously discussed) it can show that the test taker has progressed as a speaker to a point where they have established a repertoire of word strings which can be produced with minimal effort.

The ESOL criteria include reference to the former, more negative aspect. At KET level, the Common Scale recognises the likelihood of 'rehearsed or formulaic phrases with limited generative capacity', and at PET, it accepts that complex language may only occur in 'well-rehearsed utterances'. At all levels except (curiously) PET, assessors are given a warning against rote-prepared utterances: 'It is expected that some candidates' responses will sound rehearsed in Part 1 of the text as talking about oneself is the most familiar of topics . . . (L)engthy and obviously prepared speeches should be tactfully intercepted and deflected' (ISE:15, 26, 32, 38).

However, in their current form the criteria do not make specific mention of the positive role played by chunking in the development of fluency. Given the level of disagreement there has been historically about what constitutes fluency, it is entirely understandable that the criteria avoid reference to the construct[4]. The treacherous term does not appear in the Common Scale and only features, rather anomalously, at one level (CAE) in the Handbook Can Do statements. Nevertheless, with our developing understanding of the L2 speaking process, and in particular the impact upon it of the incremental storage and retrieval of formulaic items, it might in future be advisable to focus the attention of assessors more systematically upon observable features such as degree of chunking, and location of pausing – especially if empirical research continues to demonstrate correlations with listener judgements of L2 fluency. As discussion within SLA swings in favour of an emergentist view of how second language speaking skills are acquired, the importance of chunking, in particular, will need to be recognised.

A further marker of increasing competence as a speaker lies in the candidate's ability to use the more conventionalised type of chunk (*do you know what I mean? you know, kind of*) in order to gain planning time, in the way that a native speaker might. The insertion of these fillers at natural points makes speech appear less fragmented and contributes to the impression of fluency (Hasselgreen 2005:118). Again, this criterion might be a useful addition to the Common Scale, as well as to the analytic and global scales used by Oral Examiners.

Phonetic encoding, articulation

In line with the criteria discussed on pages 84–5, the specifications for the Cambridge ESOL suite strike a fine balance: giving credit for pronunciation in tests of Speaking, while at the same time not giving this facet such prominence that it inhibits the test taker's performance or imposes constraints upon their ability to produce longer and more phonologically cohesive pieces of discourse.

The focus is appropriately upon intelligibility rather than upon narrow considerations of 'accuracy'. The first sentence in each Pronunciation section of the ISE could not be more explicit: making clear that the term *pronunciation* in this context 'refers to the intelligibility of the candidate's speech'. The construct of intelligibility is defined in the examiners' glossary as follows (ISE:66): 'The candidate may have a pronounced accent but the speech can generally be understood by a non-EFL/ESOL specialist.' This addresses the reservation expressed earlier about the more sophisticated listening skills of an EFL professional who has been exposed to a range of varieties.

However, despite the foregrounding of intelligibility as a criterion, the analytical assessment criteria for raters are disappointingly vague in specifying distinctions between levels. The criteria for KET and PET thoughtfully balance intelligibility against the candidate's problems at the articulation level due to limited control of phonological features (ISE:44). But at the higher levels, the descriptor says no more than 'is intelligible'.

The more general pronunciation descriptors at the different levels of the suite are listed in Table 3.3 (taken from the Common Scale for Speaking on page 26).

Table 3.3 Pronunciation specifications for the Cambridge ESOL suite

Exam	Common Scale specifications
KET	Pronunciation is heavily influenced by L1 features and may at times be difficult to understand
PET	Pronunciation is generally intelligible, but L1 features may put a strain on the listener
FCE	Although pronunciation is easily understood, L1 features may be intrusive
CAE	L1 accent may be evident but does not affect the clarity of the message
CPE	Pronunciation is easily understood and prosodic features are used effectively

The grading relies chiefly upon a gradual reduction of elements which reflect the influence of the stored phoneme values of L1 and the automatised articulatory processes that are associated with them. The criteria are expressed in very general terms. It could be argued that it is difficult to be more specific because the precise relationship between representation and production can be expected to vary considerably from individual to individual and is not transparent to the observer.

Self-monitoring

Like articulation, self-monitoring and self-repair are aspects of speaker performance which are difficult to capture in the form of test specifications. The closest the Common Scale criteria come is in focusing upon the candidate's ability to deal with breakdowns of communication as and when they occur – specifically, the extent to which the candidate relies upon support from the interlocutor in addressing such problems.

KET:	'Requires prompting and assistance by an interlocutor to prevent communication from breaking down.'
PET:	'Has some ability to compensate for communication difficulties using repair strategies but may require prompting and assistance by an interlocutor.'
FCE:	'Does not require major assistance or prompting by an interlocutor.'

It should be noted that the term 'repair' as conceptualised here combines two distinct situations: one relating to a failure of understanding as a listener and the other relating to a failure of communication as a speaker. Another reservation is that the criteria on monitoring and repair are limited to the lower level of the suite. A more direct approach would be to provide specific reference to the extent to which candidates at different levels show themselves capable of self-monitoring and display an ability to redress a subset of their errors that threaten understanding. Higher levels of competence could then be characterised by evidence of monitoring for pragmatic effectiveness as well as for linguistic accuracy.

Cognitive task demands

The cognitive demands of speaking tasks

Two important features distinguish speech from writing (Bygate 1987). First of all, most speech takes place under *time pressure*. In normal circumstances (exceptions are rehearsed and ritualised situations and speech events that are scripted or assisted by prompts), the speaker has to formulate utterances with a considerable degree of spontaneity. Constructing a spoken sentence clearly requires an element of planning; but time does not allow for reflection, for a range of options to be considered or for initial decisions to be revised. It may not even allow for planning to extend further ahead than a few phrases. Similarly, time pressures constrain the execution of a sentence in that there has to be a rapid transition from constructing an utterance to articulating the sounds which compose it; convention requires a response to be articulated with a minimum delay (even a pause of 0.5 seconds is recognisably a hesitation). Time pressures also limit the extent to which a speaker can self-monitor: unlike a writer, a speaker has little time for checking what has been said for grammatical accuracy, pragmatic appropriacy and congruence with the speaker's intentions.

Secondly, most forms of speaking are *reciprocal*. In such encounters, the parts played by the participants switch regularly between speaking and listening. Speakers have to identify with the point of view of their partner in the exchange, just as writers do; but the role of a listening partner is a dynamic one in the way that the role of a reader is not. A conversational partner might at any point exercise the right to change the topic or to disagree with a speaker, changing the direction of the discourse in a way that is beyond the speaker's control. In addition, a response formulated in a conversational context has to conform to the topic and might even incorporate some of the language of the most recent turn by the other party – a turn which may still be in progress while the response to it is being assembled. The speaker is thus required to do more than simply answer a question relevantly: they need to acknowledge the presence of the interlocutor by picking up lexis and even syntactic patterns from the preceding turn. This imposes considerable constraints in a test of speaking. But it also affords benefits: in tasks requiring only brief responses (e.g. a question followed by single sentence answer), the interlocutor might well provide a linguistic model that the respondent can adopt (*'What is the kind of music that you like best?'* – *'The kind of music that I like best is . . .'*).

The characteristics of spoken interaction just reviewed suggest that the cognitive demands imposed by a speaking task are not simply a matter of the duration of the task or the familiarity of the content and language that has to be retrieved. The task design determines the amount of time available to the candidate for the assembly of an utterance. It also specifies the relationship between the examiner and the candidate or between two candidates in a pair. Here, one consideration is the length of turn required of each party. The shorter the examiner's turn, the greater the pressure on the candidate to formulate and respond. The shorter the turn expected of the candidate, the more likely they are to be able to construct a grammatically correct response and/or to base a response upon linguistic forms employed by the interlocutor. An additional factor in an examiner–candidate relationship (and indeed in a candidate–candidate one) is the predictability of the content. A task where the topic changes frequently makes much greater demands upon the speaker-as-listener than one where the line of conversation is relatively predictable.

Two of the task variables just identified will be considered in the sections that follow. They are firstly the *nature of the interaction* that the task requires and with it the length of turn demanded of the candidate; and secondly the *amount of time* available for the assembly of spoken utterances. Each contributes importantly to the cognitive load that is imposed upon a candidate by a speaking task.

Patterns of interaction

There are several possible interaction formats for a test of speaking (Davies, Brown, Elder, Hill, Lumley and McNamara 1999:182, Luoma 2004:35–45, Fulcher 2003:55–57). It can be one-way, with the test taker responding to a computer screen or to a voice on a CD or DVD in what is usually termed a SOPI (Simulated Oral Proficiency Interview). This interaction format is sometimes referred to as *indirect* and sometimes as *semi-direct* (Fulcher 2003:190). In this case, the course of the conversation is entirely predetermined, and the candidate has no impact upon the direction it takes. This approach may meet certain practical needs of mass testing (Stansfield 1990) but is difficult to defend in terms of cognitive validity for the following reasons:

a) The interviewer is limited to certain stereotyped questions and has no opportunity to respond to the replies of the test taker or to elaborate where the test taker shows signs of poor comprehension.

b) If the SOPI takes place in audio mode, no facial expressions or gestures are present to provide the test taker with the normal feedback indicating comprehension or support. Even in visual mode, these paralinguistic cues are necessarily depersonalised. Similarly, back-channelling is impossible.

c) The test taker is placed under a time pressure even more extreme than that which obtains in real life, since a response has to be completed before the next utterance on the recording.

d) The test taker is limited to a single role, that of respondent.

e) The test taker is unable to demonstrate the ability to seek repair or clarification in cases of uncertainty.

One can say that, in terms of the real-life cognitive processes engaged, this type of test might well provide indications as to L2 *listening* skills but cannot be said to measure the ability to participate actively in a conversation. As Fulcher puts it (2003:193) after reviewing the evidence: 'Given our current state of knowledge, we can only conclude that, while scores on an indirect test can be used to predict scores on a direct test, the indirect test is testing something *different* from the direct test.'

An alternative use of recording requires the test taker to produce a monologue on a specific question or topic. Again, it cannot be claimed that this approach replicates the conditions and demands of conversational speech: there is no interaction and the test taker usually has to be allowed time to prepare what to say. It does, of course, enable an assessment of the test taker's oral presentation skills; but, even so, an important element is absent in the form of auditors who provide signals of understanding. Furthermore, the formality of a recording tends to inhibit the test taker from stopping to rephrase points that they may have made inadequately (Luoma 2004:45). The part played in normal speaking by retrospective self-monitoring and repair is likely to be severely reduced. In short, the test does not conform to the view that most speech events entail a process of *co-construction* between interlocutors (McNamara 1997b, Swain 2001).

A second approach is to conduct the speaking test by telephone. Here, interviewer–test taker interaction is indeed provided for. The interviewer has the possibility of developing a topic more freely, reacting to initiatives by the test taker and providing support and back-channelling. However, this type of test models a single, very specific form of spoken exchange. It is qualitatively different from a face-to-face engagement in several ways that directly affect phonological processing. Most obviously, there is the absence of visual context and of the paralinguistic cues provided by facial expression and gesture. In processing terms, the consequence is that intonation assumes a much more important function for both speaker and listener. A second drawback is that the physical signal is different since a phone line employs a reduced frequency band, with the result that acoustic cues to certain phonemes are absent because they occur at frequencies above 4000 Hz. An experienced phone user learns to adjust for this (though the /f/-/s/ distinction in particular remains a problem). However, the point remains that the low-level acoustic-phonetic processing of a phone message differs markedly from that of other types of speech event. It is unsurprising that many speakers find the process of handling a phone conversation in a second language, whether as initiator or respondent, a daunting experience.

An approach which requires the physical presence of an interviewer would thus seem to be preferable in terms of cognitive validity. However, much also depends upon the role that the interviewer is required to take. One can trace a continuum in terms of the demands imposed upon the test taker. At one end, the interviewer's questions might elicit responses which are formulaic or which echo the linguistic patterns employed by the questioner. This is necessary for the purposes of controlling from task difficulty at lower levels; but it detracts from cognitive validity because relatively closed responses of this kind impose little requirement upon the speaker to engage in the process of *a novo* utterance construction. At the other end, the interviewer's role might be limited to back-channelling and follow-up questions once a discussion has been initiated. This not only places a much greater onus upon the candidate, but aligns the processing that takes place much more closely with that of normal spoken discourse.

There have also been sociolinguistic concerns (Ross and Berwick 1992, Young and Milanovic 1992) that the power imbalance between interviewer and test taker may affect the nature of the communication that takes place (at its extreme, raising the prospect of a lockstep question and answer pattern). These concerns have led test designers to introduce a further interaction format in which test takers communicate with each other in pairs (Taylor 2000b). The approach has been the subject of some criticism (for a review of the issues, see Fulcher 2003:186–190, Luoma 2004:36–39), which is discussed in detail in Chapter 4. Clearly, assessing communication between two non-native speakers can be said to possess strong ecological validity in light of the widespread use of English as a language of international communication. (See, for example, the discussion by Canagarajah 2006). On the other hand, a cognitive analysis cannot overlook the fact that the format increases the demands of the test, since the candidate *as listener* potentially has to deal with two voices (interviewer and fellow test taker), two varieties of the target language (one native and one non-native), and even potentially a three-way interaction.

This last comment draws attention again to the critical role that listening skills play in what are ostensibly tests of speaking. Clearly, it is impossible to filter out listening from an interactive communication task, and Chapter 1 noted how the ALTE Can Do statements (Council of Europe 2001) combined the Listening and Speaking descriptors onto a single scale for Interaction. Nevertheless, the extent to which achievement in a speaking test is reliant on the listening skill is an issue in an examination where listening is also tested in a separate paper. The only way of shifting the balance towards speaking is to provide a further section of the test in which the candidate speaks for a more extended period – but does so to a live audience in the form of an examiner and/or another candidate, who can provide the encouragement and feedback which would normally be available.

This discussion of patterns of interaction in speaking tests has thus identified three possible and indeed potentially desirable formats: *interviewer–candidate* (I–C), *candidate–candidate* (C–C) and *solo candidate* (C). A fourth scenario might allow for a *three-way exchange* (I–C–C) in which the interviewer engages in discussion with two test takers.

As noted, these formats vary in the cognitive demands they make of test takers. At first glance, it might appear that the most demanding is C. The reasons lie partly in the difficulties of speaking at length, even in one's first language, but also (in an L2 situation) in the reduced opportunity for repair or support by the interviewer. Fulcher comments (2003:19): 'If we accept the view that conversation is co-constructed between participants talking in specific contexts, our construct definition may have to take into account such aspects of talk as the degree of interlocutor support.'

However, the fact is that each of the four patterns of interaction poses its own cognitive challenges:

- *I–C* may well require a relatively rapid response, particularly when the interviewer's turns are short.

- *C–C* contains a major element of unpredictability (particularly in cases where the partner test taker has listening comprehension difficulties and is inclined to go off topic). It also contains an important variable in the form of the test takers' familiarity with each other's L2 variety. A further complication lies in the extent to which a test taker can accommodate to and echo the language of their partner. Whereas the language of the interlocutor can presumably be trusted as a potential source of linguistic information and emulated accordingly, fine judgements have to be made as to the extent to which a fellow learner's language is to be trusted. This kind of decision clearly imposes additional cognitive demands.

- So far as *I–C–C* is concerned, a three-way conversation clearly demands more complex processing than a two-way exchange. The test taker not only needs to process input in two different voices; but also needs to keep track of the points-of-view and foregrounded topics being expressed by two different individuals.

In addition, the cognitive demands made of the test taker may vary considerably within these various formats. Two important factors briefly touched upon have been: how much the test taker has to contribute to the discourse, and the extent to which the test taker has to engage in *a novo* utterance construction.

Planning time

The amount of time speakers have in order to prepare what to say has an important impact upon several of the phases of processing. This is true whether they are performing in a first or a second language.

Pre-planning time clearly assists *conceptualisation*. The speaker has greater opportunity to generate ideas that are relevant to the topic to be discussed. They have also has greater opportunity to organise them and to mark how they are linked conceptually. Pre-planning time also assists *grammatical encoding* and *retrieval*: increasing the likelihood of utterances that are carefully formed syntactically and of precision in the choice of lexis. One might also expect a greater degree of fluency in that retrieval of many of the appropriate lexical and syntactic forms can take place in advance of task performance. Indeed, there are opportunities for *rehearsing* fully formed utterances and committing them to long-term memory before delivering them. These utterance templates go on to assist *self-monitoring*, in that they provide the speaker with a concrete target against which to match actual performance. In short, pre-planning time supports not only the search for ideas to express and the definition of goals, but also the organisation of information, the precision of the language used and the awareness of performance errors.

That said, it has to be recognised that most speech events are interactive. They take place under time pressure and require utterances to be assembled spontaneously. Only a limited number of contexts allow the speaker the luxury of planning what to say. They include formal monologue situations such as making speeches or giving academic presentations; but also situations where a speaker knows in advance that they will be called upon to express an extended opinion, report an event, tell a story or outline a set of proposals or requirements. Applying strict ecological criteria, one might argue that it is only in conjunction with these types of speaking that it is entirely appropriate for a task to incorporate pre-planning time. This is not just an academic point. It is clear that the cognitive processing associated with a planned task is markedly different from that associated with an unplanned. One can argue that it results in a different type of discourse. A listener might reasonably expect a greater degree of coherence and cohesion, less hesitation and repetition, fewer false starts and reformulations; and this in turn might lead to setting the bar for fluency at a higher level than with an extempore speaker. The implications for the assessment of planned monologues will be obvious.

The effects of pre-planning an L2 speaking task have been quite widely discussed in the literature on task-based learning (TBL), as have the effects of repeating a task. Most of the studies that have explored the impact upon performance (e.g. Bygate 2001, Crookes 1989, Foster and Skehan 1996, Mehnert 1998, Ortega 1999) concur in concluding that preparation or repetition leads to an increase in fluency and complexity. Bygate (2001) reports unclear evidence on improvements in accuracy in the case of repetition; but accuracy must certainly be increased by pre-planning and by the opportunity of mentally rehearsing the appropriate forms of words before performing a task.

An important variable in a testing context is the length of time available for pre-planning a monologue turn. A simple analysis might assume a close correlation between the time allowed and the well-formedness of the candidate's productions. It is not quite as clear-cut as that, however. There must be a cut-off point (determined by how much language can be pre-rehearsed in the special circumstances of a test), after which additional time is unhelpful and may even lead to second thoughts and a blurring of conceptual and linguistic targets. Of course, across an entire suite of tests, this consideration is counter-balanced by the growing competence of the candidates. As they acquire greater knowledge of L2 and (above all) greater automaticity of lexical retrieval and speech assembly, they are able to make increasingly effective use of any time allowed.

Cognitive task demands: Cambridge ESOL practice

Having considered the way in which task demands can be increased or diminished by patterns of interaction and by the opportunity to plan, we now examine the way in which these cognitive variables are represented in Cambridge ESOL practice.

Interaction

Live interaction, termed *direct* testing, is very much a feature of the approach to the assessment of speaking favoured by Cambridge ESOL (see Chapter 1 for discussion of the long tradition of direct speaking assessment by this board). The suite of Speaking tests embraces all four of the possible formats that have been identified. The tests provide for an interviewer (referred to as an *interlocutor*) whose function is to initiate interaction and to keep it going. But they also include phases of test taker–test taker interaction, thus mitigating the possible 'power' effects previously mentioned as associated with the interviewer's role. Most tests also make provision for solo presentation, in which (as noted) listening skills play a minimal part. To support the interlocutor, who may be personally engaged in the exchanges that take place, a second examiner, known as an *assessor*, monitors performance. Saville and Hargreaves (1999) argue that the use of a range of interactional formats confirms to general principles of test design, in which tasks are varied so as to elicit different types of language.

Table 3.4 summarises the speaking tasks at different levels of the suite. It is clear that a range of interaction types is covered, and that they foster language processing which draws upon both interactive and presentational skills. An initial 'interview' section in all tests features the I–C relationship, while C–C appears in the specifications as 'Two-way collaboration', C as

Table 3.4 Interactional patterns in Cambridge ESOL Speaking tests

Exam	Task	mins	Interaction
KET	Q&A based on an interlocutor frame	5–6	I–C
	Q&A based on prompt material	3–4	C–C
PET	Q&A based on an interlocutor frame	2–3	I–C
	Imaginary situation with prompt	2–3	C–C
	Describe photo	3	C
	Conversation on topic of photo	3	C–C
FCE	Q&A based on an interlocutor frame	3	I–C
	Compare photos; comment	4	C
	Decision-making task with prompts	3	C–C
	Three-way discussion	4	I–C–C
CAE	Q&A based on an interlocutor frame	3	I–C
	Long turn based on visual prompt; comment	4	C
	Decision-making task and report	3	C–C
	Three-way discussion	5	I–C–C
CPE	Q&A based on an interlocutor frame	3	I–C
	Decision-making task	4	C–C
	Long turn based on written prompt; comment	4	C
	Discussion on long turns	8	I–C–C

Source: Instructions to Speaking Examiners, 2011.

Note: Timings are for a complete task involving two candidates. Timings for FCE, CAE and CPE separate Part 3 and Part 4. Actual speaking times for long turns per candidate are: PET: up to 1 minute; FCE: 1 minute (plus 20 secs. peer feedback); CAE: 1 minute (plus 30 secs. peer feedback); CPE: 2 minutes (plus up to 1 minute peer feedback).

'Long turn' and I–C–C' as 'Three-way discussion'. Test takers are required to respond to task demands involving negotiation as well as to more formal questions, both open and closed.

In grading the cognitive demands imposed upon candidates, the test developers have relied partly upon the duration of the tasks. The overall contact time for a pair of candidates increases gradually from KET (maximum 10 minutes) to CPE (19 minutes). These figures are only broadly indicative of the amount of speaking an individual candidate has to do, since there is inevitably variation in the relative contributions made. A more important criterion appears to be the way in which the test is distributed between the various types of interaction. Figure 3.3 provides evidence of how this feature has been calibrated.

At KET and PET, the Part 1 I–C interview depends quite heavily upon simple routinised Q&A exchanges. Here are some examples from KET part 1:

Where do you live / come from?

Do you work or are you a student?

Do you like (studying English)?

Figure 3.3 Interaction formats in Speaking tests: timings for tasks for two candidates

Note: the PET figure combines two C–C interactions

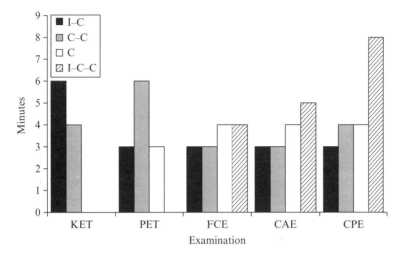

The questions are relatively predictable, allowing candidates to rehearse their answers. The answers are simple and consist of one or two sentences.

However, the cognitive demands imposed by the I–C format increase markedly in FCE Part 1. The sample materials on p. 318 include questions which are more open-ended and more difficult to predict. The questions can even invite the candidate to consider hypothetical constructs (see FCE Handbook for Teachers, p.83):

Could you tell us something about your family?

How much time do you usually spend at home?

Is there anything you would like to change about the area where you grew up?

Questions of this type demand quite extended responses from the candidate; and there is clearly a stronger requirement to engage with the interlocutor rather than simply participating in a Q&A routine.

As for grading by format, the complex three-way interaction does not appear until FCE (4 minutes) but then reappears at CAE (max. 5 mins) and CPE (max. 8 mins). The length of the 'long turn' when the candidate performs solo increases from PET (1 minute but a shorter period tolerated) to CPE (2 mins). The test designers thus treat I–C as the least demanding of the formats (especially when it is based on a simple Q&A exchange), and reserve C and I–C–C in particular for higher levels. At the same time, they attempt to redress the possible sociolinguistic constraints upon interlocutor–test taker communication by providing for a C-C phase even at the lowest level in KET – though obviously here in a very controlled form, with interlocutor prompting.

Overall, then, there has clearly been a principled approach to the grading of the task demands arising from different interaction types.

Planning time

As noted earlier, all the tests in the ESOL suite, with the exception of KET, include one task which requires extended individual performance. In cognitive terms, a long turn of this kind places heavier conceptualisation demands upon the test taker, who has to generate more ideas than when responding briefly to the comments of others and has to organise them meaningfully. It might be said to constitute a different type of discourse by virtue of the part played by forward planning (Brown, Anderson, Shillcock and Yule 1984:16– 18). From the assessor's point-of-view, coherence and cohesion would then be expected to be a greater consideration and hesitation, self-repair and loosely connected ideas might be regarded unfavourably.

The *Instructions to Speaking Examiners* (2011) make it clear that certain assessment criteria are more applicable to long turn tasks that are principally monologues. Particular attention is given to discourse features. From PET level up to CPE, these are:

* sustaining a long turn
* coherence and clarity of message
* organisation of language and ideas
* accuracy and appropriacy of linguistic resources.

(ISE:47, 51, 55, 59)

Due account has thus been taken of the part played by 'macro-planning' in extended discourse. However, there is an anomaly here. The candidate is allowed little or no pre-planning time in order to reflect upon the prompts provided and to undertake the kind of forward thinking that would feature in some types of longer turn. To be sure, the turn remains a relatively short one at most levels (indeed, the PET instructions allow the candidate to speak for less than a minute). But if candidates are to be judged on criteria such as coherence, cohesion and organisation, then the longer 2-minute slot at CPE level perhaps requires a brief period of preparation to permit macro-planning. It is true, as noted earlier, that a degree of forward planning can occur alongside speech assembly, once a monologue is underway. But one wonders whether in this type of task a speaker needs time to formulate in advance a set of 'subgoals' or 'speech act intentions' (Levelt 1989:109). The requirement that test takers speak extempore but are assessed in part by criteria based upon preplanned speech would seem to break one of Weir's test performance conditions (1993:39), namely 'processing under normal time constraints'.

However, the case is not as clear-cut as this line of argument might suggest. It would seem from the specifications[5] that the perceived function of the monologue tasks is not to test the candidate's ability to undertake a formal lecture-style presentation of the kind that would require pre-planning in a real-life context. Instead, it is to assess the extent to which the candidate is capable of engaging in a longer turn of the kind that might occur if they were called upon impromptu to tell a story, argue a point or explain a procedure. On these grounds, one might argue that cognitive validity is not compromised, though there should perhaps be some degree of latitude in applying the discourse-level criteria[6].

Summary: Cognitive processing across Cambridge ESOL levels

The main purpose of the present review was to match the specifications of the Cambridge ESOL suite of exams against an external model of the cognitive processes which the speaking skill requires of a native user. The model chosen was the most comprehensive one available: that of Levelt (1989). The Levelt model incorporates a number of components which were mentioned in the preamble as essential: a mechanism for forward-planning, a means of storing plans for forthcoming utterances while they are being articulated and a system for monitoring one's own productions to see if they accord with one's intentions.

The cognitive validity of the Cambridge ESOL suite was examined with reference to the stages of processing identified by Levelt (1999).

- *Conceptualisation.* The ESOL suite was found to provide detailed task input to the test taker in order to reduce the demands of conceptualisation. The effect is to lighten the cognitive load upon test takers, and also to reduce any potential bias towards rewarding imagination rather than linguistic performance.
- *Grammatical encoding.* The Cambridge ESOL suite specifies linguistic content in the form of language functions to be performed by test takers. It thus operationalises this phase of the Levelt model as a mapping process between the target functions and the syntactic forms which correspond to them. Two possible principles were identified for the grading of the functions in terms of cognitive demands: the first related to the semantic complexity of the function to be expressed, the second to the number of functions elicited by a particular task. The Cambridge ESOL suite was found to have borne both principles in mind in a systematic way when staging the difficulty of its Speaking tests. A marked increase in cognitive demands was noted at the FCE level, which may be intentional.

- *Phonological encoding.* There is growing support for a view of second language acquisition as a process of 'proceduralisation', in which the retrieval of linguistic forms begins as a slow and attention-demanding process but becomes increasingly automatic. Because this is a gradual and internalised development, it is difficult to represent reliably within a set of test specifications; however, a major driving force behind it is the chunking of words into formulaic strings – affecting both the way in which they are stored in the mind and the ease with which they are retrieved. Helpfully for the test designer, chunking is associated with certain observable developments in an individual's productions, which give rise to the impression of increased fluency. They include: a reduction in planning time at clause boundaries, a reduction in hesitation, an increase in length of run, an increase in grammatical and collocational accuracy within the chunk and a progression towards a more native-like rhythm. Of these, hesitation and pausing are represented at all levels of the Cambridge ESOL specifications, with clearly marked gradations between the levels. The use of formulaic language features only negatively, as an indicator of inability on the part of low-level test takers to generate novel utterances. The proposal was made that future specifications might incorporate evidence of chunking as a marker of increasing proceduralisation as the test taker moves up the scale. Test designers may also need at some point to adjust their thinking in the light of increasing support for emergentist views of language acquisition. It is not clear at present how this development might impact upon test specifications.
- *Phonetic encoding, articulation.* Potential problems of articulation were represented as deriving from two sources: inadequate phonological representations in the mind and the inability to adjust to unfamiliar articulatory settings. The L2 speaker may also face a tension between the need to hold a phonetic plan in the mind and the need to focus attention upon precise articulation. In these circumstances, it is important that test designers do not unduly emphasise the importance of accuracy in pronunciation. The Cambridge ESOL suite deals with this issue sensitively by adopting intelligibility as its principal criterion.
- *Self-monitoring.* A competent speaker monitors their own productions for accuracy and appropriacy; and is capable of introducing self-repairs both promptly and following certain norms. This aspect of the speaking process is represented in the ESOL specifications in terms of the level of support needed from the interlocutor and the test taker's ability to achieve repair. Two types of repair are combined in the descriptors, and it might be advisable to define the term more precisely. It might also be possible to grade self-monitoring more specifically by reference to the levels of attention which test takers find themselves able to allocate

to, respectively, the linguistic and semantic-pragmatic features of the utterances.

This validation exercise also considered the types of interaction which are possible in a speaking test, and the extent to which they can be said to conduce to the cognitive processes that might apply in non-test conditions. The formats employed by the Cambridge ESOL suite were found to possess greater cognitive validity than possible alternatives – providing a clear cost–benefit justification for the rather complex practical procedures which they entail. It was noted that the suite features a range of different interaction types; and thus attempts to represent the variety of speaker–listener relationships which occur in real-life speech events, and the processes that each type requires of the speaker.

A particular strength of the suite lies in the various ingenious ways in which it fosters test taker–test taker interaction but continues to control the range of language that is used. Clearly, it is not possible in test conditions to create a context identical to that of a natural speech event. However, the absence of a power relationship between test takers plus the problem-driven form of the tasks provided in this type of exchange ensure that the encounters which take place elicit processes which are as close as one can perhaps achieve to those of real life.

A second issue relating to the relative cognitive difficulty of the tasks was the amount of pre-planning time permitted. It was noted that pre-planning is not provided for – a decision which (in terms of cognitive validity) is entirely sound in the case of tasks that are designed to measure spontaneous spoken interaction. It is more open to question in relation to the monologue tasks, in that the absence of pre-planning time means that they do not replicate the cognitive processes which often accompany the preparation of a formal presentation. However, a great deal depends upon the perceived purpose of those tasks. The Cambridge ESOL test designers might argue that they are intended to provide an indication of a candidate's ability to produce an extended turn, not of their ability to engage in a markedly different type of speech assembly.

It is clear that, in grading the specifications for the five levels of the suite, designers have given careful thought to the relative cognitive difficulty both of the tasks and of the interaction formats. Task demands are increased only gradually; and the more demanding types of interaction (particularly three-way discussion) are reserved for higher levels of the suite. Overall one concludes that the Cambridge ESOL specifications do indeed correspond closely to what we know of the cognitive processes involved in the production of speech. The few reservations that have been expressed represent omissions; none constitute provisions that run counter to the findings of speech science.

It is also apparent that the cognitive requirements have been sufficiently finely graded in relation to the different levels of the suite. Full consideration has been given both to task demands and to the types of processing that can be deemed to be representative of performance at different stages of proficiency.

The focus of the present chapter has chiefly been on the cognitive demands of the speaking process, whether in L1 or in L2. The criteria for assessing cognitive validity that have been identified concern the target behaviour of the test candidate and potentially provide a framework for the cognitive validation of any test of second language speaking.

A secondary focus has been on two types of task variable present in tests of speaking: namely the nature of the interaction involved and the availability of pre-planning time. Here, the emphasis has been strictly upon the way in which these variables increase or diminish the *cognitive* demands upon a speaker. Clearly, other aspects of task design (including task setting and linguistic demands) are beyond the remit of this chapter, and will now be considered in Chapter 4.

Acknowledgements

The author is enormously indebted to Lynda Taylor for her sensitive editing and her helpful suggestions and feedback. He is also especially grateful to Kathy Gude, Chair of the Cambridge ESOL Speaking Panel, for perceptive comments and advice about the criteria and the instructions given to examiners.

Notes

1 The examples are from Aitchison (2008:254–5); for a discussion of syntactic speech errors, see Fromkin 1988.
2 It is curious that a procedural component of this kind does not feature in some standard models of test performance. The Bachman and Palmer (1996) model, for example, provides for task-related metacognitive strategies used by test takers; but does not explicitly recognise the very different type of highly learned cognitive procedure that enables a candidate to apply linguistic and pragmatic knowledge with minimal working memory demands.
3 Some caution is needed with the term *planning,* which is used in a narrow sense when discussing conceptualisation (*macro-* vs *micro planning*) but is also used more generally to refer to the process of assembling an upcoming piece of speech.
4 Chair of the Cambridge ESOL Speaking Panel, Kathy Gude, comments (personal communication) 'Perhaps it is [because] our assessment of 'fluency' is too subjective and not as easily quantified as some of the other assessment criteria'.
5 Describing the long turn section, the CAE Handbook for Teachers (2008b:76) asserts: *This part tests the candidates' ability to produce an extended piece of discourse.* On the other hand, the profile also foregrounds

the kind of criteria that might be associated with a pre-planned presentation: *Candidates have the opportunity to show their ability to organise their thoughts and ideas. . .*

6 Interestingly, a minute is allowed for selecting and preparing the topic ahead of the long turn in the Speaking papers of the specialised Cambridge tests: Business English Certificates (BEC), International Certificate in Financial English (ICFE) and International Legal English Certificate (ILEC). Indeed, in BEC, candidates are provided with pen and paper to assist them. Here one can reasonably claim that cognitive validity is not threatened since a pre-planning component is characteristic of the types of more formal real-world presentation that occur in business, financial and legal contexts.

4 Context validity

Evelina Galaczi and Angela ffrench
University of Cambridge ESOL Examinations

Chapter 3 of this volume focused on the cognitive processing underlying speaking, including the way in which particular task features can impose additional cognitive demands upon speakers. Field (this volume) comments that any consideration of task design leads us into the interface between cognitive and context validity. The aim of the present chapter is to take a closer look at context validity and the range of contextual parameters observed in the Cambridge ESOL General English Speaking tests, and to investigate the relationship between these task parameters and proficiency levels. Such an investigation has implications for the development of a validity argument supporting the Cambridge ESOL General English Speaking tests and may also have some relevance for the other Speaking tests produced by Cambridge. An investigation of this kind could also bring to light any potential areas of task design and use which may need further scrutiny.

The centrality of tasks in speaking assessment brings about a need to understand how the choice of tasks and their related contextual parameters influence the way the test taker performs. The task contextual parameters in Weir's (2005a) test validation framework (given in Figure 4.1) allow a systematic analysis of task features within a socio-cognitive approach. Such an analysis can focus on tasks in isolation, and on tasks within the same proficiency level or across different proficiency levels, thus providing insights and evidence to support claims about the usefulness of the tests in question.

An examination of tasks against Weir's (2005a) socio-cognitive framework could also contribute to the broader debate on task difficulty. There is lack of consensus in the academic literature regarding task difficulty, with at times contradictory findings from the SLA and L2 assessment literature (Bachman 2002, Fulcher and Reiter 2003, Iwashita, McNamara and Elder 2001, Skehan 1996, 1998, Skehan and Foster 1997, 1999, Weir, O'Sullivan and Horai 2006). In the absence of definitive guidance from academic research, examination boards must operationalise task difficulty themselves in order to allow for the construction of tests at different proficiency levels and thus difficulty. In the discussion to follow, the question of how task difficulty is operationalised in the context of Cambridge ESOL Speaking tests at different proficiency levels in terms of differing contextual features will be addressed.

The remainder of this chapter will explore the academic research to date on the different context validity parameters outlined in Weir's (2005a) framework for test validation. Each context validity feature will then be analysed in the light of Cambridge ESOL's General English Speaking tests. The face-to-face speaking test paradigm will be the predominant focus of the chapter, since it is a defining feature of the General English tests under review, and is of relevance for the majority of Speaking tests produced by Cambridge.

Figure 4.1 Aspects of context validity for speaking (from Weir 2005a)

CONTEXT VALIDITY

SETTING: TASK
- Response format
- Purpose
- Weighting
- Known criteria
- Order of items/tasks
- Time constraints

SETTING: ADMINISTRATION*
- Physical conditions
- Uniformity of administration
- Security

DEMANDS: TASK
Linguistic (Input and Output)
Channel
Discourse mode
Length
Nature of information
Topic familiarity / content knowledge
Lexical resources
Structural resources
Functional resources

Interlocutor
Speech rate
Variety of accent
Acquaintanceship
Number
Gender

* *Although features of Setting:Administration are undoubtedly important contextual parameters in speaking tests, they are of a slightly different order to the other elements in this box. In line with the approach taken in the Examining Reading volume (Khalifa and Weir 2009), they will be discussed in an Appendix to this volume rather than within this already lengthy chapter. See Appendix D for discussion of these features.*

Setting: Task

We begin our analysis of speaking test theory and practice by considering features of the task setting.

Response format

In speaking assessment, response format types typically refer to patterns of interaction, and can roughly be divided into *monologic* and *dialogic*. The latter usually involves response formats such as an interview, a role-play, or an interviewer–candidate or candidate–candidate discussion. The monologic response format is typically an oral presentation (also known as an individual long turn), or responses to computer/tape delivered prompts.

The effect of response format on test performance is by now widely accepted in both the L2 assessment and SLA literature and a solid body of evidence exists suggesting that different response formats can influence the resulting test taker performance (see for example, Alderson, Clapham and Wall 1995, Bygate 1999, Bygate, Skehan and Swain 2001, ffrench 2003a, Foster and Skehan 1996, Kormos 1999, O'Sullivan, Weir and Saville 2002, Taylor 1999a). This contextual parameter has fundamental implications for the cognitive validity of the test, as noted in Chapter 3, since different response formats engage different cognitive processes.

Several language testing studies have provided valuable insights and empirical evidence into the role of different response formats in terms of the quality and quantity of candidate output. Among them, O'Sullivan et al (2002) investigated the distribution of speech functions across four response formats: examiner–candidate interviews, candidate presentations, candidate–candidate discussions, and group discussions involving the candidates and examiner. The authors applied checklists covering different functions to a series of tasks from the Cambridge ESOL FCE examination. Basing their work on Bygate (1987) and Weir (1993), the taxonomy used by the authors included functions in three categories: informational (for example, providing personal information, describing or elaborating), interactional (for example, persuading, agreeing or disagreeing), and managing the interaction (for example, initiating an interaction, changing the topic or terminating the interaction). The findings indicated that different response formats produced different functional profiles. The one-to-one interview format and individual long turn tended to elicit predominantly informational functions, while the discussion tasks enabled a broader range of functions from all three categories. When the examiner joined the discussion, there was a reduction in the functional range, but this was not quite as limited as the one-to-one interview task. The results from this study are in line with an earlier investigation by Lazaraton and Frantz (1997), who also focused on the functional range in candidate output through a discourse analytic lens. The authors restricted their analysis to the frequency and range of informational functions elicited in 14 live FCE Speaking tests and found that the examiner–candidate interview and the candidate–candidate interaction tasks elicited the widest range of informational functions, whereas the individual monologic task and the discussion task involving the two (or three) candidates and examiner elicited a narrower range of informational functions.

Another group of studies has focused on the interactional opportunities provided by different response formats. An example is provided by Kormos (1999), who used discourse analysis in a comparison of interviews and guided role-play response formats in oral assessments. The author focused on the distribution of rights and duties in speaking tests and on the opportunities that test takers had to display their ability to manage conversation in the

L2 in these two tasks in terms of patterns of dominance and contingency. The results indicated that the two response formats differed: the interaction in the role-plays was more symmetrical, as the test takers introduced and ratified a similar number of topics as the interviewer. They also interrupted more, had more control of topic introduction and topic development, and had more opportunities to display the ability to open and close an interaction. The role-play format, the author concluded, provided 'circumstances for engaging in conversations' (Kormos 1999:184), echoing van Lier's (1989) and Young's (1995) appeals to incorporate response formats which provide peer–peer interactional opportunities into oral tests.

Research has also focused on the power distribution and symmetry of conversational rights and duties related with certain response formats, and has shed light on the situational and interactional authenticity of certain tasks. Young and Milanovic (1992) investigated the discourse found in the examiner–candidate interview response format and showed that it could be highly asymmetrical in terms of dominance, contingency and goal-orientation (terms introduced by Jones and Gerard 1967), as compared to a candidate–candidate discussion task, where the variables of dominance, contingency and goal-orientation are more evenly distributed among participants (see also Galaczi 2008 for a discussion of dominance, contingency and goal-orientation in a candidate–candidate interaction task). They found that the direct elicitation in an interview task made it difficult for a test taker to escape the fixed role relationship in this task format, unlike the less controlled and more open-ended response format involving candidate–candidate discussion.

Of further relevance is a group of studies which have focused on comparisons of the paired and singleton face-to-face speaking test formats. While the primary focus of these studies has been the comparison of test formats, and not specific task response formats, the findings are of importance for the present discussion since different test formats (e.g., paired or singleton) allow for a range of response formats and hold implications for the role of response format as a contextual feature. ffrench (2003a) compared the paired and singleton one-to-one Speaking test format in CPE in terms of the functional range produced in candidate output. The results suggested that the paired format, which allowed for a broader range of response formats, was capable of eliciting more speech functions than the singleton interview format, which had a narrower range of response formats. Taylor (1999a) offers another investigation into the way different response formats can achieve different outcomes. Her study focused on a quantitative comparison between singleton speaking test performances and paired speaking test performances. The findings indicated that, in terms of variables such as length of time, number of words, number of speaker turns, and average number of words per turn, the relative contribution of the candidates increased and the relative contribution of the interlocutor was reduced in the paired test format. A recent study by Brooks (2009) also sheds light on the singleton and paired test formats. The author found more complex interaction between participants in the paired format: in the paired format, which allowed for peer–peer interaction tasks, the test takers engaged in more prompting, elaboration, finishing sentences, referring to partners' ideas, and paraphrasing. Brooks' results, alongside those of Galaczi (2008), support the view that choosing the paired format allows the test designer to replicate within the testing event some of the co-construction that characterises spoken discourse between interlocutors beyond the test (as discussed in Chapter 3, and see also Fulcher 2003, McNamara 1997a, 1997b, Swain 2001). This resonates with Field's discussion in Chapter 3 on the dynamic and reciprocal nature of most forms of naturally occurring spoken interaction (see p. 97–103).

The above-mentioned research provides convincing testimony about the effect of response format on the distribution of speech functions, the quantity of language produced, the opportunities provided for candidates to manage the interaction, and the general distribution of conversational rights and responsibilities. In Chapter 3 Field has shown us how the nature of the interaction required by the task, combined with the length of turn expected and the amount of time available for assembling spoken utterances, contribute significantly to the cognitive load imposed upon the test taker, and therefore difficulty of the task. The above-mentioned research does not imply that one response format is superior to the others. Tasks with different response formats are simply tools which allow for different sampling of candidate speech. The choice of response format does not occur in a vacuum – it is dictated by the overall test purpose, and so the potential and limitations of different response formats need to be considered within the context of overall test purpose. As Bygate et al (2001:163) argue, the choice of task and its corresponding response format 'is not a neutral, technical decision: tasks introduce effects upon performance, and an unawareness of such effects may introduce error (and potential unfairness) into measurement procedures'. It is important, therefore, for test developers to understand these effects in order to make informed decisions about which response formats to include in a test and how the response format chosen links to the test purpose and the context of use of the test scores. One implication of this is the need to minimise the effect of response format in speaking tests through employing a *range* of response formats. As Alderson, Clapham and Wall (1995) note, the use of a range of response methods will ensure that the test is not biased towards one particular response format and will lead to more complex cognitive and strategic processes for the test takers, which in turn will elicit a richer range of language, and will allow for better inferences to be made about a candidate's proficiency in wider real-life contexts. The sampling across a range of response formats will broaden the evidence gathered about the test takers' skills, as it will introduce the opportunity for candidates to display a broader range of their communicative competence and will reduce the possibility of construct irrelevant variance resulting from the use of a single method. As will be seen in the following sections, these observations are reflected in Cambridge ESOL's practice in Speaking assessment across the proficiency continuum.

In addition to the call for a *range* of response formats, Weir (2005a) also discusses the need for response formats to be *appropriate* for the proficiency level they are used for. The CEFR (2001) gives little guidance on how response format as a task feature might be related to level, although it does suggest that learners at the A (i.e. lower) levels are not expected to be able to produce longer stretches of coherent text. There is undoubtedly scope for further empirical research in this area. It would be interesting to investigate in greater detail the suitability (or lack) of specific response formats at different proficiency levels, such as, for example, the use of short-response formats at higher proficiency levels or the use of presentation tasks at lower proficiency levels.

Response format: Cambridge practice

The standard format of the Cambridge ESOL Speaking tests is two candidates and two examiners engaged in a direct face-to-face test of speaking consisting of several tasks/response formats. Examples of the tasks used in each of the Main Suite examinations can be found in Appendix A; Table 4.1 provides an overview of the response formats used in the tests. As can be seen, a range of response formats is employed at all five levels and some response formats do not appear until a certain level. KET (CEFR Level A2) has two tasks with two different response formats, an examiner–candidate interview and a candidate–candidate question and answer task using prompt material. The long turn and interaction tasks are absent at this level and are introduced from PET (B1) upwards. From then on candidates are expected to be able to perform in long and short turns and with a different number of co-speakers (interviewer, other candidate, both interviewer and other candidate).

The paired test format in Main Suite Speaking tests, and the resulting range of tasks it allows for, is a reflection of the overall test purpose of the Cambridge ESOL Main Suite exams, which aims to make inferences about a candidate's communicative language ability in a general L2 context. The purpose of the Main Suite Speaking tests is driven by a socio-cognitive definition of the construct of speaking underlying this suite of tests: speaking is seen as having both a cognitive (i.e. knowledge and processing) dimension and a social dimension conceptualised in terms of reciprocity and co-construction of interaction. Weir contends that 'clearly, if we want to

Table 4.1   Response formats used in Main Suite Speaking tests

Exam	Response format			
	Part 1	Part 2	Part 3	Part 4
KET	*Interview* Each candidate interacts with the examiner.	*Candidate– candidate question and answer using prompt material* The two candidates interact with each other. Structured prompt cards are used to stimulate questions and answers.	–	–
PET	*Interview* Each candidate interacts with the examiner.	*Candidate– candidate interaction* Candidates are given oral instructions and provided with a visual stimulus (a collection of ideas in the form of a piece of artwork) to form the basis for a task which they carry out together. (Note: Though the Candidate– candidate interactions in PET, FCE, CAE and CPE are very similar in format, they differ in their concrete/abstract nature, as we shall see later.)	*Individual long turn* Each candidate is given one colour photograph to describe.	*Candidate–candidate interaction* The candidates speak to each other. The theme established in Part 3 is now used as the starting point for a general discussion.
FCE	*Interview* Each candidate interacts with the examiner.	*Individual long turn* Each candidate is given the opportunity to speak for one minute without interruption. In turn they are asked to compare	*Candidate– candidate interaction* Candidates are given oral instructions and provided with a visual stimulus (several photographs or pieces of	*Prompted candidate– candidate interaction (including interaction with the examiner)* The examiner directs the conversation by encouraging the candidates to broaden and

Table 4.1 Continued

Exam	Response format			
	Part 1	Part 2	Part 3	Part 4
		two colour photographs and to make a further comment about them in response to a question that is read out by the examiner. The prompt also appears in the form of a direct question written above the photographs. The listening candidate is also asked to comment briefly on the visual.	artwork) to form the basis for a task which they carry out together. The prompts also appear as two direct questions written above the visuals.	discuss further the topics introduced in Part 3.
CAE	*Interview* Each candidate interacts with the examiner.	*Individual long turn* Each candidate is given the opportunity to speak without interruption. In turn they are asked to select two from a set of three photographs and to comment on and react to them. Two prompts are given to the candidates in the form of two direct questions: these are written above the photographs. The listening candidate is also asked to comment briefly on the visual.	*Candidate–candidate interaction* Candidates are given oral instructions and provided with a visual stimulus (several photographs or pieces of artwork) to form the basis for a task which they carry out together. The prompts also appear as two direct questions written above the visuals.	*Prompted candidate–candidate interaction* (*including interaction with the examiner*) The examiner directs the conversation by encouraging the candidates to broaden and discuss further the topics introduced in Part 3.

Table 4.1 Continued

| Exam | Response format | | | |
	Part 1	Part 2	Part 3	Part 4
CPE	*Interview* Each candidate interacts with the examiner.	*Candidate– candidate interaction* Following an initial question which focuses their reaction to aspects of one or more pictures, the candidates are given visual and spoken prompts, which are used in a decision-making task which they carry out together.	*Individual long turn followed by prompted candidate– candidate interaction (including interaction with the examiner)* Candidates are given the opportunity to speak without interruption. Each candidate in turn is given a written question to respond to and prompts to use if they wish. This is followed by the examiner asking a series of further questions, which allows the candidates to engage in a discussion to explore further the topics of the long turns.	–

Source: KET – CPE Handbooks for Teachers, 2007, 2008.

test spoken interaction, a valid test must include reciprocity conditions' (2005a:72). Given their aim to draw inferences concerning some measure of interactional ability, the Main Suite Speaking tests have an interactional component, elicited in different response formats (candidate–examiner, candidate–candidate, candidate–candidate–examiner). Such a range of response formats 'enables a wider range of language functions and roles to be engineered to provide a better basis for oral language sampling with less asymmetry between participants' (Skehan 2001:169).

The definition of the construct underlying the Main Suite Speaking tests is supported by current theories of communicative language ability (Bachman

1990, Bachman and Palmer 1996) which include an interactional component. They presuppose the need for speaking tests which aim to make inferences about communicative language ability to provide opportunities for test takers to display their ability to manage interaction outside the restrictions of the examiner–candidate interview task or the candidate monologic task. Similarly, the CEFR advocates the importance of interaction in its division of Speaking into two skills: production and interaction, signalling that a test which purports interactional ability must tap into both these skills. We might also note here in passing that Speaking tests possess an integrative quality since they invariably test listening as well as spoken interaction and/or production; this is reflected in the ALTE Can Do statements which combine Listening and Speaking (see Table 1.1 in Chapter 1; see also Field (this volume), Nakatsuhara, forthcoming a).

The direct face-to-face format of Cambridge ESOL's Main Suite Speaking tests provides an opportunity for the inclusion of different response formats, including ones which can tap into interactional ability (e.g. question-and-answer tasks, tasks involving discussions between the examiner and test taker, and between the test takers themselves), and ones which focus on production (e.g. long turn tasks). Such a range of response formats broadens the coverage and sampling options which the test provides and allows for inferences about communicative language ability in a general context to be made. To use a metaphor, the response formats available to a test developer are a toolbox at their disposal. It is important for the test developer to understand what can be in the toolbox in the first place and what the tools can do in order to make informed decisions about which response formats would be the most suitable in the light of the specific test purpose and inferences made.

The broad construct underlying the Main Suite tests, and the corresponding test purpose and range of response formats is also supported by the interface between teaching and assessment, which will be discussed in more detail in Chapter 6. As Chalhoub-Deville (2001) notes, performance-based testing has witnessed an emphasis for assessment tasks to share features considered to be central in a classroom context. The communicative orientation in language teaching and advances in second language acquisition have argued strongly for the need to give learners opportunities to interact. The use of group work in the classroom has been shown to be beneficial to the development of the ability to interact, as it provides more opportunities for learners to use the target language than in teacher-centred approaches (Savignon 2005). A natural extension of the centrality of paired and group work in communicative classrooms is the need to use response formats in speaking tests which mirror the contextual features of a communicative language classroom. The range of response formats in the Main Suite Speaking tests, including tasks which allow peer–peer interaction, is in line with the general purpose of the tests to reflect classroom practices and the educational domain of language learning.

As noted at the beginning of the chapter, a further aim of the present discussion is to explore the progression of contextual features across proficiency levels and identify key distinguishing characteristics across levels. A useful starting point is to view response formats along a controlled/semi-controlled/open-ended continuum. As has been noted in the literature, the amount of structure/control, which is part of Foster and Skehan's (1996) task communicative demand, has implications for the cognitive load, and therefore difficulty, of the tasks. Wigglesworth (2001:203) notes that structure makes a task easier, as it 'reduces the cognitive load on the speaker by providing scaffolding upon which to build language'. This point is echoed by Field (this volume), who highlights the extent to which cognitive demands made of the test taker may vary considerably across various formats, often dependent upon how much the test taker has to contribute to the discourse or the extent to which the test taker has to engage in *a novo* utterance construction.

In the Main Suite Speaking tests the level of control of the response formats varies, as the need for higher autonomy and heavier cognitive load increases with each subsequent level. In KET (A2) both tasks use response formats which are controlled, a reflection of the required low cognitive load at this level. From PET (B1) and above, in addition to controlled, structured response formats (e.g. question-and-answer interview tasks), more open-ended response formats are used (e.g. candidate–candidate interaction tasks). There is, therefore, a transition from controlled formats used at the lower levels, to semi-controlled candidate–candidate tasks, and more open-ended discussions at the higher levels, as seen in Figure 4.2.

Figure 4.2 Level of control in Main Suite Speaking tests

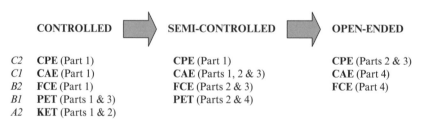

CONTROLLED	SEMI-CONTROLLED	OPEN-ENDED
C2 **CPE** (Part 1)	**CPE** (Part 1)	**CPE** (Parts 2 & 3)
C1 **CAE** (Part 1)	**CAE** (Parts 1, 2 & 3)	**CAE** (Part 4)
B2 **FCE** (Part 1)	**FCE** (Parts 2 & 3)	**FCE** (Part 4)
B1 **PET** (Parts 1 & 3)	**PET** (Parts 2 & 4)	
A2 **KET** (Parts 1 & 2)		

The same response format can be used at different proficiency levels, but manipulated in terms of the level of control, to reflect appropriate changes in difficulty level. To take the interview task as an example, in KET (A2), this task consists mostly of closed questions and focuses on giving factual information of a personal kind (e.g. *Where do you come from?*), or on talking about something very familiar (e.g. *Tell me something about your hobbies*). Field (this volume) comments on the short, routine and predictable nature of the interview questions at both KET and PET, which results in a lower cognitive load. The same response format acquires semi-controlled features at the higher levels: at FCE (B2) the interview questions become less routine and predictable, requiring longer and more engaged responses from test takers (e.g. *Is there something new you'd really like to learn about?*); at CAE (C1) and CPE (C2) the scope of the questions in the interview response format widens still further (e.g. inviting candidates to express their opinions about abstract topics).

The gradation from controlled to semi-controlled to open-ended response formats is also observed with the candidate long turn and interaction tasks. The long turn is not present in KET, it is controlled in PET, semi-controlled in FCE and CAE, and open-ended in CPE. For example, in PET the task prompt reads: *Please tell us what you see in the photograph* (PET Handbook 2007:58). The task demands a description of what is in the photo, with no opportunity to deviate from the prompt. In FCE and CAE the long turn task acquires semi-controlled features as it asks for interpretation of the given pictures by asking for candidates' opinions (FCE) or including an element of speculation (CAE). This can be seen in the following examples: *I'd like you to compare the photographs, and say why you think music is important to different groups of people* (FCE Handbook 2007a:80); *I'd like you to compare two of the pictures, and say what different aspects of train travel they show, and how the people might be feeling* (CAE Handbook 2008b:89). In CPE the extended turn takes a more open-ended character, as seen in the following example: *What are the advantages and disadvantages of 24-hour shopping?* (CPE Handbook 2008c:68). Similarly, in the candidate–candidate interaction task, there is a difference in the amount of control and support given: at KET level, the candidates engage in an information exchange activity where each candidate is supported – and limited – by matching question-and-answer written prompts (and a visual for clarification purposes). At the higher levels, in a less-controlled interaction task, candidates are provided with visual stimuli and have to draw on their own resources to produce the appropriate language.

An avenue for further exploration relating to this contextual parameter would be an investigation of the potential of a group interaction task at the C1 and C2 levels, especially given the use that is made of these exams for university entrance purposes. It would be especially beneficial to examine whether interaction in a group oral task equates with group interaction in seminars at tertiary level, which would in turn have implications for the interactional authenticity and cognitive validity of group tasks used at higher proficiency levels.

Task purpose

Typically the notion of purpose applies to overall *test* purpose (e.g. testing Business English, Academic English). While test purpose is a fundamental consideration for test developers and users, within a discussion on contextual task parameters it is also important to address the more local notion of *task* purpose. The two clearly interface and have relevance for claims of test validity, but what we manipulate as test designers are primarily the local features at task level, one of which is test purpose.

Luoma (2004) notes that one of the key decisions in task design is what the speakers will be asked to *do* with language – what, in other words, the task purpose will be. As discussed in the previous chapter on cognitive validity, the purpose of the task is central to any macro- and micro-planning that candidates are going to activate when doing the task. There is, in other words, a 'symbiotic relationship between the choices we make in relation to purpose and the processing that results in task completion' (Weir 2005a:58). A clear, precise purpose will facilitate goal setting and monitoring – two key cognitive strategies in language processing – and will potentially enhance performance. In addition to cognitive validity, clarity of task purpose has implications for the scoring validity of a task/test, as we shall see in see Chapter 5. As Shaw and Weir (2007) observe for the parallel productive skill of writing, a task with a clear and unambiguous purpose is more likely to lead to performance which can be measured with a greater degree of consistency as the macro-planning employed by the test takers will agree with the one expected by the test developer and test evaluator. Shaw and Weir (2007) cite several studies (e.g. Dudley-Evans 1988, Horowitz 1986, Moore and Morton 1999) where the wording of the task prompt had affected the candidates' interpretation of the purpose of the task, and the authors give the word 'discuss' as an example of a term open to different interpretations unless further specified.

The purpose underlying a task needs to be not just clearly stated, but also to be appropriate for the respective proficiency level and test use. Appropriateness of task purpose enhances the authenticity of the assessment as it provides test takers with a realistic and real-world based purpose which 'goes beyond a ritual display of knowledge for assessment' (Shaw and Weir 2007:71). Brown and Yule (1983), Bygate (1987) and the CEFR (2001) provide useful models for categorising task purpose by examining the macro-functions underlying speaking tasks. Brown and Yule (1983) propose four different types of informational talk: to describe, to instruct, to tell a story, to express/justify opinions; and further suggest that the list is based on a logical order of difficulty. Bygate's (1987) taxonomy is based on a two-fold distinction between factually oriented talk (description, narration, instruction, comparison) and evaluative talk (explanation, justification, prediction, decision). The author suggests that speakers' use of language is different in each of these categories and has further demonstrated (Bygate 1999) that the processing involved in performing a narrative and an argumentation leads to learners making different linguistic choices. Brown and Yule's and Bygate's categorisations have parallels with other taxonomies proposed in the literature for writing, such as Vähäpässi's (1982) tripartite distinction between reproducing, organising, inventing (which has been further developed by Weigle (2002)), and Bereiter and Scardamalia's (1987) distinction between knowledge telling and knowledge transforming. These distinctions typically refer to the extent to which information must be organised, re-organised or synthesised in order to perform the task successfully. The important point and common thread through these taxonomies is that different task purposes draw on different kinds of cognitive processing and, as such, have implications for task difficulty. The different cognitive demands of tasks with their corresponding purposes and accompanying linguistic choices illustrate the need for tests to include tasks with a range of underlying purposes. This would allow for different macro- and micro-processing to be engaged and would lead to the display of different information about learners' L2 proficiency. Following the same line of thought, Luoma (2004) notes the importance of ensuring task equivalence, in different test forms, for example, through employing tasks which have the same purpose and represent the same underlying functions.

Task purpose: Cambridge practice

The design of Cambridge ESOL's Main Suite exams takes account of the importance of giving test takers a clear purpose, and the speaking tasks are all framed by a task rubric which clearly states the purpose in the task. For example, the rubrics use words such as '*ask questions*', '*answer*', '*first talk together . . . then decide*', '*compare*', '*agree*', etc. Table 4.2 on pages 126–127 shows some examples of the rubric words and phrases used at different levels drawn from the sample tasks in Appendix A.

Additional information and guidance on the intended purpose underlying each test part, and the nature of the interaction and core functions that are to be elicited is provided in the examination Handbooks. An overview is given in Table 4.3 on pages 128–130.

Clarity of task purpose is emphasised in the instructions given to Cambridge ESOL item writers, which specify the wording of task instructions and prompts in order to make the purpose of the task clear. Item writers are also advised to ensure that the level of input language is well within the lexical and structural range of the respective level of the candidate, so that even weak candidates can understand the requirements of the task and attempt it.

Trialling of materials also plays an important role in ensuring that rubrics have a clearly stated purpose. Trialling is carried out on candidates

Table 4.2 Analysis of rubric words indicating task purpose (drawn from Main Suite sample tasks in Appendix A)

Exam	Task purpose			
	Part 1	**Part 2**	**Part 3**	**Part 4**
KET	*Interview* . . .ask. . .	*Candidate–candidate question and answer using prompt material* . . .ask. . . . . .answer. . .	–	–
PET	*Interview* . . .ask. . .	*Candidate–candidate interaction* . . .talk together about. . .	*Individual long turn* . . .talk on your own about. . . . . .show (your photograph) to. . . . . .tell us what you can see. . .	*Candidate–candidate interaction* . . .talk together about. . .
FCE	*Interview* . . .we'd like to know something about you. . .	*Individual long turn* . . .I'd like you to talk about your photographs on your own. . . . . .and also to answer a short question about your partner's photographs. . . . . .compare the photographs. . . . . .say why/what you think. . .	*Candidate–candidate interaction* + Prompted candidate–candidate interaction (including interaction with the examiner) . . .talk about something together. . . . . .imagine. . . . . .talk to each other about. . . . . .decide which. . .	
CAE	*Interview* . . .we'd like to know something about you. . .	*Individual long turn* . . .I'd like you to talk about the pictures on your own. . . . . .and to answer a question briefly about your partner's pictures. . . . . .compare the pictures. . . . . .say why/what . . . and how. . .	*Candidate–candidate interaction* + Prompted candidate–candidate interaction (including interaction with the examiner) . . .talk about something together. . . . . .imagine. . . . . .talk to each other about. . . . . .decide which. . .	

Table 4.2 Continued

Exam	Task purpose			
	Part 1	Part 2	Part 3	Part 4
CPE	*Interview* . . .we'd like to know something about you. . .	*Candidate– candidate interaction* . . .look at the pictures. . . . . .talk together about why. . . . . .imagine. . .	*Individual long turn followed by prompted candidate– candidate interaction (including interaction with the examiner)* . . .talk on your own. . . . . .listen while your partner is speaking. . . . . .you'll be asked to comment. . . . . .tell us what you see. . . . . .let X see your card. . .	–

of different ages and levels of ability and each piece of material is trialled a minimum of three times. Candidate output is recorded and reviewed to see if:

i) the task has provided sufficient stimulus (words and/or visuals) to allow the candidates to fully engage with it and display their language ability
ii) there has been any misunderstanding or misinterpretation of the task
iii) there is any ambiguity or lack of clarity in the wording of the rubric or in the visual.

Candidates are also asked to comment on the rubrics, visuals and overall task. Subsequent revisions and re-trialling result in tasks which are accessible to the target candidature and which meet the requirements of the purpose stated in the exam specifications.

Weighting

Weighting of different parts of a test or assessment criteria reflects the perceived importance, or lack of importance, of that aspect of the test in relation to other tasks. Weir (2005a) advocates that the test taker should be

Table 4.3 Description of dominant underlying purpose in Main Suite Speaking tasks

Exam	Task purpose			
	Part 1	**Part 2**	**Part 3**	**Part 4**
KET	*Interview* • to use the language normally associated with meeting people for the first time • to give factual information of a personal kind, for example, name, place of origin, occupation, family etc. • to talk about their daily life, interests, likes, etc.	*Candidate–candidate question and answer using prompt material* • to interact with the other candidate(s) by asking and answering questions about factual information of a non-personal kind • prompt cards are used to stimulate questions and answers which are related to daily life, leisure activities and social life (including references to places, times, services, where to go, how to get there, what to eat, etc.).	–	–
PET	*Interview* • to use the language of simple social interaction • to use simple everyday language • to respond to questions about personal details, daily routines, likes and dislikes, etc. • to spell all or part of candidate's name.	*Candidate–candidate interaction* • to interact with the other candidate in a simulated situation • to make and respond to suggestions, discuss alternatives, make recommendations and negotiate agreement with their partner • to give own views and opinions about the simulated situation.	*Individual long turn* • to engage in a monologic long turn (45 seconds) • to describe a colour photograph which depicts an everyday situation.	*Candidate–candidate interaction* • to interact with the other candidate in a general conversation • to discuss likes and dislikes, experiences, etc.

FCE

Interview
- to use general social and interactional language
- to give basic personal information, such as work, leisure time and future plans.

Individual long turn
- to engage in a monologic long turn (1 min)
- to compare two colour photographs, and to make a further comment about them in response to a prompt which is read out by the examiner and appears in written form above the photographs.

Candidate–candidate interaction
- to discuss a task based on a visual stimulus (several photographs or pieces of artwork), expressing and justifying opinions, evaluating and speculating. The task appears in the form of two questions written above the visuals.
- to work towards a negotiated decision towards the end of the task.

Prompted candidate–candidate interaction (including interaction with the examiner)
- to discuss further the topics introduced in Part 3.

CAE

Interview
- to use general interactional and social language
- to give some information about themselves to talk about interests, studies, careers, etc.
- to offer opinions on certain topics.

Individual long turn
- to engage in a monologic long turn (1 min)
- to compare, comment on and react to two photographs from a choice of three in response to two prompts which are read out by the examiner and appear in written form above the photographs.

Candidate–candidate interaction
- to discuss a task based on a visual stimulus (several photographs or pieces of artwork), expressing and justifying opinions, evaluating and speculating. The task appears in the form of two questions written above the visuals.
- to work towards a negotiated decision towards the end of the task.

Prompted candidate–candidate interaction (including interaction with the examiner)
- to discuss further the topics introduced in Part 3.

Table 4.3 Continued

Exam	Task purpose			
	Part 1	**Part 2**	**Part 3**	**Part 4**
CPE	*Interview* • to use general interactional and social language • to give general information about themselves and to express personal opinions • to respond to more open questions requiring speculation or an opinion.	*Candidate–candidate interaction* • to discuss a visual stimulus (one or several photographs or pieces of artwork), expressing and justifying opinions, evaluating and speculating • to work towards a negotiated decision towards the end of the task).	*Individual long turn followed by prompted candidate–candidate interaction (including interaction with the examiner)* • to engage in a monologic long turn (2 mins) • to respond to/expand on their partner's long turn • to engage in a discussion (prompted by a series of questions from the interlocutor) to explore further the topics of the long turns.	–

Source: KET – CPE Handbooks for Teachers, 2007, 2008.

advised of the weighting adopted by the test developer, as this knowledge will potentially contribute to decisions made by the test taker when participating in the test. It will, for example, have an effect on the initial goal setting, which as discussed earlier (Chapter 3) is of vital importance if the task is to result in a valid performance. Any weighting in a test must be supported by a clearly defined rationale, something that is not always easy to establish. For example, test providers may be able to demonstrate, based on a theory of language ability, that a given task is more or less important, but identifying the degree to which different tasks contribute to overall performance remains problematic, and is an avenue for further research.

Weighting: Cambridge practice

The Main Suite Speaking tests are not assessed individually by test part (or task), but for overall performance on the whole test. Cambridge ESOL speaking examiners are trained to award each task equal weight when making their final decision on a candidate's score (*Instructions to Oral Examiners* 2008). All parts in the Main Suite Speaking tests, therefore, contribute equally to the overall mark, reflecting the definition of the construct, where different types of interaction are all important in contributing to a picture of overall language proficiency.

In terms of the Main Suite analytic assessment criteria, there is no weighting applied, again a reflection of the construct underlying the test, where all assessment criteria (Grammar, Vocabulary, Discourse Management, Pronunciation, and Interactive Communication) are seen as equally important aspects of communication. The holistic Global Achievement (GA) mark receives weighting relative to the number of analytic criteria, in order to make it more comparable to the analytic marks in terms of its contribution to the overall test score. (See Chapter 5 for a fuller discussion of the scoring of the test, including the assessment criteria.)

Known criteria

Another important element of context validity is familiarity with the criteria that will be used when assessing performance. Such familiarity will naturally affect candidates' planning and monitoring of cognitive processes involved in task completion. There appears to be little or no evidence in the L2 assessment literature related to this topic, but it is logical on an intuitive level that test takers will systematically alter their communication behaviour when they know that particular aspects of this behaviour will be focused on by their examiners. If, for example, a test taker knows that not only accuracy of grammar is assessed (or given more weight), but also the range of structures and vocabulary used, this may affect the way they respond to the task.

The *Standards for Educational and Psychological Testing* (AERA/APA/ NCME 1999) also emphasise the importance of providing information about the assessment criteria used, and state that the higher the consequences of the test for the candidates, the more important it is that test takers should be provided, in advance, with as much information about the test scoring criteria as is consistent with obtaining valid responses.

Known criteria: Cambridge practice

Cambridge ESOL addresses the need to make assessment criteria known through the information it disseminates to stakeholders. Information about how the tasks are scored, including assessment criteria and a short explanation of each criterion, are provided in the Cambridge ESOL Handbooks. Detailed band descriptors, which describe spoken performance at the assessment bands, have been developed for the examiners to use in live conditions. These descriptors are rater-oriented, to use Alderson's (1991) term, and are used by all Cambridge ESOL Main Suite Speaking examiners. The performance descriptors used by the speaking examiners are also made available in the public domain, in a slightly revised user-oriented version, alongside a Glossary of Terms. Table 4.4 provides a summary of the assessment criteria used at each exam (for a detailed discussion of the development of the Main Suite scales and the performance descriptors see Chapter 5 on scoring validity).

Table 4.4 Criteria used in assessing Main Suite Speaking tests

	Scoring criteria	KET	PET	FCE	CAE	CPE
Scored by Assessor	Grammar and Vocabulary	✓	✓	✓		
	Grammatical Resource				✓	✓
	Lexical Resource				✓	✓
	Discourse Management		✓	✓	✓	✓
	Pronunciation	✓	✓	✓	✓	✓
	Interactive Communication	✓	✓	✓	✓	✓
Scored by Interlocutor	Global	✓	✓	✓	✓	✓

Source: KET – CPE Handbooks for Teachers 2007, 2008.

The range of assessment criteria underlying Cambridge ESOL Main Suite Speaking tests is an indication of the broad multi-faceted construct underlying these exams. The construct is not driven by lexico-grammatical accuracy, but includes a balance of important aspects of communicative ability, such as the ability to produce coherent and relevant contributions both in interactive and monologic tasks (Discourse Management), the ability to initiate, respond and develop the interaction (Interactive Communication), and the ability to do so with the necessary degree of intelligibility (Pronunciation). The balanced view underlying the Cambridge ESOL Speaking construct is a salient feature of Cambridge ESOL exams, which is made possible by the face-to-face interactive nature of the Speaking tests.

In addition to providing general descriptions explaining each assessment criterion, the Cambridge ESOL Common Scale for Speaking is an attempt to help users interpret levels of performance in the Cambridge tests from Level A2 (KET) to C2 (CPE). The scale identifies typical performance qualities at particular levels, and locates performance in one examination against performance in another. As explained in Chapter 1, the Common Scale is designed to be useful to test takers and other test users, since the descriptions at each level of the Common Scale aim to provide a brief, general description of the nature of spoken language ability at a particular level in real-world contexts.

Order of tasks

This task variable addresses the logic behind the order of tasks in a (speaking) test and the rationale supporting it. In objectively scored item-based tests, especially ones covering a broad proficiency range, it is generally the practice to place easier items earlier, in order to allow candidates at all ability levels to complete at least some of the initial tasks/items. In general the same principle applies to the order of tasks in a speaking test, where tasks which provide more scaffolding and require shorter candidate contributions (and are therefore less cognitively demanding) usually take initial position. A further rationale for the order of tasks in a speaking test is the existence of a thematic link between tasks, which dictates their adjacent position in a test.

There is no empirical evidence that task order may affect overall performance, but it is conceivable that the order of tasks in a test of speaking may have an effect on candidate performance. It is important to control the order of tasks as this ensures that all candidates have a similar test experience and allows for systematic comparisons to be made across a range of candidate performances.

Order of tasks: Cambridge practice

The ordering of tasks in the Main Suite Speaking tests follows a logical order from relatively structured and supported interaction under the direct control of the examiner involving topics of immediate personal relevance to more open-ended discussion with less examiner control involving more general topics. The Main Suite tasks can also be seen as ordered in terms of cognitive processing or load demands, as discussed by Field in Chapter 3 (p.87–97).

All five Main Suite tests begin with a question-and-answer interview task, which is intended to provide the candidates with the opportunity to contribute shorter answers and to serve as a warm-up activity, allowing them to settle into the test and feel comfortable with the interviewer and their test partner. The task is controlled by the examiner who directs the turn-taking; the focus is mostly on factual, personal information; the time duration of the task is relatively short. The remaining tasks loosen the examiner control through giving the candidates more freedom over the turn-taking and the content covered; they expand the focus to non-personal information at PET, familiar topics at FCE, unfamiliar topics at CAE and abstract ideas at CPE, and they take longer to complete. The progression in terms of control, length of responses and topic familiarity is a salient feature of the order of tasks in Cambridge ESOL Speaking tests and, as noted above, reflects the increasing cognitive demands placed on candidates.

There is also a thematic link built across some of the tasks in the Cambridge ESOL Speaking tests. For example, in PET and CPE the candidate monologic turn and candidate–candidate interaction tasks are thematically linked and adjacent. The same thematic relationship and adjacency of tasks is also observed in the FCE and CAE candidate–candidate interaction task and prompted candidate–candidate interaction task. A thematic link between tasks is an instance of a more natural, 'discourse-driven' sequencing in speaking tests, since it mirrors real-life development of topics in interaction, where topics are developed over a number of turns. It also provides opportunities for test takers to extend a topic both linguistically and conceptually. The first task which introduces a topic – for example, the extended turn in PET – serves to engage the candidates and develop their familiarity with the topic. The task which follows – in the case of PET, the prompted candidate–candidate interaction – can then more efficiently expand on the same topic and provide opportunities for the test takers to display a wider lexical, structural and functional range within the comfort zone of a topic which they have already engaged with.

Time constraints

This task parameter refers to both planning time and the time available to complete the task. As noted in Chapter 3, the amount of planning time impacts upon several processing phases and has implications for claims about cognitive validity. To avoid unnecessary repetition with Chapter 3, the overview here will be brief and will focus on relevant research from the L2 assessment field only.

Research on planning time from the L2 assessment context has suggested that the relationship between planning and fluency, accuracy and complexity is not linear. There is evidence that planning time interacts with the proficiency level of the learners, the cognitive demands of the task and the amount of planning involved. Wigglesworth (1997), in an investigation of planning time and fluency, focused on the *access:test* (used to screen immigrants for entry in Australia) and found only tentative support for the hypothesis that planning generated greater fluency. She further noted that planning enhanced accuracy and complexity in the most difficult task in terms of certain grammatical structures, but this effect was only found amongst the higher proficiency learners when performing cognitively demanding tasks. A later study (Wigglesworth 2001) observed that planning was, in fact, detrimental on tasks that were familiar. In another study employing both a qualitative and quantitative methodology, Iwashita, McNamara and Elder (2001) observed that planning before a monologic task had no impact on the quality of test discourse or test scores. Similarly, Elder and Wigglesworth (2006) found no significant differences in performance according to the amount of planning.

The implications seem to be that more cognitively demanding tasks benefit more from planning; if tasks are simple enough and have a clear, inherent structure, planning may be dispensable. Test tasks, the majority of which are simple enough with a clear structure, may not benefit from the inclusion of planning conditions. These findings have implications for speaking task design in assessment conditions, as they present some evidence for not using planning time, except in the case of cognitively challenging, higher proficiency tasks or where the context, e.g. business or academic, suggests it is appropriate.

The inclusion of planning time in a test also has to be considered within the context of practicality. A study carried out by ffrench (2003a) showed that for the 2-minute long turn task in CPE, 2 minutes of planning time was required before any meaningful improvement in candidates' output could be noticed. Practical considerations ruled out the inclusion of planning time, however, since the test would of necessity have been 4 minutes longer. Furthermore, the extra 4 minutes would have been silent planning time and thus perhaps even more difficult to justify to test users within the context of a large-scale testing operation.

The inclusion of planning time in L2 assessment has broader implications for a test's context validity. Skehan (1998) argues that speaking tests need to include tasks which involve both planning and non-planning conditions in order to be representative of a broader range of 'real-world' conditions. While this is an important point, it can also be argued that the majority of 'real-world' tasks involve spontaneous speaking with no planning opportunities. It is usually only tasks such as presentations (often found in academic or business settings) which may benefit from planning. Most tasks in a test are not presentations, or when they are, they are simple and brief, which would make long planning allowances unnecessary.

Response time is a further aspect of the task parameter time constraints. There is limited research addressing this issue. Weir, O'Sullivan and Horai (2006) investigated the effect of varying the response time on candidate performance and found that the amount of output expected of the candidates (as seen in the time allocation of the task) did not appear to have a significant impact on the score achieved by the high and borderline candidates in their study. In contrast, reducing the task time produced a lower mean score for the low proficiency group. This is an interesting, and perhaps counter-intuitive, finding and an area which would benefit from further research.

Time constraints: Cambridge practice

As can be seen in Table 4.5, the length of time allowed for each Main Suite Speaking task and overall test increases as language proficiency increases because of the higher cognitive and linguistic demands placed by the task. As the tasks become cognitively more challenging, the candidates need to produce longer output to allow them to produce a situationally and interactionally authentic spoken contribution.

The time allocated for similar task types also varies depending on the proficiency level the task is used at. For example, the interview task, which is relatively controlled, changes from representing 61% of the test at KET level to 16% at CPE. In contrast, the more interactional tasks, which Field has argued in Chapter 3 bring in higher cognitive demands, increase in total amount of time as the level increases. The extended turn task shows a marked difference at CPE level where the candidates are required to talk without interruption for 2 minutes rather than 1 minute for FCE and CAE, and 45 seconds at PET. Furthermore, where there is a thematic connection between two parts of the test requiring candidates to discuss a topic from different perspectives across two tasks, there is also an increase in available talking time across the levels. This can be seen in the candidate–candidate interaction plus prompted candidate–candidate interaction tasks, i.e. FCE (7 mins) and CAE (8 mins) or the long turn plus interaction tasks, i.e. PET (6 mins) and CPE (12 mins).

The time allocation for each task is specified in the relevant exam Handbooks and, equally importantly, in the 'interlocutor frame' which each speaking examiner adheres to during the test (see the section on 'Interlocutor variables' for more details). In the case of groups of three candidates, a longer time is allowed for each task and overall for the test, in order to provide suitable opportunities for all candidates to display their speaking ability.

Trialling of tasks, at both the pre-specification stage and during the production of materials for live exams, plays an important role in determining the time allocation for each task type. The time allocation for each task is

Table 4.5 Time allocation by task for Main Suite Speaking tests

	Interview	Long turn	Candidate–candidate interaction	Prompted candidate–candidate interaction (including interaction with the examiner)	Test overall
KET	5–6 mins	–	3–4 mins		8–10
PET	2–3 mins	3 mins (45-60 seconds per candidate)	2–3 mins + 3 mins	–	10–12
FCE	3 mins	4 mins (1 min per candidate, plus an approximately 20-second response from listening candidate)	3 mins	4 mins	14
CAE	3 mins	4 mins (1 min per candidate, plus an approximately 30-second response from listening candidate)	4 mins	4 mins	15
CPE	3 mins	5 mins (2 mins per candidate, plus up to an approximately 30-second response from the listening candidate)	4 mins	7 mins	19

Source: KET – CPE Handbooks for Teachers, 2007, 2008.

always checked and trialled during the test development stage before the task type is finalised for inclusion in a live exam (see ffrench 2003a). This ensures that there is sufficient time available for candidates to produce a situationally and interactionally authentic spoken contribution. Then, trialling tasks prior to their inclusion in live tests also ensures that the tasks provide sufficient stimulus for both stronger and weaker candidates to talk for the required length of time.

The Main Suite Speaking tasks do not include any planning time allocations, with the exception of a few seconds for candidates to assimilate the information for those tasks which include a visual (e.g. a photo or a drawing). The decision to exclude planning time in Main Suite Speaking tasks is supported by the previously mentioned research, which indicates that longer planning time does not necessarily aid the candidates and does not mean better production in terms of fluency, accuracy and complexity. There are, in addition, practical considerations, as shown in ffrench's (2003a) study discussed earlier.

Considerations about the inclusion of planning time are also informed by the specificity of the test. Planning is typically only present in the real world with more cognitively and thematically demanding tasks such as presentations or the description of visually dense prompts, such as charts. For example, in some Cambridge ESOL English for Specific Purposes (ESP) examinations, e.g. ILEC, ICFE and BEC (the legal, financial and business examinations offered by Cambridge ESOL at B2 and C1 level), 1 minute's preparation time is given to each candidate in turn during the appropriate section of the Speaking test to select and prepare a topic for their long turn, reflecting the higher specificity of the test content. Candidates have a choice of topics with supporting prompts to use if they wish, and they select one of the topics to talk about. A similar approach is adopted in the IELTS Speaking test where the individual candidate – IELTS does not use a paired format – is given 1 minute's preparation time to read and think about a short topic prompt and to plan what they want to say. However, in the Main Suite examinations, there is no choice of task or topic and no time is given for preparation, reflecting the general nature of the test content, and the fact that candidates are not expected to produce a formal presentation, but an impromptu long turn (as also noted by Field in Chapter 3). Examiners are advised to allow only a very short time before asking candidates to begin the task if they have not already done so.

A further aspect of the time allocated for each task relates to the issue of determining the accommodations to be made for candidates with various disabilities. Cambridge ESOL makes several provisions for candidates with disabilities, as outlined in Taylor and Gutteridge (2003). In terms of speaking, if the candidate has a disability which may cause a disadvantage to themselves or their partner (such as a stammer), they can request extra time. In these situations, the candidate would usually take the test with a 'dummy' partner or in a single format, and the examiner would give the candidate extra time as appropriate. (For detailed discussion of individual test accommodations see Chapter 2.)

Demands: Task (linguistic – input and output)

Having discussed in detail features of the task-setting parameters, we turn now to consider the demands of the task in terms of its linguistic input and output.

Channel of communication

This task feature refers to the delivery of the task input and output. In terms of input, the channel of communication can typically be:

- aural (input from examiner or from a recorded medium)
- written (a text to be read by the candidate, usually written at a level of language lower that that of the typical candidate at the proficiency level)
- visual (photos, drawings, pictures, etc.)
- graphical (charts, graphs, tables, etc.).

A key factor in the aural channel category is the distinction between speaking tests involving an examiner in a face-to-face or phone situation (also known as 'direct') and computer/tape-based tests (also known as 'semi-direct'). In a direct speaking test the test taker is required to interact reciprocally with another person (either an examiner or another test taker, or both); in a semi-direct test the test taker is required to respond to a series of pre-recorded prompts. The majority of Cambridge ESOL Speaking tests are instances of direct face-to-face speaking tests.

The main characteristic of the direct face-to-face channel is that interaction in it is bi- or multi-directional and jointly achieved by the participants in the interaction. It is, in other words, 'co-constructed' (Lazaraton 1996b, McNamara 1997a, 1997b) and reciprocal, with the interlocutors (both examiner and test taker(s)) accommodating their contributions to the evolving interaction. The construct assessed is spoken interaction. Oral computer/tape-based testing, in contrast, is uni-directional and lacks the element of co-construction. In a semi-direct speaking test the construct is defined with an emphasis on its cognitive dimension (i.e. production).

Comparisons between the face-to-face and tape/computer-mediated channel of communication have received quite a lot of attention in the academic literature, with various studies probing the differences and similarities between these two channels of communication. Some of the studies focusing on this area have indicated considerable overlap between the direct and semi-direct tests, at least in the statistical correlational sense that people who score highly in one mode also score highly in the other. For example, Stansfield and Kenyon (1992) compared the OPI (a direct test of speaking) and the SOPI (a tape-mediated test of speaking) and concluded that 'both tests are highly comparable as measures of the same construct – oral language proficiency'

(1992:363). Wigglesworth and O'Loughlin (1993) also conducted a SOPI/ OPI comparability study and found that the candidate ability measure strongly correlated; however, 12% of candidates received different overall classifications for the two tests, indicating some influence of test method. In contrast, O'Loughlin (2001:169) argued that as discourse events and assessment experiences, the two modes 'are not interchangeable as tests of oral proficiency'. Similarly, Shohamy (1994) observed discourse-level differences between the two channels, and found that when the examinees talked to a tape recorder, their language was a little more literate and less oral-like, and many of them felt more anxious about the test because everything they said was recorded and the only channel they had for communicating was speaking – no gestures or expressions could be used, or requests for clarification and repetition made. The direct and semi-direct modes have also been seen to impact differently on cognitive processing demands, as Field (this volume) argues in his discussion of the nature and patterns of interaction. Chun (2006) makes a similar argument, noting that even similar tasks may become cognitively different when presented through the different channels of communication due to the absence of body language and facial gestures.

Test taker perceptions of direct and semi-direct speaking tests have received some attention as well, and Kenyon and Malabonga's (2001) investigation of candidate perceptions of several test formats (the Simulated Oral Proficiency Interview – SOPI, the Computer Oral Proficiency Interview – COPI, as well as the Oral Proficiency Interview – OPI) found that the different tests were seen as similar in most respects. The OPI, however, was perceived by the study participants to be a better measure of real-life speaking skills. Interestingly, the authors found that at lower proficiency levels candidates perceived the COPI to be less difficult, possibly due to the adaptive nature of the COPI which allowed the difficulty level of the assessment task to be matched more appropriately to the proficiency level of the examinees. In a more recent article, Qian (2009) reported that although a large proportion of his study participants had no particular preference in terms of direct or semi-direct tests, the number of participants who strongly favoured direct testing far exceeded the number strongly favouring semi-direct testing.

Both the direct and semi-direct formats offer their unique advantages and disadvantages, and both have a role to play in L2 assessment. Careful choices need to be made, however, about what mode is appropriate in the light of overall test purpose, as argued in Galaczi (2010b).

Of relevance for the 'channel of communication' task parameter is also research which has compared the visual and written channels and found important differences between them. O'Keefe (2006a and 2006b), in research commissioned by Cambridge ESOL as part of the revision of the FCE and CAE exams, investigated the impact on candidate performance of changing the input channel from visual to verbal for the FCE and CAE long turn tasks. One task version included a visual prompt (picture) and one included a written prompt. O'Keefe's results indicated variation in the candidate output based on the different input channels in terms of the amount of hesitation (more with the picture prompt), coherence and cohesion (less with the picture prompt); quantity of lexical output (less with the picture prompt), syntactic complexity (less with the picture prompt); and use of pre-prepared language (overuse in the picture prompt, such as 'this picture', 'the second picture seems to show'). O'Keefe suggested that the pictures seemed to provide a schematically divergent prompt compared with the written prompts. They opened up many possibilities for ideas and topics, which seemed to add to the cognitive load of the candidates, who were simultaneously trying to compare pictures thematically and retrieve related vocabulary. The written prompt, on the other hand, readily provided a schema which was topic-convergent. The candidate was more task-focused, which was reflected in more 'pushed output' (i.e. more complexity), greater cohesion and coherence, and quantitatively increased output.

An obvious conclusion from the above research is the need for test developers to be aware of the strengths and limitations of the various channels of communication and attempt to address the associated caveats through the overall test design.

Channel of communication: Cambridge practice

If the purpose of a test is to draw inferences concerning some measure of interactional ability, then a speaking test must include the possibility of interaction as a channel of communication. This is the case with the 'direct' Cambridge ESOL Main Suite Speaking tests, where the test purpose is to provide inferences about communicative language ability within a general non-test context. The face-to-face channel of communication in Cambridge ESOL Main Suite Speaking tests allows the inclusion of different interactional configurations, such as question-and-answer tasks, tasks involving discussions between the examiner and test taker, and in paired format tests, discussions between the test takers themselves. Such a range of interactional configurations provides opportunities for jointly constructed interaction in a range of tasks.

In addition to the face-to-face channel of communication, the Main Suite Speaking tasks provide task input through a variety of other channels, as seen in Table 4.6. Tests at all levels include visual material as well as the (scripted) questions delivered orally by the examiner. The use of visuals provides a rich source of ideas and an efficient means of conveying information without providing the candidate with language that might be reformulated in their response. The previously mentioned studies by O'Keefe (2006a, 2006b), as well as a consultation survey with relevant Cambridge ESOL stakeholders

Table 4.6 Channels of communication in Cambridge ESOL Main Suite Speaking tests

Exam	Task input			
	Part 1	**Part 2**	**Part 3**	**Part 4**
KET	Interview • Verbal: interviewer questions	**Information exchange** • Visual: prompt card with single words and visual support	–	–
PET	Interview • Verbal: interviewer questions	**Candidate–candidate interaction** • Verbal: interviewer delivered prompt • Visual pictorial: drawing	**Long turn** • Verbal: interviewer delivered prompt • Visual pictorial: photograph	**Prompted candidate–candidate interaction** • Verbal: interviewer delivered prompt
FCE	Interview • Verbal: interviewer questions	**Long turn** • Verbal: interviewer delivered prompt • Visual pictorial: photographs, plus a question written above the visuals	**Candidate–candidate interaction** • Verbal: interviewer delivered prompt • Visual pictorial: drawings or photographs, plus two questions written above the visuals	**Prompted candidate–candidate interaction** • Verbal: interviewer delivered questions
CAE	Interview • Verbal: interviewer questions	**Long turn** • Verbal: interviewer delivered prompt • Visual pictorial: photographs, plus two questions written above the visuals	**Candidate–candidate interaction** • Verbal: interviewer delivered prompt • Visual pictorial: drawings or photographs, plus two questions written above the visuals	**Prompted candidate–candidate interaction** • Verbal: interviewer delivered questions
CPE	Interview • Verbal: interviewer questions	**Candidate–candidate interaction** • Verbal: interviewer delivered prompt • Visual pictorial: photographs	**Long turn and prompted candidate–candidate interaction** • Verbal: interviewer delivered prompt • Visual: written question • Verbal: interviewer delivered questions	–

Source: KET – CPE Handbooks for Teachers, 2007, 2008.

carried out as part of the FCE/CAE modifications project (Harrison 2007b), have also informed the use of a variety of input channels. The consultation survey indicated a split of opinion: those favouring picture prompts were concerned about the level of sophistication of some of the younger candidates and their ability to cope with the written prompts. A change to a written prompt task type at FCE and CAE would have also significantly changed the testing focus of this part of the test. The conclusion was a compromise where the visual prompts were supplemented with written questions. The ensuing trials showed that this combined visual/written format, which appealed to a broader range of individual sensory perceptions, increased candidates' confidence and allowed them to demonstrate a richer sample of language than with the picture stimulus alone.

The information given in Table 4.6 illustrates that as the level of difficulty increases, a progression can be seen from visual/pictorial to visual/linguistic sources of input, with PET, FCE and CAE using predominantly visual prompts, and CPE utilising mostly verbal prompts.

The use of visual sources of input also has relevance for the interference between speaking and reading, which could possibly have an impact on the measurement of the intended speaking construct. At each level the written prompts are worded in a clear, uncomplicated fashion in order to avoid the potential confounding of reading and speaking. At the highest level (CPE), less use is made of visual pictorial prompts, as a means of withdrawing scaffolding and thus making the task more challenging, and the written prompt is presented as bullet points, which serve to provide support for the candidates, but are not essential for the response. (See also section on 'Nature of information, page 145.)

Discourse mode

There is little agreement in the literature on the terminology that should be used to classify different discourse modes, and instead a 'plethora of different schemes for analysing discourse' exists (Shaw and Weir 2007:115). Traditionally discourse mode refers to the modes of narration, description, exposition, and argument/persuasion, which are discussed in Brown and Yule (1983), Bygate (1987), the CEFR (2001, as 'macro-functions'), and Weigle (2002, as 'rhetorical task'). Research on reading comprehension has highlighted the important role of discourse mode, showing that familiarity with the discourse mode of the text facilitates comprehension (Alderson 2000, Barnet 1989, Urquhart 1984). Brown, Anderson, Shillcock and Yule (1984) have argued that static tasks (e.g. description) were easier than dynamic tasks (e.g. narration), which in turn were easier than abstract tasks (e.g. opinion giving), while the number of elements, participants and relationships in a task also interacted with task difficulty.

Discourse mode: Cambridge practice

If appropriate for the level, the Main Suite Speaking tests make use of a range of discourse modes. Table 4.7 summarises the discourse modes to be found in the Main Suite Speaking tests (see also Table 4.3). As can be seen, a greater variety of discourse modes is used as the proficiency level increases. A gradation can be seen from factual to evaluative talk (Bygate 1987) with the role of evaluative talk increasing as the Main Suite levels progress. At the lower levels, the discourse mode is primarily description and exposition, whereas at the higher levels argument and persuasion are also elicited. KET candidates, for example, are expected firstly to engage in a question-and-answer interview task with the interviewer and then in a candidate–candidate information exchange task by asking and answering questions. The discourse mode in both tasks is description, which forms part of Bygate's (1987) 'factual talk', Bereiter and Scardamalia's (1987) 'knowledge telling', and Vähäpässi's (1982) 'reproducing' of information, all of which are relatively simple linguistic and cognitive acts. Their FCE counterparts have a broader range of discourse modes to deal with, and in addition to description, the tasks at this level also require comparison, argument and persuasion, and extend into Bygate's (1987) 'evaluative-talk' (and Bereiter and Scardamalia's (1987) 'knowledge transforming' and Vähäpässi's (1982) 'organising' of information) by requiring candidates to engage in justifying and explaining, which are higher-order cognitive acts. This gradation, which has implications for the difficulty of the tasks, is in agreement with research which has argued that cognitive difficulty increases in the progression from factual to evaluative.

Table 4.7 Discourse mode in Main Suite tests

Exam	Discourse mode			
	Part 1	Part 2	Part 3	Part 4
KET	description	description	–	–
PET	description	description; exposition	description	description; exposition
FCE	description	description; exposition; comparison	description; exposition; argument/ persuasion	exposition; argument/ persuasion
CAE	description; exposition; argument/ persuasion	description; exposition; comparison; argument/ persuasion	description; exposition; argument/ persuasion	exposition; argument/ persuasion
CPE	description; exposition; argument/ persuasion	exposition; argument/ persuasion;	description; exposition; argument/ persuasion	–

Length

Another task feature which needs consideration is the length of task input. It is general practice for test developers to use test specifications in order to control the length of the input in tests of speaking. This is based on the assumption that input length, which is part of Skehan and Foster's (1997) cognitive complexity, will affect the difficulty of a task and will show differences across proficiency levels. In general, the longer the input candidates have to process, the higher the cognitive demand on them, and the more difficult the task.

Length of input: Cambridge practice

Cambridge ESOL test developers use clearly written test specifications in order to control the length of input of tasks in tests of speaking. For example, the number of words per answer card in the KET Part 2 task must not exceed 30, with the recommendation that it is between 20 and 25 (KET *Item Writer Guidelines*, 2006d). This ensures that tasks are comparable in their reading load.

Nature of information

The nature of information in tasks – one of the features of Skehan's (1998) cognitive complexity – plays a crucial role in assessment, and influences task difficulty. Research suggests that the more abstract the input is, the more cognitively challenging it is to respond to it. Citing the literature on reading, Khalifa and Weir (2009) point out that abstract words are in general more difficult to understand than concrete words. Brown et al (1984), cited earlier in a different context, also outlined that abstract tasks are more difficult than more concrete tasks such as description.

Nature of information: Cambridge practice

Nature of information is one of the most salient features in determining the difficulty of tasks across the five Main Suite levels. It is useful to investigate this task feature in terms of two continua: personal/non-personal and abstract/concrete. An overview of the nature of information in Cambridge ESOL Speaking tasks is given in Figure 4.3. As can be seen, the tasks at all levels tap into personal and non-personal information. There is also a progression from mostly personal information (KET, PET, FCE) to mostly non-personal (CAE, CPE). A gradation from concrete/factual (KET, PET, FCE) to abstract information (CAE, CPE) can also be seen, with several tasks at FCE and CAE comprising both abstract and concrete features.

A more detailed examination across the levels and task types will illustrate

Figure 4.3 Nature of information in Cambridge ESOL Main Suite Speaking tests

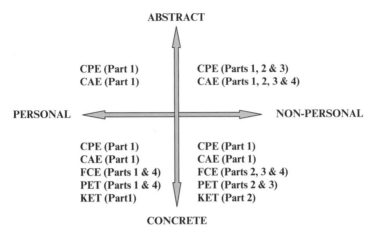

ABSTRACT

CPE (Part 1)   CPE (Parts 1, 2 & 3)
CAE (Part 1)   CAE (Parts 1, 2, 3 & 4)

PERSONAL   NON-PERSONAL

CPE (Part 1)   CPE (Part 1)
CAE (Part 1)   CAE (Part 1)
FCE (Parts 1 & 4)   FCE (Parts 2, 3 & 4)
PET (Parts 1 & 4)   PET (Parts 2 & 3)
KET (Part1)   KET (Part 2)

CONCRETE

more clearly the progression in terms of the nature of information which the tasks draw on. The discussion will expand beyond the nature of information in each task into linguistic resources, discourse mode and topic familiarity, which is inevitable, considering the closely intertwined nature of the contextual parameters discussed here.

Interview task: question-and-answer interaction between examiner and candidate(s)

At the KET, PET and FCE levels the questions asked in the Interview task (Part 1) are personal, concrete and factual, establishing who the candidates are, their likes and dislikes and what they have done recently or are likely to do at some point in the future, e.g., *'Have you got any plans for this weekend?'* (FCE Sample Papers 2008:79). At CAE and CPE, similar questions are asked in Part 1, but are followed by other, hypothetical questions, often displaced in time, e.g. *'How important do you think it is to have a routine when working or studying?'* (CAE Handbook: 2008, 88) and *'With more shopping being done over the internet, what future is there for ordinary shops?'* (CPE Handbook 2008: 66).

Candidate–candidate interaction tasks

At KET level, this task (Part 2) involves only concrete factual information within candidates' personal experience, e.g. giving information about a bookshop (its address, telephone number, opening times, how big it is, the types of books sold there) (KET Handbook 2008:52). The corresponding PET task (Part 2) also focuses predominantly on personal, concrete information, and is situated within a familiar situation, e.g. the candidates have to discuss the things a friend of theirs will need to take on a six-month trip to England and to decide which are the most important items for them to take. The suggestions include a map, camera, money and appropriate clothes (PET Handbook 2008:57). The options are simple lexical items. Candidates are not forced to say anything specific about the 'things to take' but are invited to comment in a general way about how important the objects are. In this PET task, the candidates are always either themselves in an imaginary situation, or commenting on a situation external to themselves. PET candidates are never asked to role play, take on another persona, or put forward a point of view which is not their own.

In FCE (Part 3) the scenario is still within the candidates' experience and also includes some non-personal information while still retaining factual features, e.g. *'I'd like you to imagine that a local café wants to attract more people. First talk to each other about how successful these suggestions might be. Then decide which two would attract more people'* (FCE Handbook for Teachers 2007:81), or *'Here are some pictures of things that can make living in a city enjoyable. Talk to each other about how these things can help people to enjoy life in a city. Then decide which two things are the most important'* (FCE Handbook for Teachers, 2007:85). The lexical challenge is higher than at PET and the discussion goes beyond the lexical level of, for example, deciding whether a CD player is more useful than a map. In FCE, there might be objects, situations, or concepts presented via the visuals. In the local café example given above, the candidates are presented with suggestions as to how a local cafe might attract more people, and the visuals are: a band, a free coffee, late opening hours, an international menu, comfortable chairs and sofas, an outdoor eating area, a TV showing football. Here the candidates are expected to talk about situations with which they will be familiar and are asked a specific question: *'How successful might these suggestions be?'* (FCE Handbook 2007:81).

In CAE, the task (Part 3) comprises abstract concepts based on concrete situations, e.g. *'Here are some pictures showing different ways in which computers affect our lives. First, talk to each other about how these pictures show the role of computers nowadays. Then decide which picture best reflects the difference computers have made to our lives.'* (CAE Handbook for Teachers, 2008:90). In the same example, as well as straightforward images such as a child with the controls for an electronic game and a large open plan office where each desk has a computer, there is an image of a man with his hands tied to the keyboard of his computer and his head inside the monitor. This CAE level task is more demanding than an FCE task since it requires the candidates to talk about how the pictures present the role of computers and decide which picture best reflects the difference computers have made to our lives. The FCE context is concrete and plausible and within the candidate's personal experience, whereas at CAE the context is more abstract.

Finally, at CPE level, the candidate–candidate interactive task (Part 2) is removed from the candidates' personal experience and is abstract in nature, the stimulus is less familiar, and the visuals illustrate scenarios rather than objects. It includes a medium (e.g. *'A library exhibition'*), an audience (e.g. *attendees*) and a topic, (e.g. *'The power of writing'*). In this CPE task (CPE Handbook, 2008:66), the candidates are asked to *'imagine that a library is putting on an exhibition entitled 'The power of writing'. Talk together about the importance of the written word, as represented in these pictures. Then decide which two images convey the power of writing most effectively'*. Candidates would be presented with images portraying: a sports star signing autographs, a woman using a word processor, an underpass covered in graffiti, a man reading in his study surrounded by books, a street full of signs and advertisements, the densely decorated walls of an Egyptian tomb. Not only is the lexis contained within the visuals more demanding than at the other levels; because of its abstract nature there is also less context than even the CAE pictures, so increasing the need for the candidates to use the language of speculation.

Long turn tasks

The progression in the nature of information through the levels is also seen in the visuals used in the PET, FCE and CAE long turn tasks (there is no long turn at KET and a verbal prompt is used in the CPE long turn task). In the PET long turn task (Part 3) each candidate is asked to talk about a colour photograph. As seen in the visuals in Appendix A, the photographs chosen are concrete and factual and allow candidates to use the language of description using only PET-level language; they do not require the candidates to speculate or interpret what they see. The visuals chosen are also sufficiently varied so that each candidate has something different to say. In addition, the photographs have a similar balance in terms of the quantity of information and interest. For example, it might seem unfair to the candidates if one picture was of a bright sunny setting, full of exciting activities and objects, while the other was taken on a dull day with gloomy looking people appearing to be doing very little. At this level, candidates are asked to describe their photograph so it is important that each photo contains some human activity that will allow the candidates to produce verb forms, and something in the background so that once the candidate has talked about the main focus of the photo there will be plenty more to enable the candidate to talk without support for 45 seconds.

In the FCE Speaking test, each candidate is given two photographs of people doing things in familiar situations, as seen in the visual given in Appendix A of the role of music in people's lives. A contrast is provided, e.g. indoor/outdoor, day/night, and consideration is also given to the composition of the picture, e.g. a wide-angle shot with lots of peripheral detail might be paired with a picture where the focus is closer in. For FCE the message of the visuals should be clear and unambiguous and visuals should not show situations that are unusual in any way and that would require candidates to speculate about aspects of the picture (FCE *Speaking Item Writer Guidelines* 2006). In addition to comparing the two photos, the candidates are also required to say something about them, as specified by the examiner, e.g. '. . . *and say why you think the music is important to the different groups of people'* (FCE Handbook for Teachers 2007:80). The focus of the speculation will always be concrete in nature and familiar to the candidates; in the example given in Appendix A, one picture is of a group of people in tribal costume celebrating, in the other a family group is making music. FCE item writers are also asked to take into consideration the level of lexis expected in the candidates' responses and to ensure that they are able to do the tasks without having to search for lexis that is above FCE level, or resort to paraphrasing (FCE *Speaking Item Writer Guidelines* 2006). For example, a picture of people travelling by boat is acceptable whereas a picture showing people struggling with oars to row a rowing boat would be inappropriate.

In the CAE Speaking test, candidates are required to demonstrate their ability to use the language of speculation through talking about more abstract concepts. The photographs used need to stimulate this, as can be seen in the visuals given in Appendix A of people talking to each other (page 322). The context for a picture may not be entirely clear and the situations can be more unusual and more lexically demanding, so that candidates have to go beyond description of concrete, factual content in order to speculate as to why certain things are happening. For example, a set of three pictures might show i) a referee talking to a football player, ii) a group of elderly men in a social setting, iii) a woman with a concerned expression, talking one-to-one to a younger woman and taking notes. In this case, the candidates are required to suggest why the people are talking to each other and say how they might be feeling (CAE Handbook for Teachers 2008:89).

Topic familiarity/content knowledge required

The topic familiarity or content knowledge necessary to complete a task plays a crucial role in assessment and is regarded as a fundamental variable which can impact candidate performance. Both Hughes (2003) and Weir (1993) suggest that in the testing of general proficiency, the topics chosen should be neutral, i.e. they should not favour any one group. Ellis (2003:309) advises on designing tasks which are 'content-fair', and where the content knowledge required to complete a task does not advantage specific groups of test takers. Similarly, Alderson (2000:29) argues that 'every attempt should be made to allow background knowledge to facilitate performance rather than allowing its absence to inhibit performance'.

In terms of speaking tests, Skehan (1998) contends that topic familiarity can significantly affect the fluency of the test taker's response, and as such should be taken into consideration when developing test tasks. This point is convincingly illustrated in the work of Foster and Skehan (1999), where learners were asked to watch and recount two episodes of *Mr Bean* (a British TV slapstick comedy without dialogue), one of which had a predictable storyline (a restaurant scene) while the other was unpredictable (a crazy golf scene). The authors reported significant differences in the fluency of the output, with the more predictable and familiar task resulting in higher fluency estimates. The role of topic knowledge is supported by other studies such as Papajohn (1999), who found a relationship between the topic of the input and test scores, although others have indicated that topic familiarity may not have a significant effect on test scores (Clapham 1996, Tan 1990). Lumley and O'Sullivan (2005) employed a number of tasks which were deliberately manipulated, so that they were predicted to be biased towards a particular section of the test taker population (either the men or the women). The results indicated that there was little evidence of effect attributable to topic or to audience alone. One topic, for example horse racing, favoured males, while another topic, soccer, which might have shown the same effect, showed no advantage for males.

Topic familiarity/content knowledge required: Cambridge practice

The principle that candidates should perceive topics as 'suitable, realistic, reasonably familiar and feasible' (Shaw and Weir 2007:128) underlies the development of the Cambridge ESOL Main Suite Speaking tasks and attempts are made to ensure that topics are:

- appropriate for the level of candidature from all cultures, experiences and age groups
- within the age group and experience of the candidature
- free of any cultural/UK bias (e.g. urban/rural, boy/girl, cultural, etc.)
- not potentially distressing or offensive, such as alcohol, drugs, war, death, politics, religious beliefs, racism, sexism, etc.
- likely to appeal to a broad base of candidates and will not 'date' too quickly
- able to provide a range of options in terms of sub-topics and functions
- at an appropriate cognitive level and are likely to produce answers of the appropriate level and of the required length for the particular candidature
- familiar, yet not too familiar, i.e. the candidates should have an existing schema (organised mental framework) for the topic
- not specialised or technical, so that the material does not favour candidates with specialised knowledge of a particular subject (*Item Writer Guidelines for PET – CPE*, 2006).

(See also Chapter 2 for a discussion of test taker characteristics.)

When Cambridge ESOL item writers submit materials, they are required to complete a Task Description Form which serves as a checklist to ensure all the criteria have been met. This is verified at the pre-editing stage of test construction; if the conditions have not been met, the material is rejected and the item writer's attention is drawn to the relevant section in the *item writer guidelines*. Editing by committee, trialling materials on learners who represent the target audience and the vetting of materials by independent observers provide further opportunities to ensure the materials meet all the criteria in terms of content knowledge required.

The item writer guidelines at all proficiency levels provide guidance on the selection of topics and exemplify the use of neutral topics in the Main Suite examinations. The KET, PET and FCE Speaking tests draw on the Waystage (1998), Threshold (1998) and Vantage (2001) documents (by Van Ek and Trim) in terms of the suitability of topics at different levels.

An important consideration when selecting a topic suitable for any particular level is how the topic will be treated in the task, and the language used. Topics are chosen to be accessible and of interest to the broad range of Main Suite candidates; topics which would appeal only to a minority are avoided. The item writer guidelines for each exam also emphasise that the suitability of a topic is closely intertwined with the treatment of that topic in a given task. For instance, a topic such as 'education' can be used at all five levels, but whereas CPE level candidates would be able to talk about educational policy, KET level candidates would be limited to areas connected to their own school experience, such as their favourite subjects. To take another example, in FCE, candidates might be required to discuss the merits of a range of objects that a group of explorers would find useful on a trip to the North Pole, and then to select the three most important items. This is a concrete task involving a variety of objects within the FCE candidates' lexical range (e.g. dog, gun, radio, first-aid kit, etc.). At CAE level, the same topic might require candidates to be more speculative, for example, in a discussion about the personal qualities participants might need to cope with the problems that might occur, and the selection of participants whose expertise might be most useful on an expedition of this kind.

Care is also taken to ensure that the topic is of interest to the average candidates and does not exclude any large group in terms of its standpoint or assumptions. Cambridge ESOL tests are typically constructed for heterogeneous groups of candidates, which results in the need to select tests with a wider appeal than may be the case with a homogenous group, such as ESP tests. In the latter case, it may be easier to select topics with narrower or more targeted appeal. In addition, the content is geared as far as possible to the age group and experience of the candidature, and takes account of different cultural and religious sensitivities. Cambridge ESOL routinely collects background information on the candidature by exam, which provides valuable information, such as the typical age of the candidature, which can then inform general guidelines for task construction and topic selection (see Chapter 2). For example, 75% of FCE and CAE candidates are under 25 years old, and correspondingly, topics are selected to appeal to a candidature of this age, while at the same time not seeming too childish for older candidates. Another example can be seen in the KET and PET for Schools exams which were introduced by Cambridge ESOL in 2008 and which are aimed at a younger candidature. Correspondingly, the topics are geared to a candidature at the secondary school level and topics suitable for older, mature candidates are avoided.

Lexical, structural and functional resources

In the sections to follow, the focus will shift to lexical, structural and functional aspects of the input provided in the tasks and candidate output.

Lexical resources

It is logical to expect that the lexical range of the input, which, as Skehan (1996) and others have noted, forms part of the code complexity of that input, will have a significant impact on the difficulty level of a test task. Supplementary lists giving guidance on the range of lexis at different proficiency levels have been in existence for many years (e.g. the *Cambridge English Lexicon,* Hindmarsh 1980). Such lists have been developed more intuitively than empirically, while others form part of a more functionally oriented specification (e.g. the Waystage and Threshold Levels, which underpin some of the lower reference levels of the CEFR). More recently, the development of both native speaker and learner corpora (i.e. computerised and searchable collections of written and spoken texts) and the application of corpus linguistics tools to these databases, have made it easier to derive more empirically grounded word lists for use in pedagogy and assessment contexts (see, for example, Ball 2002a on BEC wordlists, and the English Vocabulary Profile, previously known and reffered to in this volume as the English Profile Wordlists at www.englishprofile.org). Such resources provide useful guidance for test developers who need to successfully create tests targeting specific levels of difficulty or covering particular domains. At the same time, we need to keep in mind the feasibility of specifying lexis for particular domains. Vocabulary lists of core words and phrases for a few highly specific contexts are feasible (e.g., air traffic control discourse, as seen in Rubenbauer 2009). However, even for such narrow domains the specific lexis is located within a larger, more general linguistic frame of reference, as O'Sullivan (2006) suggests.

An important limitation of word lists (whether generated intuitively or by corpus linguistics tools) is the fact that they are based on frequency analyses, but do not indicate which particular words or phrases are linked to particular functions. Khalifa and Weir (2009) suggest that word lists would need to be developed by first identifying functional language use and then supplying frequencies of which words/phrases are realisations of particular functions. This is certainly a promising avenue for future research.

Khalifa and Weir (2009) contend that while it is difficult to specify which words are necessary for any particular language use context, vocabulary research has been more successful at specifying what size of vocabulary is necessary to achieve certain language aims. In this respect, Adolphs and Schmitt (2003) suggest that around 2,000–3,000 word families typically supply the bulk of the lexical resources required for basic everyday conversation. A size of 10,000 word families is typically accepted as necessary for a wide L2 English vocabulary (Hazenberg and Hulstijn 1996). These vocabulary sizes are, naturally, approximations, as Khalifa and Weir (2009) also point out, and depend on many other factors such as cognitive strategies, background knowledge, and communicative strategy use. They do, however, provide useful 'rules of thumb' for test developers.

Lexical resources: Cambridge practice

At all five levels of the Cambridge ESOL exams the lexical range of the input is general, non-specialised, without cultural references, and well within the proficiency level of the candidates at this level. Item writers are advised to use language within the level so that candidates are not tested on their listening comprehension ability, but are able to use the questions and prompts as springboards for showing off their speaking ability.

KET input includes lexical items which normally occur in the everyday vocabulary of English speakers. The lexis of the input is expected to be within the KET vocabulary list (2008), which comprises words from the Waystage Specifications List (Van Ek and Trim 1998) and other vocabulary which has been shown by corpus evidence to be relevant to the level (Ball 2002a). In terms of output, candidates are expected to know and use appropriate vocabulary normally associated with everyday situations, such as meeting people for the first time, giving factual information of a personal and non-personal kind, talking about daily life, interests, likes, leisure activities and social life.

PET input involves items which are expected to occur in the general vocabulary of native speakers using English as laid out in Threshold (van Ek and Trim 1998) and which are specified in the PET Wordlist (2009). The lexis should be sufficient for most topics in everyday life. A list of allowable prefixes and suffixes is provided in the vocabulary list; compound words are allowed if the two words appear individually in the list and the meaning of the compound word is transparent. Phrasal verbs with a fully literal meaning are also permitted, provided the individual verb and particle appear on the list. In terms of output, PET candidates are expected to use a range of appropriate vocabulary when talking about familiar topics. More specifically, they are expected to be able to deal with lexis focused on simple everyday language such as personal details, daily routines, likes and dislikes (Part 1); lexis used for making and responding to suggestions, discussing alternatives, making recommendations, negotiating agreement, etc. (Part 2); the lexis used for describing scenes/people from a colour photograph (Part 3); and lexis used for discussing likes/dislikes, experiences (Part 4).

The wordlists which are used at KET and PET level provide guidance to item writers in producing exam papers at a specific proficiency level. The word lists are dynamic and evolving documents which are reviewed every couple of years and updated with words suggested by the experts involved in the exam (e.g. exam paper Chairs and Assessment Managers). Before being added to the list, these words are explored in a range of corpora to reveal their frequency in L1 and L2 English and to provide contextualised examples. A number of the words on the list are also removed from it, usually due to being no longer relevant to today's candidature, e.g. 'cassette tape'. The quantitative evidence supplied by the corpus linguistics analysis is reviewed and discussed by a panel of experts for each examination before a decision is taken whether to add or remove a vocabulary item (Ball 2002a).

For FCE, item writers use the Vantage publication (van Ek and Trim 2001) and any other high frequency or otherwise appropriate words from corpus evidence. It is expected that candidates at this level are familiar with the vocabulary relevant to general interactional and social language, and the lexis associated with comparing, describing, expressing opinions, agreeing, disagreeing, suggesting, etc. In their output they are expected to use a range of appropriate vocabulary to give and exchange views on a range of familiar topics.

In CAE and CPE, item writers do not use wordlists to constrain lexical content and are expected to use their professional judgement of what the CAE/CPE candidature should be able to understand. At these levels, candidates need to be familiar with the vocabulary relevant to general interactional and social language, and the lexis of comparing, describing, expressing opinions, agreeing, disagreeing, suggesting, speculating, evaluating etc. In CAE, candidates are expected to use a range of appropriate vocabulary when giving and exchanging views on familiar and unfamiliar topics. In CPE, they are expected to use a range of appropriate vocabulary with flexibility when giving and exchanging views on, familiar, unfamiliar and abstract topics.

As noted earlier, trialling of materials prior to their use in live conditions plays an important role in the development of Cambridge ESOL Speaking tasks. Trialling ensures that the lexis used in the input materials (both the rubric and the stimulus represented in the visuals) is accessible to candidates, appropriate for all cohorts and able to provide enough stimulus for candidates' linguistic abilities to be displayed.

Lexical analysis of the Main Suite Speaking tests

Cambridge ESOL espouses an ongoing commitment to investigating aspects of the linguistic resources covered in the different tests. An example is a study carried out by Schmitt (2009), who examined and compared lexical features of both test input (the Speaking task prompts) and test output (the candidates' oral responses) across the five Main Suite examination levels. The details of this study are the focus of the next section.

Analysis of the Speaking task prompts (test input)

For the purposes of the study, a sample which consisted of 65 Speaking task prompts distributed across five levels (10 KET tasks, 15 PET tasks, 15 FCE tasks, 15 CAE tasks, and 10 CPE tasks) was chosen. The selected tasks were a representative sample at these levels, and were considered typical for each level. All tasks used had been previously released in the public domain. Within each level, all parts except Part 1 were used. Unlike the other test parts, the published Part 1 tasks do not include the direct prompts, but a paraphrase, such as, for example 'The interlocutor asks the candidates about where they come from/live, and for information about their school/studies/ work' (KET Part 1). As a result, the analysis consisted of only Part 2 tasks for KET, and a range of Parts 2, 3 and 4 tasks for the other four levels. The analysis was carried out using Compleat Lexical Tutor (www.lextutor.ca).

The research question guiding the study was: 'How is progression in lexical resources in the five Main Suite levels manifested in the task prompts and test taker output?' For the purposes of study, the following operationalisation of lexical resources was used:

- mean number of word tokens
- mean number of word types
- lexical variation (tokens per type ratio)
- lexical density (content words/total)
- mean word length
- frequency distribution of vocabulary.

Table 4.8 presents the number of tokens (i.e. words) and types (i.e. different words) which appear in the Speaking prompts at the different Main Suite levels.

Table 4.8 Number of tokens and types in Main Suite Speaking test prompts

	KET	PET	FCE	CAE	CPE
Tokens in test prompts	963	1,322	1,390	1,312	2,685
Types in test prompts	213	147	249	274	418
Tokens per type	4.52	8.99	5.58	4.79	6.42

As can be seen, the average number of tokens test takers would hear in the Speaking task prompts increases from the lowest to the highest level; PET, FCE and CAE show a similar profile, largely due to the similarity in task types at these three levels (i.e. there is a long-turn task, an interactive candidate–candidate task, and a prompted discussion). In terms of the occurrence of different words (i.e. types) in the prompts, again a progression can be seen as the level increases. The marked exception is at KET, which counter-intuitively has a higher frequency of types than PET. The content word-rich nature of KET Part 2 prompts, and the fact that only Part 2 was used in the analysis, is the most likely reason for this finding. The tokens per type measure is relatively high at PET, which, as Schmitt (2009) notes, is caused by task instructions being explicitly repeated by the examiner in order to ensure understanding.

The above analysis of types and tokens presents just one aspect of the investigation of lexical resources. As Shaw and Weir (2007) note in the context of lexical resources in writing exams, the number of word tokens or types to be processed by the test takers is one factor; a more significant factor is likely to be the 'difficulty' of these words. Several researchers (Laufer 1997, Schmitt 2000) have emphasised the wide range of factors which might contribute to a word's 'difficulty', and the fact that the notion of 'difficulty' may depend on many contextual and co-textual factors. Shaw and Weir (2007) make the important point that it is difficult to use contextual and co-textual criteria for word selection in an examination suite designed for candidates of multiple nationalities and first languages. These criteria will affect examinees from various L1 backgrounds differently, making it impossible to select words of equal difficulty for all of the candidates taking the test. Because of the complexity of deciding upon the difficulty of a word, language specialists generally rely on a different measure to rank vocabulary: a word's frequency of occurrence. Frequency of occurrence provides an indirect measure of a word's difficulty since higher frequency vocabulary is generally learned before lower frequency vocabulary (Schmitt, Schmitt and Clapham 2001), in line with the SLA principle that learners maximise frequently occurring linguistic properties (Hawkins and Buttery 2009). It can be assumed that on average test takers will be more familiar with higher frequency words than with lower frequency words, and that these words are, therefore, 'easier'. A useful analysis would be a comparison between the words used in the Speaking task prompts and available frequency lists. Such a frequency analysis is given in Table 4.9, and is based on the frequency lists adapted in the Lexical tutor software. The table gives the frequency distribution of words in the test prompts as compared with the first 1,000 most frequently used words in English (comparable to the Waystage Specification List, which is used to write the KET tasks), and the second band of 1,000 most frequent words, which are still considered high frequency basic vocabulary.

As can be seen, there is not much difference between the different tests in the suite, with the vast majority of words (≥95%) coming from the most

Table 4.9 Frequency analysis of prompts in Main Suite Speaking tests

Frequency level	KET %	PET %	FCE %	CAE %	CPE %
First 2,000 words	94.60	99.85	99.85	99.62	98.55
Academic Word List (AWL)	1.45	.76	1.15	1.91	2.27

frequent 2,000 words in English. Schmitt (2009) argues that as these high frequency words are usually learned towards the beginning of one's EFL/ESL education, this would suggest that the lexis in the instructions should not be a problem for the examinees. The author further notes that for texts to be easily comprehensible, learners should know 98%+ of the words in those texts. If we assume that the examinees know the first 2,000 words of English, which should be a safe assumption for the FCE, CAE and CPE levels, then these three levels clearly meet this threshold with ease. This assumption may not hold for the PET level, but because the coverage percentage is so high (virtually 100%), there is enough leeway to assume that examinees will still probably understand 98%+ of the instructions. As for the KET prompts, the actual instructions are all in high frequency vocabulary (e.g., *Here is some information about a bookshop*'), and any lower frequency items will be included on the written prompt which the candidates use, and which provides a source of scaffolding for them to aid with understanding.

A comparison with the Academic word list (Coxhead 2000) is also a useful measure of lexical resources. As can be seen in Table 4.9, the percentage of academic vocabulary is very low, as would be expected in a General English test and, with the exception of KET, it shows a slight increase as the level progresses. The highest percentage of AWL vocabulary at CAE and CPE is a reflection of the fact that both these exams are used for accessing academic study opportunities. The AWL percentage at the highest levels is nevertheless still low, and presents an avenue for research and insights for future test development and revision, as these exams become more widely used for academic course entry. KET presents an interesting case, with the percentage not following the general trend, and higher than would be expected. A possible explanation is offered by a content analysis of the KET prompts, which reveals some overlaps between the words in the KET prompts and the academic word list; for example, the words 'channel' (as in 'TV channel') is used four times in the prompts, as well as the word 'credit' (as in 'credit card'). The AWL counterparts are used as verbs (i.e. 'to channel' and 'to credit'). The limitations of the software led to the words in KET being considered academic, simply based on lexical features, whereas they have, in fact, a different functional usage. One of the limitations of this type of lexical frequency analysis is that it can only deal with prescribed, clear-cut linguistic contexts. This finding also highlights the fundamental importance of employing both quantitative and qualitative methodologies in any analyses of this kind.

Analysis of candidates' oral responses (test output)

This part of the study used speaking performances from 26 candidates, which were videotaped and filmed for rater training purposes. Only 'average' pairs for the respective level were selected. The notion of 'average' was defined as candidates who had Facets-generated fair average marks (Linacre 2006) in the 2.5–4 band range (from a 1–5 Band scale) on the Cambridge ESOL *Grammar and Vocabulary/Lexical Resource* scale. This selection process ensured that the analysis focused on clearly distinct candidates who represent the 'middle' of the proficiency level. Test takers with marks at the extreme top or bottom of the scale would have shown lexical features typical of the adjacent proficiency levels and were deemed unsuitable for the analysis (although, naturally, they are indispensible for rater training and standardisation purposes). The selection process resulted in the following sample: KET (6 candidates), PET (5 candidates), FCE (7 candidates), CAE (5 candidates), and CPE (3 candidates). The test takers displayed a range of L1s, and were both male and female. Even though small, the sample was considered adequate for an initial pilot study of an area which has received limited attention in the past. Inevitably, it will benefit from a larger-scale investigation in the future.

In the analysis of examinee output, Schmitt (2009) used similar measures to the ones employed in the analysis of prompts. This stage of the analysis was more problematic, however, since the transcripts of candidate speech contained non-lexical information, as well as incomplete or incorrectly used words. Such examples of lexical use are of fundamental importance for the rating of a sample of candidate speech. Due to the current limitations of lexical analysis software, however, only fully formed words were retained, and hesitation markers ('*erm*', '*uh*') were deleted. If a word in a transcript was shown as a partial word but it was clear from the context what the word was, or if it was produced later in the task, the word was correctly typed into the text so it could be counted by the software (e.g., '*brella*' ➡ '*umbrella*'). Thus the analysis covered the vocabulary produced to the extent discernible by the transcripts, and included vocabulary which was slightly altered for the purposes of the software used. The fact that such nuanced and important information from the transcripts was inevitably lost presents a limitation of the study, as the data used does not give an indication of the full spectrum of words produced by the examinees. It is a strong indication of the limitation of quantitative measures.

In terms of the mean number of types and tokens, a strong increasing trend was observed as the levels went up, as seen in Table 4.10. In fact, one of the clear findings of the study was that the type/token variation in candidate output was the most consistent (and perhaps only) indicator of progression in level.

We can see that as examinees develop in proficiency, they produce both more words (tokens), and display a wider range of vocabulary by using

Table 4.10 Number of tokens and types in candidate output in Main Suite Speaking tests

	KET	PET	FCE	CAE	CPE
Mean number of tokens per examinee	224	400	746	720	1,228
Mean number of types per examinee	63	83	96	127	219
Tokens per type	3.55	4.82	7.77	5.66	5.61

more different words (types). This finding is in line with Iwashita, Brown, McNamara and O'Hagan's (2008) investigation of features of spoken performance at different proficiency levels, in which the authors found that an increase in level was associated with an increase in the number of tokens and types. The tokens-per-type measure presents an interesting case, with a gradual increase observed across the levels, except for FCE. It is possible that the higher than expected result for FCE was influenced by the specific task demands and prompts, but until a follow-up qualitative analysis is carried out, the precise reason will remain unclear.

In contrast to the type and token distribution across levels, the variables 'Mean word length' and 'Lexical density' did not show consistent improvement through the Main Suite levels, as seen in Table 4.11. In fact, KET candidates counter-intuitively had the longest mean word length and highest lexical density – most probably a result of the fact that Part 2 in KET is very tightly controlled by prompts. Candidates have to use the words given in the written prompts, and many of these words are content words, which would explain the higher than expected mean word length and lexical density measure at KET. It is worth noting that a parallel study focusing on lexical resources in written output produced similar results (Schmitt 2005).

Table 4.11 Mean word length and lexical density in candidate output in Main Suite Speaking tests

	KET	PET	FCE	CAE	CPE
Mean word length	4.33	4.18	4.11	4.29	4.18
Lexical density (Content words/Total)	0.51	0.46	0.42	0.44	0.43

A similar trend of few noticeable measurable differences across levels can also be seen in Table 4.12, which gives an indication of the lexical resources of candidate output as compared to the first 2,000 most frequently used words,

Table 4.12 Frequency analysis of candidate output

Frequency level	KET %	PET %	FCE %	CAE %	CPE %
First 2,000 words	93.08	97.05	97.61	97.75	97.18
Academic Word List (AWL)	0.88	1.24	1.28	1.80	1.41

and also the use of academic vocabulary in candidate output. Several scholars (e.g. Laufer and Nation 1999) have suggested that as learners advance in proficiency, the frequency profile of their vocabulary output shifts: they use less high frequency vocabulary and more lower frequency vocabulary. However, the candidates in this study (ranging across clearly different levels of proficiency) produce frequency profiles which are very similar to each other. This can be seen in the percentage of lexis at the first 2,000 frequency band, which displays practically no variation. Counter-intuitively, KET has a lower percentage (93.08%), which Schmitt suggests is most likely influenced by the examinees using the lower-frequency vocabulary from the written prompt. Overall, Schmitt (2009:5) concludes that the candidates produce a 'relatively static frequency profile' as they move up the levels. In terms of the words in the Academic Word List, a very slight improvement can be seen across the levels, but with a reversed trend for CAE and CPE.

The strikingly similar lexical frequency profiles across the five proficiency levels indicate that these quantitative lexical variables failed to consistently show the lexical improvement in candidate speech, which is nevertheless discernible to trained raters who have awarded different marks (and therefore proficiency levels) to these candidate performances. Schmitt (2009) notes that no currently available quantitative analysis technique is able to discern 'goodness/appropriacy of usage' as well as a skilled human rater.

This finding is a very strong indicator that frequency in itself may not be the best measure of lexical resources, and has implications beyond the present study, as it raises questions about the ability of automated assessment systems to provide meaningful, adequate and complex ratings of lexical resources which go beyond the mechanical frequency counts of types and tokens. It is clear that, as Schmitt (2009) also argues, skilled raters are required to provide meaningful assessments of the lexical resources of examinees displayed during an interactive speaking test. In addition to frequency of use, a fundamental measure of improving lexical proficiency is *how well* the words are used, rather than if they are of lower frequency. For example, the limitations of current lexical software packages mean that they can only 'read' correctly formatted words. Thus errors such as *differents, *childrens, *musics must be corrected (as was the case in this study) or the software will count this as off-list (e.g., very low frequency) vocabulary. It is clear that judgements of 'correctness' of use are crucial, and yet the field is still struggling to find a way of measuring such appropriacy of use in any other way than human judgement. As such, Schmitt (2009:1) writes, 'the fact that Cambridge raters take lexical appropriacy into account in their markings is reassuring, as . . . it gives a better indication of the quality of vocabulary output than any automated method currently available'. This contention is echoed by Shaw and Weir (2007) who, in the context of written candidate output, noted that quantitative measures such as lexical density, lexical variation and lexical frequency profiling are not sufficiently robust to distinguish meaningfully between test takers of different levels.

Questions still remain, therefore, whether single-word units and frequency of occurrence are adequate criteria for distinguishing between lexical resources at different proficiency levels. The discussion above has indicated the limitations of some quantitative measures and the balance between quantity of use and appropriateness of use. As Martinez (2009) notes, single-word frequency lists are of limited validity, since the most frequent words in English 'are merely tips of phraseological icebergs'. Expanding the analysis beyond the single-word to multi-word combinations holds promise for the meaningful analysis of lexis in candidate output, as illustrated by Vidakovic and Barker (2010) in a study of lexical progression in the written candidate output of Cambridge ESOL's Skills for Life test. As Shaw and Weir (2007) argue, at more advanced levels, the influence of collocation, phraseology, idiom and register may well be more significant in distinguishing between levels, though automated rather than manual measures for confirming this are not readily available. A notable exception is the work of Martinez (2009) whose PHRASE vocabulary list is based on multi-word formulaic sequences, and would allow (when made more widely available) for a systematic way to assess the lexical profile of a text.

Despite these difficulties, efforts continue to address lexical progression in Cambridge ESOL examinations, both from a quantitative and qualitative perspective, and to engage in a research agenda which will extend our understanding of the nature and development of L2 learners' lexical resources. Investigations such as these are the aim of the English Profile Programme, a corpus-based research programme investigating criterial L2 features, i.e. key distinguishing characteristics across levels (Capel 2010, Green 2011, Hawkins and Filipovič 2011). It is clear that further work on lexical progression across levels is needed, given the limited conclusions that can be reached when employing frequency data. Qualitative investigations of how speaking examiners arrive at estimates of lexical ability might prove even more useful, especially in relation to appropriateness. It is only through such mixed-method approaches that we will be able to arrive at a comprehensive account of lexical progression across proficiency levels.

Structural resources

Specific guidance on structural resources for Levels A2 to B2 is given in the Waystage (1998), Threshold (1998) and Vantage (2001) Council of Europe series which identify and list the structures learners need in order to be able to adequately deal with the functions identified at these levels. At higher levels there is as yet no attempt to match structures with level, although the forthcoming publications from the English Profile Programme, which draw on developments in second language acquisition and on corpus linguistics evidence, aim to provide such a description.

The CEFR and the Waystage, Threshold, and Vantage documents indicate that at A1 and A2 learners have limited control of structural resources and A2 is characterised by systematic basic mistakes. By B2 there is a high degree of grammatical control of the full repertoire of verb forms and other key structures. At the C levels there is a consistent degree of control in terms of grammatical accuracy and a broader range of structural resources, allowing learners to express themselves accurately and appropriately, using a range of structures and showing some sensitivity to register.

Structural resources: Cambridge practice

With the exception of KET, the lowest-level test, the Cambridge ESOL Main Suite Speaking tasks do not force the use of specific structures – either through the design of the linguistic input or in specific expectations of the spoken output. Rather, they set tasks which give candidates the opportunity to demonstrate in their output their structural resources to the best of their ability. The success with which they do so is assessed with rating scales and descriptors which become steadily more demanding as candidates progress up the levels (see Chapter 5 on scoring validity). Task input at all levels is structurally appropriate to the level and well within the proficiency level of candidates, to ensure comprehension by the weaker candidates as well.

The difference in structural resources between KET and PET lies in the degree of control expected of candidates. At KET level the grammatical structures elicited by the tasks are expected to fall within the Waystage Grammatical Specifications (1998). Candidates at this level are expected to show sufficient control of simple grammatical forms. At PET level, the grammatical structures elicited are expected to fall within the Threshold grammatical structures specification (1998), with candidates showing a good degree of control of simple grammatical forms.

In FCE and above, Grammatical Specifications do not exist. However, the tasks are designed to ensure that candidates demonstrate an ability to produce a range of structures; for example the interview section (Part 1) includes questions with a variety of verb tenses, and the use of modals comes into play with the speculative nature of some of the tasks. Similar to PET-level candidates, FCE candidates are generally expected to show a good degree of control of simple grammatical forms in their spoken output, but also to attempt some complex grammatical forms. An FCE-level candidate who speaks simply and accurately or one who speaks in a more ambitious way but makes more grammatical errors (providing this does not result in misunderstanding) will be considered minimally adequate for this level from the point of view of grammar.

In CAE the tasks are more demanding than those in FCE in terms of the range of structures required for an adequate response. Candidates at this level need to show a good degree of control of a range of simple and some complex grammatical forms. Although the successful CAE-level candidate may still make grammatical errors, these should not result in misunderstanding. At CPE level, learners are expected to maintain control of a wide range of simple and complex grammatical forms.

A detailed analysis of the structural resources in the spoken output of Main Suite candidates would be a valuable future investigation, which could serve as a complement to the findings on lexical resources reported earlier in this chapter. Such an analysis might draw on both quantitative and qualitative methodologies and also include investigations of raters' approaches to arriving at grammatical estimates.

Functional resources

The CEFR (2001) places primary focus on language as a means of communication, and consequently puts language functions in a central position. Language learners are therefore graded in terms of what they can do with language, rather than the ability to handle specific grammatical structures or lexical items. As Shaw and Weir (2007) note, this is consistent with the communicative approach to language teaching and is reflected in most contemporary course materials, which place an emphasis on awareness of grammar and lexis within the context of coping with functional demands in the target language.

The CEFR makes a useful distinction between macro- and micro-functions. The former are general in nature and similar to the types of talk proposed by Brown and Yule (1983) and Bygate (1987), and discussed in the earlier sections on Task purpose and Discourse mode. In contrast, micro-functions are lower-level functions and are often completed within an interactional turn, such as inviting, apologising or thanking. These micro-functions are the focus of this section.

Functional resources: Cambridge practice

In line with the CEFR (2001), Cambridge ESOL examinations espouse the central role of functions in language learning, and the tasks are explicitly presented to candidates in terms of the functions which they are required to demonstrate. For example, candidates may be asked 'to describe', 'to compare', 'to agree/disagree', etc. A useful tool for investigating functional resources can be found in O'Sullivan et al's (2002) tripartite distinction between informational, interactional, and interaction management functions, which was discussed earlier in the context of response formats. Table 4.13 presents the distribution of these (micro) functions across the Cambridge ESOL Main Suite Speaking tests at different proficiency levels.

Table 4.13 Functions in Cambridge ESOL Main Suite Speaking tests

Language Functions	KET	PET	FCE	CAE	CPE
Informational					
Providing personal information					
Present	✓	✓	✓	✓	✓
Past	✓	✓	✓	✓	✓
Future	✓	✓	✓	✓	✓
Expressing opinions	✓	✓	✓	✓	✓
Elaborating	✓	✓	✓	✓	✓
Justifying opinions	✓	✓	✓	✓	✓
Comparing	✓	✓	✓	✓	✓
Speculating			✓	✓	✓
Staging			✓	✓	✓
Describing					
Sequence of events			✓	✓	✓
Scene		✓	✓	✓	✓
Summarising		✓	✓	✓	✓
Suggesting		✓	✓	✓	✓
Expressing preferences	✓	✓	✓	✓	✓
Interactional Functions					
Agreeing		✓	✓	✓	✓
Disagreeing		✓	✓	✓	✓
Modifying		✓	✓	✓	✓
Asking for opinions		✓	✓	✓	✓
Persuading		✓	✓	✓	✓
Asking for information	✓	✓	✓	✓	✓
Conversational repair	✓	✓	✓	✓	✓
Negotiating meaning					
check meaning	✓	✓	✓	✓	✓
understanding	✓	✓	✓	✓	✓
common ground		✓	✓	✓	✓
ask clarification	✓	✓	✓	✓	✓
correct utterance	✓	✓	✓	✓	✓
respond to required clarification	✓	✓	✓	✓	✓
Managing Interaction					
Initiating		✓	✓	✓	✓
Changing		✓	✓	✓	✓
Reciprocating		✓	✓	✓	✓
Deciding		✓	✓	✓	✓

Source: Compiled from information in KET – CPE Handbooks for Teachers, 2007, 2008.

The reader would also find Table 4.2 useful for the present discussion on functional resources. A more detailed overview of the functions which candidates are expected to handle at KET and PET levels can also be found in the respective examination Handbooks in the sections entitled *Inventory of functions, notions and communicative tasks*. From FCE level upwards no list of specified functions is provided in the exam handbooks.

A key aspect of a functional approach to language learning is that many functions can appropriately be tested at a range of levels, as seen in Table 4.13. In such cases, learners differ across proficiency levels in terms of the range of exponents which they can use to perform those functions and by the degree of accuracy and complexity with which they can express their views. For example, expressing preferences can be accomplished very simply even at KET, e.g. '*I like my home town more*', and persuading can be simply performed at PET, e.g. '*I think we should choose X because . . .*'.

While the majority of functions are observed at a range of levels, some are only tested at higher levels. Informational functions, such as describing a scene, summarising and suggesting are introduced at PET level, whereas speculating, staging and describing a sequence of events are introduced at FCE. A major difference between KET and the levels above is also seen in the interactional and interaction management functions. KET candidates are not expected to perform interactional functions such as agreeing, disagreeing, modifying, asking for opinions, or persuading; this is reflected in the design of the test which includes a very highly controlled and predictable candidate–candidate interaction task. Similarly, KET candidates are not expected to engage in interaction management functions, such as initiating a topic, developing it, or finding opportunities to change the topic. Such functional resources, which are mainly related to the reciprocal conditions in interaction, are only assessed from PET level upwards.

The gradation in terms of functional resources – both in terms of the proficiency level at which candidates are expected to engage with specific functions and the breadth and depth of their repertoire of functional resources – is closely linked to the cognitive demands of the task. As candidates progress up the levels, they are expected to engage with tasks which carry higher cognitive demands and to show the ability to deal with reproducing, organising and inventing information (Vähäpässi 1982), factually oriented and evaluative-oriented talk (Bygate 1987), and knowledge telling and knowledge transforming of information (Bereiter and Scardamalia 1987). Such higher cognitive demands are reflected in the micro-functions they are expected to perform. Similarly, at proficiency levels beyond the basic A level, candidates are expected to be able to deal with the higher cognitive demands of interacting with multiple speakers, which is seen in the presence of interaction management functions from PET upwards.

So far the chapter has provided a detailed description and discussion of two key task parameters: task setting, and linguistic task demands. In the following section we turn our attention to a third set of task parameters in speaking tests: Interlocutor variables.

Interlocutor variables

The interactionist approach to assessment, which emphasises the co-constructed nature of interaction, has highlighted the fundamental role of the interlocutor in affecting the discourse produced in a speaking test. The sociolinguistic, SLA and L2 assessment literature has unequivocally indicated that characteristics such as age, gender, cultural/L1 background, personality, status and degree of acquaintanceship can affect the amount and quality of interaction in an interaction (Beebe 1980, Coates 1993, O'Sullivan 2002, Wolfson 1989). Who one talks to, in other words, is not unimportant, and the characteristics of the interlocutor affect the way we speak. As such, the interlocutor, whether an interviewer or a peer test candidate, becomes a variable in speaking tasks, alongside the other task characteristics. This premise holds fundamental implications and challenges for oral performance assessment, since certain interlocutor variables could become a potential threat to a test's validity and fairness.

Weir (2005a) has highlighted several interlocutor parameters which need to be considered in any analysis of speaking tasks, such as the interlocutor's speech rate, variety of accent, acquaintanceship, number and gender. O'Sullivan (2002) has proposed the term 'interlocutor effects', which as a category covers the interlocutor variables proposed by Weir (2005a), and additionally includes the potential effect of age, cultural background, proficiency level, personality, and conversation style on the interaction constructed during the test. The available literature has mainly focused on two broad issues: the language of the interviewer and the effect of background variables on the discourse produced and scores awarded (both in a singleton and paired format). Each of these bodies of research will be reviewed in turn.

Interviewer language

A substantial body of research has focused on the language of the interviewer as an interlocutor variable and studies have convincingly documented variability in the linguistic behaviour of the examiner. For example, features of examiner talk have been shown to affect the difficulty of the interaction, as demonstrated by Brown and Lumley (1997), who suggested that factual questions, linguistic simplification and allowing candidates to control the interaction made the test easier. In contrast, the use of sarcasm, interruption, repetition and lack of co-operation contributed to making the test more difficult.

Speaking examiners have also been shown to differ in the ways in which they structure sequences of topical talk, the questioning techniques they use, and the type of feedback they provide. Brown (2003) demonstrated, for example, that one of the interviewers in her study was explicit and supportive, made elaboration requests clearly (*'Tell me more about . . .'*) and indicated comprehension and interest in her feedback turns. This, in turn, helped the examinee say more and thus made her appear a willing and able communication partner, which the raters recognised in their scores. The other interviewer's questioning strategies were much less supportive. He asked closed questions ('yes/no' and 'or' questions) more frequently and often asked for elaboration indirectly by repeating a phrase that the candidate had used. The candidate often (mis)interpreted this as a request for confirmation and simply responded with *'yes'* or *'mm'* instead of elaborating. The interviewer paused to give the examinee more time to respond, and this created an impression of a disfluent and reticent speaker. The different interviewer styles, Brown convincingly demonstrated, impacted the test taker's performance, and hence rater perceptions of test taker speaking ability.

The notion that Oral Examiners differ in the support they offer to test takers has been explored in depth by Lazaraton (1992, 1993, 1994, 1995, 1996a and b). In studies of the Cambridge Speaking tests commissioned by Cambridge ESOL she observed differences across examiners in terms of priming topics, supplying vocabulary or collaborative completions, giving evaluative responses, echoing and/or correcting responses, repeating questions (with slowed speech, more pausing, over articulation), using prompts requiring yes/no responses, and drawing conclusions for candidates. Based on the variability of examiner talk, the author argued that speaking examiners should be trained to conduct speaking tests according to a standardised prescribed role. Importantly, Lazaraton's findings fed directly into Cambridge ESOL's subsequent development of an 'interlocutor frame' (see below), extensive examiner training procedures, and a speaking examiner monitoring system.

The above studies on the variability of interviewer language have indicated that the manner in which the interviewer interacts with candidates will potentially influence how they perform and the ratings they obtain. This has obvious implications for a test's fairness. One way to ensure uniformity of interviewer language in speaking exams is through the use of an 'interlocutor frame' which scripts the language of the interviewer and reduces variation as much as possible (a practice adopted by Cambridge ESOL).

Effect of background variables

The available research on the role of interlocutor variables in paired tests (discussed in detail in Chapter 2) has suggested that background variables such as gender, age and personality, can potentially impact the discourse co-constructed in a speaking test. However, the available studies do not support any simple linear relationship between interlocutor variables and test discourse and scores, a point made by Brown and McNamara (2004:533) in the context of gender-related effects, who argued against 'any simple deterministic idea that gender categories will have a direct and predictable impact on test processes and test outcomes'. The same argument can be extended beyond gender to the whole range of interlocutor variables. These variables 'compete in the context of an individual's social identity' (Brown and McNamara 2004:533) and no linear, clear-cut behaviours based on background characteristics can be claimed, as Taylor and Wigglesworth (2009) also argue. The key questions, therefore, shift from the role of background variables (we know they play a role) to what test developers should do about interlocutor variables and whether they should try to eliminate such variability altogether or how to control for it. Swain (cited in Fox 2004:240) wisely argues that variability related to different characteristics of conversational partners is 'all that happens in the real world. And so they are things we should be interested in testing. 'She further contends that eliminating all variability in speaking assessment is 'washing out . . . variability which is what human nature and language is all about' (Swain, cited in Fox 2004:240). Coping successfully with such real-life interaction demands in a face-to-face speaking test designed to assess interactional competence, therefore, becomes part of the construct of interactional competence.

Interlocutor variables: Cambridge practice

The available research has highlighted test providers' ethical responsibility to construct tests which are fair and do not provide (intentionally or unintentionally) differential and unequal treatment of candidates based on interlocutor variables. This issue acquires fundamental importance in face-to-face speaking tests, where the potential role of interlocutor variability is highest. Cambridge ESOL addresses this important issue through the design of its Speaking tests and the training of speaking examiners, which ensure that the possible caveats introduced by the interviewer and/or peer interlocutor are addressed so as to ensure test fairness. The multi-part test structure of Cambridge ESOL Speaking tests, which includes different response formats and channels of communication, optimises the advantages of a direct paired speaking test in providing different channels of communication, while at the same time seeking to balance out possible interlocutor effects. Interaction with the other candidate(s) is generally only one part of the Speaking test. The one-to-one interview task and long turn do not involve the peer candidate, and the final part of the PET, FCE, CAE and CPE Speaking tests passes the control back to the examiner who is then able to redress any imbalance which may have occurred earlier in the test, in terms of opportunities to perform.

Interviewer variability is also addressed through the use of an 'interlocutor frame' in the Main Suite Speaking tests, which scripts the language of the interviewer and ensures consistency across the exam for all candidates, regardless of the examiner. The 'interlocutor frame' was introduced by Cambridge ESOL in the mid 1990s in response to the work carried out by Lazaraton on Cambridge ESOL Speaking tests, as reported earlier (1993, 1994, 1995 1996a, 1996b), and the body of research produced by other scholars (e.g. Brown 2003, Brown and Lumley 1997, Ross and Berwick 1992) indicating the involved role of the examiner in the discourse produced. The aim of the 'interlocutor frame' is to ensure standardisation across speaking tests and to guide and constrain examiners so that the candidates' experiences are fair and equal and the examiners' contributions are controlled. There is obviously a balance to be reached between totally scripted interviewer language and interviewer output which is less controlled. Scripting the language of the interviewer would ensure completely standardised interviewer output, but would at the same time lose the positive features of human face-to-face interaction and acquire the inflexibility of recorded prompts. It is clearly not desirable for examiners to start behaving like machines, so some flexibility in the form of follow-up questions is built into the frame. At KET level, the interlocutor is given back-up questions which can be used to paraphrase the primary question if the candidate has failed to understand. At the higher levels, if a candidate fails to extend their answer sufficiently, the examiner can prompt with *'Why? / Why not?'*, *'Why do you say that?'*. At all levels, the frame and rubrics are written in a speech-like form, using contractions and short phrases as one would in speech, to make it possible for the interlocutor to sound as natural as possible. There is also a case to be made for the use of an interviewer script which allows more flexibility and sensitivity to the candidate's comprehension of the prompts and questions, as in the case of IELTS, for example, which covers a broad proficiency spectrum. As a result, the IELTS interlocutor frame needs to provide freedom for the raters in dealing with test takers at different proficiency levels, as O'Sullivan and Lu (2006) found in their study of the use of the interlocutor frame by IELTS examiners.

In addition to using an 'interlocutor frame', the rigorous rater training and monitoring of Cambridge ESOL examiners also ensure uniformity across test events and control for possible interlocutor variables. (See Chapter 5 for a fuller discussion of speaking examiner characteristics and examiner training.)

Conclusion

The main purpose of this chapter has been to analyse the Cambridge ESOL Main Suite Speaking tests against an external framework of test validation and focus on the contextual parameters of tasks. The context validity of the tasks under review was examined with reference to the detailed taxonomy of contextual task parameters outlined in Weir (2005a). This validation exercise has revealed some important features both within and across proficiency levels, and has shown that careful consideration is given in the gradation of difficulty across the Main Suite speaking tasks at different levels.

The present chapter has highlighted the emphasis on production and interaction in the speaking construct underlying Main Suite tests (and the majority of Cambridge ESOL Speaking tests) and the corresponding use of direct, face-to-face, paired tests. As a consequence, the variability of interlocutor talk needs to be managed, at all levels, and this is done through the use of an 'interlocutor frame' and a range of task formats which allow for different types of interaction to be elicited, and for different degrees of examiner control to be embedded in the test. This in turn optimises the advantages offered by a face-to-face paired speaking test, while controlling any potential limitations.

In terms of criterial features across levels, a clear gradation is seen from controlled to semi-controlled to open-ended response formats, which accommodates the need for scaffolding and support at the lower levels, and higher communicative demand at the higher levels. There is also a progression (both within a level and across levels) from relatively structured and supported interaction, under the direct control of the examiner, involving topics of immediate personal relevance to more open-ended discussion with less examiner control involving more general topics. In addition, there is an increase in the amount of time assigned to each task type and to the overall test, as one moves up the levels. Another key distinguishing feature is the gradation from factual to evaluative discourse modes, and the larger presence at the lower levels of persuasion and description, compared with the bigger role of exposition and argumentation at the higher levels. The progression (both within a level and across levels) from personal and concrete information to non-personal and abstract information is also shown to accommodate the need for increased cognitive complexity of the task at the higher levels. Furthermore, this gradation is seen in the visuals for the tasks, which provide more scaffolding and are more content-rich at the lower levels, in contrast with visuals which convey more abstract concepts at the higher levels.

This chapter has dealt with aspects of *a priori* validation of test tasks in terms of their context validity. The next stage, *a posteriori* validation, will be dealt with in Chapter 5 with a discussion of scoring validity. Some aspects of scoring validity have already been discussed in this Chapter, such as the assessment criteria used and the role of interlocutor variables. The following chapter will broaden that discussion and will address other issues which lie at the heart of scoring validity.

5 Scoring validity

Lynda Taylor
Consultant to Cambridge ESOL
Evelina Galaczi
University of Cambridge ESOL Examinations

Introduction

In this chapter we focus our attention on the dimension of scoring validity which is linked directly to both cognitive validity (covered in Chapter 3) and context validity (covered in Chapter 4). The phrase *scoring validity* was originally adopted by Weir (2005a), and subsequently taken up by Shaw and Weir (2007) and Khalifa and Weir (2009), as a superordinate term for all aspects of test reliability, i.e. all aspects of the testing process that can impact on the consistency and dependability of test scores. The ability to place confidence in the quality of the information provided by test scores is vital if we are to use such scores for decision-making purposes. This becomes especially relevant where such decision-making is high stakes in nature, entailing significant consequences not only for an individual test taker but also for the wider stakeholder community. As Shaw and Weir explain, scoring validity 'accounts for the extent to which test scores are based upon appropriate criteria, exhibit consensual agreement in marking, are as free as possible from measurement error, stable over time, consistent in terms of content sampling and engender confidence as reliable decision-making indicators' (2007:143).

As we discussed in Chapter 1, although for descriptive and analytical purposes the various elements of the socio-cognitive framework are presented as being distinct from one another (see Figure 1.1 in Chapter 1), there exists a close relationship between these multiple elements. Chapters 3 and 4 have already highlighted the overlap between cognitive validity and context validity: for example, task context parameters may be carefully selected in advance to influence the cognitive processing provoked during task completion, whether in teaching, learning or assessment. Within the specific context of language testing and assessment, the process of scoring constitutes a third dimension that assumes a significant role. For example, a test taker's awareness of the scoring criteria for the test is likely to shape their decisions about what, and what not, to focus on in their performance and thus where to deploy their attentional resources. In the context of a speaking test, for example, this could lead to the candidate striving for spoken fluency and complexity at the expense of accuracy in a test in which effective communication is more highly prized than ability to get the grammar right all the time. At the heart of any language testing activity, therefore, we can conceive of a triangular relationship between three essential components: the test taker's cognitive abilities; the task and context; and the scoring process. These three dimensions, which are clearly reflected in the cognitive validity, context validity and scoring validity components of Figure 1.1 on page 28, essentially forming the core of the socio-cognitive framework, offer us a helpful perspective on the notion of construct validity in assessment which has direct theoretical and practical relevance for test developers and producers. As outlined in Chapter 1, by maintaining a strong focus on these three core components, and by undertaking a careful analysis of their tests in relation to these three dimensions, test providers can assemble a wealth of theoretical, logical and empirical evidence to support validity claims and arguments about the quality and usefulness of their examinations.

The two previous chapters have already identified a number of factors that can threaten the reliability or scoring validity of speaking tests. Such factors include: a narrow range of task types (and thus interaction types); variable allocation of timing or weighting; variation across different channels of communication; and interlocutor variables. To these we might add several extra factors which Shaw and Weir (2007) identified for writing tests but which apply equally to speaking tests: 'unclear and ambiguous rubrics, lack of familiarity with the test structure, inconsistent administration, and breaches of test security' (2007:143). Given the wide range of factors which can impact on the scoring validity of a speaking test, the notion that speaking test reliability can be adequately captured and expressed in the form of a single statistic, typically an inter-rater correlation coefficient, is not appropriate. This is not, of course, to suggest that rater reliability in speaking tests is unimportant. It has quite rightly been a matter of longstanding concern for Cambridge ESOL and for other large-scale testing agencies, e.g. Educational Testing Service (ETS). The reality, however, is that, in addition to rater or rating variables, there exist multiple other interacting factors in the assessment of speaking with the potential to impact on the reliability of speaking tests; so instead of simply relying on the reporting of a single statistic as an adequate measure of speaking test reliability, speaking test providers are under an obligation to acknowledge these multiple factors as they relate to their tests and to explain how they are appropriately dealt with.

As described in Chapter 1, Cambridge ESOL has employed a direct Speaking test for nearly a century, first in the Certificate of Proficiency in English (CPE) from 1913 onwards (see Weir and Milanovic 2003), and then in the Lower Certificate of English (LCE, later renamed the First Certificate in English, FCE) from 1939 onwards (see Hawkey 2009). The early experience of conducting face-to-face oral tests gained by Cambridge over a period of 25–30 years prompted Jack Roach, Assistant Secretary to UCLES from 1925 to 1945, to investigate some of the complex issues associated with the face-to-face format. In doing so, Roach was probably one of the earliest language testers to research reliability issues in speaking tests. He was particularly interested in how to describe levels of L2 speaking performance and how to standardise Oral Examiners so that they rate candidates in a fair and consistent manner – questions which continue to exercise language testers today. Roach's 1945 report *Some Problems of Oral Examinations in Modern Languages: An Experimental Approach Based on the Cambridge Examinations in English for Foreign Students* testifies to a keen understanding of the challenges facing those seeking to assess L2 speaking ability in a valid and reliable manner. Spolsky describes Roach's work as 'probably still one of the best treatments in print of the way that non-psychometric examiners attempted to ensure fairness in subjective traditional examinations, whether oral or written' (1995:108). Unbeknown to him, Roach laid the foundation for the research agenda which later emerged at Cambridge and which bore considerable fruit during the 1990s and 2000s. Milanovic and Saville (1996b) provided a useful overview of key variables that potentially impact on scoring validity and in doing so suggested a conceptual framework for setting out different avenues of research investigation. The nature and outcomes of Cambridge ESOL's research in speaking assessment over the past two decades (i.e. into the rating process, the development of rating criteria and scales, the training, standardisation and monitoring of raters) will be referred to in more detail below within the relevant sections of this chapter.

This is also the point in this volume where we move from exploring the *a priori* validation of speaking test tasks (in terms of their cognitive- and context-based validity at the largely pre-operational test design and development stages) to considering the *a posteriori* validation of speaking test tasks once they become operational and generate test scores. Thus in this chapter we shall look in greater detail at issues relating to assessment criteria and rating scales and we shall examine the rating process as a whole, from the recruitment, training and standardisation of the examiners without whom the direct testing of speaking cannot take place, through to the post-examination procedures and the reporting of scores to test takers and test users in a meaningful way. It is important to note that all of these aspects contribute in some way or other to scoring validity, and thus to the overall validation argument that is constructed in support of claims about the usefulness of test scores. If insufficient attention is paid to any one of these areas, then the risk of construct irrelevance increases and the validity argument is undermined. As Shaw and Weir astutely point out in *Examining Writing*: 'Faulty criteria or scales, unsuitable raters or procedures, lack of training and standardisation, poor or variable conditions for rating, inadequate provision for post exam statistical adjustment, and unsystematic or ill-conceived procedures for grading and awarding can all lead to a reduction in scoring validity and to the risk of construct irrelevant variance' (2007:143–4). Alderson, Clapham and Wall (1995:105) make a similar point about the need to invest comparable time and effort in ensuring the quality of test scoring as well as of test design and development. All examination boards offering speaking tests are under an obligation to demonstrate and justify the measures they take to reduce such risks and to optimise scoring validity. The publication of this volume forms part of that process of demonstration and justification.

Scoring validity parameters

In this section we begin by listing the individual parameters that can be regarded as relating to scoring validity. We then go on to survey briefly what the relevant literature has to say on each one, before examining how Cambridge ESOL deals with each parameter in practice.

Figure 5.1 Aspects of scoring validity for Speaking (adapted from Weir 2005a:46)

Perhaps the most obvious parameter for consideration under the superordinate heading of scoring validity is the *assessment criterion* (or more often criteria) and the associated *rating scale* (or scales). Several writers in the field have stressed the critical importance of the scales that are employed for assessing performance-oriented tasks such as those used in writing and speaking tests (Alderson, Clapham and Wall 1995, Bachman and Palmer 1996, McNamara 1996).

A second key parameter is the *rating process*. This concerns the nature of the decision making processes that operate when Oral Examiners assess test takers' spoken language performance. Shaw and Weir (2007:172) note the complex interaction that can take place between the writing examiner, the writing task and the written text that is generated by the test taker in response. A parallel interaction takes place in a speaking test between the Oral Examiner, the speaking test task and the spoken language performance generated by the test taker; indeed, as has already been noted in Chapter 4, the nature of this interaction becomes even more complex in cases where the Oral Examiner is directly implicated in the interaction (i.e. as an inter-locutor) and/or where there is more than one test taker (e.g. as in a paired or group format speaking test) (see pages 166–169 on why this is so). Closely linked to this parameter are the conditions under which the process of rating takes place. The conditions and circumstances under which a rater must make judgements about the quality of a test taker's spoken perform-ance can be affected by a number of factors, thus *rating conditions* may vary along a number of different dimensions, e.g. temporal, spatial, psychologi-cal, environmental. In the context of large-scale face-to-face assessment of speaking, some level of variation in test setting will be inevitable (e.g. size of room, nature of furniture, ambient temperature) since it is clearly impos-sible to replicate absolutely identical conditions and settings for all speak-ing test takers and examiners. However, features of the speaking test setting that relate to timing, or to room layout, or to the management of the test by the examiner all have the potential to impact on the rating process and on score reliability; they must therefore be controlled as consistently as possible through procedures that are carefully designed and rigorously implemented. Test producers clearly have an obligation to standardise the administra-tive requirements of their test so that the chance of systematic score vari-ability resulting from factors associated with the rating conditions can be minimised.

The parameter of *rater characteristics* has already been partially addressed in the latter part of Chapter 4 where the impact of interlocutor variables, especially the effect of the interviewer's language, was discussed in relation to context validity. Research was reported showing that in cases where an Oral Examiner functions as interlocutor–interviewer, personal background vari-ables, such as the interviewer's age, gender, cultural experience and expecta-tions, can combine with their linguistic behaviour to create an 'interlocutor effect'. Where the test taker's performance is rated during or after the test by a different Oral Examiner, then a different set of personal background variables (though not necessarily linguistic behaviour) can produce a compa-rable 'rater effect'. Like interlocutors, human raters are all individuals, each bringing their own set of personal attributes to the rating task.

McNamara (1996), for example, notes how individual rater characteristics can shape the way they interpret and apply the criteria and scale, the way they make judgements, their tendency to leniency or severity, and the consistency of their rating behaviour. The situation clearly becomes even more complex if the Oral Examiner assumes the dual role of interlocutor–interviewer <u>and</u>

rater, i.e. in addition to acting as interlocutor–interviewer to facilitate the test interaction, they simultaneously provide a rating for the spoken performance. As we shall see later, Cambridge ESOL pairs its Oral Examiners to provide ratings on test taker performance in slightly differing ways, according to whether they are fulfilling the role of an interlocutor during the test interaction or acting just as an observer.

Rater training is generally considered to be the mechanism by which the impact of individual rater differences, such as those mentioned above (and explored in depth in Chapter 4), can be mitigated to avoid construct irrelevant variance and to standardise the testing experience on grounds of consistency and equity. Much has been written over the years in the second language testing literature about the importance of rater training and standardisation, and this will be summarised below together with a detailed description and analysis of the Cambridge approach to Oral Examiner training for both interlocutors and raters.

Once the speaking test scores are available following the operational tests, a series of statistical checks can be made to identify any cause for concern in examiner performance for the session, either at the level of an individual examiner or a group of examiners. A process of *post examination adjustment* may be undertaken to ensure accuracy and fairness in the marking of this component, before *grading* takes place, first at the level of the individual skill component (i.e. the speaking test) and then at the level of the examination as a whole, in which all the skill components are combined to generate an overall grade for the examination for reporting purposes.

Assessment criteria and rating scales

We begin our detailed analysis of the scoring validity parameters for speaking tests by focusing on assessment criteria and rating scales, both in general and more specifically in the Cambridge ESOL context. We shall discuss different approaches to rating scale development that have been highlighted in the language testing literature. To conclude this section, we shall draw on the experience of Cambridge ESOL over recent years as the examination board has developed and validated criteria and rating scales for new speaking assessments and as it has researched and revised criteria and scales for its existing Speaking tests. Before embarking on our discussion of rating scales, it may just be helpful to note that some parts of the language testing community, e.g. in North America, employ the phrase 'scoring rubric' rather than rating scale. This can sometimes lead to confusion since the term 'rubric' in British English generally means the instructions given to test takers on the test paper or by an examiner, not the wording of descriptors used to assess their performance. For reasons of clarity we shall adopt the term 'rating scale' below.

Types of rating scale

At the outset it may be helpful to briefly note the various types of assessment criteria and rating scale that are typically used when assessing L2 speaking. Assessment criteria used to evaluate L2 spoken language performance generally fall into two main categories: global or holistic, and analytic or profile. A global or holistic approach seeks to evaluate the quality of performance in a unitary way, taking the performance as a whole into account and using a single rating scale in which each level descriptor provides an overall summary of performance quality that embraces multiple features; the global approach avoids breaking down the discrete qualities of a performance to report a single global score. An analytic or profile approach, on the other hand, seeks to separate out salient features of performance and to evaluate each one individually and independently on its own subscale; the analytic approach thus focuses attention on discrete qualities of performance, typically combining scores on the separate subscales to produce an overall score for speaking, and sometimes reporting the subscores as well to provide a richer level of score information, which can be useful for diagnostic purposes to guide future teaching/learning objectives. Although the global and analytic approaches are conceptually different, in reality they invariably overlap to some degree. Holistic rating scales often explicitly refer to those discrete features – such as lexical range, grammatical accuracy, and pronunciation – which are separated out as subscales in the analytic approach. These approaches are discussed more fully below with some comments on their relative advantages and disadvantages. (See also Luoma (2004) for an accessible discussion of rating scales with illustrative examples; see Fulcher (2003) for a detailed discussion of approaches to rating scale design and development.)

Holistic (or global) scoring

A holistic (or global) approach to scoring requires the rater to make an 'impressionistic assessment' of the quality of spoken language performance using a single rating scale (Davies, Brown, Elder, Hill, Lumley and McNamara 1999:75). It is commonly used in L2 speaking assessment and can be described as 'general impression marking' (Association of Language Testers in Europe (ALTE) 1998:147), in which the overall properties are more important than particular features of the performance. Examples of accessible and widely used holistic scoring scales for speaking include the ACTFL Proficiency Guidelines (American Council for the Teaching of Foreign Languages 1999) and the Test of Spoken English (TSE) scale (ETS 2001). The self-assessment grid based upon the Common Reference Levels of the CEFR (see Table 2 in Council of Europe 2001:26–27) also adopts a holistic approach for describing proficiency levels in spoken interaction and spoken production.

Several writers have commented on the relative advantages and disadvantages of this approach (Davies et al 1999, Hamp-Lyons 1991, Luoma 2004, Weir 1993). On the one hand, holistic scoring can be undertaken relatively quickly and it thus has an economic advantage, especially in large-scale testing operations where raters may need to rate large candidate volumes, or where multiple raters are assigned to rate each response. Holistic descriptors can also offer an intuitively accessible summary of skill levels, an approach that may be especially appropriate in the context of self-assessment (e.g. the English Language Portfolio) or by 'lay' or 'naïve' assessors, i.e. those who may need to make more informal judgements about a second language user's proficiency level but who are not themselves linguistic specialists. We might also argue that reading a written script or listening to a speech sample holistically is a more natural way of approaching it. On the other hand, holistic scoring offers a relatively blunt instrument, unable to credit or penalise the relative strengths and weaknesses that invariably characterise a performance. Since it generates a single overall score it can provide no diagnostic information that may be useful for corrective feedback in support of future learning. As far as speaking is concerned, Fulcher (2003) cautions that a single score may not do justice to its complexity. In addition, as Davies et al (1999) point out, in arriving at their judgements different raters may choose to focus on different performance features rather than share a common understanding. Weir (1993:164) makes the further point that global impression band descriptors lack empirical foundation and tend to be derived intuitively. In his 1993 PhD thesis Fulcher coined the phrase the 'armchair' approach to refer to this way of designing rating scales and the term is also used in his 2003 book. Since Weir's and Fulcher's comments in the early 1990s, however, greater efforts have been made within the language testing community to develop empirically based speaking scales, both global and analytic, and this will be discussed further below. For examples, see ffrench (2003b), Fulcher (2003) and Hasselgreen (1997), as well as the two case studies on rating scale development presented later in this chapter.

It is perhaps also worth noting one additional single-scale approach to scoring which can be found in performance assessment: primary trait scoring. Davies et al (1999), Hamp-Lyons (1991) and Weigle (2002) all mention primary trait scoring in the context of L2 writing assessment. According to this method a holistic score is awarded to a stretch of discourse in relation to one principal or main trait, i.e. to a specific feature of performance which is regarded as highly or most salient. In the case of writing, for example, the main trait could be structure or lexis, or it could be a criterial feature of a specific rhetorical task (Perkins 1983). The disadvantage of this approach is that it tends to be closely linked to a specific assessment task, thus the mark scheme is not readily generalisable for use with other tasks. This makes the approach more time-consuming and less flexible, especially in large-scale testing contexts, since a new mark scheme typically needs to be developed for each new test task. Although primary trait scoring is rarely found in the assessment of L2 speaking, it is nonetheless possible to envisage situations where such an approach might be appropriate; examples include a domain-specific speaking test in which the focus for assessment is performance quality on a single dominant criterion (e.g. the ability to adopt an appropriately sympathetic tone in a doctor–patient encounter), or formative assessment in a classroom context where the teacher is primarily interested in testing one particular dimension of spoken language ability as part of the teaching and learning cycle (e.g. turn-taking ability or pronunciation), while temporarily ignoring other dimensions.

Analytic (or profile) scoring

An analytic (or profile) scoring approach awards separate scores for each of a number of features of performance. Davies et al (1999:7) note that in speaking tests, 'commonly used categories are pronunciation or intelligibility, fluency, accuracy and appropriateness'. Examples of other sets of analytical criteria for speaking tests are: range, accuracy, fluency, interaction, coherence (Council of Europe 2001:28–29); grammatical resource, lexical resource, pronunciation, interactive communication, discourse management (University of Cambridge ESOL Examinations 2010a); grammatical range and accuracy, lexical resource, fluency and coherence, range and accuracy (International English Language Testing System (IELTS) 2009). One advantage of analytic scoring is that it can help to focus rater judgements more narrowly, thus contributing to rater agreement and rating reliability (Weir 1990); score reliability is also enhanced, of course, by virtue of having multiple observations. Furthermore, the analytic approach enables score reporting for diagnostic purposes, providing information on relative strengths and weaknesses. This can be especially valuable for second language learners whose spoken language performance may be characterised by an uneven, marked or 'jagged' score profile, reflecting differential development of their individual speaking sub-skills. The ability to report this level of differentiation through profiled scores may be helpful not only for teachers and students as part of formative learning; it may also assist other score users who need to ensure that particular speaking sub-skills are at an appropriate level for a certain role or context, e.g. command of pronunciation.

The advantages of analytic scoring are invariably countered by certain disadvantages. The first is that it assumes raters can reliably distinguish between specific sub-skills or performance features. Post-test analysis of scoring criteria often indicates that certain speaking criteria are strongly inter-correlated, suggesting that they are closely related, or even overlapping; they may not be functioning independently, and there may be different reasons why raters find it difficult to distinguish between them. Criteria may be conceptually inter-correlated, i.e. difficult to distinguish because the constructs overlap in some sense (e.g. Discourse Management and Interactive Communication). Or they may be inter-correlated as a result of unwelcome rater behaviour, e.g. a halo effect. Luoma (2004:80) highlights the potential impact on raters of the cognitive load if required to manage four or five criteria simultaneously and to make multiple judgements; referring to the guidance given in the Common European Framework (Council of Europe 2001:193), she suggests that five or six categories may be manageable but seven is a psychological upper limit.

One might argue, of course, that any decision on the number of criterial categories needs to take account of what *else* the rater is being asked to do during the testing event. Are they just acting as rater, and are their judgements being made in real-time, or not until after the event? Does the rater also have to participate in the speaking test, managing the test materials, acting as interlocutor, completing mark sheets – in which case there are additional cognitive demands being placed on them alongside the activity of rating? Thus any decision about the number of rating categories used and the frequency of judgement points a rater is asked to make cannot be taken in isolation; it needs to be considered alongside other aspects of the test that impact on overall cognitive load for the examiner(s) involved. As we shall see later on, awareness of the multiple sources relating to cognitive load has directly influenced Cambridge ESOL policy and practice in its Speaking tests.

In addition to the issue of cognitive load, some express concern that analytic scoring risks distorting and misrepresenting the process of evaluating L2 speaking performance, by focusing attention on specific discrete aspects that may divert from the overall communicative effect (Hughes 2003:103–4); indeed, it may well be that some of those discrete aspects are simply not salient at all points in the performance, or are not salient at all levels of the proficiency continuum. Furthermore, there is the question of how the subscores from several analytical subscales should be combined to create an overall global score for speaking. Should subscores be evenly weighted, contributing equally to the overall score? Or should their contribution to the overall score be differentially weighted or manipulated in some way, and on what basis? Finally, analytic scoring is generally recognised to be time-consuming and thus expensive, with obvious implications for large-scale assessment enterprises.

Just as we mentioned primary trait scoring under the broader heading of holistic scoring, since it uses a single scale, so we should note here the concept of multiple-trait scoring. This can be regarded as a form of analytic scoring in which the rater is required to focus on those criteria or traits that have been identified by a group of expert judges as most salient or relevant to a given task (Davies et al 1999:126). Once again, it is possible to envisage certain speaking test tasks as lending themselves more or less readily to certain assessment criteria; for example, the spoken performance elicited in an extended long turn can be evaluated for qualities of content coherence and discourse management, but the monologic nature of the spoken output may make it difficult to apply an interactive communication subscale to this part of the performance. Alderson (1981) also warned of the 'halo effect' that can occur among raters, i.e. a form of cross-contamination resulting from the tendency to give the same grade across categories. As we shall see below, a variant of the multiple-trait scoring approach can perhaps be detected in the Cambridge Speaking tests of the 1970s and 1980s.

Assessment criteria and types of rating scale: Cambridge ESOL practice

Despite almost a century of second language speaking assessment at Cambridge, information about early approaches to rating in the Cambridge Speaking tests is harder to uncover than details of the test content and format. While the archives contain some clues as to speaking tasks and topics, little information is available concerning assessment criteria or scoring methods (see Weir 2003 and Hawkey 2009 for detail on the historical development of the CPE and FCE Speaking tests). Though the exact nature of the speaking criteria and scales in the early decades remains uncertain, the CPE Regulations of 1933 tell us that 'the emphasis will be laid in the oral examination on correctness of pronunciation and intonation' (UCLES 1933:1). Phoneticians had been instrumental in the development of CPE since its inception and the study of phonetics was recommended as an aid to the acquisition of a good accent. Although the 3-hour phonetics paper had disappeared from CPE by 1932, an emphasis on pronunciation and intonation persisted in the examination. The 1958 *Instructions to Oral Examiners* note that a Proficiency candidate 'should know the pronunciation of any ordinary English word and should not have grossly foreign habits of speech. . .' (UCLES 1958:4). Interestingly, a proposal to reinstate a phonetics test in CPE in 1960 was postponed due to a lack of demand for it in test centres (see Weir and Vidakovic forthcoming).

From the mid-1970s onwards it appears that an analytical approach to rating was being adopted in the oral tests. An UCLES publication from 1973, relating to changes to CPE from 1975 onwards, refers to 'a series of oral tests separately assessing specific skills and aspects of performance' (UCLES 1973:4–5). It seems that criteria for assessing performance were also matched to specific test tasks as appropriate (a sort of primary or multiple trait approach); such criteria included vocabulary, grammar and structure, intonation, rhythm, stress and pronunciation, as well as the overall ability to communicate. Weir (2003:28–29) reports the CPE overall assessment scale for communication as having six levels or bands: *weak; inadequate; not quite adequate; adequate – satisfactory; good – very good; excellent.* A similar approach was apparently introduced for the Lower Certificate of English in 1975, when it was revised and renamed the First Certificate in English (see Hawkey 2009:42–44).

The 1984 revisions of CPE and FCE (see Weir 2003 and Hawkey 2009) maintained this trait-based approach to assessment in which relevant marking criteria and subscales were applied for each Speaking test task or sub-test, e.g. Picture Conversation (fluency, grammatical accuracy); Reading Passage (pronunciation – prosodic features, pronunciation – individual sounds); Structured Communication (interactive communication); Exercise (vocabulary resource). In most cases, a CPE or FCE candidate was interviewed by a single examiner, acting simultaneously as both interlocutor and assessor (i.e. simultaneously managing and rating the interaction). A paired or group format option for the test was also possible at this time, though it was rarely taken up; in the group format (and occasionally also in the paired format) two examiners would be present, one functioning as the interlocutor and the other as assessor, closer to the model used in the Cambridge ESOL tests today.

The assessment criteria currently used in the Cambridge Speaking tests are invariably shaped by the board's historical practices, though specification of the criteria can also be seen to have evolved over time. Hawkey (2009) notes over recent decades the increasingly detailed and explicit specification of the test construct underlying the Cambridge tests as a whole. This trend extended to the specification of assessment criteria and the development of rating scales, perhaps partly in response to the influence of the communicative movement in teaching and testing, which stressed the importance of evaluating functional ability to use language for meaningful purposes in social contexts. In turn, this required redeveloped scoring methods, whether holistic or analytic, that could incorporate communicative as well as purely linguistic features. At the same time, the development of corpus linguistics and the application of qualitative research methodologies (e.g. discourse analysis and conversation analysis) to spoken language data, including Speaking test data from interactive tests such as those offered by Cambridge, significantly improved our understanding of the nature and structure of both L1 and L2 spoken language. This influenced language test design at Cambridge, especially the assessment of L2 speaking. The advent of CAE in 1991 saw the introduction of the paired candidate format as mandatory in the Cambridge Speaking tests (rather than simply an alternative to the traditional singleton approach), partly in an attempt to elicit a broader sample of spoken language interaction. Van Lier (1989), among others, had highlighted the restricted nature of institutional talk such as occurs in interviews, including speaking tests. All CAE test candidates took a paired Speaking test, involving two examiners and two candidates (or three candidates in the case of an uneven number at the end of a test session). During the 1990s this paired format steadily became standard practice for most Cambridge ESOL Speaking tests, both for existing tests as they were revised (e.g. PET and FCE in 1996, CPE in 2002) and for new tests as they were introduced (e.g. BEC in 1993 and KET in 1994).

The paired candidate approach allows for the presence of two examiners who between them implement a combination of holistic and analytic scoring methods. In this scenario, one examiner – the interlocutor – facilitates and manages the discourse event throughout the speaking test, participating in the spoken interaction and rating each candidate holistically using a global scale (Global Achievement). The second examiner – the assessor – observes the speaking test interaction as it unfolds among the participants (candidates and interlocutor) but does not participate in the spoken interaction; this enables them to focus all their available attention on applying the analytic criteria to each candidate's spoken performance (e.g. Grammar and Vocabulary, Discourse Management, Interactive Communication, Pronunciation). Saville (2003:98) highlights the contribution to test fairness and reliability of having candidates assessed face-to-face by two independent examiners. Furthermore, though there exists an undoubted synergy between the analytical and the global scales, the use of differing yet complementary scales reflects the unique perspective each examiner has on the speaking test event, i.e. the assessor observes while the interlocutor is directly involved. This approach also takes into account the differing cognitive capacity each examiner has for making judgements during that event. The assessor can focus solely on making several analytical judgements for each candidate across the test as a whole; this may involve them in making anything from six to 15 judgements, depending on the level of the test and the number of criteria which apply, as well as on whether two or three candidates are being assessed simultaneously. The interlocutor, on the other hand, who must attend to the delivery of the paired test (managing the materials, controlling timing, etc.), makes only two overall impression judgements (or three in the case of a group), which are arrived at independently from the marks of the assessor.

Throughout the Speaking test, candidates are assessed on their language skills, not their personality, intelligence or knowledge of the world; we have already seen in Chapters 2, 3 and 4 how the examination board's detailed analysis and knowledge of the test taker population inform decisions about cognitive and contextual parameters relating to test content and format. Test takers must, however, be prepared to develop the conversation, where appropriate, and respond to the tasks set (see Appendix A for examples of speaking test tasks at each level). Candidates are assessed on their own individual performance and not in relation to one another (though see further discussion below on the inherent challenge of doing this in some parts of the test).

Depending upon the test level, the assessor awards marks on the following analytical criteria: Grammar and Vocabulary (separate scales for these operate at the CAE/C1 and CPE/C2 levels); Pronunciation; Interactive Communication; Discourse Management (not used at KET/A2). These assessment criteria have already been touched upon in Chapter 4 since they relate directly to the contextual parameters of Weighting and Known Criteria. Detailed explanations of the individual assessment criteria are provided in the relevant *Handbook for Teachers* published for each examination by the board, and the criterial definitions which follow are drawn from those that appeared in the PET–CPE Handbooks from 2007 and 2008.

Grammar and Vocabulary refers to the accurate and appropriate use of a range of grammatical forms and vocabulary. Performance is viewed in terms of the overall effectiveness of the language used in spoken interaction. At the lowest level (KET/A2), this criterion refers to the candidate's ability to use vocabulary, structure and paraphrase strategies to convey meaning. Here candidates are only expected to have limited linguistic resources and what is being assessed is success in using these limited resources to communicate a message, rather than range or accuracy. From PET/B1 level, however, this criterion includes range and accuracy of both grammatical forms and vocabulary. As we might expect, there exists a close relationship between the levels of syntactic and lexical control that are expected in KET, PET and FCE and the grammar and vocabulary specifications that were developed for the Council of Europe's Waystage, Threshold and Vantage Levels. At the CAE/C1 and CPE/C2 levels, Grammatical Resource is separated from Vocabulary (or Lexical) Resource to enable a more fine-grained evaluation at these higher proficiency levels (a decision prompted by a wide-ranging consultation with Oral Examiners, as reported in Green (2006a), and subsequently supported by positive feedback from Oral Examiners). Grammatical Resource refers to the appropriate use of a range of both simple and complex forms, including the accurate application of grammatical rules and the effective arrangement of words in utterances. At CPE level a wide range of forms should be used appropriately and competently. Vocabulary (or Lexical) Resource refers to the candidate's ability to use a range of vocabulary to meet task requirements. At CAE/C1, for example, the tasks require candidates to speculate and exchange views on unfamiliar topics, while at CPE/C2 level, the tasks require candidates to express precise meanings, attitudes and opinions, and to be able to convey abstract ideas. Test takers may lack specialised vocabulary when dealing with unfamiliar topics, but it should not, in general terms, be necessary to resort to simplification. To date, no grammar or vocabulary specifications have been available from the Council of Europe for the higher C levels to guide and shape expectations of syntactic and lexical control within assessment at these levels; however, the English Profile Programme (see Chapter 4 and also Green 2011 and Hawkins and Filipović 2011) promises to considerably expand our understanding of grammatical, lexical and functional performance at these levels and should help to inform more finely developed criteria and descriptors in the future.

Pronunciation refers to the candidate's ability to produce intelligible utterances to fulfil the task requirements. This includes stress, rhythm and intonation as well as individual sounds. Examiners put themselves in the position of the non-ESOL specialist and assess the overall impact of the pronunciation and the degree of effort required to understand the candidate. Different varieties of English, e.g. British, North American, Australian, are acceptable, and first language interference is expected and not penalised as long as it does not adversely affect communication. It is worth noting here that attitudes to pronunciation standards in teaching and assessment have changed significantly in recent years, thanks to codification of other regional varieties of English together with recognition of the growing numbers of second-language speakers using English as a *lingua franca*. Not surprisingly, the British English native-speaker criterion traditionally used in assessment has been robustly challenged and critiqued. Linguistic variation and diversity, naturally occurring phenomena that have perhaps most obvious in relation to pronunciation but which affect grammar, lexis and other linguistic features too, raise both theoretical and practical challenges for test designers and developers. The issues have been explored by various writers in the field over the past decade (see, for example, Canagarajah 2006, Davies, Hamp-Lyons and Kemp 2003, Elder and Davies 2006, Jenkins 2006, Lowenberg 2000). Several recent publications reflect upon the complex implications of linguistic variation for language testing (see Taylor 2006, 2008, 2009b); Taylor articulates a principled and pragmatic approach to setting language standards which can be adopted and implemented by large-scale, international assessment providers, such as Cambridge ESOL, as well as by smaller-scale, locally based testing agencies.

Discourse Management refers to the coherence, extent and relevance of each candidate's individual contribution, whether in monologue or dialogue. On this scale, the candidate's ability to maintain a coherent flow of language without undue hesitation is assessed, either within a single utterance or over a string of utterances. Also assessed here is how relevant the contributions are to what has gone before. Utterances should be relevant to the tasks and should be arranged logically to develop the themes or arguments required by the tasks, linked together to form coherent speech without undue hesitation. The Discourse Management criterion is applied from PET/B1 level upwards, since the tasks at KET/A2 level do not elicit sufficiently extended discourse for this criterion to be applied.

Interactive Communication refers to the candidate's ability to take part in the interaction appropriately using language to achieve meaningful communication. At lower levels, this includes initiating and responding, the ability to use interactive strategies to maintain or repair communication, and sensitivity to the norms of turn-taking. Candidates are given credit for being able to ask for repetition or clarification if necessary. At higher levels, this criterion refers to the candidate's ability to take a proactive part in the development of the discourse, participating in the range of interactive situations in the test and developing discussions on a range of topics by initiating and responding appropriately. It also refers to the deployment of strategies to maintain interaction at an appropriate level throughout the test so that the tasks can be fulfilled.

It is perhaps worth noting here the significant contribution made by discourse analytic studies of both L1 and L2 speech over the past two decades to our understanding of the structure and flow of spoken language, both monologic and dialogic. In particular, it is the application of conversation analysis to dialogic talk, and especially the talk occurring in paired speaking tests, which has helped improve our understanding of key interactional features such as turn-taking, topic development and use of feedback markers (see work by Galaczi 2008, Lazaraton 2002). This type of applied, qualitative research, often using data provided by Cambridge ESOL from its own live Speaking tests, has helped steadily refine definitions of the Discourse Management and Interactive Communication criteria, grounding them firmly in empirical evidence. The two case studies presented later in this chapter illustrate this process of empirical grounding.

Despite considerable sophistication nowadays in our specification and operationalisation of the speaking construct via assessment criteria and their associated scales, there remains one anomaly worth highlighting in relation to the Interactive Communication criteria: it concerns the requirement, mentioned above, that examiners should assess candidates on their own individual performance and not in relation to one another. This raises the interesting question of whether individual or shared scores for interactional competence should be awarded to test takers. According to traditional practice, raters assign each individual test taker their own individual scores, or set of scores, which they can then carry away with them from the testing event, as exemplified in the Cambridge Speaking tests. However, given the inherently co-constructed nature of paired interaction, one wonders how feasible it might be to consider awarding a shared score, at least for Interactive Communication, as a more authentic approach (May 2009, Nakatsuhara 2009, Taylor and Wigglesworth 2009). There undoubtedly remains scope for further research in this area.

The Global Achievement criterion relates holistically to the candidate's performance overall across the test. It is an independent impression mark reflecting the assessment of the candidate's performance from the interlocutor's perspective.

The Cambridge Speaking tests typically involve test mark bands available for each criterion scale, labelled 0, 1.0, 1.5, 2.0, 2.5, 3.0, 3.5, 4.0, 4.5 and 5.0.

In addition, verbal descriptors are attached to the bands of 1.0, 3.0 and 5.0. The band of 3.0 is seen to represent adequacy at a given level; 5.0 represents top of the range and 1.0 is seen as an inadequate performance. A mark of 0 can be awarded if a candidate fails to provide sufficient language for assessment. ffrench (2003b:415) reports how internal trialling with Cambridge's Oral Examiners during the 1990s suggested that verbal descriptors for three of the nine bands across the scales was sufficient to provide them with the information required to make their judgements. Candidates' performance may fit the exact wording of a descriptor, but often a performance may have elements of the description attached to the 5.0 band and also elements that are reflected in the wording of the 3.0 band. The Oral Examiner's judgement is based on the degree to which the performance fits the descriptors. Both assessor and interlocutor assign their marks for performance across the test as a whole, rather than for individual tasks or test parts. As noted above, this approach has a pragmatic dimension to it, taking into account the real-time cognitive demands on both examiners during the Speaking test. It would be an attractive prospect to ask examiners to award marks on each of the criteria for individual tasks (rather than across the test as a whole) as this might provide a more fine-grained evaluation with the potential for valuable diagnostic score reporting. The disadvantage, however, is that it would involve each examiner in making and recording many more judgements during the testing event. At the higher proficiency levels the interlocutor might have to make and accurately record up to eight judgements (e.g. 1 criterion x 4 tasks x 2 candidates – rising to 12 in a group test), but the assessor could have as many as 40 judgements to make (4 criteria x 4 tasks x 2 candidates – rising to 56 for a group of three). A more practical alternative to this somewhat unrealistic scenario might be to return to a more trait-based approach such as that which used to exist in the Cambridge Speaking tests, in which individual tasks or test parts attract marks on specific criteria, thus reducing the total number of judgements that need to be made within a constrained timeframe. The challenge posed by this approach, however, would lie in identifying (and justifying) precisely which assessment criteria are best matched to which tasks or test parts, and then in training examiners to attend to certain criteria for some tasks but to disregard them for other parts of the test. We might also argue that such a discrete, highly atomistic approach to the assessment of speaking moves us further away from an underlying construct of L2 speaking as a composite and holistic, albeit multifaceted, ability trait. Furthermore, the shorter speech samples elicited via each individual task or test part may not in fact constitute an adequate basis for a valid and reliable evaluation of some criteria. While the use of test parts involves potential caveats in operational test conditions, test parts can be successfully used during rater training and standardisation, as will be seen later in the chapter. Once again, there exists scope for future research to explore how a more fine-grained evaluation of test taker performance on individual tasks might be achieved, one that provides an evaluation which remains sufficiently valid and reliable to provide meaningful diagnostic feedback.

The final mark for the Speaking test is achieved by combining the assessor's analytical scores with the interlocutor's global score to produce a weighted average, which in turn contributes to the overall score for the examination as a whole when combined with scores from the Reading, Listening, Writing and Use of English components. Within this process, the interlocutor's score is weighted relative to the number of subscales by the assessor so that it makes a more balanced contribution to the overall score when combined with the assessor's marks.

Exemplar performances to benchmark the standard

As we have seen, assessment criteria and rating scales are normally laid down on paper (usually in the form of linguistic features and numerical or alphabetic bands/grades, often accompanied by verbal descriptors) to be applied and internalised by raters. However, it is perhaps important to note at this point that, no matter how comprehensive or transparent the wording of assessment criteria and rating descriptors are, criteria and scales in their written form alone are unlikely to be able to fully capture and communicate the standard or level of performance they seek to describe. Wolf (1995) highlights the importance of using students' work to communicate standards. In relation to writing assessment, Shaw and Weir comment as follows:

> . . .it is questionable whether any mark scheme can wholly capture the definition of a level in a way that examiners could reliably and consistently apply. The definition of a level is not captured merely on paper, but rather through the process of examiner training and standardisation. It depends crucially on exemplar scripts, that is, those scripts which have been identified as exemplifying the level by experienced examiners. Standards are, in this way, communicated by exemplar scripts (2007:146–147).

Writing assessment criteria, however transparent and clearly defined, and written level descriptors, however comprehensive and empirically based, are thus insufficient on their own to convey the standard; they need to be 'embodied', incarnated as some sort of concrete reality rather than simply defined in abstract isolation. The same, of course, is true for speaking assessment, as Jack Roach was keenly aware in the 1940s; so much so, in fact, that as early as 1944 Cambridge was using gramophone records of previous oral tests as examiner standardisation materials to ensure continuity of standard from one oral examination to the next. In the case of Speaking tests it is exemplar oral performances (rather than scripts) that supplement the criteria and scale descriptors to provide an 'embodied' benchmark, i.e. a benchmark which is not simply a verbal description on paper but which is also physically represented in interaction shown in film; such exemplar performances are essential in the process of examiner training and standardisation, as we shall see later in this chapter. As technology advanced down the years, so the gramophone records used for examiner training at Cambridge in the 1940s were superseded by the oral standardisation videos of the 1980s; these have in turn been replaced more recently by standardisation DVDs and, in the present day, by increasing amounts of benchmarking material made available to examiners online.

Exemplar performances can also be invaluable for communicating to test users what a test grade or level means, i.e. assisting with the process of score interpretation. It is precisely for this reason that Cambridge ESOL makes available on its website a set of video clips featuring the performance of students taking the Speaking test section of Cambridge ESOL exams at the following CEFR levels (KET/A2, PET/B1, FCE/B2, CAE/C1 and CPE/C2). Each video clip has been carefully selected to represent and demonstrate a typical performance (of at least one student) at that level. Accompanying each video clip is a commentary describing the performance and the test scores in light of the relevant assessment criteria and rating scales; the commentary also helps to explain how the elements of that particular performance make it typical of a particular CEFR level. All the video examples are drawn from materials collected and developed as calibrated samples for use by Cambridge ESOL in the standardisation of its speaking examiners. In addition, the website page provides a link to a document outlining how the video clips were selected and the processes of data analysis, verification and calibration that enabled identification of them as typical of the stated levels (see Galaczi and Khalifa 2009b for an account of this project). This documentation not only provides evidence for validity claims about the level assignment of the spoken performances but it also helps to explain the methodology of the data collection and analysis for the benefit of researchers and others interested in undertaking similar procedures.

Rating scale development

Rating scale development is acknowledged to be a complex process as several writers in the field have attested (Brindley 1998, Fulcher 2003, North 2000). The aim is to describe what learners can do and how well they can do it so that a sample of performance can be matched to a verbal description, usually according to a principle of 'best fit'. Davies et al (1999:153–4) define a rating scale as follows:

> A scale for the description of language proficiency consisting of a series of constructed levels against which a language learner's performance is judged. Like a test, a proficiency (rating) scale provides an operational definition of a linguistic construct such as proficiency. [. . .] The levels or bands are commonly characterised in terms of what subjects can do with the language (tasks and functions which can be performed) and their mastery of linguistic features (such as vocabulary, syntax, fluency and cohesion). [. . .] Scales are descriptions of groups of typically occurring behaviours.

The method is premised on a criterion-referenced approach to measurement and we have noted above the value of providing clear exemplification of the criterion by means of exemplar performances. For our purposes, it is worth noticing in the above definition the phrase 'a series of constructed levels', for this highlights the extent to which any rating scale is artificially constructed, shaped both by an underlying linguistic construct and the intended function of the scale. It is worth drawing a distinction here between scales that are designed for the purpose of rating and other scales which may look like rating instruments but which are actually designed with a different purpose and audience in mind. Alderson (1991) provides a well-reasoned and conceptually accessible discussion of the nature of different scales, the principles and practice of scale development and the various challenges associated with scale construction. His categorisation of scales into three main types – user-oriented, constructor-oriented and assessor-oriented (or rater-oriented) remains a useful heuristic because it reminds us that scales can be designed for different audiences and purposes, offering different kinds of statements about student ability. Chapters 1 and 4 in this volume provide several examples of user-oriented and constructor-oriented scales. A user-oriented scale is designed to communicate information about typical or likely test taker behaviours at a given level, while a constructor-oriented scale guides test writers in their choice of tasks to include in a test. In this chapter, our focus is firmly upon assessor-oriented scales which 'guide the rating process, focusing on the quality of performance expected' (Fulcher 2003:89).

Shohamy (1996) and Luoma (2004) comment on how rating scales may or may not be derived from well-developed theoretical models of language ability. Shohamy discusses the 'theory-free' language tests of the 1980s in which it was the performance tasks and rating scales that came to articulate the construct: 'Describing language in behavioural/functional terms rather than implicational terms was easy to comprehend' (Shohamy 1996:145–146). In a similar way, Luoma categorises some rating scales as 'behavioural' and others as 'theory-derived' (Luoma 2004:67). Behavioural scales, suggests Luoma, tend to describe different types of task handled by learners at different levels along with some indication of how well they do this. Both Shohamy and Luoma cite the ACTFL Speaking scale as an example of this.

Theory-derived scales, on the other hand, are generally derived from a model of communicative competence and refer to language skills and describe degrees of ability without close reference to tasks or situations, and Luoma cites the TSE scale as an example of this approach.

Traditionally, the design and construction of rating scales for direct tests of speaking ability depended upon an *a priori* approach, in which assessment criteria and rating scale descriptors are developed by 'experts' (i.e. teachers, applied linguists and language testers) using their own experience and intuitive judgement, either individually or in committee (i.e. adopting the 'armchair' approach (Fulcher 2003)). McNamara (1996) suggests that rating scale development was also strongly influenced by original assumptions underlying the construction in the 1950s of the first scale for the Foreign Service Institute's (FSI) Oral Proficiency Interview (OPI). In the 1990s, however, writers in our field advocated a more empirically based approach to rating scale construction (Fulcher 1996, Milanovic, Saville, Pollitt and Cook 1996, Shohamy 1990, Upshur and Turner 1995). McNamara called for more research into the validation of rating scales on the grounds that scales are 'central to the construct validity of the instruments with which they are associated' (1996:212). An empirically based approach involves analysing samples of actual language performance in order to construct (or reconstruct) criteria and rating scale descriptors; it also involves investigating the way these are likely to be interpreted and applied by human raters. Fulcher (2003) helpfully discusses these two basic approaches to rating scale development, i.e. intuitive and empirical, illustrating the different methods with real-world examples, including database-based, data-driven scales (Fulcher 1996), empirically derived, binary choice, boundary definition scales (Upshur and Turner 1995) and scaling descriptors (North 2000). More recently, in association with scale development for the Common European Framework of Reference (CEFR), the value of a mixed-methods empirical approach has been recognised, in which both qualitative and quantitative methods make a complementary contribution to rating scale development (Council of Europe 2001). Quantitative methods rely on statistical analyses and the careful interpretation of results, while qualitative methods involve interpretation of the information obtained. Work on the CEFR also highlighted the importance of several practical features when developing scale descriptors: positiveness; definiteness and clarity; independence; and brevity. We shall return to these features later in the chapter (e.g. see the two case studies) since they can impact directly on the rating process itself, particularly the extent to which raters can successfully interpret and apply the scale. Interestingly, on the question of brevity, Luoma (2004:68) critiques the ACTFL scale for its long and detailed verbal descriptors, which she speculates must be difficult for raters to internalise; however, she believes it brought advantages to teachers and learners when it was introduced in 1986 through its focus on language in use (rather than simply language knowledge).

Rating scale development: Cambridge ESOL practice

Having examined the general issues surrounding the development of criteria and rating scales for assessing L2 speaking, this section describes and discusses work conducted by Cambridge ESOL over the past 20 years to develop the assessment criteria and rating scales for the Speaking tests offered by the examination board.

In practice it is rarely possible for an examination board to begin the task of rating scale development with a blank sheet of paper; this is usually only the case when developing a brand new test which stands in isolation from all other assessment measures. Even in the case of new test development, it may be that the new test must sit alongside existing tests within a larger framework of reference, e.g. a suite of tests covering the proficiency continuum, such as the Cambridge Main Suite tests. As a result, a new test may need to take on a 'family resemblance' and share pre-existing delivery systems, such as the examiner cadre or processing procedures. This practical reality is likely to affect decisions about the assessment criteria and rating scales as well as test content and format. This was certainly the case for Cambridge in the 1990s when developing the CAE and KET examinations which were specifically designed to fit alongside their older siblings CPE, FCE and PET in order to provide an ordered and accessible 'ladder' that supported English language learning and certification. There are also advantages, of course, to adopting tried and trusted approaches in this area, drawing on existing knowledge and previous experience rather than reinventing the wheel.

With the growth during the 1990s of additional Cambridge Speaking tests targeted at different proficiency levels came the opportunity to develop a Common Scale for Speaking (see Chapter 1, page 26) which sought to standardise the assessment criteria across the tests and to articulate as clearly as possible for Oral Examiner training explanation of the terms and guidance on how to apply the criteria. At the same time, Cambridge ESOL was actively responding to calls from the academic assessment community, as discussed above, for more attention to be paid to the empirical development and validation of assessment scales prior to live use. The examination board has been committed to such research and validation work in this area since the early 1990s, as evidenced by the use of Rasch analysis in developing the rating scales for the Cambridge Assessment of Spoken English (CASE), an exploratory prototype speaking test (see Lazaraton 2002, Milanovic, Saville, Pollitt and Cook 1996). Angela ffrench's Chapter in Weir and Milanovic (2003) provides further evidence of this trend in her comprehensive account of how the CPE revision project during the late 1990s used both operational feedback and statistical analyses to redevelop the examination's assessment criteria and rating scales (see in particular pages 414–445, and also Appendices 7.5–7.11 to that chapter).

Two more recent case studies from the past decade are presented here to illustrate the complex enterprise of rating scale development and the many phases and processes which constitute such an endeavour for an examination board.

Case Study 1 describes the revision in 2006–08 of the Main Suite and BEC rating scales for Speaking, which entail both global and analytic criteria and scales. Case Study 2 overviews an earlier project to revise the IELTS Speaking test in 2001, in which the previous holistic approach was replaced by an analytic approach. The summaries of these case studies demonstrate the extent to which rating scale development requires careful planning and sound project management, involving the examination board in iterative cycles of design, review, revision and research over a significant time frame (2–3 years). They show how outcomes from previous research were combined with insights from expert judgement and findings from analyses of actual candidate performance, test scores and rater experience. They also emphasise the point that developing or revising criteria and rating scales entails far more than just addressing these elements in isolation from the rest of the test format and its delivery system. Finally, the case studies highlight the extensive stakeholder consultation which should form part of any development and revision process, with the rater cadre, not surprisingly, at the forefront.

Case Study 1: Revising the Main Suite and BEC rating scales for Speaking (2006–08)

Background

The extensive revision of the CPE examination in December 2002 was an opportunity to introduce updated assessment scales for all the Main Suite and BEC Speaking tests as part of a move towards greater coherence and harmonisation across the Speaking tests. It was agreed, however, that a further review would take place once the new criteria had been used in live conditions. The review of the FCE and CAE examinations instigated in the mid 2000s provided just such an opportunity to do this (see Hawkey 2009 for a full account of the FCE/CAE review project). The 2006–08 project to review and revise the Main Suite/BEC rating scales for Speaking followed the tradition of *a priori* validation in performance assessment as recommended within the literature and among the wider assessment community (for a more detailed discussion see Galaczi, ffrench, Hubbard and Green in press).

The 2002 assessment scales for Speaking

The revised assessment scales for Speaking introduced in 2002 followed a generic model, where the descriptors at each level were written in a similar way, but were interpreted at the level of the examination (see ffrench 2003a). At each level, 10 marks were available (0; 1.0; 1.5; 2.0; 2.5; 3.0; 3.5; 4.0; 4.5; 5.0), and descriptors were provided for Bands 1.0, 3.0 and 5.0. While examiners found these easy to use, analysis of data from live examinations from 2002 onwards showed that little use was being made of the 5 marks available from 0 to 2.5, thus truncating the 10 point scale. The descriptors of the 2002 scales included negative statements in all bands at all levels, and it was felt that this contributed to the under-use of marks 0 to 2.5. As a result, it was agreed to revise the criteria.

Using the CEFR 2001 as a starting point, the following guidelines were adopted to develop refined descriptors:

- *Positiveness* – Positive formulation of descriptors should be attempted, given that levels of proficiency are to serve as objectives rather than just an instrument for screening candidates.

- *Definiteness and Clarity* – Vague descriptors should be avoided since they can mask the fact that raters are interpreting them differently, which makes the ratings less reliable. As far as possible, the descriptors should refer to concrete degrees of skill, i.e. what a candidate can be expected to do at a given level. To assist with making descriptors definite, concrete and transparent, a glossary of terms should be introduced which defined each concept in specific terms with relevant examples.

- *Brevity* – Research has consistently shown that short descriptors are to be preferred to longer ones (see Appendix A of the CEFR 2001) and that a descriptor which is longer than a two clause sentence cannot realistically be referred to during the assessment process. An attempt should be made, therefore, to produce short, succinct descriptors.

- *Independence* – Each descriptor should have meaning without reference to any other descriptors, so that each would be an independent criterion.

Revising the 2002 assessment scales for Speaking

In line with contemporary thinking in the literature advocating an empirically based approach to rating scale construction (Council of Europe 2001, Fulcher 1996, Shohamy 1990, Upshur and Turner 1995), several scale development methodologies were followed in the design of the revised MS and BEC assessment scales: intuitive, qualitative and quantitative methods. The full methodology supporting the revision project took place in three phases, as outlined below.

Intuitive phase (January – March 2006)

- Reports from external experts, which included reviews of current ESOL practice in the light of the literature and the experts' experience.
- Review of the reports by internal staff and an external reviewer and the setting out of design principles for the revised assessment scales.
- Production of Draft 1 descriptors.

Qualitative phase (May – September 2006)

- A scaling exercise, which involved a rank ordering of the descriptors.
- A verbal protocol trial, which involved raters' perception of the descriptors while rating performances.
- An analysis of test performances at PET and FCE level by an external expert using a Conversation Analysis methodology. The aim was to identify discourse features associated with differently ranked performances and thus review the extent to which such features were captured by the scales.
- Production of Draft 2 descriptors.

Quantitative phase (October 2006 – April 2007)

- Setting of 'Gold Standard' marks. This involved using the revised criteria to assess performances on existing standardisation videos so that the marks could be used to standardise raters who would be involved in the marking of new standardisation videos.
- Further extended trial to confirm the soundness of the scaler prior to the live roll out.

In addition to the design principles outlined above, the descriptors for each level were mapped on to a common scale, so that, for example, the descriptors at A2 Band 5 were identical to those at B1 Band 3 and B2 Band 1. This was felt to be important since it suggested some rough equivalencies between different bands for different levels. There were, however, deviations from the 'stacking up' of levels: the descriptors for Pronunciation at Levels C1 and C2 were identical, in line with current thinking on the assessment of Pronunciation (CEFR, Phonological Control Scale) and the descriptors for Grammar and Vocabulary were worded somewhat differently in the transition from B2 to C1, since at C1 they were divided into two separate assessment criteria ('Grammar/Vocabulary' at A2–B2 and 'Grammatical Resource' and 'Lexical Resource' at C1–C2).

The rest of this case study overview highlights some of the research undertaken to inform the drafting of the analytical descriptors, namely the scaling of the descriptors, the verbal protocol study and the final extended trial.

Research study 1: Scaling of the descriptors

In order to explore the validity of the revised descriptors, draft descriptors were distributed to 31 speaking examiners, who were divided into four groups. The participants were selected so that they represented all the levels in the speaking examiner cadre: Senior Team Leaders, Regional Team Leaders, Team Leaders and speaking examiners. It was felt important that the participating examiners should bring with them different levels of expertise and experience and so provide a more representative view on the revised descriptors. Each descriptor was sub-divided into different aspects of a sub-scale: altogether 64 sub-descriptors were identified.

Each group received a set of 20 of the 64 new descriptors and each participant was asked to match the descriptors to a test level on the Cambridge ESOL Common Scale (provided in Chapter 1). The relative 'difficulty' of the descriptors, based on examiner ratings, was estimated through FACETS (Linacre 2006). The examiner ratings were then compared to the levels intended by the scale developers. In addition, the consistency in the performance of examiners was investigated since lack of consistency might suggest difficulties in the interpretation of the descriptors.

Encouragingly for the validity of the revised scale, there was broad agreement between intended levels and examiner ratings. Descriptors placed at A1 by the developers were generally rated as the easiest by the examiners, and those placed at C2 were generally rated as the most difficult. There was some evidence that examiners were unwilling to use the extreme points of the scale with ratings clustering in the B1 to C1 range. In some cases the rank ordering did not match the anticipated level and in such cases the wording of the descriptors was looked into and revisited.

In terms of rater severity, the range fell between -2.41 and +2.58 logits. There was a significant (p<.01, reliability of separation =.91) difference in harshness of examiners. This finding was in line with the available literature on performance assessment which indicates that rater variability is an inevitable part of the rating process and, as McNamara (1996:127) notes, 'a fact of life'. The results also indicated generally high levels of agreement between the raters involved shown in the high point biserial correlations between the ratings made by each single examiner and by the rest of the examiners. The lowest point biserial correlation was at .63, which nonetheless suggested an acceptable level of agreement between this individual's ratings and those of the other examiners.

In summary, this exercise showed that examiners were able to rank the draft descriptors in much the same order as intended by the scale developers. However, it was felt that there was a need to address through training the use of the full range of the scale since the consensus view of the descriptors resulted in a narrower clustering than was intended. There were also a number of issues of wording and clarification raised by the exercise which pointed to a need for rewording or careful exemplification of some of the descriptors in the glossary which accompanied the new scales.

Research study 2: Verbal protocol study

The guiding question in this study was, 'What do raters pay attention to when using the revised descriptors?' Similar to the study reported above, the participants ranged in terms of experience and expertise. Eight raters were asked to use the draft descriptors and award marks to a set of standardisation videos. In addition, they were asked to fill in a questionnaire which invited their comments on the usefulness of the revised descriptors and their experience of using them. In general, the comments focused on four themes:

– The greater specificity, transparency, brevity and clarity of most of the descriptors

'More concise; it's easier to see the main points.'

'Clear and succinct.'

'Tight, objective language of the descriptors is very welcome.'

'It is clearer what is expected at each band of each level, with less subjective interpretation.'

– The need for greater clarity with some of the descriptors

'What constitutes "a good degree of control", "limited control"?'

'The "range" aspect was quite difficult to judge.'

– The greater ease of processing and applying the descriptors

'Much easier to process when marking.'

'Easier to apply perhaps just because they aren't quite so wordy.'

– The use of positively worded descriptors

'I'm all in favour of positive statements at all levels – it is a matter of mindset.'

'The greater emphasis on positive achievement is welcome. One is encouraged to concentrate on what the candidate is capable of.'

The extended feedback received from the participants was a very rich source of information which informed the further revision of the descriptors for each criterion.

Research study 3: Marking trial

After the descriptors were finalised a large-scale trial was carried out in order to investigate the consistency and level of agreement of raters using them. The general aim was to confirm the soundness of the revised assessment scales prior to their being used in live conditions. In other words, it was important to provide evidence of the extent to which the assessment categories worked consistently at the five levels under investigation in terms of examiner severity, examiner agreement and misfit.

A total of 28 raters participated in this study, divided into seven groups. The raters provided a spread in terms of experience and position within the Cambridge ESOL speaking examiner framework. In terms of location, most of the raters were based in Europe (in 10 countries), one in Asia and one in Latin America.

A total of 48 test performances were rated, divided into five levels and eight exams: A2 (KET), B1 (PET and BEC Preliminary), B2 (FCE and BEC Vantage), C1 (CAE and BEC Higher), and C2 (CPE). The examinees had volunteered to participate in 'mock' Speaking tests and had given consent to be video recorded. Recordings took place at centres in the UK and Greece.

Each group of raters viewed a selection of test performances at different levels. The groups were constructed to ensure overlap between raters, levels and examinees. Multi-Faceted Rasch measurement (MFRM) was used as the method of analysis.

The findings indicated that there were different levels of rater severity. However, taking account of the view that rater variability is an inevitable part of the rating process, the important issue is how pronounced the differences in rater severity are. If the differences fall within acceptable parameters, this would indicate that the raters are interpreting the scales in similar ways and, by extension, that the scales are performing at an acceptable level. For practical purposes, Van Moere (2006) provides a range of -1.00 and +1.00 logits as being useful cutting-off points of severity range. Applying these standards to the marks awarded in this trial, the majority of raters were found to be within acceptable parameters for harshness/leniency, indicating that they were following the expected standards and rating as a homogenous group. In addition, the majority of raters were internally consistent. Only two examiners gave cause for concern because they were consistently too harsh and 'noisy' (i.e. showed too much unpredictability in their scores). The acceptable range of examiner severity and levels of consistency for the majority of raters in this trial was seen as providing validity evidence for the revised assessment scales for speaking.

Conclusion

The new set of assessment scales for Speaking for Main Suite and BEC examinations was introduced in live conditions in December 2008. As this case study summary shows, a great deal of time and effort was devoted to the *a priori* development and validation of the new scales. The triangulation of different methodologies (expert judgement, qualitative and quantitative studies) engendered confidence in the scales and provided encouraging validity evidence for their subsequent use. Implementation of the new scales has been followed up with research and validation activity to monitor their performance and to identify any additional issues arising that may need to form part of a future revision (Chambers 2010, Galaczi 2010a).

Case Study 2: Revising the IELTS Speaking test criteria and scales (1998–2001)

Background

A major revision of the International English Language Testing System (IELTS) in 1995 left the Speaking Module unchanged for various reasons. At that time, there was no clear consensus on the approach to take; a number of research studies were in progress, some under the auspices of the IELTS grant-funded research programme, and the findings of these were still awaited. Furthermore, revising a face-to-face speaking test is an especially complex matter, involving not only re-design of the test format, re-development of assessment criteria, revision of rating scales, re-drafting of performance descriptors, and re-engineering of delivery and processing systems, but also the re-training and re-standardisation of the worldwide examiner cadre in readiness for the revised test becoming live. It thus requires careful planning and management as well as considerable resources.

A project to revise the IELTS Speaking Module began in 1998 with identification of the issues that needed addressing. This was informed by a number of sources:

- a review of the routinely collected candidate score and test performance data for the operational IELTS Speaking test
- a review of theoretical and empirical studies on the test conducted between 1992 and 1998 (e.g. Brown and Hill 1998/2007, Ingram and Wylie 1993, Merrylees and McDowell 1999/2007)
- a review of other research into speaking assessment, together with work on speaking test design for the other Cambridge ESOL tests (see Lazaraton 2002).

The project set out to revise (among other aspects of the test) the approach to assessment to ensure that the IELTS band-level descriptors matched more closely the spoken output of candidates in relation to specified tasks and that raters could apply these in a more standardised and reliable manner. Attention focused on several key areas:

- the salient/non-salient features of spoken performance for assessment purposes
- the nature of the rating scale/s (holistic or analytic? which criteria, and how many?)
- the behaviour of raters.

Phase 1: Consultation, initial planning and design (May–December 1998)

Some initial investigative work was commissioned in June 1998 from specialists in the field of oral proficiency assessment: Alan Tonkyn of Reading University, UK, reported on his own study of grammatical, lexical and fluency features of IELTS candidates' oral proficiency at different bands, including the rater perspective (Tonkyn 1998, Tonkyn and Wilson 2004). Anne Lazaraton reported on discourse features observed during her transcription analysis of 20 IELTS Speaking tests (using conversation analysis (CA) methodology), ranging from Bands 3 to 7 (Lazaraton 1998). This work, together with findings from earlier studies, raised the question of how well the existing holistic IELTS rating scale and its verbal descriptors were able to articulate key features of performance at different levels or bands. It was felt that a clearer specification of performance features at different proficiency levels might enhance standardisation of assessment. For this reason, the Project Working Party, which included specialists in speaking assessment and also active IELTS raters, reviewed the test specifications and rating scale descriptors to abstract the key analytical criteria and to develop working definitions; they then deconstructed the existing holistic scale into several analytical subscales for more detailed investigation, deciding finally on four subscales: pronunciation, fluency, grammatical range and accuracy, and lexical resource. A maximum of four analytical scales was felt to be manageable given that each IELTS examiner also has to conduct the face-to-face interview, managing the test and being an interlocutor/facilitator as well as providing an assessment.

Phase 2: Development (January–September 1999)

In May 1999 the Draft 1 assessment criteria and four rating subscales were applied to a subset of four audio-recorded test performances gathered in Australia during trialling of the prototype for the revised test format. (See

Taylor 2001a, 2001b and 2007 for discussion of revisions to the IELTS Speaking test format.) When applying the draft descriptors to these samples using the revised test format, careful attention was paid to features of candidate performance which distinguished the critical boundaries of Band 5/6 and Band 6/7, i.e. the central section of the Band 1–9 proficiency scale, and the Bands which are most frequently used for decision-making purposes. This exercise led to production of second draft assessment criteria and rating subscales. Draft 2 was trialled in a similar way in July 1999, but using a new set of four audio-recordings, and further minor adjustments were made to some rating scale descriptors. At this point the Draft 3 assessment criteria and rating scales were considered ready for larger scale trialling.

Phase 3: Validation (October 1999 – September 2000)

This phase focused on setting up an experimental study to investigate the way the assessment criteria and scales were functioning. The research design involved gathering a sample of video performances using the revised IELTS test format and then arranging for each of these performances to be rated by several experienced IELTS examiners. The video-rating was preferred over the audio-rating option on the grounds that it approximated more closely to the actual IELTS rating experience. In addition, though the literature on the issue is not conclusive, there exists some research evidence suggesting that examiners may rate audio-performances more harshly (Ingram 1984, Lowe 1978, McNamara 1990). For practical reasons, multiple rating of live performances was not an option. A total of 29 video performances were filmed in the UK and Australia, using a range of materials (in revised test format), proficiency levels, first languages and IELTS examiners, to ensure as representative a sample as possible of the conditions that exist with the operational test. From these a dataset of 20 performances was selected for the multiple rating exercise. The subjects included 10 male and 10 female candidates, represented 15 different L1s and ranged in proficiency level from Band 3 to Band 8 on the IELTS scale. Candidates scoring below Band 3 or above Band 8 rarely appear in the live test so were not included in the study.

The 20 performances were rated under controlled, on-site conditions by two teams of experienced IELTS examiners – a team of four in the UK and a team of nine in Australia. Using the Draft 3 assessment criteria and rating subscales, they provided entirely independent ratings; any group discussion which took place immediately after rating was audio-recorded for future reference. Data for analysis therefore included both score data for the 20 candidates and retrospective feedback from the raters themselves.

In line with Lynch and McNamara's (1998) advice that generalisability theory and multi-faceted Rasch measurement offer complementary approaches that provide useful information for developers of performance assessments, the candidate score data was analysed using generalisability theory (GENOVA) and multi-faceted Rasch measurement (FACETS) analysis programs to investigate several research questions, as outlined below (Jones 2000b).

1. *Do the four subscales measure distinct aspects of speaking ability?*

   Pronunciation was a distinct trait, correlating most weakly with the other scales. The three other scales appear to be more closely related, with the grammatical and lexical scales being the closest, as might be expected:

Table 5.1 Correlations between the four subscales Pearson correlations

	Fluency	Lexical resource	Grammatical range and accuracy	Pronunciation
Fluency	1			
Lexical Resource	0.974	1		
Grammatical Range and Accuracy	0.951	0.981	1	
Pronunciation	0.829	0.865	0.843	1

2. *Do the four subscales contribute consistently to the candidate's final score?*

   The FACETS graphical plot indicated that the band thresholds were fairly similarly spread in each of the four subscales. There was a small difference in the difficulty of the subscales, i.e. it seemed slightly harder to score highly on Grammatical Range and Accuracy. Interestingly, this was consistent with findings from post-test analyses for other Cambridge Speaking tests (Galaczi 2005).

3. *Do raters use and interpret the subscales in the same way?*

   Generally it appeared that raters did use and interpret the subscales in the same way. This was confirmed by the relatively good generalisability coefficient established for the single-rater condition (0.862).

4. *How reliable will the rating procedure be when applied by a single rater in operational conditions?*

   Operational requirements meant that the IELTS test adopted a one-to-one format, i.e. one candidate and a single examiner. The reliability of the test when rated by nine examiners was predictably high (above 0.95), but it was important to be able to model what could be expected in a single rater condition. For a single rater the modelled reliability was still reasonable at 0.857.

   Since some of the subscales (Grammatical Range and Accuracy and Lexical Resource) appeared not to be strongly distinct in what they were measuring, one further question was considered:

5. *What if fewer subscales were used?*

Interestingly, modelling indicated that although the Phi coefficient dropped substantially from 0.857 with four subscales to 0.731 with one subscale, reducing the number from four to three (i.e. by conflating Grammatical Range and Accuracy with Lexical Resource) would lead to only a small reduction in generalisability (i.e. 0.841).

Phase 4: Implementation (October 2000 – June 2001)

The findings from Phases 2 and 3 directly influenced decisions on the nature and number of rating criteria and subscales which were subsequently adopted for the revised IELTS Speaking test. For example, examiner feedback from Phase 2 argued for the usefulness of maintaining the grammar vs lexis distinction especially when assessing higher level IELTS candidates, so despite evidence in Phase 3 of the closeness of the grammatical range and accuracy and the lexical resource subscales, it was decided not to conflate these criteria but to keep them separate, thus retaining four subscales. Additional analyses were also undertaken to compare the original and revised approaches to rating IELTS Speaking performance. The new criteria and scales were applied to existing standardisation videos in order to confirm that speaking band scores resulting from the revised approach matched those that were generated by the original holistic scale and that the assessment standard was therefore being maintained. Retrospective, qualitative feedback from raters in the early stages of trialling and during the multiple rating study helped to inform production of IELTS examiner training and standardisation materials, e.g. the development of an IELTS Examiner Induction Pack (with video and accompanying notes) to familiarise examiners with the revised test format prior to their attending the face-to-face training and standardisation session. It also led to further studies in both the UK and Australia to investigate examiners' experience as they simultaneously delivered the test using its revised format and rated performance using the new criteria and scales in real time. The worldwide re-training of all IELTS examiners, based on a cascade system of regionally based, face-to-face training sessions, took place between January and June 2001 and is described by Taylor (2001c, 2007).

Phase 5: Operational (from July 2001)

The revised assessment criteria and scales became fully operational from July 2001 when the revised format of the IELTS Speaking test was introduced worldwide. Following its introduction, candidate score and test performance data was systematically gathered and analysed to monitor the functioning of the individual subscales as well as examiner behaviour (Brown and Taylor 2006, DeVelle 2008, 2009).

Rating process

The *rating process* parameter in scoring validity concerns the nature of the decision making processes that operate when Oral Examiners assess test takers' spoken language performance. We noted earlier the complex inter-action that takes place in a speaking test between the Oral Examiner, the speaking test task and the spoken language performance generated by the test taker, and the way in which that complexity increases in speaking test formats where the Oral Examiner is directly implicated in the interaction (i.e. as an interlocutor) and where there is more than one test taker (e.g. as in a paired or group test). We should not ignore here the closely related param-eter concerning the physical and psychological conditions under which the rating process takes place; factors such as time constraints, the nature of the local environment, and the cognitive demands placed upon the examiner all have the potential to influence the nature of the rating process (see brief comments on this below and more fully in Appendix D).

From the early 1990s language testing researchers became increasingly interested in the nature of the rating process, particularly the decision-making strategies used by raters in both speaking and writing assessment (see, for example, Brown 1995, Lazaraton 1996b, Lumley 2000, Meiron and Schick 2000, Milanovic, Saville and Shuhong 1996, Pollitt and Murray 1996). The need to investigate what raters take into account when awarding scores in oral proficiency assessment is essential for informing the design of speaking test tasks, the choice of criteria for assessment, and the construc-tion of rating scales; furthermore, a sound and comprehensive understanding of rater behaviour can help shape effective procedures for rater training and standardisation ensuring that these are as valid and reliable as possible. For example, both Bachman (1990:36) and Brindley (1998:63) note the impor-tance of raters being able to clearly distinguish between levels, and Pollitt and Murray (1996) suggest the rating process should be characterised by simplic-ity and transparency. As we have already seen, work on scale development associated with the CEFR (Council of Europe 2001) suggests that the rating process is more effective when scale descriptors are positive, definite and clear, independent and brief. Specific questions of interest to speaking test devel-opers include: How do raters understand the construct of oral proficiency? Which aspects of spoken performance do they find salient, why and when? Are these aspects more or less salient at different levels of proficiency? What is the best way to train/standardise raters? The availability of newly emerging and effective methodological approaches, such as conversation analysis, dis-course analysis, and, in particular, verbal protocol analysis, has made it much easier since the 1990s to investigate these questions and to provide test devel-opers with some tentative answers. Today, verbal protocol studies (see Green 1998) are widely regarded as an effective way of gaining helpful insights into how raters make their judgements when assessing oral and written language proficiency, and what factors are likely to constrain this process. Since much of what we have learned about the rating process derives from research investigations into rater characteristics and rater training, we shall leave the main literature review and discussion to those sections (see below). Here we shall simply note some specific research studies into the rating process which have been conducted using data from Cambridge ESOL Speaking tests.

Rating process: Cambridge ESOL practice

Investigating the nature of the rating process in performance assessment is never easy, but it becomes particularly challenging in the context of direct Speaking assessment, as it is operationalised by Cambridge ESOL, for two main reasons. Firstly, rating has to take place in real time during the actual speaking test event. This is different from what happens in the rating of writing performance, where the rater accesses and evaluates a script either online or in hard copy after the test has finished. Secondly, the process of rating can vary according to whether the rater is taking the role of the assessor or the interlocutor. As we saw earlier in this chapter, the interlocutor role combines the rating process (holistic) with other responsibilities such as managing the materials, controlling timing and co-constructing the interaction, while the assessor stands outside the interaction and evaluates as an observer (analytically). This too is somewhat different from the writing assessment scenario in which, even if there are two raters, both are generally applying the same assessment criteria and rating instrument to the performance, rather than adopting differing approaches. It is important to acknowledge that any insights gained on the oral examining process via verbal protocol analysis must be treated with some caution, since the methodology risks interfering with the very processes we are seeking to investigate – focus group, semi-structured interview and survey questionnaire methodologies – have the advantage of being slightly less intrusive but still have the capacity to potentially colour or distort the actual rating experience after the event. Despite this caveat, several small-scale investigations conducted specifically into the rating process are worth noting here for the insights they offer us.

Pollitt and Murray (1996:77) attempted to measure and analyse the 'essentially private or subjective experiences' of raters by bringing together two methods or techniques – Kelly's 'Repertory Grid' procedure and Thurstone's 'Method of Paired Comparisons'. A small group of naïve raters (but with TESOL experience) were asked to behave first as quantitative raters and then as qualitative describers of pairs of candidates in video recordings taken from the CPE Speaking test. The study's findings raised some interesting questions about how naïve raters naturally select their judgement criteria, about individual and somewhat contrastive approaches to rating, about the role of comprehension in a test of oral proficiency and about the significance of paralinguistic features on raters' decision-making.

Following revision of the IELTS Speaking rating approach in 2001 (see Case Study 2 earlier in this chapter), Cambridge ESOL commissioned a large-scale survey in 2005 to explore examiners' views and experiences of the revised rating process; the outcomes are reported and discussed in Brown (2006) and Brown and Taylor (2006). A general finding was that examiners felt the pronunciation bands and descriptors did not discriminate sufficiently clearly between different levels of proficiency. Insights from this study led to further research and subsequent development to adjust the Pronunciation scale, which had been an innovation in 2001 (DeVelle 2008), as well as to enhanced certification procedures for IELTS examiners (DeVelle 2009).

Hubbard, Gilbert and Pidcock (2006) report one of very few studies in the field using verbal protocol analysis methodology with speaking test examiners to explore how raters make their assessments in real time. The small-scale study, conducted with CAE Speaking test data, sought a better understanding of how examiners approach their work in order to use that understanding to inform examiner training and development programmes and to provide feedback to raters on how they use the scales. A small group of raters used a Verbal Protocol Analysis (VPA) 'think-aloud' methodology to evaluate a small number of speaking test performances. The study also trialled three variants of the 'think-aloud' model to see which might be most productive for a larger-scale study in the future. The findings provided interesting albeit tentative insights into: how much raters focused on the different analytical scales; how raters appeared to be using and interpreting the subcriteria within each criterion; and what aspects of performance raters focused on during individual parts of a test. Each of the examiners involved in this study was found to be focusing on different aspects of performance in different parts of the test. For example, Interactive Communication was clearly the focus of rater attention in Part 3 (the candidate–candidate interaction task). Pronunciation was key in Part 1 of the test but much less so thereafter, suggesting that raters may make a general decision on pronunciation quite early on, perhaps because they feel that it is likely to remain fairly constant throughout the test. Cambridge's current examiner training instructs raters to consider all the criteria throughout the whole test so this observation raises the question about how feasible it is for examiners to apply multiple scales continuously throughout a test. Hubbard et al speculate as follows: 'Is the differential attention to criteria due to features of the assessment scales and aspects of the language elicited by particular tasks, or is it more fundamental to the nature of the assessment process?' (2006:18). Further research is needed in larger scale studies before we can be sure of the answers to these questions and of their implications for rater training.

Studies such as these, even on a small scale, offer speaking test designers valuable insights which can inform a range of test development activities, including construct definition and specification, test format and task design, selection of assessment criteria, construction of rating scales as well as procedures for training and standardising Oral Examiners. The way in which such investigations are now routinely built into Cambridge ESOL's ongoing test development and revision programme reflects the examination board's commitment to ongoing quality management of its Speaking tests.

Rating conditions

As previously mentioned, closely linked to the *rating process* parameter are the conditions under which the process of rating takes place. *Rating conditions* may vary along a number of different dimensions, e.g. temporal, spatial, psychological, so test producers must consider carefully the extent to which these can or should be standardised. Compare, for example, the difference between the *temporal* constraint experienced by a rater who is required to make a real-time judgement on a test taker's performance immediately at the end of one speaking test (before moving on to examine the next test candidate), and another examiner who has to rate the recording of a speaking test performance after the event, and who is at liberty to replay the recording more than once if they wish. Rating conditions may vary *spatially*; for example, the rating process is likely to be different for a rater who is physically present in the same room as the test taker during the test, as compared with a rater who is assessing a test taker's performance at a distance, e.g. via computer link. Empirical research specifically into temporal and spatial rating conditions as they relate to speaking assessment is difficult to find, though some of the issues that arise in the context of computer-based assessment of speaking are discussed in Galaczi (2010b).

There are also likely to be significant *psychological* differences in the rating process for the rater who assumes the role of interlocutor–examiner in a speaking test, thus co-constructing as well as assessing the performance, as compared with the rater who acts as a non-participatory observer to assess the performance. Most of the empirical work relating to this aspect has been done as part of the research agenda into rater characteristics which is dealt with in the following section. As we have seen, this scenario typically applies in Cambridge ESOL Speaking tests where there are two Oral Examiners, one taking an interlocutor role and the other an assessor role. As previously explained, the differing nature of these two roles, and the psychological processing capacity available to the examiners for the purpose of rating, has informed examination board decisions about the nature of the assessment criteria and the number of rating scales associated with each role.

Finally, the delivery of any speaking test generally entails complex administrative procedures and for a face-to-face speaking test, involving multiple participants, these are likely to be even more complex. In light of their complexity and comprehensiveness, procedures for the administrative setting and management of oral examining in the Cambridge tests at the local test centre level are outlined in a separate appendix to this volume (see Appendix D).

Rater characteristics

As mentioned towards the start of this chapter, the parameter of rater characteristics has already been addressed to some degree in the latter part of Chapter 4 on context validity, within the discussion of the impact of interlocutor variables. We saw there that personal background variables, such as the interviewer's age, gender, cultural experience and expectations, could combine with their linguistic behaviour to create an 'interlocutor effect' (O'Sullivan 2002). Where the test taker's performance is rated during or after the test, either by the interviewer or by another Oral Examiner, then the examiner's personal background variables (though not necessarily linguistic behaviour) can produce a comparable 'rater effect'. Like interlocutors, human raters are all individuals, each with their own set of personal attributes that they bring to the rating task, helping to shape the way they interpret and apply the criteria and scale, the way they make judgements, their tendency to leniency or severity and the consistency of their rating behaviour. The situation becomes even more complex if an Oral Examiner simultaneously assumes the dual role of interlocutor–interviewer _and_ rater, i.e. in addition to acting as interlocutor–interviewer to facilitate the test interaction, they also provide a rating for the performance so that interlocutor variables and rater variables combine to influence rating outcomes.

Second/foreign language research has for many years explored the subjective influence of the rater on performance assessment, or the so-called 'rater effect'. The available research has extensively documented rater variability in speaking and writing assessment, with studies demonstrating variability in test scores associated with rater effects. More than a century ago, Edgeworth (1890, quoted in Linacre 1989:10) rather pessimistically cautioned that due to rater variability, only 'a fraction – from a third to two thirds – of the successful candidates can be regarded as safe, above the danger of coming out unsuccessfully if a different set of equally competent judges had happened to be appointed'. More recently, Eckes (2005:198) wrote about the 'pervasive and often subtle ways in which raters exert influence on ratings'. The fact that the rating process is affected by rater variability has obvious implications for the scoring validity of a test, because rater variability may threaten the validity of the assessment procedure, as it may introduce construct-irrelevant variance. The available research, however, has also clearly demonstrated that raters can succeed in awarding consistent scores provided they are supported by adequate and rigorous training and standardisation (to be discussed in more detail later).

Our understanding of rater variability has evolved, and the consensus in the field of language assessment is that there are various sources of rater variability. Myford and Wolfe (2003, 2004; see also McNamara 1996) present a useful summary of rater effects:

- the 'leniency/severity' effect, where raters may differ in their overall harshness/leniency as compared to other raters or benchmark reference marks
- the 'halo' effect, which occurs when the assessment of one trait (e.g. grammar and vocabulary) influences the evaluation of a different, conceptually independent trait (e.g., discourse management)
- the 'central-tendency' effect, which refers to the overuse of the middle category of a rating scale and the avoidance of the extremes
- the 'randomness' effect, where raters show a tendency to apply one or more categories of the rating scale in an inconsistent way, showing random variation
- the 'bias' effect, which occurs when raters may show a pattern of harshness/leniency with regard to one or more aspects of the rating process, e.g., a certain group of students, a certain task or certain criteria of the rating scale.

Considering the inherent variability in rater judgements, a range of widely used practices have been adopted to increase the reliability of their' judgements. One such practice of moderating the influence of rater effects is the use of assessment scales, scoring criteria and performance descriptors. Studies have also shown that the use of analytic rating scales, alongside holistic ones, has a positive effect on scoring validity (Hamp-Lyons 1991, North 1995, North and Schneider 1998, Upshur and Turner 1995, 1999). Rater variability is also addressed through double or triple assessments (ratings) of candidate performance, or through the use of sophisticated statistical methods, such as multi-faceted Rasch measurement, which allow for statistical adjustments to be made to a candidate's marks after the live exam. Another method for reducing rater variability is the beneficial effect of rater training and standardisation.

Rater training and standardisation

The need for and importance of rater training has been strongly recognised and advocated in the assessment literature (e.g. Alderson, Clapham and Wall 1995, Bachman and Palmer 1996, Elder, Knoch, Barkhuizen and von Randow 2005, Fulcher and Davidson 2007, McNamara 1996, Weigle 1994a, 1994b, 1998, Weir 2005a). As would be expected, rater training is a vital element in the assessment of speaking (and performance assessment in general), and a small but significant body of research has investigated various aspects of rater training. The areas of enquiry within rater training have mainly focused on:

(a) the general and specific effects of rater training

(b) the effect of individualised feedback on rater performance; and

(c) the attrition of training.

The remainder of this literature overview will focus on each one of these areas in turn. The review will draw on both the speaking and writing literature on rater training. Although there could potentially be differences in speaking and writing assessment and potential effects on rater training, the focus will be on common training themes in performance assessment in general, which applies to speaking tests as well.

Effects of rater training

There is strong evidence about the beneficial role of rater training. Lunz, Wright and Linacre (1990) and Stahl and Lunz (1991) found that training can make examiners more consistent in their individual approach to marking, but that it cannot wholly eradicate differences in severity. Weigle (1994a, 1994b) observed that rater training in writing assessment increases the self-consistency of individual raters by reducing random error and extreme differences between raters. She also found that rater training clarifies understanding of the rating criteria, and modifies rater expectations in terms of the characteristics of the candidates and the tasks. Other research found that training cannot eliminate variation in the harshness of raters' marking (Lumley and McNamara 1995, Weigle 1998), but it can make them more internally consistent. Lumley and O'Sullivan (2000) observed that there was a tendency for raters who had been newly trained and accredited to be harsh, though consistent, in their judgements, while experienced raters trained in previous years tended to have become more lenient, and a small number of them were also prone to inconsistency. This finding to some extent contradicts that of Weigle (1998), who showed that newly trained raters of writing tended to be both less consistent and harsher than more experienced raters. While there is some contradiction in their results, both of these studies highlight the need for rater training beyond the initial standardisation process. In another study relevant to this discussion, Furneaux and Rignall (2000/2007) investigated the effects of standardisation on rater judgements for the IELTS Writing Module over a six-month training period. The authors found that the mark scheme itself had some standardising effect even without training. In addition, there was an increase in standardisation of rating between the first and last occasion on which marking took place; the number of marks that were in perfect agreement with the standard/reference mark rose from

4% to 35% over the four occasions. The marks within one band of the standard mark rose from 83% to 92%. The authors also found that examiners became less harsh and more in line with reference marks during training.

While there are clearly benefits to training, some researchers have cautioned about the possible negative effects of training. Weigle (1994a), citing Charney (1984) and Barritt, Stock and Clarke (1986), notes that if raters of writing scripts can be trained to show exceptionally strong agreement on ratings, it is likely that they are agreeing on superficial aspects of a text, such as handwriting and spelling (which have a clearer right/wrong aspect), rather than any substantive criteria. In addition, an emphasis on very strong agreement during training tends to force raters to ignore their own experiences and expertise, thus denying the possibility that there may be more then one 'correct' judgement of a performance. This chimes with Lumley and McNamara's (1995:57) assertion that in the 'assessment of human performance, which is a matter of some complexity, no one judgement may be said to be definitive, although there is likely to be a considerable area of overlap between judgements'. It is important to question, therefore, what the aim of rater training should be, given the complexity of the judgement process. This is especially true at higher proficiency levels, where candidate output is extremely complex and very difficult to reduce to a set of ratings. No single opinion, therefore, is definitive. McNamara's (1996:233) contention that we need to accept rater variability as a 'fact of life' seems especially appropriate. It is not surprising that rater variability is not only present, but inevitable, since raters are not machines, but human beings who are influenced (often unconsciously) by their previous experience, expectations, knowledge, preferences, and subjective interpretation of assessment scales and their categories and descriptors. In this respect, McNamara (1996:233) argues that the traditional objective of rater training – to eradicate any differences between raters – may be 'unachievable and possibly undesirable'. Instead, he suggests that the appropriate aim of training is to get raters to become more focused and to encourage new examiners to be self-consistent.

Individualised feedback and rater performance

One promising aspect of rater training is the provision of individualised feedback to raters on their performance. The issue of raters' attitudes and responsiveness to feedback on their ratings was investigated by Elder, Knoch, Barkhuizen and von Randow (2005) in the context of an analytically scored writing test, and in general the study emphasised the positive effect of individualised rater feedback. The feedback given to the raters was generated using multi-faceted Rasch measurement, focusing on three aspects of rater behaviour: the relative severity of the rater, the internal consistency of the rater, and any bias with respect to particular categories of the rating scale. The findings indicated that most raters had a positive attitude to receiving individualised feedback, as it allowed them to focus more precisely on their rating patterns. The authors also reported that many raters were able to modify their scoring, resulting in greater intra-group consistency and a reduced incidence of bias. This positive effect of training came, however, at a price, since the authors found that the test had less discriminatory power after the feedback, as the raters became 'overcautious or fearful and less inclined to use the full range of the scores available to them' (Elder et al 2005:190). In line with the discussion above, this is again an illustration of the tension between rater agreement and individual opinions.

A study by Knoch (2009) also investigated the effectiveness of individualised feedback on rating behaviour in a longitudinal study, producing mixed findings: only some raters were able to incorporate the feedback into their ratings. The findings suggested that raters found it comparatively easy to adjust their relative severity, but it was more difficult for them to make changes to internal consistency or to reduce any individual biases towards categories on the rating scale.

In an earlier study (Knoch, Read and von Randow 2007) which focused on online versus face-to-face training, Knoch and her colleagues indirectly addressed the value of providing individualised feedback which gave raters information on their performance (e.g. in terms of their severity, consistency and bias). The authors found that one of the benefits of the training programme which had incorporated individualised feedback (in this case the face-to-face training format) was that it helped to reduce the 'flat profiles' in the ratings and enabled raters to treat the different assessment categories as separate, thus reducing the halo effect. The authors also made the important point that raters need to *notice* specific issues in their rating patterns before they can start addressing them, which again signals the value of individualised feedback.

Shaw's (2002) investigation also focused on the effect of individualised feedback and found that an iterative standardisation process of training and successively delivered feedback to CPE writing examiners did not significantly enhance inter-rater reliability. However, the author suggested that this was perhaps affected by the fact that inter-rater reliability was already encouragingly high.

The effect of feedback on ratings has also been investigated in the context of speaking assessment by Wigglesworth (1993). The author observed that bias evident in various aspects of the ratings was reduced as a result of feedback, and suggested that formal feedback reports (based on multi-faceted Rasch bias analysis and giving rater feedback on their severity and consistency, for example) might contribute to the quality of ratings. Wigglesworth's (1993) investigation was replicated by O'Sullivan and Rignall (2007) within the context of the IELTS General Training Writing examination. In addition to graphic feedback similar to that provided by Wigglesworth, the authors also provided feedback in the form of a brief written description. Even though the findings indicated that the feedback did not result in significantly more consistent or accurate scoring, questionnaire feedback collected as part of the study indicated that the raters saw the feedback as a very positive and beneficial addition to their marking. The feedback had also motivated the raters to become more reflective about their decision-making processes during the rating process.

Stability of training over time

A further strand of research on rater training has focused on the stability of training over time. Focusing on this line of research, Lumley and McNamara (1995) investigated the stability of ratings by a group of raters on three occasions over a period of 20 months. Their findings indicated that the results of training 'may not endure for long after a training session' (Lumley and Mcnamara 1995:69). More recently, a study by Congdon and McQueen (2000) investigated the stability of rater severity in a large-scale assessment programme and suggested constant monitoring of rater stability over a training period, accompanied by ongoing training. The authors concluded with a cautionary note about 'the danger of certifying raters on the basis of a once-off calibration' (Lumley and McNamara 1995:176). The findings from both these studies clearly highlight the importance of ongoing rater training and standardisation.

To sum up, while differences in rater judgements will evidently exist despite training, the research on speaking and writing assessment has indicated the value of training as a cyclical, iterative process which goes beyond the initial standardisation phase. Rater training can reduce the extent of rater variability usually through reducing extreme differences in terms of harshness or leniency. Rater training can also be successful in reducing the random error in rater judgements and in making raters more self-consistent.

Online rater training

A relatively recent development in rater training has been the delivery of training online. Online rater training has been relatively little investigated in the academic literature. A study by Hamilton, Reddel and Spratt (2001) which focused on teachers' perceptions of online rater training and monitoring is a notable exception, alongside an investigation conducted by Knoch et al (2007).

Hamilton et al's (2001) findings provided support for the value of an online rater training system, highlighting several advantages of online over face-to-face rater training, such as time saving and flexibility, and the increased opportunity for reflection. The raters in the study commented that 'online communication was felt to be less "intimidating", could produce "more honest opinions" and more "varied" discussion' (Hamilton et al 2001:515). The authors also noted several caveats associated with online training, mainly the loss of the 'synergy that comes by people all sitting in a room and doing [rater training]' (2001:515). In addition, the study indicated the potentially poor receptiveness to online training among raters who may feel uncomfortable working with a computer or have a low degree of familiarity with computers, website navigation and discussion forums.

In a more recent study, Knoch et al (2007) investigated the effectiveness of online vs. face-to-face training. The authors focused on rater performance in terms of severity, internal consistency, central tendency and bias in the online and face-to-face training modes. They also investigated the raters' perceptions about online training, as compared to face-to-face training. Their findings indicated that both online and face-to-face training were successful, with a suggestion that the raters trained online might have become slightly more consistent. In terms of the raters responding to individual biases, the authors found that after training the face-to-face group was able to reduce all biases that were found before training, and speculated that this could be because the face-to-face raters were given individualised feedback in which the biases were specifically pointed out. As noted earlier in the discussion of individualised feedback, raters are more successful in eliminating individual biases if they notice them.

To sum up, the available literature on raters in performance assessment has demonstrated (not surprisingly) the value of rater training, as well as its inevitable limitations. The need for ongoing training has been shown, as well as the potential synergy between online and face-to-face rater training. As online training becomes more widespread, it is worth reminding ourselves that a blended approach which includes both online and face-to-face features would perhaps reap the biggest benefits, as it would allow flexibility, while preserving the rich atmosphere and profitable debate of a face-to-face context.

We now turn to a reflection of how Cambridge ESOL practice reflects some of these findings from the literature.

Rater registration, induction, training, certification and performance feedback: Cambridge ESOL practice

Rater training has been much discussed in the literature on performance assessment; however, very little information exists about how training is actually carried out by examination providers. This section attempts to address this lack of information by providing details of the procedures and stages which Cambridge ESOL speaking examiners (SEs) go through as part of their preparation for examining in live Speaking tests. As will be seen in the sections to follow, Cambridge ESOL SEs undergo rigorous procedures of training and standardisation as part of a cyclical, recurrent process of certification (see DeVelle 2009 for a more detailed overview of IELTS examiner certification).

Background

There are currently approximately 16,000 approved Cambridge ESOL Main Suite/BEC speaking examiners around the world. The international standardisation of Speaking test conduct and assessment is achieved by:

- a network of professionals in a hierarchical structure called the Team Leader System
- a set of quality assurance (QA) procedures for trainers.

The Team Leader system (see Figure 5.2) operates in a majority of countries where Cambridge ESOL examinations are taken. At the operational level there are the speaking examiners (SEs). Team Leaders (TLs) or

Figure 5.2 Cambridge ESOL Speaking Examiner Network

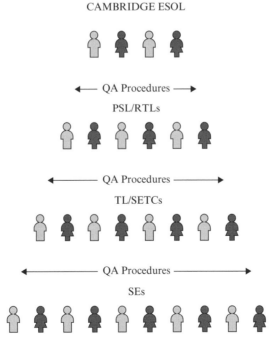

CAMBRIDGE ESOL

←— QA Procedures —→

PSL/RTLs

←—— QA Procedures ——→

TL/SETCs

←—— QA Procedures ——→

SEs

speaking examiner trainer/co-ordinators (SETCs) carry out training and certification of speaking examiners. In countries with large numbers of Team Leaders, Regional Team Leaders (RTLs) are employed to help manage the Team Leaders. At the highest level of the hierarchy, Professional Support Leaders (PSLs) are appointed by Cambridge ESOL to manage the professional aspects of the operation. They communicate directly with Cambridge ESOL on matters relating to the Team Leader system in their countries.

The quality assurance procedures which regulate the activities of the levels in the Team Leader system involve Registration, Induction, Training, Certification (comprising two stages: the Certification of Procedures and the Certification of Assessment), and Performance Feedback. Each of these procedures is defined by a set of quality assurance requirements appropriate to the level of professional responsibility. The speaking examiner level, which is of most relevance to the current discussion, is discussed in more detail below. (In order to avoid confusion with other terms used in the field, the 'Certification of Procedures' and 'Certification of Assessment' stages will be referred to as rater standardisation, the outcomes of which lead to certification.)

The first three stages – Registration, Induction and Training – typically apply only once to an applicant SE for a given examination or group of related examinations (e.g. PET and KET). The remainder of the procedures are recurrent and cyclical for each examination, in so far as the outcome of Monitoring of Performance feeds into certification and any re-training required in specific circumstances.

The discussion will now move on to a description of each of these stages, starting with examiner registration.

Registration of Cambridge ESOL speaking examiners

The objective of this stage is to ensure that the background, experience, language competencies and interpersonal skills of applicants meet the minimum eligibility requirements for a given examination or group of examinations. In terms of professional recruitment, prospective SEs need to have education to first degree level or equivalent, a recognised language teaching qualification, and at least three years or 1,800 hours of relevant and recent teaching experience. Applicants do not have to be native speakers of English. However, they need to have overall language proficiency relevant to the examination level (in principle, at least two CEFR levels higher than the CEFR level of the exam).

In addition to professional background requirements, prospective SEs need to demonstrate certain personal qualities and inter-personal skills, such as a willingness to observe the need for confidentiality and security in all aspects of the role; a responsible and conscientious attitude to work; attention to detail; the ability to interact appropriately with the type of candidates for the examination in question in such a way as to ensure that the candidates provide an adequate sample of English representative of their speaking ability; and readiness to respond to TL guidance and advice given in the context of training and standardisation meetings and, monitoring, or informally. For the Young Learner English (YLE) tests, applicants need to have recent experience of dealing with children, either socially or professionally, and must be prepared to sign a declaration that they are suitably responsible to examine children. Within the UK, all speaking examiners for the YLE tests (where only one examiner and one candidate are present) are required to undergo a Criminal Records Bureau (CRB) check in accordance with the UK government's current Vetting and Barring scheme operated nationally by the Independent Safeguarding Authority (ISA) (<www.direct.gov.uk/en/campaigns/Vetting/DG_183221>). Speaking examiners for the other Cambridge Speaking tests are not currently required to undergo CRB checks or be ISA-registered since their contact with minors is limited, as defined by the national vetting scheme, and because the examinations are in paired format, i.e. there are two candidates and two examiners present. Overseas test centres are expected to adopt similar principles and to comply with all local laws and regulations relating to child protection. The issue of child protection is emphasised to all Cambridge ESOL speaking examiners and a set of 'Guidelines for Adults conducting Speaking Tests with Minors' is included in training materials. This highlights appropriate behaviour for conducting assessments.

Finally, prospective SEs need to satisfy certain administrative professional requirements, such as access to PC and broadband for standardisation and other online activities; the aptitude to fulfil the administrative aspects of performing in the role of SE, e.g. dependability, ability to maintain confidentiality of the work involved (of test materials, assessments, etc.), flexibility; availability to undertake assignments during a substantial proportion of the examining period of the examinations for which they are applying, and to attend relevant training and standardisation meetings.

Induction of Cambridge ESOL speaking examiners

The main objective of this stage is to familiarise prospective examiners with what is required of a Cambridge ESOL speaking examiner from both a professional and an administrative point of view.

In order to proceed to the training stage, applicant SEs must have a reasonable grasp of the main principles of Cambridge ESOL Speaking tests, namely: general issues related to singleton, paired and group formats; the roles of the interlocutor and assessor in Speaking tests; the function of stimulus material in Speaking tests and the functions of different question types/ elicitation techniques; limitations on choice of materials relating to age, cultural factors, etc.; the need to ensure that candidates are not disadvantaged or advantaged by the way the SEs conduct Speaking tests; the function of interlocutor frames; the importance of adhering to rubrics and prescribed timings; the difference between global/holistic and analytical scales; the Cambridge ESOL Common Scale for Speaking; the affective impact of SEs on candidates (dress, demeanour, etc.); and sensitivity to different types of candidate (age, gender, ethnicity, etc.).

The induction stage, therefore, has a more general purpose of familiarising SEs with global issues underlying Cambridge ESOL Speaking tests. The more specific aim of familiarising SEs with the features of specific exams lies in the Training stage.

Training and certification of Cambridge ESOL speaking examiners

The aim of this QA procedure is to familiarise speaking examiners (during a face-to-face event) with aspects of each examination relevant to them. Rater training is carried out by Team Leaders and is attended by new speaking examiners or existing examiners who are being trained for a new Cambridge ESOL Speaking test. SEs also need to attend trainings sessions if there are significant changes to any Speaking test, or if they have not examined for any Cambridge ESOL examination for more than two years.

Speaking rater training differs from writing rater training in that Speaking Examiners have two roles: as an interlocutor in the test and as a rater of test taker performance. Training, therefore, has two aims: the first is to familiarise prospective speaking examiners with the format of the test, how to conduct the test, and the types of test materials used, and to give them practice in test conduct with volunteer candidates. The second aim is to familiarise prospective SEs with the assessment aspects of the test, such as the assessment scales, criteria and performance descriptors.

The training session includes an overview of key features of Cambridge ESOL Speaking tests, such as the standardised nature of each part of the test, the focus of each task, the interaction patterns, the nature of the prompts, the timing and anticipated response in each case. During training, prospective speaking examiners are also provided with specific training in managing the test effectively by using a script (the 'interlocutor frame') while speaking naturally; handling the test materials and ensuring their security, being familiar with them, handling them efficiently and discreetly; timing and adhering to prescribed timing in each part of the test; the manner and level of involvement and the need to provide support and encouragement while giving candidates space to complete the task; and providing equal opportunities to candidates. This is accomplished through peer practice with sample materials. The aim of this part of the session is to give trainees time to become familiar with the sample materials that will be used later with volunteer candidates, including practice in delivering scripted rubrics and handling materials. After peer practice, the prospective speaking examiners conduct practice speaking tests with volunteer candidates. The purpose of these practice tests is not to assess the volunteer candidates, but to ensure that trainees are familiar with the procedure and can handle the interlocutor frame and test materials effectively. At this stage, Team Leaders observe the potential new SEs, give support and advice where necessary and may have to decide at this or any other stage of training that a trainee is not suitable to continue to the next stage.

Another aspect of the training process is to familiarise the trainee SEs with the assessment aspects of the test, such as the level of the examination (*vis à vis* the CEFR, ALTE and other Cambridge ESOL examinations). In addition, the trainee SEs are also familiarised with the criteria and descriptors of the holistic and analytic scales used, and receive practice in the application of the analytic criteria and in the accurate completion of the mark sheets. The training session ends with an open discussion where the trainees share their impressions of the practice tests and discuss any other issues of interest. Feedback from Cambridge ESOL PSLs indicates that some of the typical issues which arise at this stage involve the accurate and meaningful delivery of the interlocutor frame and the controlling of the timing of the test. The degree of standardisation of procedures can be a great surprise to some SEs, who may be used to speaking tests which allow a much greater degree of freedom for the examiner. As noted earlier in the chapter, standardisation in delivering the test is important in order to control for the potential effect of different interlocutors, who could influence the performance of the candidate, as has convincingly been demonstrated by Brown (2003). The challenge, however, is to balance the tension between following a tight script but at the same time preserving the human element which is, after all, one of the distinguishing features of direct tests of speaking. Training to deliver the script in a natural way is, therefore, important at this stage. The rigorous control of timing is another feature of the management of the test which may be difficult for some SEs to accept or manage at first. Standardised timing of the test parts is an important test feature with implications for the scoring validity of the test. The challenge for SEs is to get training in controlling the timing without overly interrupting.

In addition to training in the role of interlocutor–examiner, the training stage also involves extensive training in applying the speaking test assessment criteria to candidate performances. The goal of this stage is to minimise rater effects and reduce psychometric errors introduced by leniency/harshness, central tendency, restriction of range, etc., while acknowledging the fact that there will be some level of divergence in the examiner's judgements and that rater training cannot – and, more importantly, should not

– make raters into duplicates of each other. Investigations of SE performance during standardisation, for example, indicate that the majority of speaking examiners (94%) are within a one-band divergence from the reference mark (on a 10-point scale), indicating satisfactory level of agreement with the standard (Galaczi 2009) and by extension, an acceptable level of rater variability.

Cambridge ESOL practice involves both face-to-face and online rater training, standardisation and certification. All speaking examiners are required to attend a face-to-face standardisation session at least once every 12 months, and standardisation takes place as close as possible to the start of the main examining period. Attendance at these sessions is an absolute requirement for SEs, and any required follow-up rating activities must also be successfully completed before a speaking examiner can rate in live exam conditions.

The purpose of these sessions is to standardise areas of SE assessment, procedures and conduct through familiarisation with, or review of (in the case of experimental examiners) the assessment scales (assessment criteria, bands, performance descriptors) and with examples of Speaking test performances at several bands (accompanied by commentaries justifying each mark for each assessment criterion). The specific objectives are to set the benchmarks for SEs to use in assessing candidates by providing examples on video, to give SEs practice in applying the criteria to candidates in sample tests, and to collect a sample of SEs' marks to ensure that assessments are within the acceptable parameters of divergence (in this case, +/- 1 band on a 10-point scale).

At the standardisation meeting the assessment criteria and scales are examined closely and any differences in interpretation are clarified. Examples of performances at different levels (bands) are provided on video in order to ensure a common interpretation of the assessment scales, and supporting commentaries are given for each performance justifying the mark. The materials used for rater standardisation are samples of Speaking tests (both full tests and test parts) at the relevant CEFR level, marks for each assessment criterion, and commentaries supporting the marks.

The careful exemplification of adjacent bands is an especially important stage of the standardisation process and every effort is made to exemplify the full range of bands with appropriate benchmark performances. At the end of the standardisation process, examiners go through a marks collection exercise where their marks are evaluated against divergence parameters. Examiners whose marks fall outside these parameters are required to carry out further standardisation.

Feedback from some Cambridge ESOL PSLs has indicated that at this training stage, which aims to standardise the marks awarded, the greatest focus (and debate) is about clearly conceptualising the assessment criteria and performance descriptors, and distinguishing reliably between them. The areas which SEs need most training in are: noticing both the positive and negative aspects of a performance; becoming aware of the non-grammatical aspects of a performance (e.g. issues of Interactive Communication) and the relevant assessment categories and descriptors in the scales; reducing the halo effect, which could be common with new SEs; reducing an over-emphasis on the Grammar and Vocabulary scale; increasing an SE's ability to accurately assess candidates who are outside the language group the SE is most familiar with; dealing with the 'pendulum effect', where SEs who are excessively divergent in their marks will then overcompensate and be divergent in the other extreme. The first issue in the list above has perhaps been the most challenging for raters, since the scales follow the CEFR guidance for positively worded descriptors about what learners 'can do', and yet raters need to make decisions both about what learners 'can do' and 'can't do' in order to discriminate between different levels of ability. In addition to the scales, guidance is further provided in the standardisation materials and accompanying commentaries which justify the given reference marks. The following examples from FCE standardisation materials (*Guidelines for Oral Examiners* 2010), which draw raters' attention to both positive features of learner performance and limitations, provide an illustration: *'Despite some hesitation, Charline produces extended stretches of language throughout the test'* (p. 42) or *'Word stress is generally accurately placed, but not throughout the test'* (p. 44). The tension between positive/negative features of performance and performance descriptors is an issue to be revisited during the next cycle of scale revision and addressed more explicitly in the scale descriptors themselves.

All these issues emphasise the need for the standardisation stage to provide examiners with a wide range of candidate performances which can help them to understand, apply and internalise the assessment criteria and benchmark performances and apply them reliably and consistently over time in live test conditions. As one Cambridge ESOL Professional Support Leader put it, the standardisation stage shouldn't 'become a kind of "MOT" [i.e. a UK annual test of automobile safety] test that you "pass" and then don't think much about [it] again. In this case it would be counter-productive as a tool for maintaining and improving standards. The need for SEs to reflect on their own rating techniques and skills is more important in the long term' (Gilbert 2010, personal communication).

Standardisation (benchmark) marks

Before proceeding further, it is worth explaining how the reference marks used during rater standardisation are arrived at. The reference standardisation marks provide the benchmarks for assessment, and due to their fundamental role, standardisation marks are arrived at after extensive analysis and consultation with experienced examiners worldwide (Galaczi 2009).

The standard procedure for arriving at standardisation marks at Cambridge ESOL is through the use of a mixed-method approach which involves both statistical procedures (multi-faceted Rasch measurement) and expert judgement. This approach involves the collection of multiple marks which are given independently by a group of experienced raters, and the calculation of a Fair Average Score (through FACETS, Linacre 2006), which adjusts for examiner harshness/leniency and task/criteria difficulty. In addition to the statistically derived Fair Average marks, expert judgement is considered in the selection of benchmark performances.

The marking exercise which produces standardisation marks is typically carried out annually for every Cambridge ESOL Speaking exam as new sets of standardisation materials are created. The raters participating in the marks collection exercise are experienced Oral Examiners, who represent a spread in terms of examining experience, responsibilities (Professional Support Leaders, Regional Team Leaders, Team Leaders, speaking examiners) and geographic location (Europe, Latin America, Asia, Australia). The raters are given access to video recordings of candidates taking a 'mock' speaking test, which is recorded for the purposes of rater training and standardisation. Typically about 15 speaking examiners mark about 20–25 candidates at each proficiency level in a fully crossed design (e.g. 15 raters x 20 candidates x 4 assessment criteria). Each rater gives a separate rating for each assessment criterion.

The ratings are analysed through FACETS, where candidate, rater and assessment criterion are treated as separate facets. As a preliminary stage, rater performance is scrutinised to detect rater effects and potentially remove from the analysis any raters who are excessively harsh/lenient or are rating inconsistently. As a general rule, any raters with infit/outfit mean squares greater than 2 are removed from the dataset and the analysis is re-run. The infit/outfit mean square cut-off point attempts to achieve a balance between removing raters who are drastically misfitting, but at the same time preserving a balance between divergent individual judgements and the need for rater agreement. As Linacre (2007, personal communication) has said:

> Removing misfit is like cleaning a window. After you clean it the first time, you can see the faint smudges you missed the first time. Then you clean them. Now you can see the fine scratches in the glass. So you polish them out. Now you can see the pane of glass is not exactly flat. So you remedy that. Now you can see that the glass is not all equally transparent. So you . . . Following this process, you will finally have no glass left at all!

Our experience with such benchmarking multiple-marking projects at Cambridge ESOL has indicated that cases of severe rater divergence are very rare, largely due to the high level of experience and training of the raters who take part.

After the performance of the raters is scrutinised for any rater effects, the candidate Fair Average marks are reviewed and rounded up or down to match bands in the Cambridge ESOL assessment scales. Any candidates with Infit Mean Square values greater than two are removed from the sample. The recorded Speaking tests, accompanying transcripts, and Fair Average marks are then given to a group of experienced examiners who provide commentaries to justify each given mark. The commentaries include references to the assessment scales and examples from the candidate output. The commentary writers can query any Fair Average mark which they find difficult to support, and in such cases they provide justification for why they feel that a mark should be raised/lowered. This is a crucial stage of the process of providing standardisation marks, as it allows a synergy between the power of statistical analysis and the depth and richness of expert judgement. The queried marks are reviewed by an internal team, and the decision whether to change or not a given Fair Average Mark is made after considering the statistical support, the expert recommendation, and the remaining candidates at that and adjacent levels.

Use of test parts and full tests as standardisation material

As mentioned earlier, another feature of rater training at Cambridge ESOL is the use of both full tests and test parts during the standardisation process. This practice was adopted in an effort to provide SEs with more opportunities to mark sample tests during the standardisation stage, while taking into account time and resource limitations. The use of more samples was also aided by the use of online rater standardisation, which has raised new opportunities for the development of rater standardisation. In an internal Cambridge ESOL study focusing on the potential use of test parts in rater standardisation, Green (2006b) investigated the ability of speaking examiners to assess candidate performance on the basis of relatively brief samples. He also focused on the degree of agreement between marks awarded to full tests and marks awarded to test parts. Green reported an encouragingly high level of agreement between rater marks and benchmark marks, which provided support for the use of test parts in rater standardisation. However, we also highlighted some important issues to be considered when asking examiners to mark test parts during standardisation, namely the difficulty of awarding marks on certain assessment criteria to certain tasks. For example, the 'Interactive Communication' assessment criterion, which captures basic turn-taking principles, such as initiating, responding and developing the interaction, was difficult to apply to the long turn task in the test, as well as to the parts which have higher interlocutor control, such as the Interview in Part 1 (for a fuller discussion of the parts of the Cambridge ESOL Main Suite Speaking tests, see Chapter 4). Similarly, the 'Discourse Management' assessment criterion was difficult to apply accurately to test parts which require short turns. The application of some of the criteria, most notably 'Discourse Management' and 'Grammar and Vocabulary', was hindered by brevity of response in some of the test parts, and it was difficult to identify performances at the highest band, where descriptors call for certain features of performance to be exhibited 'throughout [the test]' or for a 'range' of certain features to be present. As a result, some of the raters in the study commented that they tended to be more lenient when marking brief responses provided by test parts, or to give 'safe' ratings from the middle of the scale. From all four assessment criteria, 'Pronunciation' seemed to be the easiest to apply to both full tests and test parts, due to its stable nature and minimal deviations in performance on 'Pronunciation' across all parts of the test. Considering the findings, Green recommended that it is possible to arrive at scores on test parts that are generally consistent. Even if there is a small loss of accuracy in marking test parts, this was felt to be offset by the advantages of collecting more scores from each speaking examiner during the standardisation process, which would in turn lead to a greater level of accuracy in identifying off-target raters. Following on from the report findings, Cambridge ESOL now uses test parts in addition to full tests as an integral part of the standardisation of Main Suite and BEC speaking examiners. However, it is seen as imperative that the standardisation process includes an adequate number of full tests as well, to reflect the real-life assessment situation where SEs mark full tests. In order to ensure better fit between test parts and assessment criteria, when marking test parts examiners are asked to apply only two pre-selected criteria to the performance. In addition to providing more opportunities for prospective raters to apply the assessment scales and criteria, the use of test parts can also be used to raise awareness of the issues relating to specific assessment criteria.

In a more recent study focusing on the use of test parts, Galaczi (2010a) investigated the use of test parts and full tests by raters who were going through standardisation prior to the live November/December 2009 exam session. She found a non-significant difference in divergence from the benchmark mark when raters were marking full tests as compared to test parts. This finding confirmed the value of using test parts as part of SE standardisation, since it indicated that SEs can mark test parts to an acceptable standard, while at the same time giving them the opportunity for more practice before a live test. The practice of using test parts also provides a larger number of observations per SE, which increases the accuracy of decisions about an SE's readiness to examine in live conditions.

Feedback from Professional Support Leaders has indicated that the use of test parts during rater standardisation has been received positively by SEs, after an initial ambivalence about rating test parts, which is different from the live-test focus on marking the whole test. Generally, however, SEs have felt that working on test parts during the standardisation stage is a useful training exercise, as it requires them to focus on specific criteria at specific moments during the test, which in turn raises their awareness about details of the performance descriptors and gives them more fine-tuned practice in applying the scales, assessment categories and descriptors in a live-test environment. In addition, using test parts (alongside full tests) during rater training allows raters to focus on a wider range of performances and language backgrounds. An issue which needs further consideration, however, is the use of test parts during rater certification, i.e. the final stage of the training and standardisation process which goes beyond training in setting the standard and applying the standard to a collection of marks from the raters which determines their certification status. This practice has been seen as too demanding and stressful by raters, since it gives them access to a relatively small sample and does not fully replicate real examining conditions. The use of shorter segments for rater certification purposes is an issue which has implications beyond Cambridge ESOL, as raters these days are asked to do more in less time and with fewer resources. It is an issue worth exploring empirically and operationally in the future, and will shed light on the most appropriate use of full tests and test segments for rater training, standardisation and certification purposes.

The experience of Cambridge ESOL SEs with using test parts for training purposes could potentially feed into future revisions of the assessment model for Main Suite Speaking tests. As explained earlier in the chapter, raters need to mark the whole test, partly as a result of the cognitive overload associated with providing a mark for each part. As technology becomes more prominent in Speaking tests and the recording and dissemination of Speaking test performances to raters around the world become less onerous, the possibility to provide marks by test part becomes a more realistic possibility, which could enhance the scoring validity of Speaking tests.

Finally, a few words about the Certification stage of SEs. This Quality Assurance stage takes place annually for each CEFR level and comprises two stages: the Certification of Procedures and the Certification of Assessment. Certification of Procedures is carried out annually during a face-to-face meeting, which every SE must attend. Certification of Assessment is also carried out face-to-face for one CEFR level, and is completed online for any CEFR levels not covered at the face-to-face meeting. This procedure aims to optimise the advantages of both face-to-face and online training environments, and also acknowledges the need for ongoing examiner certification, which is carried out periodically.

Performance feedback for Cambridge ESOL speaking examiners

In addition to the rigorous process of rater training, standardisation and certification outlined above, there are additional quality assurance checks built into the Team Leader system to ensure quality assurance of rater conduct and assessment. The practice at Cambridge ESOL involves a range of QA checks, which include face-to-face monitoring of SEs during live Speaking tests at least once every two years, and statistical monitoring several times a year.

Each of these monitoring systems will now be overviewed in turn.

Monitoring by a more experienced speaking examiner (The expert-judgement approach)

This kind of monitoring is carried out by a Team Leader (TL) and consists of the TL sitting in on a number of Speaking tests, observing how they are conducted, what marks are given, and discussing aspects of the exam procedure and marks allocation after the test. The monitoring observation is captured in a checklist, which records a 'snapshot' of examining on a particular day and with a particular group of students.

The categories in the checklist are (Cambridge ESOL PSL Handbook, 2009):

- Appearance and manner: SEs are expected to be suitably dressed and behave in an appropriate manner.
- Environment: SEs are expected to do the best they can to create a suitable test environment with the resources provided. Important aspects are light, space, air, tidiness and organisation, a non-intimidating atmosphere, and the relative positions of the assessor and interlocutor in relation to the candidates.
- Procedure: This refers to following the test procedure exactly, using the correct materials as instructed, including every part and phase of the test, giving out and taking back materials at exactly the right time and asking questions to the candidates in the order indicated in the SE booklets.
- Timing: This category refers to keeping to the prescribed timing. While some tests have more internal flexibility of timing among the test parts than others, SEs must keep to the prescribed timings given in the *Cambridge ESOL Instructions to Speaking Examiners* booklets, both for the whole test and for the various parts.
- Delivery: SEs are expected to read the rubrics with meaning and a natural use of emphasis to aid understanding. They should use word

and sentence stress effectively. They should also be sufficiently familiar with the rubrics to be able to make eye contact with candidates to check understanding. They should adapt their speed to the level of the exam, but maintain a natural rhythm. Where indicated and/or appropriate, they should use gesture to aid understanding.

- Frame: SEs are instructed to keep to the interlocutor frame at all times; some exams specifically allow additional words (e.g. the follow-up question 'why?' or feedback through words such as 'good' in YLE), but SEs must not add other questions or comments or leave out parts of the rubric. Back-up questions are provided in some tests, which SEs must use as instructed and when necessary.

- Handling materials: SEs are required to have all the equipment they need for the test and to organise it efficiently so that they can run the test without hesitations and any potential distraction to the candidates. They should organise the test materials appropriately and use all the materials provided, making sure candidates do not misuse them or take them away. SEs are also responsible for the security of test materials at all times.

- Sample/Equality: SEs are responsible for making sure all candidates leave the room feeling they have had a fair test with sufficient opportunity to speak and that there has been equality of treatment between candidates. In paired tests, interlocutors must be aware of candidates who dominate or fail to participate and must do their best to correct any imbalance, either with gesture during the task or with follow-up questions. They must never give the impression of favouring one candidate over another during any part of the test.

- Courtesy: SEs are expected to manage the test in such a way that the candidates feel supported and respected from the moment they come into the room until they leave.

- Problems: The *Cambridge ESOL Instructions to Speaking Examiners* booklet deals with Special Circumstances, but it is impossible to predict everything that can happen during a Speaking test. SEs are expected to have understood the principles of examining and be able to respond appropriately when unforeseen events happen.

- Global mark: SEs acting as interlocutor must also give global marks and be able to justify them according to the criteria.

- Analytical marks: Assessors must give analytical marks and be able to relate these to the criteria.

- Scales: Both assessor and interlocutor must have the printed assessment scales where they can be consulted easily during the test. They must also have the relevant *Cambridge ESOL Instructions to Speaking Examiners* booklet easily available for reference during tests.

- <u>Marksheets</u>: Assessors are responsible for the correct completion of the mark sheets. They must write in the marks as the test finishes, having already completed all the other information during the test, such as test packs used, SE identification number, etc. The correct procedure for collection and checking of the Interlocator (i.e. the global mark) must be followed.

Feedback from Professional Support Leaders indicates that this stage of professional quality assurance is very important and valuable, as it highlights issues for improvement at the individual SE level. The issues which are most often in need of improvement are controlling the timing of the test and delivery of accurate rubrics and test procedures. As part of rater feedback, in some Team Leader groups a spontaneous 'critical friend' culture has developed, with a real interest among SEs in improving team performance, not just when the more senior Examiner is there to monitor. This SE monitoring stage also encourages continuous improvement among SEs, which in turn allows them to take responsibility for developing their examining skills. These are strong examples of the value of a network of professionals who work together and provide professional feedback for one another, which in turn enhances their ratings and ultimately the scoring validity of the test.

Statistical post-exam monitoring

In addition to monitoring by a more experienced speaking examiner, Cambridge ESOL routinely conducts post-exam statistical monitoring of Speaking examiners. Even though these monitoring procedures do not result in any statistical post-exam adjustment of scores, the findings do feed into further training, standardisation or monitoring of examiners or examination centres that have been identified.

One aspect of statistical monitoring focuses on the level of agreement between the interlocutor and assessor. This analysis identifies examination centres which have a level of agreement that is too low (indicating excessive examiner disagreement beyond the acceptable divergence criteria) or too high (indicating potential examiner collusion). Examination centres which are consistently identified as deviating from the acceptable range are then contacted and further monitoring/training of SEs carried out.

Another monitoring procedure focuses on over- or under-marking tendencies in individual examiners. The methodology rests on a comparison between candidate scores on the Speaking paper and scores on the other four papers (Reading, Writing, Listening, Use of English), and the subsequent flagging up of candidates with very jagged profiles (i.e. very strong in Speaking and very weak in the other four papers or vice versa). The methodology allows for the fact that learners' skills do not necessarily develop in tandem and at the same rate, and that many learners do show a difference in performance on the different skills. As a result, only candidates where the difference is exceptionally large are identified. The clustering of flagged-up candidates around SEs is investigated next, and speaking examiners who show an unusually high clustering of flagged-up candidates are identified. SEs who are consistently identified through this monitoring analysis receive additional monitoring, training and/or standardisation if necessary. The analysis carried out so far (for sessions covering November/December 2007 to present) consistently indicates that the vast majority of centres and SEs are marking within acceptable parameters.

Post-exam analysis/adjustment: Cambridge ESOL practice

The beneficial use of multi-faceted Rasch analysis in the moderation of scores has been widely recognised in the literature. However, major drawbacks to using multi-faceted Rasch analysis are the large size of the sample required and the relative complexity involved in ensuring that there is some level of duplication or connectivity for all raters. If done with a small dataset, the analysis would result in error figures that call into question the value of the exercise, while the complexity of the research design requires connectivity between raters and/or candidates to be built into the process, which may not always be practical (or even possible) during tight examination schedules. Due to this reason of practicality, Cambridge ESOL does not carry out any post-adjustment of Speaking scores. As noted above, however, a great deal of effort and resources are devoted to examiner training, standardisation and performance feedback, and the practice of double marking in the majority of Cambridge ESOL tests. Standard procedures for grading and awards, explained below, allow for some adjustment of the score boundaries should this be needed.

Grading and awarding: Cambridge ESOL practice

Grading is the process of setting cut-off scores for various grade boundaries prior to reporting final score results to test users. The Cambridge ESOL approach to grading the examinations involves comparing candidates' results from session to session and from year to year to ensure that standards across different forms of a particular examination remain constant. This aspect of fairness is of particular importance, not only to the candidates themselves, but also to test score users looking to recruit people with a specific level of language ability.

The performance of large groups of candidates or cohorts is compared with cohorts from previous years, and performance is also compared by country, by first language, by age and a number of other factors, to ensure that the standards being applied are consistently fair to all candidates, and that a particular grade 'means' the same thing from year to year and throughout the world. Any requests for Special Consideration are reviewed at this stage, together with any reports from centres about specific problems that may have arisen during the examination (see Chapter 2); such problems could include unexpected environmental problems during the test, e.g. power failure or excessive noise, as well as suspicion of malpractice, i.e. risk of cheating.

Although the different skill-based papers (i.e. Reading, Use of English, Speaking) within an examination contain different numbers of items or tasks, and thus generate different numbers of marks, the marks are usually equally weighted in terms of the contribution they make to the overall examination score. The revised FCE for example, has five papers weighted to 40 marks each, the marks being summed to an exam score out of 200. Mark distributions are not scaled to have an equal standard deviation. The papers are graded in such a way that the marks indicating a satisfactory level of performance in each paper sum to a passing grade in the exam (Grade C).

In practice, candidates will not pass or fail an individual skill paper within a Main Suite examination. An overall grade is provided to show how a candidate has performed on the examination as a whole. Several steps are taken to arrive at the overall grade. The cut-off raw scores on the objectively scored papers, i.e. Reading, Listening and Use of English, are combined and added to the cut-off scores on the criterion-referenced adequate performance on Writing and Speaking papers; this generates an aggregate pass score. At this stage various other considerations such as examiner reports, relative performance of big cohorts and candidates' overall language ability may result in adjusting the final cut-off score for passing the examination.

This begs the question of how the expected levels of performance are defined for each level of Cambridge ESOL examinations. The approach has normative as well as criterion-related features. In criterion terms, each exam level can be seen as representing a level of proficiency characterised by particular abilities to use English to some purpose (see Chapters 3 and 4 on cognitive and context validity). The normative aspect relates to the way that the target difficulty of each component paper is set, with the aim of making each paper in an exam of similar difficulty for the 'typical' candidate. A mean facility of around .6 is the test construction target for objectively scored papers at the three upper levels, i.e. FCE, CAE, CPE (B2 to C2) which should indicate a satisfactory level of performance for the criterion level if repeated across all papers.

A system of graphical profiling provides information to show how close a candidate's marks on each component of the assessment, e.g. Speaking, was compared to the average performance of other candidates in that paper (see the following section on reporting results for further discussion).

After the grading meeting, results are generated in the form of grades for the test as a whole. At this stage a procedure known as Awards is carried out to ensure the fairness of the final results before they are issued to candidates. As part of this procedure an Awards Committee looks particularly closely at the performance of candidates who are close to the grade boundaries – particularly the pass/fail boundary.

Reporting results and certification

Once the Awards procedure is complete, centres are sent a statement of provisional results, together with individual results slips, known as a Statement of Results, for each candidate. The Statement of Results gives not only a candidate's overall grade for the examination (e.g. A, B), but also their standardised score (out of 100) and a candidate profile. These results are known as provisional results because they are still subject to a final quality check, e.g. to ensure that the candidate's name is spelled in the correct or preferred way before the official examination certificates are printed.

The candidate score is a standardised score between 0 and 100, which is converted from the total number of marks available in the exam. It enables candidates to see how well they performed within a grade boundary, i.e. whether their score is near the top of the grade, in the middle or at the bottom. So, for example, a candidate with a score of 62 on the FCE examination would have just succeeded in achieving a C grade, whereas a candidate with a score of 73 would have performed significantly better within the C grade band. Because this score is standardised, it also allows comparison across different sessions of an examination.

The Statement of Results also provides the candidates with a 'graphical profile' showing the profile of their performance across the various components of the whole examination.

Approximately three months after the examination, certificates are issued (via the test centre) to successful candidates. These documents incorporate a number of security features to make them extremely difficult to forge. Cambridge ESOL keeps detailed records of the certificates awarded to candidates (additionally score data is stored for an indefinite period) so that, if necessary, any claim about which an employer or university is dubious can be verified.

Main Suite certificates do not have a fixed 'shelf-life' and do not expire. They attest to the fact that at the time of the examination, the candidate had achieved and demonstrated a specified level of English. The length of time since the certificate was obtained is a factor that potential test score users are encouraged to take into account when using the test score in their decision-making processes.

Users of the Cambridge ESOL Main Suite examinations appear to support the current approach to grading, with a single exam grade; at the same time, however, there is growing demand for more information concerning the way the grade was arrived at and what it means qualitatively, in terms of performance. This largely reflects the pedagogical context in which Cambridge ESOL examinations are generally taken – feedback on performance in each paper is seen as a useful guide for further study, particularly in the case of failing candidates who may wish to re-take the exam. For this reason, Statements of Results containing a graphical profile of the candidates' performance were introduced in 2000. The following explanatory notes were issued to explain how the information should be interpreted:

> Every candidate is provided with a Statement of Results which includes a graphical display of the candidate's performance in each component. These are shown against the scale Exceptional – Good – Borderline – Weak and indicate the candidate's relative performance in each paper.
>
> In looking at this graphical display it is important to remember that the candidates are NOT required to reach a specific level in any component, i.e. there are NO pass/fail levels in individual components. Thus different strengths and weaknesses may add up to the same overall result.
>
> We recommend that fail candidates planning to resit an examination, or pass candidates who plan to continue their studies, do not focus only on those areas where they have a performance which is less than Borderline, but try to improve their general level of English across all language skills.
>
> The profile indicates a candidate's performance on the specific occasion when they sat the exam – this may be influenced by a number of different factors, and candidates can find that they have a somewhat different profile on another occasion. Evidence of candidates who resit exams indicates that in some cases performance declines overall and in other cases declines in some papers while improving in others (Saville 2003:104).

The purpose of the profiled result slips is to give useful information about performance in each paper. The graphical candidate profile shows candidates how they performed on each paper in the exam, compared to the standard of all the other candidates taking that paper at the same time. The information plotted in the result slips is not candidates' raw marks, but marks which are scaled to implement the normative frame of reference which has been presented above. The candidate with a borderline pass, if their skills profile were completely flat, would be shown as having all papers just above the 'borderline' boundary. A very good candidate, achieving an A grade, would most probably have at least one paper in the 'exceptional' band. In each paper a similar proportion of candidates fall in the 'exceptional' and 'weak' bands. If a candidate did not attain the grade they hoped for or needed, then the information in the Statement of Results can sometimes help them to decide on specific skill areas for improvement.

The profiled result slips attempt to achieve a balance between the need to provide more information about performance in components, and a full-blown system of component-level grading. This latter option, as explained above, is not wholly appropriate for the construct of English language proficiency embodied in the Cambridge ESOL Main Suite exams. Cambridge ESOL's introduction from December 2008 of standardised score reporting on the 0–100 scale constituted an attempt to further improve on the Statement of Results. Feedback from consultative exercises with stakeholders on the use of these result slips has generally been positive as shown by questionnaire data gathered from a number of test centres worldwide.

Conclusion

This chapter has addressed the multiple and complex issues associated with the scoring validity parameter in speaking test development and validation activity. We have reviewed the available theoretical and empirical research as it relates to the various scoring validity parameters identified in Figure 5.1. We have described in some detail the approach and procedures adopted by Cambridge ESOL, an examination board with a long history and experience of the direct assessment of second language speaking proficiency, as well as a strong commitment to an ongoing research agenda in the field, the results of which feed into the continuous improvement of the Speaking tests that it offers in the public domain.

Having scrutinised what happens within the context of one examination board in relation to its Speaking tests in terms of their design, development, production, delivery, processing and validation, this is the point in the narrative so far at which to broaden our horizons to look beyond the borders of the actual testing event into the wider world where the tests and test scores take on something of a life and meaning of their own, sometimes beyond the influence or control of those who gave them birth. Chapters 6 and 7, therefore, will explore issues concerning the consequential validity and the criterion-related validity of speaking tests respectively, before the final Chapter reflects upon how far the current Cambridge ESOL tests operationalise contemporary thinking and research insights, and what issues and areas for further research and development can be identified.

6 Consequential validity

Roger Hawkey
Consultant to Cambridge ESOL

Introduction

This chapter begins with background and definitions of exam impact and washback. It then investigates their role in test validation, the structure of impact studies, the complexity of the variables involved, ethical issues and their codification, taking some account of critical testing, formative assessment and exam impact by design. Finally, we survey impact-related research for Cambridge ESOL exams, including some examples of findings from actual impact studies. Throughout, the main interest will be aspects of the consequential validity of tests of speaking.

Impact and washback: background and definitions

There is no doubt that the work of Samuel Messick (e.g. 1989, 1996) is a major influence on the Consequential validity box of the Weir (2005a) socio-cognitive test validation model referenced throughout this book. Although, as McNamara (2006:43) argues, Messick never actually used the term consequential validity (preferring to refer to 'the consequential aspect of construct validity' (1996:241)), his concern for the 'consequences of test use' has been a key factor in 'the significant upsurge of interest over the last ten years' (McNamara 2006:43). Alderson (2004:ix), among others, notes the increasingly acknowledged importance of the consequences of exams and tests: 'Washback and the impact of tests more generally has become a major area of study within educational research'.

From a Cambridge ESOL viewpoint, between 2005 and 2007 four new volumes focusing on major consequential validity related studies appeared in the *Studies in Language Testing* (SiLT) series to which this volume belongs: Liying Cheng (2005), Dianne Wall (2005), Roger Hawkey (2006) and Anthony Green (2007). Weir and Milanovic (Eds 2003) and Hawkey (2009) also cover significant recent Cambridge ESOL test impact research, the former for CPE, the latter for FCE and CAE. In addition, Taylor and Falvey (Eds 2007) select research studies on the IELTS test, a significant proportion of them impact-related.

In fact, Cambridge ESOL, and previously UCLES EFL, have long claimed a concern for the effects of their exams for speakers of English as a second or foreign language, ESL or EFL, on their test takers and other stakeholders. Hawkey (2009:37) cites a 1943 *Cambridge Examinations in English for Foreign Student Survey* as asking 'how far examinations of this kind may act as a stimulus and a focusing point for both teachers and taught, and thereby promote the expansion of the studies which they are designed to test'. In her review of the 1984 FCE exam, Hamp-Lyons (1987:19) appears to answer this question, encouraged by 'the Syndicate's [now Cambridge ESOL] attempts to bring it in line with pedagogic developments, particularly in communicative teaching/learning'. We shall see below evidence that Cambridge ESOL now investigates and reports on such matters regularly and transparently. A concern with evidence-based research into a test's consequential validity within a validation framework has now, as already illustrated in Chapters 1 to 5, grown into a systematic and evidence-seeking test validation framework. Alderson (2004) refers to two of the key elements of consequential validity, namely *washback* and *impact*. These need some immediate definition in the consequential validation context of this chapter.

Washback (Hughes (2003) and Green (2007) call the same phenomenon 'backwash') is generally taken to refer to an exam's influences on teaching, teachers, learning, curriculum and materials (see, for example, Alderson and Wall 1993, Gates 1995, Hamp-Lyons 1998, Hawkey 2006 and 2009, Shohamy, Donitsa-Schmidt and Ferman 1996). Messick refers to washback as 'the extent to which the introduction and use of a test influences language teachers and learners to do things they would not otherwise do that promote or inhibit language learning' (1996:241), and indicates the possibility 'that a test's validity should be appraised by the degree to which it manifests positive or negative washback, a notion akin to the proposal of "systemic validity" in the educational measurement literature'. Frederiksen and Collins (1989:189) suggest that systemic validity is achieved 'if the activities employed to help students achieve an instructional objective do not merely increase test scores but increase performance on the construct cited in the objectives as well'.

Impact, washback and validation

In a personal communication to Alderson (Alderson 1995:3) Messick warns against too glib a view of the relationship between test washback and test validation:

> Washback is a consequence of testing that bears on validity only if it can be evidentially shown to have been an effect of the test and not of other forces operative on the educational scene . . . Washback is not simply good or bad teaching or learning practice that might occur with

or without the test, but rather good or bad practice that is evidentially linked to the introduction of the use of the test.

Significantly, Messick links positive washback to 'direct' assessments and stresses the need to minimise construct under-representation and construct-irrelevant difficulty in such tests (see further below).

Green's comprehensive (2007) review of the interpretations of washback in the language testing literature confirms it as a neutral term (as in Alderson and Wall 1993 and 1996) which may refer to both positive effects (Bachman and Palmer 1996, Buck 1988, Davies, Brown, Elder, Hill, Lumley and McNamara 1999, Hughes 2003) and negative effects (Bachman and Palmer 1996, Buck 1988, Davies et al 1999, Hughes 2003). The term *impact,* also neutral in itself, as instanced in the literature (e.g. Hawkey 2006, Shohamy 2001), now appears generally to be agreed to cover 'the total effect of a test on the educational process and on the wider community' (McNamara 2000:133). So, impact is concerned with wider influences, the broader social contexts of a test, and washback with the micro contexts of the classroom and the school (see Hawkey 2006 and Hamp-Lyons 2000). Impact is the superordinate consequential validity construct, washback thus a part of impact (see Green 2007, Green and Hawkey 2004, Hamp-Lyons 1998, McNamara 1996, 2000, Shohamy 2001). The two earlier companion exam construct-focused volumes in this series, *Examining Writing* (Shaw and Weir 2007) and *Examining Reading* (Khalifa and Weir 2009), agree that the consequential validation of Cambridge ESOL exams must cover both impact and washback.

When Bachman and Palmer (1996:29) envisage impact as operating on a 'macro' level 'in terms of educational systems and society in general' and a micro level, 'a local and personal level, in terms of the people who are directly affected by tests and their results', they appear to be making a distinction similar to that between impact and washback. In its Bachman and Palmer (1996) definition, test 'usefulness' entails six qualities: reliability, construct validity, authenticity, interactiveness, *impact* and practicality. There is considerable conceptual overlap here with the validity, reliability, impact and practicality (VRIP) criteria used to guide UCLES EFL test validation procedures from 1995 (Milanovic and Saville 1996a).

Bachman (2004a) expresses concern that validity and *test use* are not always accepted as related in language assessment: 'Both the construct validity of our score-based inferences and the impact, or consequences, of test use need to be considered from the very beginning of test design, with the test developer and test users working together to prioritise the relative importance of these qualities' (2004:7). If this is not the case, 'we are left with validity at one end and consequences at the other, with no link between' (2004:7). Bachman's two-part assessment argument (building on Kane, Crooks and Cohen 1999, Mislevy, Steinberg and Almond 2002, 2003, and Toulmin 2003) seeks to embrace the twin concerns of validity and test use. The proposed logic here combines the assessment *validity* argument linking assessment performance and interpretation, with the assessment *use* argument, linking score-based interpretations with intended uses or decisions (2005:31). See Bachman and Palmer (2010) for a full discussion of the Assessment Use Argument (AUA).

Such an approach could perhaps answer Spolsky's two key questions about test use (1981:19): 'How sure are you of your decision?' and 'How sure are you of the evidence that you're using to make that decision?' There is evidence later in this chapter (and elsewhere in this volume) on research into how Cambridge ESOL's Speaking tests are structured to facilitate valid scores and valid use of the scores. In any case, Bachman's insistence that test impact should be designed systematically into test design and validation is in line with the view taken in this chapter and with current Cambridge ESOL policy and practice on the validation of its exams.

A socio-cognitive validation framework

Messick's consequential validity construct was originally interpreted by Weir in his 2005 test validation framework as embracing <u>three</u> aspects of test validity: impact on institutions and society; washback on individuals in classroom/workplace; and avoidance of test bias. Since that time, however, thinking in this area has evolved and we have, at Weir's suggestion, relocated avoidance of bias to the test taker and test taker populations sector of the model. For this reason, matters relating to bias were discussed in Chapter 2 rather than here in Chapter 6; in this chapter we will restrict our focus to matters of washback and impact.

Table 6.1 Consequential validity (adapted from the Weir 2005a framework for conceptualising speaking test validity)

CONSEQUENTIAL VALIDITY
• Impact on institutions and society • Washback on individuals in classroom / workplace

Weir appears to situate consequential validity both in the *a posteriori* phase of impact on institutions and society, and in the *a priori* phase of washback on the teaching and learning related to the test before it happens. This inclusion of both washback and impact under the consequential validity heading is significant. We will include in this chapter Cambridge ESOL consequential validation research related to both the impact of exam preparation and of exam scores on test takers and test users. This implies some overlap between research for other socio-cognitive validity categories in Weir 2005a, for example, his context and cognitive validities. As Saville (2009:25) points out, the impact : washback 'distinction is useful for conceptualising the notion of impact, but it does not imply that the levels are unconnected. On the contrary, the potentially complex relationships between individuals, the institutions to which they belong, and broader systems in society are clearly of crucial importance in reaching an understanding of what impact is and how it works.'

The Cambridge ESOL internal report *FCE/CAE Modifications: Building the Validity Argument: Application of Weir's Socio-Cognitive framework to FCE and CAE* (ffrench and Gutch, 13 July 2006) operationalises and implements the socio-cognitive framework for validity evidence on each area and sub-area within Weir's model, including the time-scale for completion of this and reference to activities which support the decisions made (in the *Notes* column). Table 6.2 presents the section of the report on the Weir (2005a) Consequential validity categories as interpreted by ffrench and Gutch in their application. The questions posed for each Consequential validity sub-category help clarify the nature of the validity information to be sought.

Table 6.2 Grid for the application of Weir's socio-cognitive framework, consequential validation section

CONSEQUENTIAL VALIDITY		
Score Interpretation		
Framework	Skills areas	Notes
Differential Validity: *Are the items free from bias towards candidates with different cultural backgrounds, background knowledge, cognitive characteristics, native languages, ethnicity, age and gender? Is there potential for unsuitable topics (e.g. religion, war) to be included?* **Washback in classroom or workplace:** *Does the test have beneficial impact on FCE/CAE classroom activities, FCE/CAE text books and teaching resources, and the attitudes and related practices of FCE/CAE stakeholders towards the exam?* **Effect on individual within society:** *Does the test have beneficial impact on the wider community?*		

The place of impact studies

Figure 6.1 below reminds us of where washback and impact *studies* may fit in the cycle of test impact study and validation, the assumption now being that washback and impact must indeed be investigated as part of test validation. Figure 6.1 (from Hawkey 2006:12) indicates the points (▰) where potential washback and impact may occur (i.e. the effects of an international gate-keeping language test such as IELTS on test preparation programmes, or the effects of the test on candidates' futures at receiving institutions and the admissions policies of those institutions). The data collected on test washback and impact may inform changes designed to improve the test and related systems.

Figure 6.1 Sequence of washback and impact study actions in relation to a high-stakes test

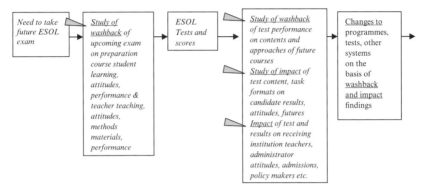

As Figure 6.1 indicates, washback occurs throughout the implementation of a new language test preparation course because a curriculum associated with the specifications of the new exam is known in advance and this shapes the teaching and learning that occurs. Washback also takes place in subsequent courses because of the experience of the first preparation course and because of the test performances and scores of learners on the tests at the end. The first occurrence of washback in Figure 6.1 is more like a 'bow-wave' than washback from the exam specifications and/or curriculum. The second occurrence is indeed wash*back* from the course and the test(s) that have already taken place. The examples of 'impact' in Figure 6.1 take account too of the use of the term to include the effects of a programme or test *beyond* washback, on stakeholders, domains and systems *in addition to* language learners and teachers and their immediate context. Notice also in Figure 6.1 the final arrow indicating continuing washback and impact and the iterative nature of its study. The data collected on test washback and impact should inform changes designed to improve the validity of an exam provider's test and related systems.

The range and complexity of the variables

Though defined as a hyponym of the superordinate concept of impact, washback is still broad in its coverage, as indicated, for example, by Alderson (2004:ix), Bailey (1996), Cheng and Curtis (2004:12), Hawkey (2006:13), Spratt (2005:5) and Watanabe (2004:19). Alderson and Wall (1993) identify

15 washback hypotheses, including the potential influence of a test on *the teacher and the learner, what and how teachers teach and learners learn, the rate and sequence of learning*, and *attitudes to teaching and learning methods*. These hypotheses suggest that investigations of any aspect of test washback, for example, the effect of a speaking test on the teaching of a particular skill or strategy required in it, may be complicated by one or more intervening variables operating between the learning and the teaching and the target test. This means that we must beware of washback assumptions that are too clear-cut. Hamp-Lyons (2000) cautions against the over-simplification that exam washback necessarily leads to 'curricular alignment'; Green and Hawkey (2004:66) warn that washback should not be assumed to be a 'harmful influence'. Alderson (1995:3), while agreeing that 'test consequences are important and may relate to validity issues (bias being perhaps the most obvious case)', has 'difficulty seeing the washback and impact as central to construct validity' because of the 'myriad factors' impacting on a test, e.g. a teacher's linguistic ability, training, motivation, course hours, class size and extra lessons. For Alderson this 'is not, of course, to deny the value of studying test impact and washback in its own right, but it underscores the need to gather evidence for the relationship between a test and its impact on the one hand, and of the futility, given current understanding and data, of making direct and simplistic links between washback and validity' (Alderson 1995:3).

Green (2007:3), who adopts the term 'backwash' rather 'washback', agrees that the concept 'is not generally considered to be a standard for judging the validity of a test', because 'backwash can only be related to a test indirectly, as effects are realised through the interactions between, *inter alia*, the test, teachers and learners'. Green cites Mehrens (1998) on 'the lack of agreed standards for evaluating backwash' and the fact that 'different stakeholders may regard the same effects differently'. There is interesting food for thought in Messick's 1996 advice, also cited by Green: 'rather than seeking backwash as a sign of test validity, seek validity by design as a likely basis for backwash' (1996:252). Alderson and Wall (1993) and Wall (2005) add that we should not even take for granted that teachers will use methods advised by exam syllabuses or teacher guides. Wall (2005) finds empirical evidence suggesting that teachers may not be driven by the exam rather than the textbook or that they over-focus on skills in the textbook that are tested in the exam (see also Hawkey 2006). Nor should we assume that what teachers claim they teach necessarily coincides with their actual teaching (Wall 2005), or that teacher and student perceptions of exam-preparation lesson content are always in tune (Hawkey 2006:138). Hawkey also reminds us that washback is not necessarily unidirectional, i.e. from exam to textbook and teaching, rather than bi-directional, i.e. also from textbook and teaching to exam (see also Wall 2005, and the Cambridge ESOL CPE *Handbook* 2002).

A substantial research literature now exists that illustrates the range and complexity of potential variables associated with washback and impact. Interested readers are advised to consult Wall's 2005 and Green's 2007 volumes in this series, Spratt's 2005 survey, and Cheng, Watanabe and Curtis (2004), whose edited volume on washback-related research contexts and methods illustrates both the *a priori* and *a posteriori* focus of test washback and impact concerns. Readers may also find it helpful to consult the recent work of Wall and Horak who conducted and reported on a washback study for TOEFL on behalf of ETS (Wall and Horak 2006, 2008). Their study stresses the importance of gathering proper baseline data in washback studies so researchers can have confidence that washback evidence can be attributed to the test in question and not to other factors. These and other publications make clear the multiple variables involved across the language test candidacy. It is also likely that a direct speaking test construct will bring more of these into play than a non-direct speaking test.

Globalisation, international communication, values and codes

Graddol (2004, 1,329–1,330) reminds us of the importance of English in international business, global communications, science and technology, social and cultural affairs. 'Most scientific papers (80 – 90%) are written in English,' he notes, 'and many technical terms do not have equivalents in other languages'. Furthermore, 80% of the information stored in the world's computers is in English (McCrum, Cran and MacNeil 1986). Learners worldwide use English-usage tips on their mobile phones and English language teachers refer to 'Microsoft English', where learner/users draft letters in English with assistance from pop-up guides and Windows Spellcheck. Economic globalisation is leading to increased demand for English language skills, written and spoken, among future managers of companies and institutions. In particular, 'the increasing demand for performance assessment of speaking skills' (McNamara and Lumley 1997) makes the need for the valid and reliable measurement of their oral communication skills crucial.

In an era of globalisation and interconnectivity, the tendency for such developments to come under closer comparative scrutiny is strong. McNamara (2006:43–44) confirms the strong influences of values-concerned testers such as Messick. Messick has contributed to the test impact construct, has 'informed debate on ethics, impact, accountability, and washback in language testing' by putting validity theory firmly 'in the area of values' and highlighting the social construction of language test constructs (see McNamara 2006:31). Spolsky (1995:354–7) had also made the strong connection between impact considerations and test ethics: 'Post-modern testing adds a sincere, ethically driven consideration of the potentially deleterious effects of testing on the test taker, on the instructional process, and on other facets of the social context in which we test.'

In this view, testers, in particular high-stakes testers, need to accept both professional and social responsibility to stakeholders for a test's washback and impact consequences, doing everything possible to ensure their consequential validity. The view accepts that high-stakes language tests *can* be ethical as long as ethicality is a key argued and evidenced part of the consequential validation applied by the test developers.

Even earlier, Spolsky (1981) had encouraged testers to consider the ethical issues involved in the use of language test scores for decisions that would affect people's lives. Language testers should, says Kunnan (2003), develop a test fairness framework covering five qualities: *validity, absence of bias, access, administration* and *consequences.* Kunnan (2008) sees the issue of fairness as the most important challenge in large-scale assessment. In the large-scale, direct assessment of speaking, of course, the qualities of *access* and *administration* are significant factors impacting on fairness. Kunnan defines fairness in terms of the use of fair content and test methods (see Weir's Cognitive and Context validities) and in assessing language ability and the fair use of the scores obtained from the test (Weir's Consequential validity). These are clearly useful criteria for checks on fairness as an aspect of test validation although Bachman (2005:7) regrets the apparent absence here of any 'logical mechanism for relating these'.

Test providers are thus concerned *a priori* with the washback of a test on curricula, course design, materials, teachers, teaching/learning, learners, schools, parents and so on. They are equally concerned, *a posteriori,* with the impacts of test scores on candidates' further/higher studies, careers, attitudes, getting the right people into the right jobs or places, thus with institutional, regional, national performances and ethos. Figure 6.2 (Saville 2009:53 adapting Taylor 2000a) reminds us of the number and diversity of stakeholders 'impacted by assessment or who contribute to assessment processes and mechanisms'.

Taylor (2000a:2) notes, with reference to the stakeholder community summarised here, the *a priori : a posteriori* distinction above: 'Some of the stakeholders listed (e.g. examiners and materials writers) are likely to have more interest in the 'front end' of a test, i.e. the test assessment criteria or test format. Others may see their stake as being primarily concerned with the test scores. Some stakeholders, such as learners and teachers, will naturally have an interest in all aspects of the test'. The kind of consequential validity claims made in this volume, particularly with reference to Cambridge ESOL exams, must be supported by validation studies of the type exemplified below, as well as other kinds of evidence that can be assembled in support of claims for consequential validity. These should be informed by codes of ethics and practice, formative assessment ideas and the warnings of the critical testers,

Figure 6.2 Stakeholders in the testing community (Saville 2009: 53 from Taylor 2000a:2)

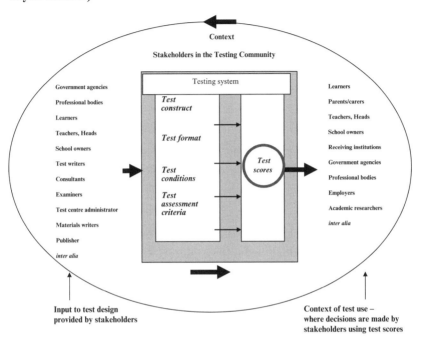

for example Shohamy (1997, 2001, 2008), who sees all tests as a potential instrument of power and control in society.

It is to be expected in an era of increasing high-stakes testing and such high-profile concern for their implications that the question of *common* standards and codes of practice should be advocated and developed. As Saville and Hawkey (2004:75) put it: '[i]n tune with increasing individual and societal expectations of good value and accountability, testers are expected to adhere to codes of professionally and socially responsible practice'. This, they argue: 'tends to increase the concern of high-stakes exam providers with the ethics of language testing. Such codes (for example, of the International Language Testing Association (ILTA), or the Association of Language Testers in Europe (ALTE)), were intended to improve test development rigour and probity.' Alan Davies, who chaired an ILTA Code of Practice Committee, considers that a Code of Ethics 'demonstrates to the members of an association or of a profession what its standards are' (2005:46); in the words of the Code of Ethics itself (adopted at the annual meeting of ILTA, March 2000), the ILTA Code of Ethics was 'to offer a benchmark of satisfactory ethical behaviour by all'. A Code of Practice, Davies adds, then 'instantiates that Code of Ethics' (2005:46–47). (For more on the ethics and professionalisation of language testing, see Taylor pages 5 to 9, this volume.)

McNamara (2006:x) sees three main areas of responsibility in ethical testing practice: accountability (Norton 1997), mainly to test takers and test score users; washback (Alderson and Wall 1996); and impact as McNamara describes it, as the 'waves the test makes in the wider educational and social world'.

Impact by design

Given the acknowledged impact of tests, in particular high-stakes tests, educational authorities and test developers will consider how to optimise this impact. The concept of *impact by design* has 'emerged as a key feature of the impact model' (Saville 2009:254), 'related to the principles of social impact assessment (SIA), a form of policy-oriented social research . . . concerned with the consequences of planned developments'.

Saville sees SIA as relevant to test impact study and part of test validation, the process of 'identifying the future consequences of a current or proposed action . . . related to individuals, organizations and macro systems in society (e.g. stakeholders at both the macro and micro levels of the educational system in which a test or testing system is to operate)'.

Green (2007) and Hughes (2003) suggest the kind of conditions that need to be in place for positive washback. These include emphasising the importance, demandingness, but attainability of the test tasks; making them direct and criterion-referenced; ensuring the test takers and teachers are familiar with the test; and providing optimal support for teachers. Weir (2005), Wall (2005) and Cheng (2005) argue the centrality of teacher support provision if beneficial washback is to occur. One of our aims in this chapter is to explore how these conditions can be controlled in relation to the testing of speaking, and specifically the direct tests of Speaking offered by Cambridge. But the potential intervening variables remain.

Chalhoub-Deville (2009) indicates some of the dangers of impact by design in language testing and education, with reference to the No Child Left Behind (NCLB) Act, a recent US educational reform targeting the testing of all English language learners according to state-wide standards. Chalhoub-Deville, showing a concern redolent of the fears expressed above by Shohamy, notes that 'past experience indicates that test-driven educational reform had repeatedly fallen short in delivering the desired educational change' (<http://www.alte.org/2008/section05.html>).

Hamp-Lyons (2000:586) links the increasing importance attached to some tests with the washback : impact relationship, claiming that the 'shift from washback to impact suggests a growing awareness by language testers that the societies in which and for which we work are, whether we approve or not, using tests as their levers for social and educational reform'. Actually, as

Alan Davies points out (personal communication), this is by no means a new phenomenon, being a feature, for example, of the Civil Service examinations in India in the 19th century.

Impact study and Cambridge exams

Whether impact is intended or unintended, it would seem to be a legitimate and crucial focus of research, both 'micro' and 'macro', to 'review and change' tests and programmes in the light of findings on, among other aspects, 'how the stakeholders use the exams and what they think about them' (Saville 2003:60). This is a justification, of course, for studies of the effects of exams as part of the test *validation process*, that is 'the process of investigating the quality of test-based inferences, often in order to improve this basis and hence the quality of the test' (McNamara 2000:138).

Thus almost all test development and validation research may have a relationship with consequential validity in the sense that changing a test will also tend to affect its washback *a priori* and/or its impact *a posteriori*. In Chapters 2 to 5 of this book, Cambridge ESOL validation research has been described, which claims to be in the interests of cognitive, contextual and scoring validity as it relates to the assessment of L2 speaking. In this section of the present chapter, examples are cited of Cambridge ESOL research on aspects of its tests relevant to consequential validity and some of its decisions on appropriate action. We shall focus on:

- the impacts of the Cambridge ESOL direct Speaking tests construct
- examples of speaking test research with possible consequential validity implications as reported in Cambridge ESOL's *Research Notes*
- examples of other Cambridge ESOL Speaking test research carried out for consequential validation purposes
- the design and speaking test-related findings of some major Cambridge ESOL impact studies.

Earlier chapters have described and discussed the theoretical construct underpinning the Cambridge ESOL Speaking tests and the way this is operationalised. The format adopted is intended to create a positive washback on the teaching of speaking, to help learners develop their speaking skill to deal with 'reciprocal oral interaction with others'.

A second, well-documented implication, for example by Spolsky (1995) and Bachman, Davidson, Ryan and Choi (1995), is the use of *examiner scoring*. In the assessment of speaking in the Cambridge exams there are typically two examiners. One examiner, the test *interlocutor*, facilitates, guides and participates in the test interactions, and awards each test taker a mark for global achievement. The second examiner, the *assessor,* who does not participate in the spoken interaction, has an observer role and awards marks according to several analytical criteria: *Grammar, Vocabulary, Discourse Management, Pronunciation, Interactive Communication.*

The scope and range of washback and impact research

Relevant to the themes of this chapter is the growing number of articles on impact and washback research which have appeared since 2000 in Cambridge ESOL's quarterly publication *Research Notes*, publicly available via the website archive. Articles cover a wide range of single or related impact study aspects, including: impact study approaches and methods; impact studies of particular ESOL exams; the (comparative) exam washback and impact on particular stakeholder groups; ethical impact; exam washback on textbooks. It is clear, in relationship to the main points on impact made in this chapter above, that the studies focus on both impact and washback, and have both mainly *a priori* or mainly *a posteriori* emphases. It is also clear that the numerous studies listed cover a complex of test impact and validation issues beyond their titles. The frequency with which Cambridge ESOL's own quarterly presents washback and impact study research, along with the numerous other impact references, including books and chapters in books published by Cambridge ESOL and Cambridge University Press (CUP), again underlines the significance of impact study in the thinking of the exam board, particularly in relation to the assessment of speaking.

The speaking test research projects, reported in *Research Notes* and elsewhere, relate potentially to all sectors of the socio-cognitive framework, reflecting its unified approach to gathering validation evidence. Examples of particular relevance to consequential validity would be those relating to speaking test tasks (likely to have preparation course washback relevance) and those relating to assessment criteria and rater behaviour (clearly relevant to test scores and their impacts). In this connection, Taylor (personal communication) draws attention to test impact in relation to raters of speaking test performances, and, in the case of Cambridge direct Speaking tests, to examiners who act as interlocutors as well as raters. Taylor comments that studies investigating examiner behaviour and rating issues tend to be conducted and reported under the *scoring validity* heading and are rarely perceived as having a consequential validity dimension, though in reality, of course, they do. As Figure 6.2 above indicates, the examiner cadre constitutes an important part of the larger test stakeholder constituency. It is thus valid to regard studies that investigate examiner perceptions, attitudes and experiences as sources of consequential validity evidence.

A brief overview now of the impact-related research into the International English Language Testing System (IELTS) Speaking test over the past 15 years illustrates this point quite well.

Impact issues and insights from IELTS Speaking test research

A survey of 10 volumes of IELTS-related research (1995–2009) carried out under the joint-funded programme, sponsored by the IELTS partners (Cambridge ESOL, British Council and IDP Australia) reveals interesting further points about the study of impact and the nature of research into the Cambridge ESOL direct face-to-face Speaking assessment model, a model which is also used in the IELTS Speaking test, though in a one-to-one (rather than paired) format. Of 55 research studies included in the 10 volumes, 28 are impact studies of various kinds and 12 are studies related to the IELTS oral interview. Again, we note that the impact studies include a focus on washback from preparation course teaching, learning and materials (11); IELTS results impact on academic and professional futures (15); stakeholder attitudes (10), the studies sometimes including more than one impact focus, of course.

The coverage of the studies which focus on the IELTS oral interview illustrates clearly the range of direct speaking assessment aspects carrying potential consequential validity implications, including the specific point made earlier about the relationship between test impact and examiners: test format and candidate/examiner discourse produced (Merrylees and McDowell 1999); interviewer style (Brown and Hill 1998); examiner attitudes and behaviour in the IELTS oral interview (Merrylees and McDowell 1999); rater behaviour and rater orientation in awarding scores (Brown 2000, 2003); gender in the oral interview (O'Loughlin 2000, 2002); examiner behaviour and the rating process in the revised IELTS Speaking test (Brown 2006); examiner deviation from the interlocutor frame (O'Sullivan and Lu 2006); the lexical dimension of the Speaking test (Read and Nation 2006); speaking task difficulty (Weir, O'Sullivan and Horai 2006); the effectiveness and validity of planning time in the Speaking test (Elder and Wigglesworth 2006); interactional organisation (Seedhouse and Egbert 2006); phonology and inter-examiner variation in the rating of pronunciation (Carey and Mannell 2009). The *Studies in Language Testing* volume *IELTS Collected Papers* (Taylor and Falvey Eds 2007) also presents four studies on IELTS Speaking conducted under the grant-funded research programme between 1995 and 2001, including some of those mentioned above.

At the time of the revision of the IELTS oral interview Taylor (2001a) reminded stakeholders of the particular validation demands of the direct model of speaking (and writing) assessment including issues of 'assessment criteria, rating scales, test format and task design' (2001a:9). But Taylor is also referring here to a further example of speaking test impact, to 'the need to prepare examiners in readiness for the revised test becoming live'. The washback/impact dimension of direct speaking tests with regard to speaking test examiners, namely that the test format provides rich opportunities for professional development, is covered more fully in Chapter 5 above, on scoring validity. But Oral Examiners are a core and an extensive stake-holder constituency. Taylor (2001c:9) also mentions how the revised IELTS oral interview test required the development of 'appropriate methods and materials for retraining and standardising existing examiners, often in large numbers and in many places' (2001c:9). Cambridge ESOL acknowledge-ment of the importance of examiner training is well noted elsewhere (e.g. Saville 2003:98). It is important, Taylor (2001c:9) suggests, 'both in terms of its impact on the reliability and validity of performance testing (Alderson, Clapham and Wall 1995) and also in terms of the call for increased profes-sionalisation in language testing (Bachman 2000)'.

Cambridge ESOL Speaking test-related consequential validation research

Regular reviews of its key exams (see, for example, Weir and Milanovic 2003, Hawkey 2009) are a systematic part of Cambridge's approach to test validation. These typically involve surveying a wide range of stake-holders; in the case of the CPE exam Milanovic (2003:xviii–xix) describes 'an extensive consultation exercise on a scale not previously attempted by a British Examination Board', with questionnaires sent to 25,000 students, 5,000 teachers, 1,200 Oral Examiners, 800 Local Secretaries and 120 UK further education institutions. The FCE and CAE updating project (2004–08) included an early three-questionnaire survey (online and hard copy) for Cambridge ESOL exam candidates, for Local Secretaries, the third of these (the 'in-depth questionnaire') targeting stakeholders involved in the administration of the examinations, including examiners. Responses were received from 1,900 candidates, 101 Local Secretaries across 20 countries, and 625 stakeholders completed the in-depth questionnaire (including Local Secretaries, Directors of Studies, Examiners and Examinations Officers, teachers and teacher trainers, and materials writers). The 2004–08 FCE and CAE review process also included key ESOL management, administrative, research and business management staff, Principal Examiners, Senior Team Leaders and Local Secretaries, stakeholders from major ESOL partners (e.g. the British Council, the European Association for Quality Language Schools (EAQUALS), Reading University, Cambridge University Press). As the review and updating of the exams reached firm decisions on the modifications to be implemented, communication was reported with thousands of stake-holders through face-to-face presentations and seminars round the world, around 20,000 website hits on the proposed FCE and CAE *Specifications*, and hits in the thousands on the special exam update project *Bulletin 5* and *Bulletin 6*. Similar numbers of hard copies of the bulletins and of the *Specifications and Sample Papers for examinations from December 2008* had been delivered. Work was in progress on promotional DVD video clips, speaking packs for classroom use, FAQs on the website, and the creation of a brochure through redirecting the contents of *Bulletin 5* (the bulletin outlining all five papers for both updated exams). Standard seminar presentation packs had been developed for use at such events. Note the clear consequential validity, as well as a publicity, intention in all these stakeholder communication efforts, adding to the increasing amount and quality of stakeholder support material seen as related to exam consequential validity (see above). There is also a clear consequential (as well as context) validity element in the summaries of the predicted benefits of the FCE and CAE review communicated through formal presentations on the changes to FCE and CAE during 2007 and 2008, namely:

- more straightforward progression from FCE to CPE, with FCE and CAE structured more similarly, 'thus encouraging candidates to progress from one level to the next: from CEFR B2 to C1 to C2'
- reduced exam length, more appealing and accessible for test takers, perhaps enabling exams to be taken in a day (possibly with the exception of the Speaking test)
- additional results information to help candidates to understand how they have performed, and assist exam users in the interpretation of results
- a further claimed benefit, namely 'an updated format to help teachers and students with exam preparation', a further reminder of Cambridge ESOL's concern for exam washback'(Hawkey 2009:165).

An example of work towards Speaking test modifications may be seen in Table 6.3, as reported in 2004 by a CAE and FCE modifications project skills meeting taking account of survey research data:

Table 6.3 FCE and CAE Speaking test modifications for 2008

Paper and Part	Proposed action
FCE and CAE Paper 5 Speaking: analyse candidate performance for data of potential use to Item Writers and future candidates	follow up report *Analysis of Speaking Tests* (2003) re: • comparison of scores for Speaking test pairs and trios of candidates • rater interpretations of Paper 5 rating scales • relationships between global achievement and analytical scores and their relevance to construct validity of the rating scheme • the Common Scale for Speaking check with Senior Team Leaders *re* possible sensitivity issues in Part 1 (conversation)

Hawkey (2009:166–167) discusses in some detail Cambridge ESOL's work to investigate validity-related issues. He categorises the various types of evidence – consultative, qualitative research-based and

quantitative-empirical research-based – that are gathered in support of consequential and other validity claims. He explains how such research, including washback, impact and test bias studies relating to the Speaking tests,
informed changes in the 2008 update of the FCE and CAE examinations.
This kind of public reporting of the process of test change is an example
of the increased transparency attempted by the exam provider in tune with
the evidence-based and stakeholder oriented test validation times. It meets
Fulcher and Davidson's expectation that language test providers should
'document upgrade retrofits and place the information in the public domain
(2009:134).

Some Cambridge ESOL impact studies

Saville (2003:60), writing from his standpoint as Cambridge ESOL Director
of Research and Validation, stresses that a 'taxonomy of stakeholders' [see
Figure 6.1 above] places demands on an exam provider to ensure that, as an
organisation, it can 'review and change what it does in the light of findings on
how the stakeholders use the exams and what they think about them'. This
requirement provides a primary justification for impact studies being part of
the test validation process.

   In the final sections of this chapter we refer to two such studies to illustrate
their part in supporting the validation argument for the positive consequences
of certain exams. Thus, impact studies associated with various ESOL exams,
or particular aspects of the washback and impact of those exams, are now
part of the organisation's exam validation systems. The IELTS Impact Study
(IIS) constitutes a major long-term programme of research by Cambridge
ESOL into the impact of IELTS, one of the most widely used language tests
for those needing to study or train in the medium of English. The *Progetto
Lingue* 2000 (*PL2000*) Impact Study was carried out by Cambridge ESOL
with the support of the Italian Ministry of Education. It aimed to ascertain
the effects of the *PL2000* foreign language reform measures on English language learner performance in state schools in Italy and to analyse the effects
of the use of external examinations for the certification of *PL2000* learner
language levels. Given the focus of this volume, we shall review and reflect on
both these studies in terms of the insights they provided for the assessment of
speaking.

The IELTS Impact study: findings on the Speaking test

The IELTS Impact study (see Hawkey 2006 for a detailed account, Saville
2009 for a particular focus on it as a case study for the development of
Cambridge ESOL exam validation systems) sought evidence of the washback and impact of the test on:

- the test-taking population
- classroom activity in IELTS-related classes
- teaching materials, including textbooks
- other users of the test.

Phase 1 of the study was commissioned in the mid-1990s by the then UCLES EFL from Alderson and his research team at the University of Lancaster. This first phase identified target impact study areas and developed appropriate data collection instrumentation to be validated in Phase 2 of the project (see Alderson and Banerjee 1996, Banerjee 1996, Bonkowski 1996, Herington 1996, Horak 1996, Milanovic and Saville 1996a, Winetroube 1997, Yue 1997). In Phase 3 these instruments were used for the main data collection from a case study sample reflecting the IELTS test taker and teacher population. A total of 572 test takers, 83 IELTS preparation course teachers, and 45 textbook evaluators responded through the questionnaires; 120 students, 21 teachers and 15 receiving institution administrators participated in face-to-face interviews and focus groups to enhance and triangulate questionnaire data from student and teacher participants.

The study probed the perceived influence of the IELTS test on preparation courses since both participants' perception of content and the materials writer's or teacher's intended content are relevant to the analysis of test washback. Table 6.4 summarises activities selected by high percentages of both the teachers and the students as *prominent* in their IELTS preparation courses, the implication presumably being that oral communication skills were perceived as being given high priority in their courses.

Table 6.4 Candidate and teacher perceptions of prominent IELTS preparation course activities

Activities	Students %	Teachers %
Practising making a point and providing supporting examples	78	88
Group discussion / debates	83	76
Practising using words to organise a speech	74	83

Teachers' views on their IELTS courses (91% of the 83 feeling that these were successful in comparison with other courses they taught) are relevant to washback aspects of IELTS consequential validity. The main reasons mentioned by the teachers questioned in the IELTS impact study for their positive views were: clear course goals and focus (in 21 teacher responses out of 83), high student motivation (16), clear-cut student achievement potential (12) and course validity (11) in terms of student target language needs, topics and skills. On the *negative* side of the teacher perceptions of their IELTS preparation courses, 19 of the teachers were concerned about the narrowness of their students' focus, and six about pressure on the students.

Phase Three IELTS impact study participants who had already taken IELTS were asked whether they thought IELTS a fair way to test their proficiency in English. Table 6.5 summarises the responses (of the 190 concerned) with the option to explain why/why not.

Table 6.5 IELTS takers' perceptions of the fairness of the test

Do you think IELTS is a fair way to test your proficiency in English? (N=190)	
YES	72%
NO	28%
If No, why not?	
1 opposition to all tests	
2 pressure, especially of time	
3 topics	
4 rating of writing and speaking	
5 no grammar test	

Note the concern, in fourth place in the table, with the rating of the IELTS Speaking (and Writing) test. These are the two *qualitatively* assessed modules. As noted above (see Taylor 2001c) and as evidenced in the focus of several Cambridge ESOL research studies also referenced (e.g. Galaczi 2005, Vidakovic and Galaczi 2009), it is a consequence of the direct Speaking test format that participants are required to communicate with each other and that performance is assessed by human raters, though with strongly validated assessment criteria, highly trained raters and rigorously applied standardisation systems. If the reliability of assessments of the productive skills tests continues to washback, as a cause for concern, on test takers and other users, then the need for research and other action to improve this situation is clear.

The 72%:28% split on perceived test fairness indicated in Table 6.5 may be considered a reasonably positive response. Interestingly, we find the most frequent of the 49 follow-up responders (some making more than one point) was opposition to *all* tests. Among the 25 comments indicating that tests in general were seen as unfair were the following:

- 'Any test is unfair as they're tested for a day while they have done a lot before'
- 'It just depends on one test'
- 'Because it is a test, it is different from doing it at home'
- 'It is a test – some students can get a good mark in the test but are not able to use it in real life'
- 'I usually cannot perform well on exam day'
- 'Because sometimes it depends on your fate'.

Some of these responses seem to be focusing on the *pressure* of high-stakes tests *per se,* others on the time factor in IELTS specifically, for example, and relevant to the testing of speaking: *'Not fair to test speaking proficiency in a 10 minute test.'* This is interesting feedback on the speaking test model, accepting the construct of a face-to-face event but finding the timing too tight. In fact, the official duration of the IELTS oral interview module is 11 to 14 minutes, including short-answer questions, the opportunity to speak at length on a topic and some interaction with the examiner. For the FCE Speaking test, a test taker participates with another candidate or in a group of three, and is assessed through different types of interaction: with the examiner, with the other candidate(s) and speaking alone. Interestingly, candidates who had already taken IELTS were asked, in the impact study, for their *likes* and *dislikes.* The problems raised by the IELTS impact study respondents could well be addressed through studies of speaking test timing and resources. Table 6.6 summarises the top *likes* and *dislikes* and IELTS Speaking emerges from this albeit limited data as one of the more popular modules with candidates.

Table 6.6 Comparison of test taker IELTS likes and dislikes

IELTS LIKES	n
1 VALIDITY [fair (17), 4-skills / comprehensiveness (15), recognition (7), language *and* study skills (2)]	41
2 SPEAKING	17
3 STRUCTURE, ORGANISATION, FORMAT	16
4 WRITING	15
5 INCENTIVE, CHALLENGE, INTEREST, VARIETY	14
6 LISTENING	13

Indications from the impact study data on test fairness and test *likes* and *dislikes* are, unsurprisingly, that the IELTS test does indeed cause anxiety. Perhaps that is inevitable, as Alderson indicated (2004: ix–x):

> We know that high-stakes tests – tests that have important consequences for individuals and institutions – will have more impact than low-stakes tests, although it is not always clear how to identify and define the nature of those stakes, since what is a trivial consequence for one person may be an important matter for another.

Table 6.7 indicates that both candidates and IELTS preparation teachers have similar perceptions on the relative difficulties of the IELTS skills modules, with the Reading module seen as the most difficult across our candidate and preparation course teacher participants, the Speaking module the least difficult, this latter finding fitting, perhaps, the relative popularity of the oral interview among candidates indicated in Table 6.6 above. The relatively positive perception of the IELTS Speaking test may well be a compliment to the skills of the interlocutors, who tend to be adept at making candidates feel at ease.

Table 6.7 IIS student and teacher perceptions of IELTS module difficulty

Most difficult IELTS Module? (%)	Students	Teachers
Reading	49	45
Writing	24	26
Listening	18	20
Speaking	9	9

Hawkey (2006:123) reports that the inter-relationships between perceived difficulties emerging from the questionnaire data were investigated through second-level analysis of other factors perceived as affecting candidates' performance. The time factor was also frequently mentioned as a cause of worry for candidates. Table 6.8 below emphasises the dominance of the Reading test module as the most difficult according to IIS test-takers, of time pressure as the most prominent problem with the Reading test, and confirms that the Speaking test is perceived as the least difficult module across the selected factors. The fact that the test is rated as the least difficult on *all* the features rated as affecting candidate test performance must be of interest to a range of stakeholders and warrants further investigation.

Table 6.8 Relationship between perceived skill difficulty and other factors perceived as affecting candidate test performance

	Difficulty of language	Difficulty of questions	Unfamiliarity of topics	Time pressure	Fear of tests	Others	Total
Listening	4	7	6	16	4	1	38
Reading	13	20	28	51	14	2	128
Writing	10	10	19	26	8	0	73
Speaking	**2**	**4**	**6**	**9**	**3**	**1**	**25**

With its current 1.5 million candidacy worldwide, IELTS is a case for particularly strong validation research and action. The examples of consequential validity related research in Cambridge ESOL *Research Notes* and in the joint-funded IELTS research programme discussed in this chapter are evidence of the importance attached to this area of test validation.

The *Progetto Lingue* 2000 Impact Study: impact and speaking

The Cambridge ESOL *Progetto Lingue* 2000 (*PL2000*) Impact Study investigated the impact of state foreign language teaching reforms on English language learner performance and of external examinations, in particular the Key English Test (KET) and the Preliminary English Test (PET) as used for the certification of *PL2000* student language levels. The *PL2000* aimed to provide state school foreign language education to better meet the communication and certification needs of students as defined by the *Common European Framework of Reference for Languages* (Council of Europe 2001). One of the project's key policies was to encourage the *external* certification of learners' language proficiency through the examinations of providers such as Cambridge ESOL. The Ministry of Education (Italy) reasoning on this is germane to our test impact discussion and redolent of the globalisation trends:

> External certification represents an added value in quality of "transparent credit" which may facilitate the re-orientation of students in their educational programmes (the transition from one academic direction to another or from a formal system of instruction to professional education) constituting a negotiable certification in the professional world and across national borders (Ministry of Education (Italy) *Progetto Lingue in Communicazionedi Servizio,* September 1999 *[www.istruzione. it/argomenti/autonomia/documenti.]*).

Cambridge ESOL carried out a study of the impact of the *PL2000* during the 2001–02 school year, with the encouragement of the Education Ministry in Italy, collecting data from stakeholders including students, teachers, parents, education managers and language testers. The *PL2000* Impact Study was to provide small-sample quantitative and qualitative impact information on the teaching/learning module organisation, content, methodologies, media and learner success, as seen by the learners themselves, their teachers, their school Heads and their parents.

On the use of external certification as a key element of *PL2000,* a project official commented as follows:

> Teachers were surprised at first, at the idea of external certification, they didn't think it suited their teaching; but external certification is important as it means that students can be checked for their level of competence at any stage, from A1 to C2. Teachers are used to the idea now (Hawkey 2002:65):

PL2000 teacher comments tended to support this view of the status and impact of external exams used for certification within a national education system. Typical are these teacher opinions:

> The KET programme impact is positive; good tests lead to good teaching. KET Speaking is OK, but the writing test is difficult . . . (from a comprehensive school English teacher) (Hawkey 2002:70).

> Exams such as FCE encapsulate the communicative approach, the four skills, especially speaking and writing, and the testing of real communicative abilities (from a three-teacher *liceo* focus group) (Hawkey 2002:71).

Despite the intention that *Progetto* classes should provide good opportunity for spoken communication by the students, the data in Table 6.9 suggested quite a heavy proportion of teacher-to-whole-class talk, perhaps at the expense of learner speaking opportunity.

Table 6.9 Student perceptions of frequency of activities in their English classes at school

Activities in class	Frequently	Quite Often	Sometimes	Never
Individual students				
1. listening to the teacher talking to the whole class	35	20	9	2
2. reading texts (from books or other materials)	25	24	17	1
3. writing notes, letters or compositions	18	27	20	2
4. reading then writing answers to questions	22	23	20	2
5. discussions with whole class	20	24	17	5
Two classes (total 42 students) negotiating block votes				
1. listening to the teacher talking to the whole class	√	√		
2. reading texts (from books or other materials)		√√		
3. writing notes, letters or compositions	√	√		
4. reading then writing answers to questions			√√	
5. discussions with whole class	√	√		

We noted in this case that the students appeared to regard the speaking activities as somewhat *less* prominent in their *PL2000* classes than their teachers did, reminding us, as mentioned in this chapter above, of the difference in perceptions between learners and teachers of the shape and elements of a classroom lesson. However, of the 161 responses to the questionnaire item concerned, more students (35%) felt that it was their English language *speaking* skills that had improved most over the year, compared with writing (34%), reading (16%) and listening (15%). There was further possible evidence of the positive washback of *PL2000* as an educational project and of the tests, including KET and PET, which participants would be taking, both these exams, of course, also following the Cambridge ESOL Speaking test construct of live conversational language use. All 11 teachers from the case-study schools who completed the impact study teacher questionnaire in April 2002 agreed that *communication skills relevant to students' language needs* was a project objective which had been achieved 'very well' or 'well' in their schools.

Hawkey (2006:153) identifies a further exam consequential validity related matter suggested by *PL2000* impact data:

> It was commonplace during the study to hear school Heads, teachers and students refer to 'the PET (FCE or CAE) *course*'; or to see curriculum specifications expressed in exam preparation terms. Making sure that students are prepared for the formats and conventions of external exams is, of course, an important and natural part of an examined course. School language courses that are simply exam cramming, however, would not have been in the spirit of the needs and task-based communicative approaches suggested by the *PL2000*.

What emerges clearly here is the responsibility of high-stakes exam providers to try to minimise the dangers of negative washback (and thus impact) through systematic processes, impact-by-design based, so as to encourage positive consequential validity. But typical of stakeholder feedback on this issue was the project teacher comment: 'KET Speaking tasks seem to reflect PL2000 objectives', or the response of a CAE (C1) course student: 'I think my English is better than the past year probably because with the Cambridge course I can improve my vocabulary and my skills of listening and speaking'. But the macro-skill of speaking is a complex matter, of course, as the Cambridge ESOL Speaking tests attempt to reflect. In the CAE Speaking test candidates are expected to 'demonstrate a range of oral skills: interactional, social, transactional, negotiation and collaboration' (CAE Handbook, 2005:1). The Speaking test, which involves a pair of candidates, includes a 'collaborative task'.

One *PL2000 liceo* teacher is reported in the impact study as finding that although her PET (B1) students could 'speak in English', they were 'not good at *interacting* in the language, i.e. co-operating, using language that helped others, as they would in actual communication, which is often likely to be with people they would not know or would not be like. Such skills, as well as purposeful reading skills, have to be developed with the help of the teacher' (Hawkey 2002:23).

There is thus, in the objectives, approaches and findings of an impact study such as that carried out for the *PL2000*, a fair amount to inform the consequential validity related development of Cambridge ESOL Speaking tests. The importance given to them by key stakeholders such as ministries of education, school directors, teachers, students and parents is underlined by evidence from the *PL2000* impact study.

Conclusion

Chapter 6 has sought to build upon the earlier chapters in this volume. The chapter has explored the constructs and implications of the consequential validity box within the socio-cognitive framework for test validation that provides the context for analysing the assessment of L2 speaking and its operationalisation in the Cambridge ESOL Speaking tests. We have re-visited the background and definitions of test washback and impact and attempted to establish where they belong in the complex process of validating high-stakes exams such as those offered internationally by Cambridge ESOL. We have noted the effects of globalisation leading to the rapid growth of English as a worldwide *lingua franca*, and particularly the prioritisation of oral communication skills. The growing concern with the consequences of increasingly high-stakes English language tests is seen as leading to the expectation they will meet the requirements of stricter and more critical international codes of practice and ethics taking account of current assessment trends and values. We have surveyed and exemplified Cambridge ESOL research initiatives and studies to analyse and adjust positively the consequential validity of its exams taking account of the many complex variables involved.

Chapter 7 will examine the final set of parameters that examination boards need to consider in generating evidence on the validity of their tests, namely those of criterion-related validity.

7 Criterion-related validity

Hanan Khalifa and Angeliki Salamoura
University of Cambridge ESOL Examinations

The previous chapter of this volume introduced the *a posteriori* notion of validity by looking at elements that are external to the test process, i.e. the effect the test score has on various stakeholders. Chapter 7 continues this thread of *a posteriori* validity evidence by examining the extent to which the test correlates with a suitable external measure of performance (see Anastasi 1988:145, Messick 1989:16), in other words, by investigating its criterion-related validity.

As Khalifa and Weir (2009:7–8) point out, evidence of criterion-related validity can come in three forms:

- Firstly, as mentioned above, if a relationship can be demonstrated between test scores and an external criterion which is believed to be a measure of the same ability. This type of criterion-related validity is traditionally subdivided into two forms: concurrent and predictive. Concurrent validity seeks an external indicator that has a proven track record of measuring the ability being tested (Bachman 1990:248). It involves the comparison of the test scores with this other measure for the same candidates taken at roughly the same time as the test. This other measure may consist of scores from some other speaking tests, or ratings of the candidate by teachers (Alderson, Clapham and Wall 1995). Predictive validity entails the comparison of test scores with another measure of the ability of interest for the same candidates taken some time after the test has been given (Alderson et al 1995).

- Demonstration of the qualitative and quantitative equivalence of different forms of the same test is a second source of evidence.

- A third source of evidence results from linking a test to an external standard such as the Common European Framework of Reference (CEFR) through the comprehensive and rigorous procedures of familiarisation, specification, standardisation and empirical validation (Council of Europe 2009).

The discussion of criterion-related validity in this chapter will therefore be structured around the three parameters sketched above and summarised in Figure 7.1.

Figure 7.1 **Aspects of criterion-related validity for speaking (from Weir 2005a)**

Criterion-related validity
• cross-test comparability
• comparison with different versions of the same test
• comparison with external standards

Cross-test comparability

Taylor (2004a:2) argues that test users want to know how one test compares with other available tests which claim to perform a similar function. University admissions officers want to know how to deal with students who present them with TOEFL, IELTS, PTE Academic, CAE or CPE scores; employers need to know how to equate different language qualifications presented by job applicants; educational institutions, teachers and students have to choose which test to take from those on offer. As reported in Khalifa and Weir (2009), the importance attached by test users to test comparability information has increased in recent years, and test providers have had to pay greater attention to issues of *cross-test comparability* – both in terms of the relationships between their own tests and with those offered by other examination boards.

Cross-test comparisons usually take the form of score equivalences, in other words, whether a score on one test is equivalent to a score on another. This of course assumes that both tests measure the same ability. However, if a comparability study is to be informative for the end users, it needs to take account of more than score equivalences. It needs to compare the intended purposes, test content and test performance under live conditions. There have always been informal as well as formal attempts by language schools, individual researchers, and examination providers to compare language proficiency measures. In the following section we note one of the earliest comparability attempts by an examination provider.

Cross-test comparability: Cambridge ESOL practice

Cambridge ESOL and ETS tests

In 1987, Cambridge ESOL commissioned a team of academics under the direction of Professor Lyle Bachman to conduct a three-year comparability study between Cambridge ESOL examinations and examinations offered by the Educational Testing Service (ETS). Although this study is now of primarily historical interest as both FCE and TOEFL have since been substantially revised (and were not testing similar constructs), its value lies in being a pioneering example of a cross-national comparison of two different testing approaches and traditions – the British tradition with a 'flexible but complex system' and the US tradition with a 'rigid and relatively simple psychometric system' (Bachman, Davidson, Ryan and Choi 1995:136), as illustrated in the two speaking tests described below. The study focused on the comparison of FCE (a level-based test targeting what is now known as CEFR B2 level) and TOEFL/TWE/SPEAK (a multi-level test battery, that included reading, listening, structure and vocabulary items, as well as a direct test of written English and a semi-direct speaking test). The researchers carried out content analysis of the two examinations and investigated the reliability of the two test batteries, the abilities measured, the effect of test preparation on test performance, and the interchangeability of FCE and TOEFL scores. With regard to test preparation, Bachman et al (1995) investigated whether there is any difference in test performance on the two tests as a function of whether or not test takers had specifically prepared (by attending a course) to take one of the tests. Using regression analysis, they examined whether participation in an FCE preparatory course would yield a significant effect on performance on either the FCE papers or the ETS tests.

Of relevance to this volume is the finding related to the FCE Speaking test, i.e., Paper 5. In order to investigate score equivalence, the researchers opted for using linear regression analysis as IRT modelling was deemed unsuitable in this case. FCE Paper 5 was regressed on SPEAK (the institutional version of ETS' semi-direct Test of Spoken English), and vice versa, yielding two sets of predictions – FCE Paper 5 scores with corresponding predicted scores for SPEAK and SPEAK scores with predicted scores for FCE Paper 5 (Bachman et al 1995:96–98). The result of the regression did not show high score equivalence (R^2 = 0.327, Bachman et al 1995:97–98). Moreover, the researchers stressed that any statistical correspondences between Cambridge ESOL and ETS tests 'should not be taken as sufficient evidence that they are arbitrarily interchangeable for any or all of the uses for which they are intended. Decisions regarding which test to take, or which scores to accept, for any given test-use situation should also be based on test content considerations . . .' (Bachman et al 1995:99).

The above statement/observation becomes all the more important when one considers the qualitative differences between the two speaking tests under comparison – FCE Paper 5 is a direct test of oral performance, whereas SPEAK is a semi-direct one. This difference is highlighted in the following description of the two tests in Bachman et al (1995):

Paper 5 consists of a face-to-face oral interview, the conduct of which is determined by two sets of choices. First, the number of candidates and interviewers, or examiners, may vary. Some interviews consist of one candidate and one examiner while others may include several candidates and one or two examiners. A second set of choices pertains to the "information package" that provides the content basis for the interview. For each interview, the examiner may choose one information package from among a large number of such packages that contain prompt material such as short reading passages, photographs and charts, and that determine, to a large extent, the content of the interview. Topics vary, and include areas such as holidays, sports, and food and drink. One information package is called a "set book" package, and this contains prompt material based on reading texts which the candidate can prepare before the interview. . . In general, all interviews should follow four stages:

Stage 1: general conversation (brief)
Stage 2: discussion of one or more theme (package)-related photos
Stage 3: discussion of one or more theme-related short reading passages
Stage 4: discussion talk, problem-solving task, role-playing task, etc., related to the theme

(1995:25–26)

The SPEAK is intended to measure speaking, but does not involve a live face-to-face interaction with an interlocutor. Rather, the candidate listens to a number of prompts from a cassette source tape, looks at some stimulus material in an accompanying booklet, and responds on a target cassette tape, which also records the prompts from the source tape.

(1995:27)

The Bachman et al (1995) study is an example of cross test comparisons between examinations offered by two different test providers. It highlighted the need to place any such comparisons within the broader context of the differences between distinctive approaches to test development and test use. It is worth noting here that 20 years on, when the Language Policy Division of the Council of Europe conducted a cross-language benchmarking seminar to calibrate examples of spoken production in five languages across the six levels of the CEFR, the data collection methodology and the research design paid particular attention to the fact that the seminar was dealing with different pedagogic cultures associated with the five languages (see seminar report by Breton, LePage and North 2008). The Bachman et al 1995 study also underlines Cambridge ESOL's early interest in examining the criterion-related validity of its tests.

Cambridge ESOL's Common Scale for Speaking

Of relevance to this discussion is the comparability of assessment scales. In the 1980s and early 1990s, Cambridge ESOL used different assessment scales for its different examinations, mainly because each examination had developed independently rather than as part of a comprehensive and coherent 'suite' of examinations. However, as more examinations were added during the mid-1990s to the product range offered by Cambridge, so the board worked towards integrating its examinations into a coherent system or interpretative framework, developing, among other things, a common assessment scale on which speaking ability can be measured and speaking test scores can be reported. The driving factor for this movement was the desire to foster a common understanding of assessment for speaking across the board's exams, to establish a relationship between its different exams and to foster common practices among its growing network of thousands of Oral Examiners. Hence the introduction of the Cambridge ESOL Common Scale for Speaking in 1996 (also mentioned in Chapters 1 and 4), later revised in 2007 (see below).

As Galaczi and Khalifa (2009a:24) explain, the Common Scale for Speaking spans five global levels (KET/A2 to CPE/C2), which in turn branch out into sublevels (bands) in order to provide the possibility for a more fine-tuned dispersion of candidates taking Cambridge ESOL exams. Each global level in the Cambridge ESOL Speaking scale is broken down into 10 bands (Band 0, 1, 1.5, 2, . . . 4.5, 5). The assessment criteria covered in the scale comprise of four categories: Grammar and Vocabulary (Grammatical Resource and Lexical Resource at Levels C1 and C2), Discourse Management, Pronunciation, and Interactive Communication. The descriptors for each level are stacked into a common scale, so that, for example, the descriptors at KET/A2 Band 5 are identical to those at PET/B1 Band 3 and FCE/B2 Band 1. This suggests some rough equivalences between different bands for different levels. Taking into account the overlap between some of the bands in the different levels, the result is a 25-point common scale covering levels A2–C2 (see Table 7.1; also Galaczi and ffrench 2007 for a more detailed account of the development of this scale).

Cambridge ESOL's exams in the ALTE Framework

In addition to the ESOL Common Scale, Cambridge examinations are also linked to the Association of Language Testers in Europe (ALTE) Framework and the ALTE Can Do descriptors which we will refer to below in this chapter. Here, we provide a brief description of the Framework and descriptors.

At the same time of the development of the ESOL Common Scale for Speaking, ALTE members were working on a 5-level Framework. This was a descriptive framework that sought to locate different foreign language examinations administered by various European test providers on common levels of proficiency, to promote transnational recognition of certification in Europe (Milanovic and Saville 1992b). The original development process of the ALTE Framework went through the following steps (Milanovic and Saville 1992b:2):

1. Members of the ALTE group provided a general (i.e. non-detailed) description of each of their examinations.
2. The group agreed on its external reference points where appropriate (e.g. Threshold and Waystage 1990).
3. The descriptions of each examination were translated and circulated together with sample papers to members.
4. On the basis of Step 3, members placed their examinations provisionally alongside others on the basis of content analysis and expert judgement.
5. Members discussed the groupings and made adjustments.
6. The provisional Table with five levels was drafted and circulated.
7. A research programme was initiated to check the judgements based on content inspection (Steps 4–5).
8. Refinements to descriptions, levels and groupings were made as necessary based on Step 7.
9. The comparison was extended to examinations in specialist areas (e.g. French, German, etc. for business).
10. The Table and descriptions were circulated to the user groups (students, teachers, employers, agencies, etc.) and other examinations providers for feedback.

For the most up-to-date version of the ALTE Framework Table and a comprehensive description of the five levels, the reader is referred to www. alte.org

This ALTE Framework was subsequently linked to the CEFR via the development of ALTE Can Do statements and their anchoring to the CEFR (for details see Jones 2000a, 2001, 2002). The ALTE Can Do Project formed part of the development and exemplification of the ALTE Framework. It aimed at developing descriptions of what learners can or cannot do at each of the ALTE levels. As Jones (2001:5) notes, '[t]he ALTE Can Do Project has a dual purpose: to help end users to understand the meaning of exam certificates at particular levels, and to contribute to the development of the Framework itself by providing a cross-language frame of reference'.

The ALTE Can Dos are language-neutral, user-oriented descriptors which were designed to assist communication between test stakeholders and specifically the interpretation of test results by non-specialists. They are organised into three general areas: *Social and Tourist*, *Work*, and *Study*, following assessment of learner needs. Each of these areas is subdivided into more specific areas, e.g. the Social and Tourist area has sections on *Shopping*, *Eating out*, *Accommodation*, etc. The descriptors cover all four skills with Listening and Speaking combined into one scale relating to interaction. For examples of the ALTE Can Do descriptors see Jones and Hirtzel (2001: 251–257) or www.alte.org . Table 7.1 below (adapted from Jones and Hirtzel 2001) sums up salient features of the ALTE levels and provides an example of Can Do descriptors per level.

Table 7.1 The ALTE Framework

ALTE levels	Salient features	Example descriptor
ALTE Level 5 (Good User)	the capacity to deal with material which is academic or cognitively demanding, and to use language to good effect, at a level of performance which may in certain respects be more advanced than that of an average native speaker	*CAN scan texts for relevant information, and grasp main topic of text, reading almost as quickly as a native speaker.*
ALTE Level 4 (Competent User)	an ability to communicate with the emphasis on how well it is done, in terms of appropriacy, sensitivity and the capacity to deal with unfamiliar topics	*CAN deal with hostile questioning confidently. CAN get and hold onto his/her turn to speak.*
ALTE Level 3 (Independent User)	the capacity to achieve most goals and express oneself on a range of topics	*CAN show visitors round and give a detailed description of a place.*
ALTE Level 2 (Threshold User)	an ability to express oneself in a limited way in familiar situations and to deal in a general way with non-routine information	*CAN ask to open an account at a bank, provided that the procedure is straightforward.*
ALTE Level 1 (Waystage User)	an ability to deal with simple, straightforward information and begin to express oneself in familiar contexts	*CAN take part in a routine conversation on simple predictable topics.*
ALTE Breakthrough Level	a basic ability to communicate and exchange information in a simple way	*CAN ask simple questions about a menu and understand simple answers.*

Finally, Table 7.2 on page 266 brings all three frameworks/scales together.

Cambridge ESOL test development and revision activities during the late 1990s and early 2000s increasingly involved both alignment to the Common Scale for Speaking and also cross-test comparisons across individual speaking tests from various examinations, the scores these generate and the assessment criteria employed (ffrench 2003b). The development of the CELS Speaking test offers a good example of the process of aligning a speaking test to the Common Scale for Speaking and we shall examine this next.

Table 7.2 The relationship between the Cambridge ESOL Common Scale, ALTE Framework and CEFR

Cambridge ESOL Common Scale	ALTE Framework	CEFR
5 / CPE	Level 5	C2
4 / CAE	Level 4	C1
3 / FCE	Level 3	B2
2 / PET	Level 2	B1
1 / KET	Level 1	A2
	Breakthrough Level	A1

Alignment of the CELS Speaking test to the Cambridge ESOL Common Scale for Speaking

The CELS Test of Speaking, which was offered by Cambridge ESOL from (May) 2002 until 2007, was a standalone test of speaking in the context of general English proficiency. It was offered at three levels – Preliminary, Vantage and Higher; these three levels were designed to equate to the existing Cambridge/ALTE Levels 2, 3 and 4, as well as to the CEFR Levels B1, B2 and C1. In developing the new suite of CELS Speaking tests for 2002 (see Hawkey 2004a for a full account of this project and its predecessor tests), a key issue was to ensure their horizontal link to equivalent levels or tests within a wider framework as well as their vertical relationship within the suite (Taylor and Shaw 2002). A rating study was therefore carried out in order to:

- confirm the relationship of CELS speaking proficiency levels to the Cambridge Common Scale for Speaking
- provide an empirical link between CELS speaking proficiency levels and performance levels as described by the ALTE Can Do statements
- verify that CELS rating scales provide a sound vertical equating.

Nine samples of CELS Speaking test performance on video were selected for the study. The sample tests were taken from the CELS standardisation videos and covered the three CELS levels: Preliminary (two tests), Vantage (three tests) and Higher (three tests). Candidate performances in each sample test had previously been rated using the Main Suite Global and Analytic scales to place them at the same proficiency level as performances in PET, FCE or CAE. Two experienced raters were asked to rate candidate performances in the nine sample tests using:

(a) the Cambridge Common Scale rating descriptors

(b) the ALTE Can Do statements.

The two raters observed and 'blind' rated each test twice. Both examiners were very familiar with the Main Suite levels and assessment approaches for

PET, FCE and CAE, but were unfamiliar with the test format for CELS. During the first rating the raters were asked to match the observed performances to the Common Scale for Speaking levels 2 (PET/Threshold), 3 (FCE) and 4 (CAE) using Common Scale Descriptors (see Taylor and Shaw 2002 for an example of these descriptors). During the second rating the raters were asked to link the observed performances to the ALTE Can Do statements for level and skill (see Taylor and Shaw 2002 for the ALTE Can Do descriptors used in this study). In both cases, the raters were required to make notes as they assessed each performance and their follow-up discussions were audio-recorded.

The results revealed a good inter-rater agreement (0.75 using Pearson product-moment correlation coefficients) between the two raters assessing CELS performances (based on Common Scale Band Descriptors) across the three levels of CELS proficiency: Preliminary, Vantage and Higher. A good level of agreement (nearly 95%) was also achieved between these rater assessments derived from the Common Scale Band Descriptors and the original 'standardised' assessments based on Main Suite Band Descriptors. In this way, both CELS and Main Suite performance thresholds were specified in terms of the Common Scale for Speaking.

Performance on CELS was, in addition, empirically linked to the ALTE Can Do statements (Jones 2000a, 2001, 2002). The raters were in general agreement about what candidates were able to do in terms of the ALTE speaking Can Do statements at the Preliminary level. At Vantage and Higher levels, however, there was more variation between raters about which Can Do performance descriptors should be ascribed to which candidates. The raters' observations and recommendations fed directly back into the test development process for the CELS Speaking test.

In the next part of this section, we consider a subsequent cross-test comparison study conducted among the Main Suite examinations and the suite of Business English Certificates (BEC) offered by Cambridge ESOL.

Alignment of the Main Suite and BEC assessment scales for Speaking

Revising the oral assessment scales for the Main Suite examinations and Business English Certificates (BEC) in 2007–08 involved substantial cross-test comparisons across their individual Speaking papers, the scores these generate and the assessment criteria employed, and it is to these projects that we shall turn now.

Before the release of these revised scales, several research studies were set up and are reported in Galaczi (2007a), Galaczi and ffrench (2007), Galaczi, ffrench, Hubbard and Green (in press). They aimed at:

- providing evidence of the extent to which the revised assessment criteria and their descriptors (Grammar/Vocabulary, Discourse Management, Pronunciation, Interactive Communication) performed consistently well at CEFR Levels A2 to C2 in terms of examiner severity, examiner agreement and misfit
- providing recommendations for Oral Examiner/rater training, based on how well specific criteria performed
- comparing the marks awarded using the revised scales with the marks previously awarded on the existing scales.

The methodology followed included the use of expert judges in critiquing the existing descriptors, the use of verbal protocols, a scaling exercise in which examiners matched descriptors to proficiency levels, and a marking trial. The research studies showed that the revised assessment scales performed generally well, as evidenced by the generally acceptable range of examiner severity and levels of agreement between raters. Applying van Moere's (2006) ±1.00 logit cut-off standards to the marks awarded, the majority of raters were found to be within acceptable parameters for harshness/leniency. No more than three raters (out of 28) were outside these limits at any level (Galaczi and ffrench 2007, Galaczi et al in press). In terms of rater consistency, the majority of raters showed acceptable fit statistics (average infit mean square ± 1 standard deviation, O'Sullivan 2005), except two raters, out of 28, who showed too much unpredictability in their marks across levels. Overall, the small number of inconsistent raters suggested that the inconsistency was idiosyncratic, and not a fundamental issue with the scales (Galaczi et al in press). In addition, the marks awarded using the revised scales were on a par with marks awarded using the previous scales; a comparison between the revised and current marks indicated typically a decrease of approximately half a band (Galaczi 2007a, 2007b).

Main Suite and BEC examinations are targeted at different audiences: candidates who want to use English in everyday situations, for general work, social or study purposes, and candidates who wish to gain an English language qualification that is more closely linked to a business context and domain of language use. The growing internationalisation of business and the need for employees to interact in more than just a single language has led to an increase in the teaching of English (and possibly other languages) which is contextualised within a more explicitly business or commercial context. Chapter 1 discussed the issue of test purpose and specificity (see pages 16–19), particularly the challenge of determining precisely how general or specific a test is designed to be. Though BEC is associated with a particular language use domain (i.e. the business context), it remains closer to the 'less specific' rather than the 'more specific' end of the specificity continuum. For a full discussion of the notion of general versus specific language testing and how this informs the constructs underpinning BEC, see O'Sullivan 2006. Because of the targeted audiences, differences between the two examinations are seen in the choice of topic and its associated lexis, structures and functions. For example, BEC topic areas would typically include talking about the office, general business environment, entertainment of clients, relationships with colleagues and clients, travel and meetings, using the telephone, health and safety, buying and selling, products and services, company structures/systems/processes to a list a few (see BEC Handbook 2008:4). On the other hand, Main Suite would typically include more general topics related to personal life and circumstances, living conditions and environment, occupational activities and interests, leisure activities and social life. Despite these differences, both exams share common ground in terms of being level-based, having similar task types, following the same test construction process and applying the same administration procedures. In addition, many of the Main Suite speaking examiners are certificated as BEC examiners and vice versa. Furthermore, both exams are marked using the same criteria and foci for each criterion.

A close look at the analytical scale used for assessing oral performances in PET and BEC Preliminary (both targeting CEFR B1 level) would illustrate how one scale can be used for two examinations despite the differences in targeted audiences and topic selection. It is the less (rather than more) specific nature of BEC that makes this possible. From Table 7.3 on page 270 we see that whether the topic is on business meetings or on personal life, or whether the candidate is using English for social purposes or to participate in a business meeting, the criteria below and their foci would apply (see Chapter 4 for a discussion of the assessment scales). However, if the task requires use of specific lexis and specialist knowledge of vocabulary then this is an issue for examiner training. Such a requirement would be more obvious in other more specific Cambridge ESOL examinations like ILEC (International Legal English Certificate) and ICFE (International Certificate in Financial English). Given their much more specific orientation and purpose, ILEC and ICFE have different assessment scales from those used for Main Suite and BEC.

As a result of the aforementioned cross-test comparability studies and related internal ESOL work, a conceptual framework gradually emerged mapping Cambridge ESOL exams within a shared frame of reference. This built on the earlier work of Common Scale development, the Cambridge/ ALTE 5-level system and the ALTE Can Do project (Jones and Hirtzel 2001), as well as the emergence of the CEFR. Taylor (2004a) presents this framework as it stood in 2004, showing the links as they were understood at that time between Cambridge ESOL suites of level-based examinations or syllabuses, i.e. Main Suite, BEC and YLE (Young Learners English). These suites are targeted at similar ability levels as defined by a common measurement scale based on latent trait methods (see Chapter 7 in Khalifa and Weir 2009 for a discussion of Cambridge ESOL's item banking system); many are also similar in terms of examination content and design (multiple skills components, and similar task/item-types). Taylor (2004b:3) notes that alignment between examinations is based not only on the internal research at Cambridge ESOL referred to above, but also on the 'long established experience of test use within education and society, as well as feedback from a range of examination stakeholders regarding the uses of test results for particular purposes'. At the time of writing, 2004, she suggested it would continue to be refined as further evidence was generated.

Table 7.3 Selected analytic criteria for PET and BEC Preliminary (CEFR B1)

	Criteria & Foci	
	Grammar & Vocabulary Foci: Control, Range, Appropriacy	Discourse Management Foci: Extent, Relevance, Coherence, Cohesion
0	Performance does not satisfy the Band 1 descriptor	
1.0	• Shows sufficient control of simple grammatical forms • Uses a limited range of appropriate vocabulary to talk about familiar topics	• Produces responses which are characterised by short phrases and frequent hesitation • Repeats information or digresses from the topic
1.5	More features of 1.0 than of 3.0	
2.0	Some features of 3.0 and some features of 1.0 in approximately equal measure	
2.5	More features of 3.0 than of 1.0	
3.0	• Shows a good degree of control of simple grammatical forms • Uses a range of appropriate vocabulary when talking about familiar topics	• Produces responses which are extended beyond short phrases, despite hesitation • Contributions are mostly relevant, but there may be some repetition • Uses basic cohesive devices
3.5	More features of 3.0 than of 5.0	
4.0	Some features of 3.0 and some features of 5.0 in approximately equal measure	
4.5	More features of 5.0 than of 3.0	
5.0	• Shows a good degree of control of simple grammatical forms, and attempts some complex grammatical forms • Uses a range of appropriate vocabulary to give and exchange views on familiar topics	• Produces extended stretches of language despite some hesitation • Contributions are relevant despite some repetition • Uses a range of cohesive devices

The 2004 conceptual framework was subsequently revised to accommodate further evidence produced over the following five years. Figure 7.2 illustrates how, based on current evidence, Main Suite, BEC, YLE, ILEC, ICFE, BULATS and IELTS examinations are believed to align with one another and with the levels of the CEFR. Note that the IELTS band scores are the overall scores, not the individual module scores. The issues associated with aligning tests within a wider framework of reference are complex and

Figure 7.2 Alignment of Main Suite, BEC, YLE, ILEC, ICFE, BULATS and IELTS examinations with the Common European Framework of Reference

Source: http://www.cambridgeesol.org/exams/exams-info/cefr.html

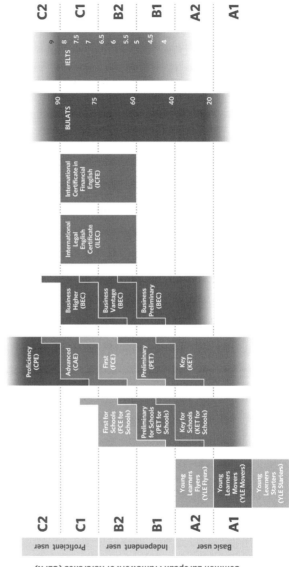

we shall return later in this chapter to consider the potential implications of alignment claims and the challenges they pose for examination providers.

Comparison with different forms of the same test

Whereas in the previous section we talked about the issue of *test comparability*, here we will focus on the issue of *test form equivalence*. The Cambridge ESOL range of tests displayed in Figure 7.2 above share one important feature in that they assess the language proficiency of the candidates attempting the tests and measure this along a common measurement scale based on latent trait theory. For security reasons and to meet the needs of the test users, test providers who operate on a global scale need to produce 'alternate' or 'parallel' forms, i.e. different forms of the same test to be administered on different test sessions over a period of time. But what is test equivalence and how can it be achieved?

The ALTE *Multilingual Glossary of Language Testing Terms* (1998:144) uses comparability and equivalence synonymously. It offers the following definition of equivalence in test forms:

> Different versions of the same test, which are regarded as equivalent to each other in that they are based on the same specifications and measure the same competence. To meet the strict requirements of equivalence under classical test theory, different forms of a test must have the same mean difficulty, variance, and co-variance, when administered to the same persons.

According to Weir (2005a:208), *test equivalence* is established if 'a relationship can be demonstrated between test scores obtained from different versions of a test administered to the same candidates under the same conditions on two different occasions' (see also Mislevy 1992 for a comprehensive discussion of this area).

As is evident from the above definitions, test equivalence is quite challenging to achieve in practice especially in performance testing where human raters are involved. Despite the difficulties, several studies that attempt to measure form equivalence within the context of performance testing are now available in print (Bae and Bachman 2010, Bae and Lee in press, Weir and Wu 2006). As described in Shaw and Weir (2007:236–237), Weir and Wu used checklists to investigate content parallelness of three trial speaking test forms from the viewpoint of raters, in addition to measuring parallel form reliability statistically in a quantitative way (correlation, ANOVA, MFRM). An individual checklist was specifically developed for each of the three task types in which potential variables affecting difficulty of the task were detailed for raters' judgements.

In addition to the use of checklists eliciting raters' views on task difficulty, this study adopted the use of observation checklists to validate Speaking tests as proposed by O'Sullivan, Weir and Saville (2002). Through raters' observations, a comparison of the intended functions in Task B (Answering Questions) of the three trial test forms was made so that the extent to which the tasks across different test forms are similar in the area of test content coverage was also measured. It was reported that the language functions covered in the tasks of answering questions in the three tests were indeed similar. Moreover, *a posteriori* studies on content coverage using candidates' transcripts were carried out. Raters were asked to map the language functions which they observed from candidates' actual performance to confirm previous findings in terms of equivalent coverage of language functions.

The results of the Weir and Wu 2006 study show that without the necessary steps to control cognitive and context variables affecting test difficulty (see Chapters 3 and 4 for a full discussion of this area), test quality may fluctuate over tasks in different test forms. They argue that high correlations in themselves do not provide sufficient evidence that two tests are equivalent. This clearly highlights the important role of the specifications, test design and interlocutor frame in controlling the key variables.

We use below the terms 'qualitative equivalence' or 'cognitive and context comparability' to investigate how parallel test forms are comparable in terms of their cognitive and contextual parameters; and we use the term 'quantitative equivalence' to examine how the alternate test forms are equivalent in terms of their measurement characteristics.

Comparison with different forms of the same test: Cambridge ESOL practice

Cambridge's concern with the equivalence of its speaking tests started very early on. In a 1945 report entitled *Some Problems of Oral Examinations in Modern Languages: An Experimental Approach Based on the Cambridge Examinations in English for Foreign Students*, John Roach (then Assistant Secretary at UCLES) raised concerns about the consistency of speaking examiners' practices underlining the importance of what we would call now examiner standardisation procedures. Half a century later, Taylor notes that Cambridge ESOL puts 'considerable effort and expertise into ensuring examination equivalence through the implementation of a comprehensive set of standard procedures applied at each stage of examination production' (2004a:2). Chapter 5 above gives a detailed account of Cambridge's current approach to examiner training and standardisation.

Qualitative equivalence

Cambridge ESOL ensures qualitative equivalence or cognitive and context comparability between the different test forms through the use of checklists for comparing speaking task design and output of different forms, through its item writer guidelines and through its rigorous procedures of test production. These are discussed below since other elements contributing to context comparability such as uniformity of administration, interlocutor variables, rater training and standardisation have been dealt with in Chapters 4 and 5 respectively.

Checklists

In 1993 Cambridge ESOL and other ALTE members developed a series of skill-related checklists for the purpose of exam evaluation or comparison (Stevens 2004). The ALTE Speaking Content Analysis Checklist (downloadable from <http://www.alte.org/downloads/index.php>) includes: a component on task presentation and layout which is related to practical considerations; a component on guidance provided to candidates in terms of instructions and rubrics; several components describing the examination in terms of its contextual parameters, i.e., task format, task type, topics and prompts used, language ability tested, expected response and marking. It is perhaps not surprising that the ALTE checklists focus primarily on capturing and demonstrating the contextual features of test tasks, given that contextual features of test tasks are more observable and thus easier to determine and describe than the cognitive parameters. The latter are typically hidden, lending themselves less readily to systematic or convenient analysis.

In 1999, Cambridge ESOL commissioned the development of an observation checklist designed for both *a priori* and *a posteriori* analysis of speaking task output. It was envisioned that such a checklist would enable language samples elicited by the task to be scanned for these functions in real time, without resorting to the laborious analysis of transcripts (see Chapter 4 Table 4.14 for the checklist; for details of its development process see O'Sullivan et al 2002). More importantly for our discussion, the checklist has great potential for enabling comparison between different test forms. For example, by allowing the observer-evaluator multiple observations (stopping and starting the recording of a test at will), it is possible to establish whether there are quantifiable differences in the language functions generated by the different tasks, i.e. the observer-evaluator will have the time they need to make frequency counts of the functions. In addition to this *a posteriori* validation procedure, the checklist can also inform *a priori* analyses of tasks (Weir and Wu 2006). By taking into account the expected response of a task (and by describing that response in terms of functions), it is possible to compare predicted and actual test task outcome, thus informing task design. It can also be a useful guide for item writers in taking *a priori* decisions about content coverage as it relates to both cognitive and contextual parameters.

When used as an evaluative tool, the checklist provided valuable insights: into the language functions elicited by the different task types in Main Suite Speaking papers; into how the language elicited by the paired format differs in nature and quality from that elicited by a single format; and into the extent to which there is functional variation among Main Suite Speaking test papers (see Chapter 4 Table 4.13).

Of course, the effective use of the observation checklist requires a degree of training and practice similar to that given to speaking examiners if a reliable and consistent outcome is to be expected. To achieve this, Cambridge ESOL developed, alongside the checklists, standardised training materials for speaking examiners (Saville and O'Sullivan 2000). Observation checklists have been used with Main Suite Speaking tests (O'Sullivan et al 2002) and BEC Speaking tests (Booth 2002). They have also been tailored for application to IELTS Speaking tests (Brooks 2003).

It is worth noting that, while considerable progress has been made in recent years to develop user-friendly and effective checklists for establishing the comparability of contextual factors across test forms, there remains more work to be done to develop instrumentation which is capable of investigating and demonstrating cognitive comparability across tests. Cognitive processing questionnaires have been used successfully in recent years to investigate the cognitive validity parameters of IELTS test tasks (see Weir, O'Sullivan and Horai 2006 for speaking, Weir, O'Sullivan, Yan and Bax 2007 for writing, and Weir, Hawkey, Green and Devi 2009 for reading). However, these investigative studies all involved experimental, one-off research designs which were both time-consuming and labour-intensive for those involved (both test takers and researchers), and they are for this reason not entirely practical for a large-scale test producer to use on a routine, operational basis. Converting such cognitive processing questionnaires for test takers into instrumentation that an examination board can use routinely and efficiently to establish cross-task or cross-test cognitive comparability presents a significant challenge. Nevertheless, just as the observation checklist mentioned above (O'Sullivan et al 2002) was developed as a practical and economically viable alternative to the more heavy-duty methodology of transcribing and analysing oral test data, so it is to be hoped that a similar solution can be found in the future for investigating and demonstrating cognitive comparability across test forms.

Item Writer guidelines

For each Cambridge ESOL examination, there are corresponding item writer guidelines. These provide item writers with guidance regarding the writing of tasks and selection of visuals for Speaking test materials. The item writer guidelines (IWG) document provides a description of the Speaking test paper: format, task type and focus, length of each task, overall timing, and mark scheme. The IWG provide advice on selecting materials. For example, content must be accessible, avoiding as far as possible bias for or against any candidates whatever their age, interests, field of specialisation or country of origin. Similarly, the message of visuals should be clear and unambiguous. The IWG also provide advice on writing the Speaking test tasks, for example with respect to the input language (rubric and stimulus material) and the expected candidate output (structure and lexis).

Standard procedures for the production of examination materials

The development of any Cambridge ESOL Speaking examination passes through the following stages: commissioning, pre-editing, editing, trialling, trial test review, test construction, examination overview and question paper preparation (see Appendix C for a full description).

At the commissioning stage, external test material writers are commissioned to write speaking test material. The pre-editing stage is intended to select materials which will progress into the production process and to improve the quality and maximise the quantity of material available at the editing stage. The editing stage ensures that, as far as possible, material is of an acceptable standard for inclusion in trial tests. Trialling helps determine how well individual speaking tasks function and informs the development of marking criteria. The participants used for trialling reflect, as far as possible, the variety found in the target population in terms of age, proficiency level, L1 and educational background. The trial test review stage considers trial results in terms of candidate performance and feedback received from examiners, candidates and test administration centres. At this stage, recommendations are made as to which material to take forward to future live speaking tests. The test construction stage is a key activity in the production of speaking test papers to ensure that they meet required standards in terms of proficiency level, coverage, content and comparability. The examination overview stage is where the content of the examination as a whole (i.e. all the skills papers) is reviewed to confirm earlier decisions made at the paper construction stage and take remedial action where necessary; to check that topics are not repeated across test papers and that there is a range of cultural contexts where appropriate. The question paper preparation is the process whereby the constructed test paper is prepared for printing, printed and stored ready for use.

Quantitative equivalence

The 1987 Cambridge–TOEFL Comparability study reported above also looked into the equivalence of different test forms of FCE (Bachman et al 1995). For speaking, in particular, the study examined the equivalence of the 15 FCE Paper 5 forms (Speaking test packages) that were administered during the study. Using multiple regression analysis, with FCE Paper 5 scores as the criterion variable and FCE Paper 5 form as one of the predictors, it was found that the different forms of Paper 5 and the interaction between speaking ability and form accounted for only 2% of the variance of Paper

5 test scores after controlling for speaking ability. This variance is not large and suggests that form was not a major source of measurement error in this case, providing useful evidence to support a claim about form equivalence across the 15 Paper 5 forms.

Quantitative methods such as classical analysis and MFRM are regularly used as a means of checking the equivalence of the alternate forms of the Cambridge ESOL Speaking tests. Table 7.4 provides distribution statistics for KET Speaking test papers over a number of sessions in a 4-year period; the mean speaking scores in this table are reported as overall raw scores out of 30. The table shows no major differences between the test papers in terms of their measurement characteristics.

Table 7.4 Distribution statistics for candidate performance on KET (2004–07 sessions)

Session	June A 04	June B 04	Nov 04	Dec 04		
Mean	22.11	22.2	22	21.7		
S.D	3.19	3.0	3.1	3.3		
Session	**Mar 05**	**May 05**	**June A 05**	**June B 05**		
Mean	22.2	22.2	22.2	22.36		
S.D	3.2	3.1	3.1	2.96		
Session	**Mar 06**	**May 06**	**June A 06**	**June B 06**	**Nov 06**	**Dec A 06**
Mean	22.35	22.43	21.9	22.44	22.36	22.04
S.D	2.94	2.95	3.11	2.9	2.96	3.12
Session	**June A 07**	**June B 07**	**Nov 07**	**Dec A 07**	**June A 07**	**June B 07**
Mean	22.33	22.48	22.02	22.43	22.33	22.48
S.D	3.05	2.88	3.23	2.97	3.05	2.88

The picture is replicated if we consider another Main Suite examination. Table 7.5 below provides the distribution statistics of FCE over a period of two years; here the mean scores shown are the scaled speaking values out of 40.

Cambridge ESOL's Research and Validation Group provides annual internal reports on the performance of the individual Speaking tests of Main Suite examinations (Bell 2009a, b, c, d, e). Typical questions addressed by these reports would include the following:

- Which tasks proved popular or unpopular by part, as measured by the frequency of their use?
- What is the overall performance of candidates on each task per part?
- What is the level of agreement between the Global Achievement mark and the analytical scale marks?
- How many assignments did each examiner undertake per year?
- What is the level of agreement between the scores given by the interlocutor and the assessor by session and administration centre?

Table 7.5 Distribution statistics for candidate performance on FCE (2008–09 sessions)

	Sessions	Mean	Std. Dev.
2008	March	32.03	4.61
	June A	32.46	4.77
	June B	31.96	4.67
	December A	30.27	5.10
	December B	30.22	5.14
2009	March	30.63	5.08
	June A	31.09	5.14
	June B	30.79	5.00
	December A	30.43	4.92
	December B	30.02	5.23

• What is the overall performance by candidates by session, by country, as well as by marking criteria and session?

Answers to these questions provide information on the use and performance of test materials, on inter-rater correlations, on candidate performance, on examiner quality; all of these contribute to the decision making process and to continuing monitoring of qualitative and quantitative equivalence of different test forms.

Comparison with external standards

There is a growing interest worldwide in *comparability with external standards* such as PIRLS (Progress in International Reading Literacy Study), PISA (Programme for International Student Assessment) or, in the case of language curriculum and examinations, the CEFR. These standards tend to be influential as they provide policy makers with tools that can be used for gathering baseline data, for benchmarking and for evaluating current practices. External standards are of particular benefit to governments implementing educational or test reform initiatives. The external standard which is of relevance to our discussion here is the CEFR.

Less than a decade after its publication in 2001, the CEFR (Council of Europe 2001) seems to be the dominant external framework of reference in the field of language assessment. The CEFR has been endorsed by a European Union Council Resolution (November 2001) which recommended its use in setting up systems for the validation of language competences (<http://www. coe. int / T / DG4 / Portfolio/?L = E&M = /documents_intro/common_frame work.html>). More recently, many countries in Europe and beyond increasingly couch their foreign language requirements in terms of CEFR levels and Khalifa and Weir (2009:201–203) provide a detailed account of the situation as it appeared in 2009.

For examination providers, therefore, it has become increasingly necessary to make the case that their exams are aligned to the CEFR. Since 2003, the CoE has attempted to facilitate the alignment process by providing a toolkit of resources, including a draft Manual for relating language examinations to the CEFR and a technical reference supplement to this (Council of Europe 2003a, 2004) and by providing fora where practitioners share their reflections on the use of the Manual and their experience in using the different linking stages as suggested in the Manual. Examples of such fora include a seminar entitled 'Reflections on the use of the Draft Manual for Relating Language Examinations to the CEFR: Insights from Case Studies, Pilots and other projects' held in Cambridge in December 2007, and a research colloquium, entitled 'Standard Setting Research and its Relevance to the CEFR' (Athens, May 2008). Cambridge ESOL was one of several different test providers who piloted the draft Manual, and suggested improvements to it in the aforementioned fora (Khalifa, ffrench and Salamoura 2010); contributions from a variety of testing agencies informed a full revision of the Manual in 2009. (See Martyniuk (ed) (2010) for a full published report on the 2007 Cambridge Colloquium together with a selection of CEFR-related case studies).

In addition to the Manual, the CoE has published learner samples illustrating the CEFR levels. For speaking in English, for example, it released two DVDs with oral performances in 2003–04 – one comprising samples from Cambridge ESOL's Main Suite and Certificate in English Language Skills (CELS) examinations that were calibrated to the CEFR, and the other comprising a set of samples provided by Eurocentres. Recently, the CoE published online a new set of speaking performances compiled by the Centre International d'Etudes Pédagogiques (CIEP). These are available at <www.coe.int/T/DG4/Portfolio/?L=E&M=/main_pages/illustrationse. html> and <www.ciep.fr/en/publi_evalcert/dvd-productions-orales-cecrl/videos/english.php>.

Linking tests to an external standard or framework is not straightforward, however, and the role and status of the CEFR in this regard remains controversial. Several writers in the field highlighted early on the limitations of the CEFR in terms of its relevance and implications for language testing (Fulcher 2004, Weir 2005b). More recently, Milanovic and Weir (2010) present a comprehensive and in-depth overview of the issues involved. While they acknowledge that the CEFR has raised awareness of language issues, helping to articulate objectives for language learning and teaching, at the same time they express their concern that the CEFR may be subject to misinterpretation and misuse. They highlight the deliberately underspecified and incomplete nature of the CEFR 'which makes it an appropriate tool for comparison of practices across many different contexts in Europe and beyond' (2010:x). However, this also means it is not (and was never intended to be) applicable to all contexts without user intervention to adapt it flexibly to suit local purposes and to take account of local conditions and features. This has direct implications for questions of test alignment, since an overly prescriptive approach or over-interpretation of the *illustrative* scales of descriptors in standard setting exercises risks resulting in unhelpful and misleading claims that two tests are 'doing the same thing' or 'mean the same thing' simply because they have both been placed at the same CEFR level. As Jones and Saville (2009:54–55) astutely point out:

> . . .some people speak of applying the CEFR to some context, as a hammer gets applied to a nail. We should speak rather of referring a context to the CEFR. The transitivity is the other way round. The argument for alignment is to be constructed, the basis of comparison to be established. It is the specific context which determines the final meaning of the claim. By engaging with the process in this way we put the CEFR in its correct place as a point of reference, and also contribute to its future evolution.

Comparison with external standards: Cambridge ESOL practice

The previous section acknowledged that the role and status of the CEFR remains contentious with regard to language tests and attention was drawn to some significant reservations, expressed both within the Cambridge ESOL organisation and more widely in the language testing profession, about the process of aligning tests to the CEFR and the meaningfulness of test alignment claims. (See Milanovic and Weir 2010 for a fuller discussion of the issues and of Cambridge ESOL's position.) Despite these reservations, real-world demands for statements about the nature of the relationship between a given test and the CEFR cannot easily be ignored, and test providers such as Cambridge ESOL have to address public and governmental expectations in some meaningful and responsible way, as the case studies below aim to illustrate.

The historical, conceptual and empirical relationship between Cambridge ESOL exams and the CEFR is well documented by Taylor and Jones (2006) and Milanovic (2009), while Khalifa and Weir (2009) detail in Chapter 7 of their volume how the CEFR is embedded in the Cambridge ESOL test development and validation cycle. In this section we will discuss Cambridge ESOL's practice in aligning or maintaining alignment to the CEFR, bringing forward examples that illustrate the alignment stages and practices proposed by the Manual (Council of Europe 2003a, 2009), and how these practices have been further extended and adapted to suit the Cambridge ESOL context where appropriate. We provide two case studies for the purpose of illustration.

Case study 1: Cambridge ESOL's 2008–09 CEFR DVD of speaking performances

Cambridge ESOL recently developed a set of Speaking test performances which exemplify a range of the CEFR levels. This newly developed selection of Cambridge ESOL Speaking test performances was planned to coincide with the update of Cambridge ESOL FCE and CAE examinations in December 2008, the revision of the assessment scales for speaking for Main Suite and BEC and the release of the final version of the CoE Manual for relating language examinations to the CEFR (2009). The set consists of Main Suite tests and is intended for use as calibrated samples in CEFR standardisation training and ultimately in aiding a common understanding of the CEFR levels. They can be found at Cambridge ESOL's website: <www. cambridgeesol.org/what-we-do/research/speakingperformances.html>.

In order to select oral performances exemplifying CEFR Levels A2–C2, an internal research project was initiated and implemented. The following provides a brief summary of the study and the reader is referred to Galaczi and Khalifa (2009b) for a detailed discussion.

Video recordings of 28 test takers distributed in 14 pairs were selected for the purpose of this study. Eight raters participated in the project. They were chosen because of their extensive experience as raters for Main Suite Speaking tests. They had also participated in previous Cambridge ESOL marking trials and had been shown through FACETS analyses to be within the norm for harshness/leniency and consistency. Two scales from the CEFR Manual were used: a global scale (Table C1, Council of Europe 2009:184) and an analytic scale (Table C2, Council of Europe 2009:185) comprising five criteria: Range, Accuracy, Fluency, Interaction, Coherence; this generated a total of six criteria. A CEFR familiarisation exercise was carried out to refresh raters' understanding of the CEFR scales for oral assessment and to establish a common interpretation of the descriptors. A fully crossed design was employed in which all raters marked all of the test performances on all of the assessment criteria.

The marks awarded were analysed using a multi-faceted Rasch model where candidate, rater and criterion were treated as facets. The results indicated a very small difference in rater severity (spanning from 0.37 to -0.56 logits), which was well within an acceptable severity range and gave no cases of unacceptable fit (all cases were within the acceptable range of 0.5 to 1.5 logits), indicating high levels of examiner consistency. These results signalled a high level of homogeneity in the marking of the test, and provided scoring validity evidence (Weir 2005a) for the ratings awarded. The results also illustrated very strong rater agreement in terms of typical and borderline performances at Levels A2 to B2. At Levels C1 and C2 there was a lower level of agreement among raters regarding the level of the performances; in addition, the marking produced mostly candidates with differing proficiency profiles and so no pair emerged as presenting two typical candidates across all assessment criteria at the respective level, which led to extending the project into a second phase. Galaczi and Khalifa (2009b) attributed the lower degree of agreement among raters at the higher proficiency levels to the higher degree of difficulty when marking higher-level candidates whose output is more complex and therefore leaves more room for divergent evaluations.

Due to the lower rater agreement for the C levels as described above, it was decided to select new C level performances and to rate them afresh following the same procedures. The results of this phase produced a typical pair of test takers at C1 level across all CEFR assessment criteria, with very high rater agreement. The pairs used at C2 had more varied performances and no pair emerged as having two typical C2 performances across all assessment criteria. According to Galaczi and Khalifa (2009), this result is expected since the performances used in the study came from the rater training pool where both typical and borderline cases should feature to allow raters to develop familiarity with a range of test taker abilities.

Taking the statistical evidence into account, five pairs of candidates emerged as the most suitable Main Suite illustrations for Levels A2 to C2, with the C2 pair including one typical candidate at that level across all criteria, while the second test taker in the pair showed borderline performance at the C1/C1+ level (see Table 7.6 below).

Commentaries were also provided for each selected performance; these included positive comments about what this learner Can Do, as well as an explanation of why the learner is not at the level above. An example from a C1 level candidate is given in Table 7.7, and the full set of commentaries can be found online at <www.cambridgeesol.org/what-we-do/research/speaking-performances.html>.

In this case study we outlined the development of a tool for exemplifying the CEFR – the selection of speaking performances from Cambridge ESOL

Table 7.6 Selected performances

Candidate	Overall level	Range	Accuracy	Fluency	Interaction	Coherence
Mansour	A2	A2	A2	A2	A2	A2
Arvids	A2	A2	A2	A2	A2	A2
Veronica	B1	B1	B1	B1	B1	B1
Melissa	B1	B1	B1	B1	B1	B1
Rino	B2	B2	B1+/B2	B2	B2	B2/B2+
Gabriela	B2	B2	B2	B2	B2	B2
Christian	C1	C1	C1	C1	C1	C1
Laurent	C1	C1	C1	C1	C1	C1
Ben	C1/C1+	C1	C1	C1/C1+	C1+	C1
Aliser	C2	C2	C2	C2	C2	C2

Table 7.7 Sample candidate commentary

Laurent: Level C1

Laurent communicates very naturally. He has sufficient range and accuracy to express himself on a wide range of subjects, with occasional slowing down when speaking about more complex issues. He could not be said to have the degree of fluency, nor the ability to express "finer shades of meaning" which would place him in the C2 band.

Range (C1):
Laurent has command of a wide range of linguistic resources (*"I don't take time to do enough sport because I'm always busy with other things", "they want to show us how we use oil and how dirty it can be [. . .] all these people who are working very hard and they are so dirty", "dumping rubbish everywhere", "you can't see it immediately, but maybe you will see it in the future", "maybe it was a wood before that they had to burn down . . . and . . . and where are the animals who lived there?"*). He uses a tag question very naturally (*"isn't it?"*).

Accuracy (C1):
Laurent demonstrates a sufficiently high degree of accuracy throughout the test, although there are a few errors (*"take attention", "a contact with the client", "animals who lived", "if you can change something in your life it can make you more happy"*). He corrects himself (*"to work . . .to walk, sorry"*).

Fluency (C1):
At times the delivery is slowed down and becomes rather measured: this is noticeable in the more conceptually difficult areas where coherence is maintained but at the expense of flow.

Interaction (C1):
Laurent comments on his partner's statements (*"I think it's kind of old, really. . .sorry!"*), and invites comment from his partner, (*"What d'you think about. . .", "it's also the same with the last picture, isn't it?"*). He responds (*"yes indeed!", "yes, that's right", "Oh yes, I see"*), takes up his partner's comments in Part 4 very naturally (*"it depends which way, of course . . ."*), and moves the discussion on by relating his contributions skilfully to those of his partner.

Main Suite exams which are typical of each CEFR level. In the following case study we will be looking into how such tools as well as procedures suggested by the Manual can be used to maintain (or establish) alignment to the CEFR within the context of an international exam body.

Case study 2: Maintaining FCE alignment to the CEFR

Khalifa et al (2010) focused on the relationship between the CEFR and the FCE (a well-established examination which pre-dates the CEFR). In their study, they provide reflections from piloting the Manual procedures, in particular Familiarisation and Specification, as a means of: a) maintaining the FCE/CEFR alignment, and b) weaving Manual prescribed procedures into Cambridge ESOL practices. Their work demonstrates how the Manual activities can be constructively used and extended, not only to build a linking argument, but also to maintain it. Here we will report on study methodology and findings that are of relevance to speaking (for details on other skill areas, the reader is referred to Khalifa et al 2010).

Familiarisation

The Manual perceives the familiarisation procedure as 'a selection of activities designed to ensure that participants in the linking process have a detailed knowledge of the CEFR' and considers it an 'indispensable starting point' before a linking exercise can be carried out effectively (Council of Europe 2003a:1).

Cambridge ESOL implemented a number of Manual prescribed and non-Manual prescribed Familiarisation activities in a face-to-face workshop with internal and external staff responsible for FCE test construction, marking, analysis and grading. The workshop included a variety of activities relevant to the FCE context. The non-Manual prescribed activities were designed by Cambridge ESOL to complement the Manual activities and to ensure full coverage of the needs and purposes of the workshop. The aim of the workshop was to enable reflections on:

- how effective the Manual activities are in familiarising participants with the CEFR
- how the activities can be complemented to reflect the FCE context more appropriately (see the non Manual prescribed activities in Table 7.8
- how effective they are as a means of maintaining the FCE–CEFR alignment
- how best they can be incorporated in the FCE test cycle.

The full day workshop brought together a total of 14 FCE expert judges. All participants had extensive experience in developing and validating tests. The event also included pre- and post-workshop activities, all of which are shown in Table 7.8 below. The majority of the tasks dealt with the CEFR B2 level – the FCE exam level – and its adjacent B1 and C1 levels. The focus on the B2 level and comparisons with the B1 and C1 levels was a feature introduced to aid understanding of the characteristics of this level and its differences from the adjoining levels.

Before the workshop, participants carried out preparation tasks, such as background reading, to update their knowledge of the CEFR and its associated projects such as the European Language Portfolio and how the CEFR has affected the development of Cambridge ESOL examinations. They also reflected on how the use of the CEFR has affected their own work on Cambridge ESOL examinations, e.g. in terms of item writing, scale construction, marking productive skills, etc. Other pre-workshop tasks aimed at ensuring common understanding of the CEFR global scale and a selection of B1 to C1 language use descriptors related to the four language skills:

Table 7.8 The FCE–CEFR workshop programme

The FCE–CEFR workshop programme	
Pre-workshop activities: Introduction to the topics and activities of the face-to-face workshop	
Manual Prescribed	**Non-Manual Prescribed**
• Descriptor-sorting activity: sorting out mixed up descriptors from a variety of CEFR scales into B1–C1 levels • Self-assessment of foreign language ability using CEFR	• Background reading: Taylor & Jones (2006:1–5) • Juxtaposing the target B2 level with its adjacent B1 & C1 levels in all descriptor-sorting and rating activities throughout the workshop
Face-to-face workshop	
Manual Prescribed	**Non-Manual Prescribed**
• Descriptor-sorting activity • Rating activity: rating of spoken and written performances as well as reading and listening tasks across B1–C1 levels	Presentations on the origins, aims and nature of the CEFR
Post-workshop activities: Consolidation of knowledge gained and feedback on workshop effectiveness	
Manual Prescribed	**Non-Manual Prescribed**
Descriptor-sorting activity	Workshop evaluation questionnaire

listening, speaking, reading and writing. A descriptor-classification exercise was used to achieve this aim. A further task involved using the CEFR global scale to self-assess own ability in a second language.

The face-to-face workshop itself started with an introductory focus on the origins, aims and nature of the CEFR, its relevance for language assessment and its implications for participants as professional language testers working with Cambridge ESOL. The workshop then moved on to a descriptor-sorting activity where participants classified language use descriptors into CEFR levels, building on one of the pre-workshop tasks. The workshop ended by training participants in applying skill-specific CEFR B1 to C1 level scales to CEFR-calibrated spoken and written performances, as well as CEFR-calibrated reading and listening tasks (rating activity in Figure 7.3) The CEFR-calibrated materials used were those published by the Council of Europe (2003b, 2003c, 2005).

In the post-workshop tasks, participants were asked to evaluate the effectiveness of the activities used before and during the workshop in terms of familiarising participants with the CEFR. Figure 7.4 below summarises the responses to the workshop evaluation questionnaire. Overall, the participants found the workshop activities effective. Figure 7.3 shows that juxtaposing the B2 level with its adjacent B1 and C1 levels was judged to be the most effective feature of the workshop. This was followed by a self-assessment activity, background reading, and a descriptor sorting activity.

After the workshop, participants were also asked to revisit their earlier classification of descriptors into CEFR levels, building on the knowledge

Figure 7.3 Participant evaluation on the effectiveness of the workshop activities

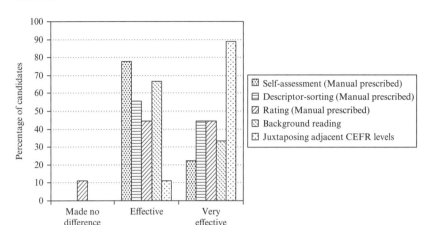

gained and the discussion that took place at the workshop. A comparison of the results from the pre- and post-workshop descriptor-sorting tasks was carried out to check the effect of the workshop descriptor-sorting on familiarising participants with the CEFR scales used in these tasks.

Figure 7.4 below presents the mean percentage of rater responses matching the target CEFR level in the pre- and post-workshop descriptor-sorting sessions and shows how many descriptors were placed at the correct CEFR level. Exact agreement in all sessions is satisfactory as it has an average of 77% and never fell below 66%. Although there is some variation across the four skills, on average raw scores improved or stayed the same from the pre-workshop exercises to the post-workshop ones.

Figure 7.4 Mean percentage of rater responses matching target CEFR level in the pre- and post-workshop descriptor-sorting activities

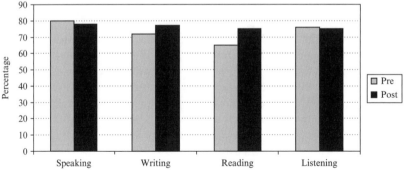

Improvement varies but this may be due to the high level of previous familiarity and experience of participants with the CEFR. The majority of the participants claimed (in a pre-workshop questionnaire) that they were fairly familiar with the framework before the workshop. As a result, they scored quite high in the pre-workshop sessions where they had been instructed to classify the descriptors based on their *own* background knowledge and experience with the framework. For Speaking in particular, they scored around 80% correct in both the pre- and post-workshop activity.

Intra-rater reliability (Spearman correlations) is satisfactory across all four scales of the descriptor-sorting activity which ranged on average from 0.85 to 0.94 (the average for Speaking was 0.90), meaning that the raters were sufficiently consistent with themselves. Average values of inter-rater reliability are also satisfactory.

The study concludes that the Manual prescribed activities appear to be effective in terms of familiarising participants in the linking process with the CEFR. However, the type and amount of familiarisation activities need to be considered depending on the extent of participants' familiarity with the CEFR, as discussed above. In the contexts where participants are not yet familiar with it, it may be appropriate for them to start with some scaffolding activities, such as background reading on the origin, aims and aspirations of the CEFR. Their awareness should also be raised to the existence of the CEFR toolkit of resources. In contexts where participants are quite familiar with the CEFR (such as the group in this study), activities like the one Cambridge ESOL introduced which focus on carefully examining adjacent levels and identifying criteria differences between these levels may prove to be beneficial in understanding the CEFR levels/descriptors/scales.

For Cambridge ESOL, familiarisation with the CEFR is seen as part of consolidating and building on existing knowledge as well as an awareness-raising activity, especially for staff and networks just entering the organisation. As a direct consequence of the FCE–CEFR workshop, four self-access CEFR induction worksheets were designed as CEFR 'familiarisation tools' for use as part of Cambridge ESOL's staff training and induction programme. The worksheets focus on different aspects of the CEFR and the relationship between Cambridge ESOL examinations and the CEFR (see Table 7.9 below for an overview and Appendix E for a sample worksheet).

Cambridge ESOL staff are required to complete at least two of the four worksheets, the selection being guided by their work focus and needs. The current Cambridge ESOL process for recruiting, training, monitoring and evaluating item writers and examiners includes explicit reference to the CEFR where appropriate.

Table 7.9 Topic and focus of the Cambridge ESOL CEFR induction worksheets

Topic — Focus	Theoretical	Practical
CEFR	Induction Worksheet 1 Provides general introduction to the CEFR.	Induction Worksheet 3 Hands-on activities both based on the Manual familiarisation tasks (Chapter 3): self-assessment in a foreign language using the CEFR and descriptor-sorting.
ESOL exams & CEFR	Induction Worksheet 2 Discusses the relationship of the Cambridge ESOL exams and the CEFR.	Induction Worksheet 4 Asks participants to compare and contrast one Cambridge ESOL assessment scale with an equivalent one from the CEFR.

Specification

According to the Manual, *Specification* involves 'mapping the coverage of the examination in relation to the categories of the CEFR' (Council of Europe 2003a:6). It aims to build a linking claim of how an exam relates to the CEFR via a thorough description of the exam content, implemented by filling in the Specification Forms A1–A23 provided by the Manual in Chapter 4 (Council of Europe 2003a:34–63).

To complete this phase, Cambridge ESOL commissioned an external consultant who is familiar with both the FCE exam and the CEFR, being at the time of the study a Principal Examiner and item writer for FCE. Other roles have helped the consultant develop a thorough knowledge of the CEFR (e.g. presenter on the topic of the FCE–CEFR link within the Cambridge ESOL network, inspector of EAQUALS schools including their work on mapping their class levels to the CEFR). The consultant worked individually and with a number of internal staff (from the Assessment and Operations and the Research and Validation Groups of Cambridge ESOL) in order to fill in Forms A1–A23 and to map the construct of the FCE to the CEFR. This process involved:

- Reading thoroughly Chapter 4 of the Manual on Specification, as well as Chapters 1 and 2 to obtain introductory and background information.
- Consulting all the CEFR scales suggested in the Specification forms, a variety of FCE related documents, including the FCE test specifications (FCE Handbook) and task specifications (item writer guidelines), as well as *Vantage* (Van Ek and Trim 2001).
- Completing relevant forms. Forms A15–18 and A22 were not completed as the FCE exam does not explicitly test integrated or mediation skills. The content of the forms was also discussed and agreed on by the FCE Subject Manager and Subject Officers.
- Providing a written report on the process.

The FCE was classified as B2 level across all four skills – reading, writing, listening and speaking. Overall, the procedures suggested and the forms completed were found useful in mapping the FCE construct to the CEFR. Here we provide an example of the B2 justification compiled for speaking. Table 7.10 shows the B2 and B2+ descriptors of the CEFR scale 'overall Spoken Interaction' (Council of Europe 2001:74).

Table 7.10 The B2 (and B2+) descriptors from the CEFR scale 'Overall Spoken Interaction' (Council of Europe 2001:74)

Overall Spoken Interaction
B2   *Can use the language fluently, accurately and effectively on a wide range of general, academic, vocational or leisure topics, marking clearly the relationships between ideas. Can communicate spontaneously with good grammatical control without much sign of having to restrict what he/she wants to say, adopting a level of formality appropriate to the circumstances.*
B2+   *Can interact with a degree of fluency and spontaneity that makes regular interaction, and sustained relationships with native speakers quite possible without imposing strain on either party. Can highlight the personal significance of events and experiences, account for and sustain views clearly by providing relevant explanations and arguments.*

The B2 justification for the FCE was as follows:

In the FCE Speaking test candidates are required to express their views on a wide range of topics and to organise what they say ('Do you have a favourite newspaper or magazine?' 'Why do you like it?'). The candidate is required to provide reasons and explanations. There is no preparation time given in Parts 1, 3 and 4 and the candidates are required to answer spontaneously. They have to handle different levels of formality, one with the interlocutor (likely to be older and not viewed as a peer) and another with the second candidate, likely to be a peer ('Let's go for that, OK?' 'What about you?' etc.).

We will now move on to discuss how the information required by the Manual can be embedded within examination board practice. The Manual Specification forms aim at providing:

(i) a general and detailed description of the examination content with regard to issues of test development, marking, grading, data analysis, results reporting and rationale for decisions (Forms A1–A7)

(ii) mapping of the examination content onto the CEFR (Forms A8–A23) along individual and integrated skills as well as the language competence required by the examination.

Cambridge ESOL already makes available the information outlined in (i) in relation to FCE via internal documents, such as item writer guidelines, routine test production documentation, standard operational procedures for exam production, and grading manuals, as well as via publicly available documents, including the FCE Handbook and annual reports on FCE performance which can be accessed through the Cambridge ESOL website. These documents describe the objectives and the content of the FCE and explain how they are implemented.

Mapping an exam onto the CEFR, as envisaged in the Manual, corresponds to the planning and design phases of the FCE, and in general Cambridge ESOL's test development model (for a detailed description of the model see Saville 2003). In these phases, test specifications are produced linking needs to requirements of test usefulness and to frameworks of reference such as the CEFR. Decisions are made with regard to item types, text features, range of topics etc. Task design and scale construction take place which include explicit CEFR reference. This is documented in research publications (e.g. Khalifa and ffrench 2009 on the comparison of the CEFR and the FCE speaking scales; Galaczi and ffrench 2007 on the revised speaking assessment scales for Main Suite and BEC), examiner instruction booklets and item writer guidelines, and is fed back to examiners and item writers via training and co-ordination.

Spoken corpora and criterion-related validity

Although there is a considerable literature now discussing the potential of written corpora for language assessment (cf. Barker 2010, Taylor and Barker 2008), there is relatively little reported on the use of spoken corpora in validating speaking tests. This, however, comes as no surprise given the fact that there are as yet no publicly available spoken corpora of test performances (Anne O'Keeffe 2009, personal communication). And yet, spoken corpora can play a very similar role to that of written corpora for Writing tests. Realising this potential, Cambridge ESOL started building corpora of spoken learner data using recordings of their Speaking tests in the early 2000s (e.g. Ball and Wilson 2002). A number of studies have already made use of small scale oral corpora consisting of speaking data from Cambridge ESOL exams. These studies have investigated a variety of topics: the investigation of the difficulty of the oral story-telling task for young learners in YLE through the qualitative analysis of task responses (Ball 2002b); the patterns of interaction in Paper 3 ('two-way collaborative task') of the FCE and the salient discourse features of these interactional patterns (Galaczi 2003); the relations between discourse performance and linguistic, discourse and overall oral proficiency scores in FCE speaking (Lu 2003); vocabulary use by applying various lexical statistical measures on IELTS oral performances (Read 2005); the impact of proficiency level on conversational styles in paired speaking tests in the FCE (Nakatsuhara 2006). Although none of these studies specifically investigated criterion-related validity issues, it is evident from the aforementioned range of topics that spoken corpora allow the in-depth investigation of many test taker and test characteristics that may have an impact on criterion-related validity. As Taylor noted, 'over time, analysis [of such corpora] should provide us with rich additional insights into the nature of spoken language proficiency *across different levels* (preliminary, intermediate, advanced) and *across different linguistic domains* (general, business, academic)' (2003:our emphasis). In other words, spoken corpora can be a valuable additional tool for cross-test comparability and thus investigating criterion related validity.

Conclusion

The criterion-related validity of speaking tests is an aspect that Cambridge ESOL has been exploring for a number of years and in an increasingly systematic way. The studies discussed in this chapter provide evidence of the criterion-related validity of Cambridge ESOL Speaking examinations in several different ways; they show strong links between various Cambridge ESOL Speaking tests, between different forms of the same speaking test and with external standards, such as the CEFR. In particular, Chapter 7 discussed how Cambridge ESOL has linked or maintained the link between its examinations and the reference levels of external internationally accepted frameworks such as the CEFR and the ALTE framework.

In many cases Cambridge ESOL has not only followed the suggested methodologies in the literature for generating criterion-related validity evidence but it has also developed and tested new ways of doing so (e.g. observation checklists and non-Manual mandated activities for linking examinations to the CEFR). With respect to comparison with external standards, it has also shown how the CEFR/Manual suggested procedures can be complemented with non-Manual activities which are in line with the aims of the CEFR/Manual but are more appropriate to an examination's context (e.g. the FCE context) and how best they can be incorporated in test development and validation processes as a means of maintaining the alignment with external standards.

Chapter 7 is the last of the six chapters in this volume that have explored the socio-cognitive validation framework, seeking to examine it in detail with reference to the Cambridge ESOL Speaking tests. Chapter 8 will draw together the threads of the previous chapters, summarising the findings from the overall exercise and making recommendations for further research and development which would benefit not only Cambridge ESOL but also the wider testing community.

Acknowledgement

This chapter builds on previous work published by the authors in the *Studies Language Testing* series (UCLES/CUP) and in *Research Notes* (UCLES/ Cambridge ESOL). It also draws on the work undertaken by Shaw and Weir for their 2007 *Examining Writing* volume, as well as on various internal ESOL Research and Validation reports.

8 Conclusions and recommendations

Cyril Weir
University of Bedfordshire
Lynda Taylor
Consultant to Cambridge ESOL

In this volume the theoretical framework for validating language examinations first outlined in Weir (2005a) remains the springboard for reflecting upon our understanding and conceptualisation of the second language speaking ability construct for assessment purposes. The systematic application of the framework initially to the productive skill of second language writing as operationalised in the Cambridge ESOL tests (Shaw and Weir 2007) and then to the receptive skill of second language reading (Khalifa and Weir 2009) proved to be both a practical and a useful exercise. It enabled an in-depth analysis of key test features regarding quality and fairness, and at the same time was effective in highlighting issues likely to need future attention and meriting further research. The framework has shown itself able to accommodate and strengthen Cambridge ESOL's existing Validity, Reliability, Impact and Practicality (VRIP) approach (see Saville 2003). The new framework seeks to establish similar evidence, but in addition it attempts to describe the constituent parts more fully and explicitly and to reconfigure validity to examine how these parts interact with each other.

This third volume (following the earlier volumes on second language writing and reading) describes the successful extension of the theoretical framework to explore the construct of second language speaking ability and to examine in depth how it is operationalised in Cambridge ESOL's Speaking tests, which, as Chapters 1 to 7 have suggested, have a long history and, in recent years, a strong research base. As before, it has proved helpful to conceptualise the validation process in a temporal frame thereby identifying the various types of validity evidence that need to be collected at each stage in the test development and post implementation cycle. A separate chapter was dedicated to each of the validity components within the framework with the aim of identifying and analysing the relevant criterial parameters and understanding how these can be manipulated to distinguish between adjacent proficiency levels.

The importance of the relationship between the contextual parameters which frame a task and the cognitive processing involved in task performance has been emphasised throughout this volume. We believe it is important in language testing that we give both the socio- and the cognitive elements an appropriate place and emphasis within the whole, resisting any temptation to privilege one over another. The framework reminds us that language use – and also language assessment – is both a socially situated and a cognitively processed phenomenon. The socio-cognitive framework seeks to marry up the individual psycholinguistic perspective with the individual and group sociolinguistic perspective, ensuring a complementary balance of these two fundamental perspectives.

In our view, the socio-cognitive framework allows for serious theoretical consideration of the issues but it has also proven itself capable of being applied practically; it therefore has direct relevance and value to an operational language testing/assessment context – especially when that testing is taking place on a large, industrial scale such as in Cambridge ESOL. While other frameworks developed during the 1990s (e.g. Bachman's 1990 Communicative Language Ability (CLA) model and the Council of Europe's Common European Framework of Reference (CEFR)) undoubtedly helped Cambridge ESOL to consider key issues from a theoretical perspective, they generally proved somewhat difficult for the examination board to operationalise in a manageable and meaningful way.

The results from developing and operationalising the framework in this volume with regard to second language speaking ability are encouraging, and evidence to date suggests that where it has been applied to other Cambridge examinations and tests it has proved useful in generating validity evidence in those cases too, e.g. Main Suite Writing tests (Shaw and Weir 2007), Main Suite Reading tests (Khalifa and Weir 2009), the International Certificate in Financial English (ICFE) (Ingham and Thighe 2006, Wright 2008 and 2010), the International Legal English Certificate (ILEC) (Corkhill and Robinson 2006 and Thighe 2006), the Teaching Knowledge Test (TKT) (Ashton and Khalifa 2005, Harrison 2007a and Novakovic 2006), Asset Languages (Ashton 2006 and Jones 2005), the SurveyLang project (see <www.surveylang.org> and SurveyLang 2008), and BEC and BULATS (O'Sullivan 2006).

It would be illuminating for other examination boards offering English language tests at a variety of proficiency levels to compare their own exams in terms of the validity parameters mapped out in this volume. In this way the nature of language proficiency across levels in terms of how it is operationalised through examinations and tests might be better grounded. Similar comparisons across languages may also be worth considering though these are likely to be more problematic with regard to certain parameters, for example structural progression (Hardcastle, Bolton and Pelliccia 2008).

In any evidence-based approach to validation it is essential to clearly specify each of the parameters of the validity model first and then to generate the data appropriate to each of these categories of description. Such data provides the evidential basis for inferential 'interpretative argument' logic. Important and valuable contributions to the conceptualisation of the broad nature of such an argument are provided by Toulmin (1958), Kane (1992), Mislevy, Steinberg and Almond (2002 and 2003), Bachman (2004a) and Chapelle, Enwright and Jamieson (2004 and 2008). These researchers all make a case (in slightly differing ways) for the need for clear, coherent, plausible and logical argument in support of validity claims based on evidence. Saville (2004) argues that this sort of systematic approach to the reporting of a validity argument is essential for an examination board; it enables Cambridge ESOL 'to set out our **claims** relating to the usefulness of the test for its intended purpose, explain why each claim is appropriate by giving **reasons** and justifications; and provide adequate **evidence** to support the claims and the reasoning'.

At the heart of any validity argument, of course, must be the evidence. As Weir and O'Sullivan (in press) argue, 'Unless the model of validation clearly accounts for the evidence that needs to be collected in support of a validity claim one is left with the form and not the substance'. The considerable resources, time and effort required to specify and then generate this evidence should not be underestimated. This volume has sought to demonstrate one way in which this can be done, by identifying the elements of validity we need to collect data on, documenting what evidence is available in relation to Cambridge ESOL examinations across the range of cognitive, contextual and scoring parameters we have established in our framework, and then *beginning* to explain their inter-relationships.

Most of the analysis carried out on context and cognitive validity in Chapters 3 and 4 covers only a small sample of speaking papers from Cambridge ESOL Main Suite examinations and any conclusions drawn from that analysis, while nonetheless being enlightening, must therefore be seen as tentative. Additionally, the analysis is based on the opinions of a group of expert judges only and findings will need to be more firmly grounded in the future by having students take the various Speaking tests and complete retrospective verbal protocols (or other appropriate instrumentation) on their experiences. An example of this sort of research on IELTS is provided by Weir, Hawkey, Green and Devi (2009) who comment also on the complexities and time consuming nature of undertaking such procedures.

In the remainder of this chapter we attempt to summarise the findings from applying the socio-cognitive validity framework to the Cambridge ESOL Speaking examinations that have been sampled. We summarise the data that provides the evidence to support the claims and the reasoning for the validity of Cambridge Speaking examinations in terms of each element of the socio-cognitive model of validity (context, cognitive, scoring, criterion related and consequential).

Messick (1989) has pointed out, however, that validity is a question of degree, not an all or nothing concept. Validity should be seen as a *relative* concept which examination boards need to work on continually. Much of the substantial validity evidence generated by Cambridge ESOL on its Speaking examinations has been brought together in this volume. Additionally, critical evaluation in Chapters 2 to 7 has helped clarify a number of areas in examining speaking where further research would be beneficial. As well as drawing conclusions on this data below, we therefore indicate the areas where research will take place at Cambridge ESOL to inform judgements on future revisions to its Speaking examinations.

Test taker characteristics

In Chapter 2 O'Sullivan and Green addressed a range of issues associated with the test taker. We would argue that a socio-cognitive approach can help to maintain a 'person-oriented' view of the testing and assessment process rather than an 'instrument-oriented' view in which the decontextualised language use or the test instrument risks being placed centrally while the language user or test taker remains more peripheral. A socio-cognitive perspective implies a strong focus on the language learner or test taker as being at the heart of the assessment process, rather than the test or measuring instrument being the central focus. We see this approach as consistent with the humanistic tradition that has been a key feature of the Cambridge ESOL examinations since their inception in 1913 (see Weir 2003 for further discussion of this point).

Nowadays, analysis of data gathered via Cambridge ESOL's Candidate Information Sheet (CIS) (see Appendix B), which is completed by all candidates taking Cambridge ESOL examinations, helps to provide a clear picture of the experiential profile of the test taker population in terms of their *educational level, preparedness, reasons for* and *experience of taking examinations,* as well as *L1, age* and *gender.* It allows the examination board to monitor how well speaking test topics and tasks used in the test are matched to the test takers. This is done both qualitatively through review processes during the test production cycle (see Appendix C) and quantitatively through analysis of the test's psychometric and other qualities via task bias studies. Such analyses are also crucial for informing test revision projects since changing trends in the intended population must necessarily be reflected in appropriate changes to test format and content.

For a commercially successful but also ethically responsible testing programme it is important both that test developers understand the nature of the test takers and that test takers (together with other score users and test stakeholders) have a good appreciation of the content and purpose of the test. Chapter 2 outlined some of the ways in which test takers can be informed about test content and how this can be shaped to reflect their level of maturity and knowledge of the world. The chapter also suggested ways in which an examination board can build and maintain its knowledge of test takers and how it can seek to use this knowledge to enhance fairness, whether by taking account of demographic trends in the candidature or by responding to individual circumstances. A good deal of research remains to be done to explore how such efforts may impact on test validity, but such concerns do not detract from the ongoing need to ensure equality of access to the opportunities that tests of this nature can open up.

One particular area meriting future research is that of language testing accommodations, i.e. tests which are modified to meet the special requirements of certain test taker populations. There exists relatively little research in the area of accommodations for testing second language speaking that is directly relevant to the testing of English as a Foreign Language (EFL) in the international context. Most of the published research relating to accommodations in language assessment has been conducted in the US with English language learners (ELLs) who are typically immigrants and indigenous groups in US school-based learning and assessment contexts (see Abedi 2008). This research tends to focus on the language of instruction, and while some studies have investigated the effectiveness and validity of accommodations for language learners with disabilities, we still know very little about the effect of special arrangements on test takers whose spoken language is tested under the different conditions discussed in Chapter 2. The very small numbers of test takers and the diversity of the disabilities involved mean that conducting research into the effects of special arrangements is extremely challenging. Nonetheless, it is clearly essential that the relevant issues are investigated in the interests of ensuring fair access to assessment opportunities, which is the fundamental principle underlying the provision of special arrangements. From a validation perspective, it is also important that test score users can place confidence in the meaningfulness of scores from tests involving special arrangements and test providers therefore need to be able to bring forward evidence in support of any claims they make about the usefulness of scores from their modified tests. Given that examination boards are often in direct contact with test candidates requesting special arrangements, a large and experienced organisation such as Cambridge ESOL may in fact be well-placed and well-equipped to undertake some of this much needed research, in the form of small-scale but well-designed case studies (see, for example, the multi-faceted case study investigating provision for candidates with dyslexia in writing assessment, reported in Shaw and Weir, 2007:20–27).

Despite the growing range of provision for candidates with disabilities offered in recent years by the examination board, the number of candidates requesting accommodations remains extremely small as a proportion of the overall candidature. The fact that the number of requests for accommodated tests seems not to reflect the likely distribution of EFL learners with disabilities in the wider population constitutes some cause for concern and we might speculate on possible reasons for this. There may be a genuine lack of awareness among teachers and candidates, and even testing centres, concerning the wide range of test accommodations now available, despite the provision of information in published documentation and on the examination board's website. Alternatively, it may be that the administrative procedures associated with requesting modified tests discourage some from applying because it can sometimes involve a longer lead-time as well as additional paperwork. Finally, as O'Sullivan and Green (this volume) point out, not all cultures have similar attitudes towards disability, both in terms of definitions of what constitutes a disability and of how disabilities should be dealt with; this may well affect the take-up of language learning as well as assessment opportunities. This touches upon matters of test washback and impact, and Cambridge ESOL may wish to consider how to promote its accommodations more widely so that students with disabilities are encouraged to learn English and to take advantage of assessment opportunities.

A further area of potential investigation for the future relates to the testing of second language speaking ability among younger learners which, as was noted in Chapter 2, is a growing area of interest given the rapid development of English language teaching and learning within primary education systems worldwide. Given Cambridge ESOL's strong commitment to the paired interaction format in so many of its Speaking tests, it might be interesting to explore whether this peer–peer format could reasonably be extended into its tests for Young Learners, in which to date the interaction has been limited to a one-on-one format between a single test taker and an examiner. Research questions of interest here might relate to whether there are significant developmental reasons for maintaining the current singleton format with young learner test takers, or whether this group is in fact capable of engaging in peer–peer interaction (in pairs or a small group) and thus providing a richer language sample for assessment purposes. Once again, this sort of research is valuable in informing the ongoing process of test review and revision, ensuring that tests continue to be well-matched to the target population and that the resulting scores are as meaningful and useful as possible.

The previous two paragraphs touch upon matters of test bias, i.e. the concern that particular test taker populations or subgroups should not be unfairly disadvantaged. Following any test, it is important in post-examination procedures to check for bias and O'Sullivan and Green describe in Chapter 2 how this is done statistically in relation to candidate biodata for the Cambridge tests. It is also clearly essential to establish *a priori* evidence for context and cognitive validity before candidates sit an examination to ensure that no potential sources of bias are allowed to interfere with measurement. The means of achieving this were extensively discussed in Chapters

3 and 4, while Chapter 5 addressed the systems and procedures to ensure scoring validity. It would be useful to see evidence of a lack of bias in all examinations being researched and reported in the public domain.

Cognitive validity

It is hard to see how one can build a convincing validity argument for any assessment practice without assigning cognitive processing a central place within that argument. Given our desire to extrapolate from test tasks to real world behaviour, it is essential to carry out research to establish with greater certainty that the test tasks we employ do indeed activate the types of mental operations that are viewed in the cognitive psychology literature as essential elements of the speaking process which are relevant to the contexts and purposes of test use. To the extent that this is not the case, extrapolation from the test data to speaking in the wider world is clearly under threat. With this in mind, we believe that Chapter 3 in this volume on cognitive validity, by John Field, represents a significant and timely contribution to the wider field of language testing, especially those who are working in speaking assessment, since it assembles the latest theoretical and empirical findings from cognitive psychology and discusses their direct relevance for the design and analysis of speaking tests.

The main purpose of the review in Chapter 3 was to match the specifications of the Cambridge ESOL suite of exams against an external model of the cognitive processes which the speaking skill requires of a native user. The model chosen was the most comprehensive one currently available to applied linguists and language testers, that of Levelt (1989). The Levelt model incorporates a number of essential components: a mechanism for forward-planning, a means of storing plans for forthcoming utterances while they are being articulated and a system for monitoring one's own productions to see if they accord with one's intentions. The cognitive validity of the Cambridge ESOL suite was examined with reference to the stages of processing identified by Levelt (1999).

- *Conceptualisation.* The ESOL suite was found to provide detailed task input to the test taker in order to reduce the demands of conceptualisation. The effect is to lighten the cognitive load upon test takers, and also to reduce any potential bias towards rewarding imagination rather than linguistic performance.

- *Grammatical encoding.* The Cambridge ESOL suite specifies linguistic content in the form of language functions to be performed by test takers. It thus operationalises this phase of the Levelt model as a mapping process between the target functions and the syntactic forms which correspond to them. Two possible principles were identified for the grading of the functions in terms of cognitive demands: the first related to the semantic complexity of the function to be expressed, the second to the number of functions elicited by a particular task. The ESOL suite was found to have borne both principles in mind in a systematic way when staging the difficulty of its speaking tests. A marked increase in cognitive demands was noted at the FCE level, which may be intentional, and may also be appropriate.

- *Phonological encoding.* There is growing support for a view of second language acquisition as a process of 'proceduralisation', in which the retrieval of linguistic forms begins as a slow and attention-demanding process but becomes increasingly automatic. Because this is a gradual and internalised development, it is difficult to represent reliably within a set of test specifications; however, a major driving force behind it is the chunking of words into formulaic strings – affecting both the way in which they are stored in the mind and the ease with which they are retrieved. Helpfully for the test designer, chunking is associated with certain observable developments in an individual's productions, which give rise to the impression of increased fluency. They include: a reduction in planning time at clause boundaries; a reduction in hesitation; an increase in length of run; and an increase in grammatical and collocational accuracy within the chunk and a progression towards a more native-like rhythm. Of these, hesitation and pausing are represented at all levels of the Cambridge ESOL specifications, with clearly marked gradations between the levels. The use of formulaic language features only negatively, as an indicator of inability on the part of low-level test takers to generate novel utterances. The proposal was made that future specifications might incorporate evidence of chunking as a marker of increasing proceduralisation as the test taker moves up the scale. Test designers may also need at some point to adjust their thinking in the light of increasing support for emergentist views of language acquisition. It is not clear at present how this development might impact upon test specifications.
- *Phonetic encoding, articulation.* Potential problems of articulation were represented as deriving from two sources: inadequate phonological representations in the mind and the inability to adjust to unfamiliar articulatory settings. The L2 speaker may also face a tension between the need to hold a phonetic plan in the mind and the need to focus attention upon precise articulation. In these circumstances, it is important that test designers do not unduly emphasise the importance of accuracy in pronunciation. The Cambridge ESOL suite deals with this issue sensitively by adopting intelligibility as its principal criterion.
- *Self-monitoring.* A competent speaker monitors their own productions for accuracy and appropriacy; and is capable of introducing self-repairs both promptly and following certain norms. This aspect of the speaking

process is represented in the ESOL specifications in terms of the level of support needed from the interlocutor and the test taker's ability to achieve repair. Two types of repair are combined in the descriptors, and it might be advisable to define the term more precisely. It might also be possible to grade self-monitoring more specifically by reference to the levels of attention which test takers find themselves able to allocate to, respectively, the linguistic and semantic-pragmatic features of the utterances.

This validation exercise also considered the types of interaction which are possible in a speaking test, and the extent to which they can be said to align with the cognitive processes that might apply in non-test conditions. The formats employed by the Cambridge ESOL suite were found to possess greater cognitive validity than possible alternatives – providing a clear cost–benefit justification for the rather complex practical procedures which they entail. It was noted that the suite features a range of different interaction types; and thus attempts to represent the variety of speaker–listener relationships which occur in real life speech events, and the processes that each type requires of the speaker. A particular strength of the suite lies in the various ingenious ways in which it fosters test taker–test taker interaction but continues to control the range of language that is used. Clearly, it is not possible in test conditions to create a context identical to that of a naturally occurring speech event in the world beyond the test. However, the absence of the power relationship between test takers plus the problem-driven form of the tasks provided in this type of exchange ensure that the encounters which take place elicit processes which are as close to those of real life as one can reasonably expect to achieve. Despite the obvious attraction and strengths of the current approach, there is always room for ongoing exploration of ways to increase the range of speech types sampled in the test and their approximation to what happens during spoken interaction in the world beyond the test.

A second issue relating to the relative cognitive difficulty of the tasks was the amount of pre-planning time permitted. It was noted that pre-planning is not provided for in the Cambridge Main Suite Speaking tests – a decision which (in terms of cognitive validity) is entirely sound in the case of tasks that are designed to measure spontaneous spoken interaction. It is more open to question in relation to the monologue tasks, in that the absence of any pre-planning time means that they may not necessarily replicate the cognitive processes which often accompany the preparation of a formal or semi-formal presentation. However, a great deal depends upon the perceived purpose of those tasks. The Cambridge ESOL test designers might argue persuasively that the monologues are intended to provide an indication of a candidate's ability to produce an extended turn, not of their ability to engage in a markedly different type of speech assembly. Interestingly, however, a short 1-minute pre-planning phase (prior to a 1/2-minute 'mini-presentation') is included in the IELTS, BEC, ILEC and ICFE Speaking tests, presumably with the intention of echoing the formal and semi-formal presentation skills that are typically required in the higher education and professional employment contexts. Given that both CAE and CPE are used for admission to academic and professional domains, we might speculate on whether there is a case for this pre-planning feature (with or without pen and paper for making notes) to be mirrored in the higher level Cambridge Main Suite Speaking tests. Perhaps this could constitute an area for further research investigation and comparative analysis in the future.

It is clear that, in grading the specifications for the five levels of the suite, designers have given careful thought to the relative cognitive difficulty both of the tasks and of the interaction formats. Task demands are increased only gradually; and the more demanding types of interaction (particularly three-way discussion) are reserved for higher levels of the suite. One concludes that the Cambridge ESOL specifications correspond closely to what we know of the cognitive processes involved in the production of speech. The few reservations that have been expressed represent omissions; none constitutes provisions that run counter to the findings of speech science. It is also apparent that the cognitive requirements have been sufficiently finely graded in relation to the different levels of the suite. Full consideration has been given both to task demands and to the types of processing that can be deemed to be representative of performance at different stages of proficiency.

Context validity

In Chapter 4 Galaczi and ffrench examined the context validity of Cambridge ESOL Speaking tasks with reference to the detailed taxonomy of contextual task parameters originally outlined in Weir (2005a) and which has been further refined since then. This validation exercise revealed a number of important features both within and across proficiency levels, and demonstrated that careful consideration is given in the gradation of difficulty across the Main Suite levels.

It highlighted the emphasis on production and interaction in the speaking construct underlying Main Suite (and BEC) tests and the corresponding use of direct, face-to-face, paired tests. As a consequence, the variability of interlocutor talk needs to be managed at all levels; this is done through the use of an 'interlocutor frame' and a range of task formats (examiner/test taker, test taker/test taker, test taker long turn). It is worth noting that some elements of the interlocutor frame are shaped by the proficiency level, e.g. at the lower levels the interlocutor is provided with standardised alternative 'back-up' prompts to ensure that, as far as possible, the input language remains accessible in cases where the test taker appears to encounter a comprehension challenge.

A range of response formats is used at each of the Cambridge ESOL Main Suite proficiency levels. Some response formats do not appear until a certain level, and sometimes the same response format is used at multiple levels, but manipulated in different ways. In terms of criterial features across levels, a clear gradation is seen from controlled to semi-controlled to open-ended response formats, which accommodates the need for higher communicative demand at the higher levels (Skehan 1996).

There is also a progression (both within a level and across levels) from relatively structured and supported interaction, under the direct control of the examiner, involving topics of immediate personal relevance to more open-ended discussion with less examiner control involving more general topics. In addition, there is an increase in the amount of time assigned to each task type and to the overall test, as one moves up the levels.

Another key distinguishing feature is the gradation from factual to evaluative discourse modes, and the larger presence at the lower levels of exposition and description, compared with the increased role of exposition/argumentation at the higher levels. The progression (both within a level and across levels) from personal and concrete information to non-personal and abstract information is also shown to accommodate the need for increased cognitive complexity of the task at the higher levels. Furthermore, this gradation is seen in the visuals for the tasks, which provide more scaffolding and are more content-rich at the lower levels, in contrast with visuals which convey concepts at the higher levels.

In terms of future research, an investigation of the potential of a group interaction task at C1 and C2 with three candidates (see Nakatsuhara forthcoming b) might be beneficial, especially given the use that is made of CAE and CPE for university entrance purposes, e.g. exploring whether interaction in a paired group task equates with group interaction in seminars at tertiary level.

Further work on lexical analysis across the proficiency levels is clearly needed given the limited conclusions that can be reached by employing only frequency data. A starting point for this might be to examine frequencies for word types elicited only, rather than relying upon a general frequency analysis of tokens which risks skewing the data. This would simply involve extracting types from discourse samples and running the frequency analysis on these alone. Qualitative investigation of how examiners arrive at estimates of lexical ability, e.g. through use of verbal protocol analysis or prompted recall studies, might prove even more useful especially in relation to the criterion of lexical appropriateness. It might also be instructive to undertake a more detailed analysis of the structural resources which are made manifest in the spoken output to set alongside the findings on lexical resources. Fortunately, this area of research investigation is now receiving significant attention through the work of the English Profile Programme which is beginning to bear fruit after several years of intense investment. The same research programme is providing valuable insights into the nature of functional resources at the higher proficiency levels (C1 and C2); functional capability and use at the higher C levels have always been less well understood or specified than at the lower KET, PET and FCE levels which are themselves linked to the Council of Europe's Waystage, Threshold and Vantage linguistic specifications respectively. Further research into all these areas – lexical, structural and functional resources – would be beneficial to inform not only contextual aspects of the speaking tests but also key features relating to their scoring validity, namely speaking assessment criteria, rating scale descriptors and examiner training. Conducting qualitative and quantitative research into first and second language spoken interaction has tended to be much more challenging than comparable analyses of written language data, but it is likely to be easier to undertake in the future as the available technology for automatic speech recognition becomes more sophisticated and as research methods for analysing spoken language become increasingly sensitive to its multi-faceted complexity and ephemeral nature.

Cambridge ESOL takes considerable care to ensure appropriate physical conditions for taking its Speaking examinations, to maintain uniform delivery and administration across centres and to achieve complete security of test materials. The procedures which are currently in place and which are described at some length in Appendix D will continue to be monitored, evaluated and enhanced by the examination board to ensure that they do not pose a threat to test reliability and that they safeguard valid measurement of the construct in Speaking tests.

Scoring validity

The ability to place confidence in the quality of the information provided by test scores is vital if we are to use these for decision-making purposes, especially high stakes decision-making. Chapter 5, by Taylor and Galaczi, outlined the multiple factors which can impact on the reliability or scoring validity of speaking assessment, especially direct Speaking tests such as those offered by Cambridge ESOL, and the wide range of measures taken by the examination board to control these factors. Attention focused on assessment criteria and rating scales, the rating process and rating conditions, the recruitment, training and standardisation of examiners, as well as the post-examination procedures and the reporting of scores to test takers and test users in a meaningful way. All examination boards offering speaking tests are under an obligation to demonstrate and justify the measures they take to reduce threats to test reliability and to optimise scoring validity. It would be interesting to see more speaking test providers report detailed information on their policy and practice for achieving this.

In terms of criteria for evaluation in the Cambridge Speaking tests, candidates are assessed on their language skills not their personality, intelligence or knowledge of the world, and Chapters 2, 3 and 4 explained how the examination board's detailed analysis and knowledge of the test taker population inform decisions about cognitive and contextual parameters relating to test content and format to ensure as far as possible that this is the case. Rather than adopting a 'one-size-fits-all' approach, some linguistic criteria (e.g. Grammar, Vocabulary, Interactive Communication and Discourse Management) are treated flexibly and are given greater or less prominence according to the proficiency level of interest and their relevance to the overall evaluation. Discourse Management, for example, is only assessed from PET level upwards. The paired candidate scenario in Cambridge ESOL's Speaking tests enables a complementary approach, combining the benefits of holistic and analytic scoring methods and taking account of the cognitive capacity available to examiners depending on their respective roles in the speaking test event. The use of differing yet complementary scales also acknowledges and reflects the unique perspective each examiner has on the Speaking test event, i.e. the assessor observes the interaction while the interlocutor is directly implicated in it.

Though candidates are, in theory and in practice, assessed on their own individual performance overall and not in relation to one another, Chapter 5 highlighted the complex question of whether in fact individual or shared scores for interactional competence should be awarded to test takers. Given the inherently co-constructed nature of paired (and group) interaction, there is undoubtedly scope for further research in this area to explore how feasible it might be to consider awarding a shared score as a more authentic approach (Taylor and Wigglesworth 2009). A further research focus could explore the potential for examiners to award marks for individual speaking test tasks (rather than across the test as a whole) so as to provide a more fine-grained evaluation for diagnostic score reporting. This would involve each examiner making and recording many more judgements during the testing event than at present and it may prove so cognitively burdensome and distracting as to be impractical and unreliable. Alternatively, a more trait-based approach could be explored in which individual tasks or test parts attract marks on specific criteria, thus reducing the total number of judgements that need to be made within a restricted timeframe. The challenge here lies in identifying (and justifying) precisely which assessment criteria are best matched to which tasks or test parts, and in training examiners to attend to certain criteria for some tasks but to disregard them for other parts of the test. Chapter 5 reported some preliminary research findings on this issue in relation to examiner standardisation practice, but the idea of introducing a similar practice into live test rating is clearly more controversial and would need extensive research to underpin and justify it. Nevertheless, it would be instructive to explore how a more fine-grained evaluation of test taker performance on individual tasks might realistically be achieved, an evaluation which remains sufficiently valid and reliable to provide meaningful diagnostic feedback for test score users.

The specific issues highlighted above for further investigation are part of a broader research agenda which, if pursued, could significantly improve our understanding of the rating process in speaking assessment and of the operational conditions that influence it. As noted in Chapter 5, this type of research is particularly challenging in the context of direct speaking assessment as operationalised by Cambridge ESOL, where rating takes place in real time and where the actual process of rating can differ according to the role assumed by the rater. While verbal protocol analysis methodology has provided us with some valuable insights into the oral examining process, new and innovative methodologies probably need to be developed which are less intrusive and thus less likely to colour or distort the actual rating experience associated with a direct speaking test. There is undoubtedly much more to be learned about how naïve raters naturally select their judgement criteria, about individual and contrastive approaches to rating, about the role of comprehension in tests of speaking proficiency and about the significance of paralinguistic features on raters' decision-making in face-to-face encounters. There is also a need to explore in greater depth how much raters focus on different analytical scales, how they use and interpret sub-criteria within each criterion, and what aspects of performance raters focus on during individual parts of a test. Finally, there is a considerable potential research agenda associated with the computer-based assessment of speaking, not only concerning the impact of various rating conditions on human raters but also the comparability of human and electronic rating of spoken interaction.

Though rater training is widely discussed in the literature on performance assessment, very little information exists about how training is actually carried out by examination providers so Chapter 5's description of the procedures and stages which Cambridge ESOL speaking examiners go through as part of their preparation for examining in live Speaking tests constitutes a major contribution in the public domain. The examination board's approach is based on *a network of professionals* with various levels of (overlapping) responsibility, and on *a set of standard procedures* that apply to each professional level. Quality assurance procedures, which have been developed and refined in light of experience from implementing this system over more than 20 years, set down the minimum levels and standards (for registration, induction, training and standardisation programmes) that must be achieved in order to meet the professional requirements of administering Cambridge ESOL Speaking tests and sustain a fully effective Team Leader System. The first three stages – Registration, Induction and Training – typically apply only once to an applicant SE for a given examination or group of related examinations (e.g. PET and KET). The remainder of the procedures are recurrent and cyclical for each examination, in so far as the outcome of performance monitoring informs Certification and any re-training required in specific circumstances. The outcomes of these quality assurance procedures are recorded on a central speaking examiner database held in Cambridge. Each SE, once approved, is given a unique identifier, which they retain if they are engaged in different geographic locations, whether in the same country or different countries. The database then records recruitment details (qualifications, first language, etc.) and also attendance at training sessions, annual standardisation meetings and performance feedback.

Within this system, as we have seen, there appears to exist considerable scope for ongoing research exploring not only the efficacy of examiner training and standardisation procedures, but also examiners' views and experiences of new or refined rating procedures arising out of a test revision project. For example, examiners are encouraged to deliver the interlocutor frame in a natural way and it would be interesting to explore how effective current training is in achieving this. In future, it would be helpful to see more SE-related management data reported in the public domain, e.g. outcomes from SE monitoring and evaluation, subject of course to confidentiality and commercial constraints. It would also be good to see more outcomes reported of the post-revision validation studies involving examiners, not least because the methodologies employed to garner examiner reactions following changes to a test could usefully be adopted and adapted by other boards working in similar areas.

It is worth noting that Cambridge ESOL's worldwide speaking examiner cadre represents a considerable research asset. It is an expert community of committed, motivated and well-trained professionals, many with high-level skills in applied linguistics, language assessment and research methods. As such, they constitute a valuable stakeholder constituency who can directly support the board's research agenda on speaking assessment, collaborating in studies as informants or co-ordinating and replicating small-scale case-study projects in their own contexts for which they have important and unique local knowledge and expertise. It would be good to see more research and validation studies such as that undertaken by Hubbard, Gilbert and Pidcock (2006), involving close collaboration between the research team in Cambridge and research-qualified speaking examiners in the field. Further research is particularly encouraged to explore raters' real-time use of criteria and subscales across tasks and test parts, e.g. the extent to which it is reasonable to expect raters to apply multiple criteria and subscales throughout the test. Outcomes from this type of research have potentially useful implications for rater training and practice.

Chapter 5 explained that, for reasons of practicality, Cambridge ESOL does not carry out any post-adjustment of speaking scores based upon statistical analyses, e.g. Multi-faceted Rasch measurement. Instead, effort and resources are devoted to the training, standardisation and performance monitoring stage, and to the practice of double marking by two examiners in most Cambridge ESOL Speaking tests. Standard procedures for grading and awards, however, allow for some adjustment of the score boundaries should this be needed. Routine analysis is carried out on all the test components and reports are produced for use in the Grading and Awards process as well as to feed into the ongoing refinement of test production procedures. The aim is to ensure that the awarding of overall grades for the examination at each level is as fair as possible and that the examinations continue to be improved over time. The performance of large groups of candidates is compared with cohorts from previous years, and performance is also compared by country, by first language, by age and a number of other factors, to ensure that the standards being applied are consistently fair to all candidates, and that a particular grade 'means' the same thing from year to year and throughout the world. Any requests for Special Consideration are reviewed at this stage, together with any reports from centres about specific problems that may have arisen during the examination. After the grading meeting, results in terms of grades are generated. At this stage a procedure known as Awards is carried out to ensure the fairness of the final results before they are issued to candidates. As part of this procedure an Awards Committee looks particularly closely at the performance of candidates who are close to the grade boundaries – particularly the pass/fail boundary.

Consequential validity

Chapter 6 re-visited the background and definitions of test washback and impact, attempting to establish where these phenomena belong in the complex process of validating examinations, particularly high-stakes tests, such as those offered internationally by Cambridge ESOL. Hawkey surveyed and exemplified Cambridge ESOL research initiatives and studies to analyse and adjust positively the consequential validity of its Speaking exams taking account of the many complex variables involved.

The need to monitor a test's effects on language materials and on classroom activity (see, for example, Hawkey 2004c and Green 2007) and to seek information on the views of a full range of stakeholders (Taylor 2000a) is now accepted by most serious examination boards and it has been the hallmark of Cambridge examinations at least since the modern revisions commenced in the 1980s, and in the case of stakeholder consultation since much earlier according to Weir (2003, and see also Hawkey 2009). In the recent CPE revision and FCE/CAE modifications, conscious efforts were made to elicit feedback on the existing forms from test takers and a wide variety of stakeholders contributed to the decisions that were taken concerning changes in the examination (see Weir and Milanovic 2003 for a full account of the CPE revision, Hawkey 2004a for a description of the CELS examination change process and Hawkey 2009 for that in FCE and CAE). Hawkey (this volume) notes the frequency with which Cambridge ESOL presents washback and impact study research, along with numerous other impact references, including books and chapters in books published by Cambridge ESOL and CUP, thus underlining the significance of impact study in the thinking of the examination board. For our purposes, it is worth noting that a significant portion of the available documentation in *Research Notes* articles and the SiLT volumes concerns washback and impact associated with the Cambridge Speaking tests.

We should not ignore the fact that the direct approach to speaking assessment, as operationalised by Cambridge ESOL, has the potential to significantly influence a variety of individuals involved directly or indirectly in the assessment, not only the language learners and their teachers, but also the human examiners who conduct and score the speaking test. In consequential validity terms, the Cambridge ESOL Speaking test format, with its face-to-face encounter and its paired arrangement between peer test takers, is intended to create a positive washback on the teaching of speaking, helping language learners to develop their speaking skill to deal with reciprocal interaction with others. This, as we have seen throughout this volume, has been a dominant feature of Cambridge's approach to language test construct and structure over almost a century. A further feature of the Cambridge ESOL Speaking test format with the potential to influence language pedagogy in the classroom is the use of human examiners for managing and scoring the tests. The publication of sample speaking tasks, criteria for evaluation and exemplar performances provides language teachers with convenient access to resources and expertise which can support their own pedagogic knowledge and skills in the speaking class, leading to a form of washback that relates directly to professional development. Indeed, many English language teachers actively choose to train as Cambridge speaking examiners for purposes of professional development, a potential aspect of test washback that is rarely acknowledged or discussed in the literature perhaps because it is less obviously true for tests of L2 Reading, Listening or Writing. Similarly, a direct speaking test's potential to influence the human examiners involved (whether they function as interlocutor or rater or both) is rarely acknowledged as a form of test washback in its own right, though clearly there are elements of this phenomenon at work. In the case of Cambridge's Speaking test research and validation agenda, studies investigating examiner behaviour and rating issues tend to be conducted and reported under the *scoring validity* banner. It would not be unreasonable, however, to conceive of these studies as having a consequential validity dimension too. Since the examiner cadre constitutes an important part of the larger test stakeholder constituency, it seems valid to regard studies investigating examiner perceptions, attitudes and experiences as potential sources of consequential validity evidence. We might argue that this dimension of 'examiner-related' or 'examiner-oriented' washback has received relatively little attention in any systematic way from within a consequential validity paradigm. It might be interesting therefore to explore this angle further, both theoretically and empirically, perhaps in collaboration with current research into the development of assessment literacy or the nature of professional expertise. This is something that Cambridge ESOL is probably uniquely placed and sufficiently well-resourced to be able to undertake, given its longstanding commitment to direct speaking assessment and its extensive experience of examiner management.

Criterion-related validity

In Chapter 7 Khalifa and Salamoura examined the extent to which the Cambridge Speaking tests correlate with external measures of performance, i.e. what evidence can be assembled to support claims about the criterion-related validity of the board's speaking tests. According to Weir (2005a), criterion-related validity can be seen from three perspectives: in terms of cross-test comparability; through comparison with different forms of the same test; and via comparison with external standards.

As reported in Khalifa and Weir (2009), the importance attached by test users to test comparability information has increased in recent years, and test providers have particularly had to pay greater attention to issues of cross-test comparability – both in terms of the relationships between their own tests and with those offered by other examination boards. Attempts to compare tests meaningfully are not straightforward, however, since two tests may well be testing differing constructs, as demonstrated by Cambridge 20 years ago in the FCE/TOEFL comparability study (Bachman, Davidson, Ryan and Choi (1995). It is generally accepted nowadays that high correlations in themselves do not provide sufficient evidence that two tests are equivalent. This is particularly true for speaking assessment, where examination boards may adopt very different speaking test methods, e.g. direct vs semi-direct, or where even use of the same test method may entail significant content variation: compare, for example, a direct test involving a one-on-one interview format vs a multi-phase test involving peer interaction and tasks that elicit both monologic and dialogic talk. Any comparison between tests needs to be placed within the broader context of the differences between distinctive approaches to test development and test use, and even different pedagogic or assessment cultures.

Without the necessary steps to control cognitive and context variables affecting test difficulty, test quality risks fluctuating over tasks across different test forms. Cambridge ESOL seeks to ensure qualitative equivalence or cognitive and context comparability through the use of checklists for comparing speaking task design and output of different forms, through its item writer guidelines and through its rigorous procedures of test production (see Appendix C). As Chapter 7 notes, while considerable progress has been made in recent years to develop user-friendly and effective checklists for establishing the comparability of contextual factors across test versions, there remains a great deal of work to be done to investigate and demonstrate cognitive comparability across test forms. Experimental, one-off research designs are time-consuming and labour-intensive and may well not be entirely practical for large-scale test producers to implement, but it is clearly important that further systematic investigation is undertaken into the cognitive validity elements identified in Chapter 3 so that an examination board can provide adequate evidence for claims of cross-task or cross-test cognitive comparability. Cambridge ESOL could have a significant role in developing new types of instrumentation to assist in this endeavour.

From the 1980s onwards Cambridge ESOL worked towards integrating its examinations into a coherent system or interpretative framework, developing, among other things, a common assessment scale on which speaking ability can be measured and speaking test scores can be reported. The driving factor for this movement was the desire to foster a common understanding of assessment for speaking across the board's exams, to establish a relationship between its different exams and to foster common practices among its growing network of thousands of speaking examiners. As new Speaking tests were added to its product range, so evidence of criterion-related validity needed to be routinely generated by Cambridge ESOL. The studies discussed in Chapter 7 show strong links between Cambridge ESOL suites of level-based tests, i.e. Main Suite, BEC, and CELS. These suites are targeted at similar ability levels as defined by a common measurement scale.

Chapter 7 also detailed how Cambridge ESOL has linked its examinations closely to the levels laid out in internationally accepted frameworks such as the CEFR and the ALTE framework. It is this level system which provides an interpretative frame of reference for all the exams in the suite. Although these European levels remain underspecified for testing purposes (see Weir 2005b and Milanovic and Weir 2010), they nevertheless have the advantage of according with the proficiency levels familiar to teachers and are supported by the work of the Council of Europe over the last 30 years; this important work is based on a consensus view that adequate coverage is afforded by six broad levels for the purposes of organising language learning, teaching and assessment in the European context (Council of Europe 2001:22–3). Khalifa, ffrench and Salamoura (2010) discuss a range of procedures used by the board to build and maintain a linking argument between a test and the CEFR levels, at the same time demonstrating how some of these procedures have been embedded into Cambridge ESOL routine practices. All examination boards should be encouraged to consider carefully how they approach the process of linking their tests to external frameworks of reference in a valid and systematic manner.

The scale of levels which is used by Cambridge ESOL provides a set of common standards and is the basis of the *criterion-referenced approach* to the interpretation of examination results. The Cambridge Main Suite examinations are linked to the CEFR scale for speaking. Referencing to the criterion is undertaken by means of scalar analyses using the Rasch model to relate the results from the whole range of Cambridge examinations to the global scale of common reference levels of the CEFR (Council of Europe 2001:24). In addition, the ALTE Can Do scales provide criterion-related statements at each level in relation to the specified domains which are covered in the examinations (i.e. situated language use for social, tourist, work and study purposes). The criterion scale and the Can Do descriptors provide representations of the external reality, which helps to ensure that the test results are as meaningful and as useful as possible to the key stakeholders (the candidates, their sponsors and other users of examination results). Work to date in this area will be supplemented by the ongoing English Profile programme which uses, among other tools, the analysis of spoken language corpora. This allows in-depth investigation of test taker and test characteristics that may impact on criterion-related validity and it should provide us with rich additional insights into the nature of spoken language proficiency across different levels (preliminary, intermediate, advanced) and across different linguistic domains (general, business, academic).

As Chapter 7 points out, linking tests to an external standard or framework is not straightforward and the role and status of the CEFR in this regard remain controversial. Attention was drawn to some significant reservations, expressed both within the Cambridge ESOL organisation and more widely in the language testing profession, about the process of aligning tests to the CEFR and the meaningfulness of test alignment claims. (Milanovic and Weir 2010 offer a fuller discussion of the issues and of Cambridge ESOL's position.) Despite these reservations, real-world demands for statements about the nature of the relationship between a given test and the CEFR cannot easily be ignored, and test providers such as Cambridge ESOL have to address public and governmental expectations in some meaningful and responsible way.

While the criterion-related validity of speaking tests is an aspect that Cambridge ESOL has been exploring for a number of years, in an increasingly systematic way, there nonetheless remains some critical work still to do in this area.

Endnote

Hopefully readers will have found the detailed description and discussion of operational language testing practices in this book useful. Practical real-world testing, as opposed to language testing research, so often has to concern itself with far more than just the issues of construct definition and operationalisation, assessment criteria and rating scale development. Operational tests, especially large-scale commercial tests conducted on an industrial scale, are usually located within a complex ecology comprising multiple, interacting factors, many of which are simply not present or relevant in more academically oriented language testing research; these include sustainability issues to do with test production, delivery, processing; practical issues concerning test timing, security, cost, accessibility; organisational issues relating to personnel (e.g. developing and sustaining the rater cadre) or to management (e.g. the revision of an existing test, or development of its replacement). This is particularly true for the direct testing of L2 speaking ability, for which practicality and sustainability are core considerations. Hopefully, the explication of theory and practice presented in this volume will lead to a broader and deeper understanding of the issues in all their breadth and depth.

The issues of what a language construct is and whether it is possible to identify and measure developmental stages leading towards its mastery are critical for all aspects of language learning, teaching and assessment. Examination boards and other testing institutions need to demonstrate evidence of the context, cognitive and scoring validity of the test tasks they create to represent the underlying real life construct. They also need to be explicit as to how they operationalise criterial distinctions between levels in their tests in terms of the various validity parameters discussed above. Use of a socio-cognitive validation framework can help to clarify, both theoretically and practically, the various constituent parts of the testing endeavour as far as 'validity' is concerned; it can offer a valuable means of revisiting many of our 'traditional' terms and concepts, to redefine them more clearly and to grow in our understanding.

Following *Examining Writing* (Shaw and Weir 2007) and *Examining Reading* (Khalifa and Weir 2009), *Examining Speaking* marks the third comprehensive attempt to expose the totality of Cambridge ESOL academic practice in a particular domain to scrutiny in the public arena. As we have demonstrated, much has already been achieved by Cambridge and other researchers towards a better understanding of the nature of second language speaking proficiency and how it can be assessed; perhaps not surprisingly, this volume also shows that there are plenty of questions still to be answered and a great deal of work still to be done. Future research needs to investigate whether further work on refining the parameters identified in this volume, either singly or in configuration, can help better ground the distinctions in speaking proficiency that are represented by levels in Cambridge ESOL examinations and its external referent the CEFR, as well as in the level-based tests produced by other language examination boards.

Appendix A

Sample Speaking tasks at five levels

KET

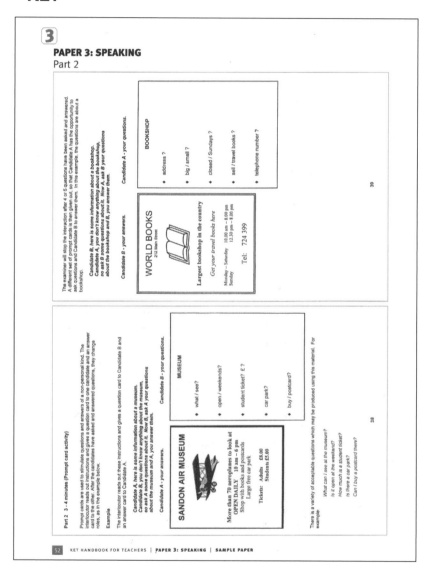

PET

3

PAPER 3: SPEAKING
Part 1

Phase 2

Interlocutor

(Select one or more questions from the list to ask each candidate. Use candidates' names throughout. Ask Candidate B first.)

Do you enjoy studying English? Why (not)?

Do you think that English will be useful for you in the future?

What did you do yesterday evening / last weekend?

What do you enjoy doing in your free time?

Thank you.

(Introduction to Part 2)
In the next part, you are going to talk to each other.

Part 1 (2-3 minutes)

Phase 1

Interlocutor

A/B   Good morning / afternoon / evening.
Can I have your mark sheets, please?

(Hand over the mark sheets to the Assessor.)

A/B   I'm .... and this is ....
He / she is just going to listen to us.

A   Now, what's your name?
Thank you.

B   And, what's your name?
Thank you.

B   Candidate B, what's your surname?
How do you spell it?

Thank you.

A   And, Candidate A, what's your surname?
How do you spell it?

Thank you.

(Ask the following questions. Ask Candidate A first.)

Where do you live / come from?

Adult students
Do you work or are you a student in .....?
What do you do / study?

School-age students
Do you study English at school?
Do you like it?

Thank you.

(Repeat for Candidate B.)

Back-up prompts

How do you write your family / second name?

Do you live in .....?

Have you got a job?
What job do you do? / What subject(s) do you study?

Do you have English lessons?

PET

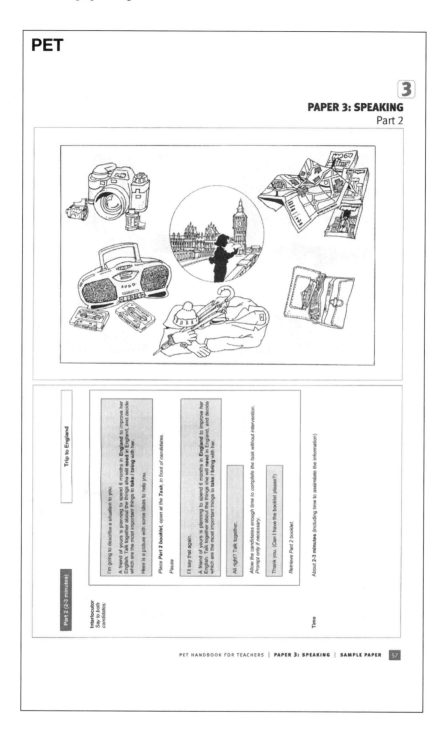

Part 2 (2-3 minutes)

Trip to England

Interlocutor
Say to both candidates:

I'm going to describe a situation to you.

A friend of yours is planning to spend 6 months in **England** to improve her English. Talk together about the things she will **need** in England, and decide which are the most important things to **take / bring** with you.

Here is a picture with some ideas to help you.

*Place **Part 2 booklet**, open at the **Task**, in front of candidates.*

Pause

I'll say that again.

A friend of yours is planning to spend 6 months in **England** to improve her English. Talk together about the things she will **need** in England, and decide which are the most important things to **take / bring** with her.

All right? Talk together.

Allow the candidates enough time to complete the task without intervention. Prompt only if necessary.

Thank you. (Can I have the booklet please?)

Retrieve Part 2 booklet.

Time   About 2-3 minutes (including time to assimilate the information)

PET

3

PAPER 3: SPEAKING
Parts 3 and 4

People reading and writing

Part 3 (3 minutes)

Interlocutor
Say to both candidates:

Now, I'd like each of you to talk on your own about something. I'm going to give each of you a photograph of people reading and writing.

Candidate A, here is your photograph. (*Place Part 3 booklet, open at Task 1A, in front of Candidate A.*) Please show it to Candidate B, but I'd like you to talk about it. Candidate B, you just listen. I'll give you your photograph in a moment.

Candidate A, please tell us what you can see in your photograph.

(Candidate A)

Approximately one minute

If there is a need to intervene, prompts rather than direct questions should be used.

Thank you. (Can I have the booklet please?)

Retrieve Part 3 booklet from Candidate A.

Interlocutor

Now, Candidate B, here is your photograph. It also shows someone reading and writing. (*Place Part 3 booklet, open at Task 1B, in front of Candidate B.*) Please show it to Candidate A and tell us what you can see in the photograph.

(Candidate B)

Approximately one minute

Thank you. (Can I have the booklet please?)

Retrieve Part 3 booklet from Candidate B

Part 4 (3 minutes)

Interlocutor
Say to both candidates:

Your photographs showed people reading and writing. Now, I'd like you to talk together about the different kinds of reading and writing you did when you were younger, and the kinds you do now.

Allow the candidates enough time to complete the task without intervention. Prompt only if necessary.

Thank you. That's the end of the test.

Time

Parts 3 & 4 should take about 6 minutes together.

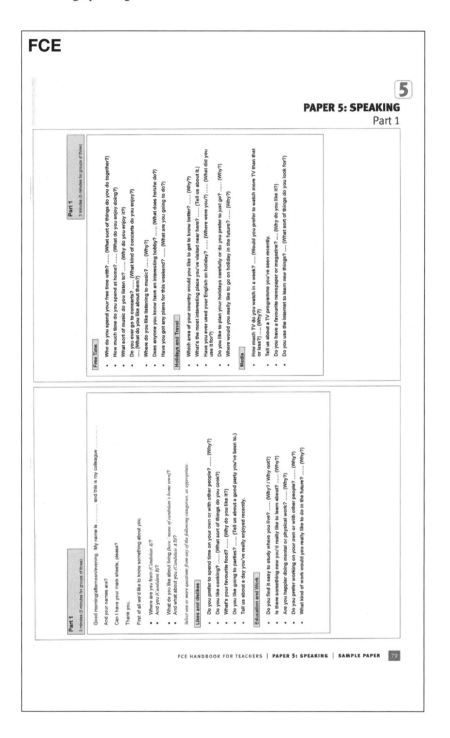

FCE

Part 1
3 minutes (5 minutes for groups of three)

Free Time
- Who do you spend your free time with? ...... (What sort of things do you do together?)
- How much time do you spend at home? ...... (What do you enjoy doing?)
- What sort of music do you listen to? ...... (Why do you enjoy it?)
- Do you ever go to concerts? ...... (What kind of concerts do you enjoy?) ...... (What do you like about them?)
- Where do you like listening to music? ...... (Why?)
- Does anyone you know have an interesting hobby? ...... (What does he/she do?)
- Have you got any plans for this weekend? ...... (What are you going to do?)

Holidays and Travel
- Which area of your country would you like to get to know better? ...... (Why?)
- What's the most interesting place you've visited near here? ...... (Tell us about it.)
- Have you ever used your English on holiday? ...... (Where were you?) ...... (What did you use it for?)
- Do you like to plan your holidays carefully or do you prefer to just go? ...... (Why?)
- Where would you really like to go on holiday in the future? ...... (Why?)

Media
- How much TV do you watch in a week? ...... (Would you prefer to watch more TV than that or less?) ...... (Why?)
- Tell us about a TV programme you've seen recently.
- Do you have a favourite newspaper or magazine? ...... (Why do you like it?)
- Do you use the Internet to learn new things? ...... (What sort of things do you look for?)

Part 1
3 minutes (5 minutes for groups of three)

Good morning/afternoon/evening. My name is .... and this is my colleague ......

And your names are?

Can I have your mark sheets, please?

Thank you.

First of all we'd like to know something about you.

- Where are you from (*Candidate A*)?
- And you (*Candidate B*)?

- What do you like about living (*here / name of candidate's home town*)?
- And what about you (*Candidate A/B*)?

Select one or more questions from any of the following categories, as appropriate.

Likes and dislikes
- Do you prefer to spend time on your own or with other people? ...... (Why?)
- Do you like cooking? ...... (What sort of things do you cook?)
- What's your favourite food? ...... (Why do you like it?)
- Do you like going to parties? ...... (Tell us about a good party you've been to.)
- Tell us about a day you've really enjoyed recently.

Education and Work
- Do you find it easy to study where you live? ...... (Why / Why not?)
- Is there something new you'd really like to learn about? ...... (Why?)
- Are you happier doing mental or physical work? ...... (Why?)
- Do you prefer working on your own or with other people? ...... (Why?)
- What kind of work would you really like to do in the future? ...... (Why?)

FCE

PAPER 5: SPEAKING
Part 2

Why is the music important to the different groups of people? **1**

What will the people learn on their visits? **2**

| 1 Making music | Part 2 |
| 2 Educational visits | 4 minutes (6 minutes for groups of three) |

Interlocutor
In this part of the test, I'm going to give each of you two photographs. I'd like you to talk about your photographs on your own for about a minute, and also to answer a short question about your partner's photographs.

(Candidate A), it's your turn first. Here are your photographs. They show **people making music in different ways**.

Place Part 2 booklet, open at Task 1, in front of Candidate A.

I'd like you to compare the photographs, and say why you think the music is **important to the different groups of people**.

All right?

Candidate A
⏱ *1 minute*

Interlocutor
Thank you. (Can I have the booklet, please?) *Retrieve Part 2 booklet.*

(Candidate B), **which type of music would you prefer to listen to?**

Candidate B
⏱ *approximately 20 seconds*

Interlocutor
Thank you.

Now *(Candidate B)*, here are your photographs. They show **people of different ages on educational visits.**

Place Part 2 booklet, open at Task 2, in front of Candidate B.

I'd like you to compare the photographs, and say what you think the people will learn on their visits.

All right?

Candidate B
⏱ *1 minute*

Interlocutor
Thank you. (Can I have the booklet, please?) *Retrieve Part 2 booklet.*

(Candidate A), **which of these things would you like to learn about?**

Candidate A
⏱ *approximately 20 seconds*

Interlocutor
Thank you.

319

FCE

- How successful might these suggestions be?
- Which two would attract most people?

21 Jon's café

Parts 3 and 4
(7 minutes (9 minutes for groups of three))

Part 3

Interlocutor Now, I'd like you to talk about something together for about three minutes.
(4 minutes for groups of three)

I'd like you to imagine that a local café wants to attract more people. Here are some of the suggestions they are considering.

Place Part 3 booklet, open at Task 21, in front of the candidates.

First, talk to each other about how successful these suggestions might be. Then decide which two would attract most people.

All right?

Candidates *(3 minutes (4 minutes for groups of three))*
....

Interlocutor Thank you. (Can I have the booklet, please?) *Retrieve Part 3 booklet.*

Part 4

Interlocutor *Select any of the following questions, as appropriate:*

- Would you like to spend time in a café like this?
  ...... (Why? / Why not?)
- Would you like to work in a café?
  ...... (Why? / Why not?)
- What sort of restaurants are most popular with visitors in your country? ......
  (Why?)
- What sort of things do people complain about in cafés and restaurants?
- Young people usually go to different places to relax than older people. Why do you think that is?
- Some people say that going out to relax is a waste of time and money. Do you agree? ...... (Why? / Why not?)

Thank you. That is the end of the test.

Select any of the following prompts, as appropriate:
- What do you think?
- Do you agree?
- And you?

CAE

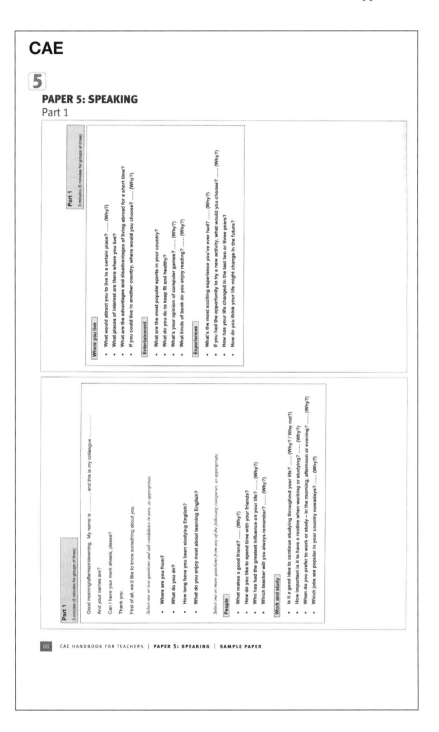

5

PAPER 5: SPEAKING
Part 1

Part 1
3 minutes (5 minutes for groups of three)

Good morning/afternoon/evening. My name is .... and this is my colleague ....

And your names are?

Can I have your mark sheets, please?

Thank you.

First of all, we'd like to know something about you.

Select one or two questions and ask candidates in turn, as appropriate.

- Where are you from?
- What do you do?
- How long have you been studying English?
- What do you enjoy most about learning English?

Select one or more questions from any of the following categories, as appropriate.

People

- What makes a good friend? ...... (Why?)
- How do you like to spend time with your friends?
- Who has had the greatest influence on your life? ...... (Why?)
- Which teacher will you always remember? ...... (Why?)

Work and study

- Is it a good idea to continue studying throughout your life? ...... (Why? / Why not?)
- How important is it to have a routine when working or studying? ...... (Why?)
- When do you prefer to work or study – in the morning, afternoon or evening? ...... (Why?)
- Which jobs are popular in your country nowadays? ...... (Why?)

Part 1
3 minutes (5 minutes for groups of three)

Where you live

- What would attract you to live in a certain place? ...... (Why?)
- What places of interest are there where you live?
- What are the advantages and disadvantages of living abroad for a short time?
- If you could live in another country, where would you choose? ...... (Why?)

Entertainment

- What are the most popular sports in your country?
- What do you do to keep fit and healthy?
- What's your opinion of computer games? ...... (Why?)
- What kinds of book do you enjoy reading? ...... (Why?)

Experiences

- What's the most exciting experience you've ever had? ...... (Why?)
- If you had the opportunity to try a new activity, what would you choose? ...... (Why?)
- How has your life changed in the last two or three years?
- How do you think your life might change in the future?

CAE

CAE

5

PAPER 5: SPEAKING
Parts 3 and 4

- How do these pictures show the role of computers nowadays?
- Which picture best reflects the difference computers have made to our lives?

21

21 The computer generation

Parts 3 and 4
8 minutes (12 minutes for groups of three)

Part 3

Interlocutor   Now, I'd like you to talk about something together for about three minutes.
(5 minutes for groups of three)

Here are some pictures showing different ways in which computers affect our lives.

Place Part 3 booklet, open at Task 21, in front of the candidates.

First, talk to each other about how these pictures show the role of computers nowadays. Then decide which picture best reflects the difference computers have made to our lives.

All right?

Candidates   ....
(3 minutes (5 minutes for groups of three)

Interlocutor   Thank you. (Can I have the booklet, please?) *Retrieve Part 3 booklet.*

Part 4

Interlocutor   *Select any of the following questions, as appropriate:*

- Some people say that computers are helping to create a generation of people without social skills. What's your opinion?

- What are the advantages and disadvantages of shopping by computer?

- How far do you agree that the computer is the greatest invention of modern times?

- A lot of personal information about all of us is now kept on computers. Do you find this worrying? ...... (Why? / Why not?)

- In future, what role do you think there will be for people who are not interested in technology? ...... (Why?)

Thank you. That is the end of the test.

Select any of the following prompts, as appropriate:
- What do you think?
- Do you agree?
- How about you?

CPE

5

PAPER 5: SPEAKING
Parts 1 and 2

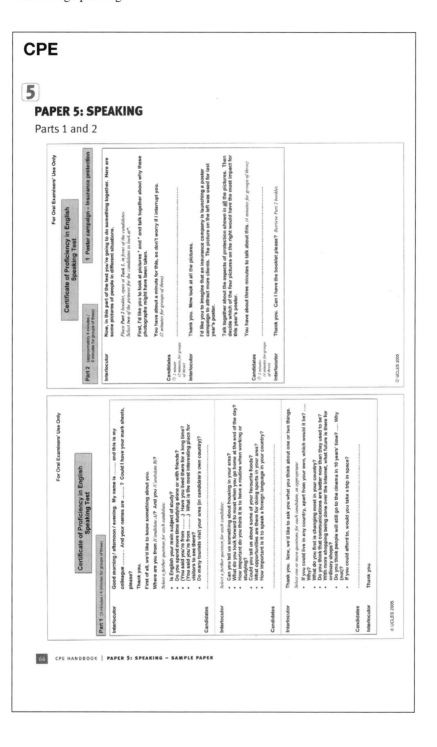

CPE

PAPER 5: SPEAKING
Part 2

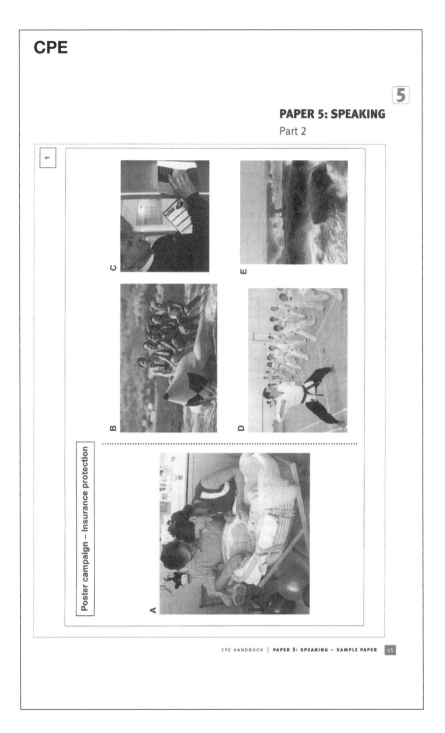

Poster campaign – Insurance protection

CPE

5

PAPER 5: SPEAKING
Part 3

Certificate of Proficiency in English
Speaking Test

Part 3 *(approximately 12 minutes)*

	15 Sound

Interlocutor

Now, in this part of the test you're each going to talk on your own for about two minutes. You need to listen while your partner is speaking because you'll be asked to comment afterwards.

(A)

So *(Candidate A)*, I'm going to give you a card with a question written on it and I'd like you to tell us what you think. There are also some ideas on the card for you to use if you like.

All right? Here is your card.

Place Part 3 booklet, open at Task 15(a), in front of Candidate A.

Please let *(Candidate B)* see your card. Remember *(Candidate A)*, you have about two minutes to talk before we join in.

[Allow up to 10 seconds before saying, if necessary: Would you like to begin now?]

Candidate A
2 minutes

Thank you.

Interlocutor

Select one appropriate response question for Candidate B:

- What do you think?
- Is there anything you would like to add?
- Is there anything you don't agree with?
- How does this differ from your experience?

Address one of the following follow-up questions to both candidates:

- Do you think everyone has musical ability?
- What kinds of music do you strongly dislike?
- How has your taste in music changed?

Candidates
1 minute

Interlocutor Thank you. Can I have the booklet please? *Retrieve Part 3 booklet.*

Task 15(a)

Why is music important to people around the world?

- traditions
- entertainment
- emotions

© UCLES 2005

---

15 Sound (cont.)	

Interlocutor

Now *(Candidate B)*, it's your turn to be given a question. Here is your card.

Place Part 3 booklet, open at Task 15(b), in front of Candidate B.

(B)

Please let *(Candidate A)* see your card. Remember *(Candidate B)*, you have about two minutes to tell us what you think, and there are some ideas on the card for you to use if you like. All right?

[Allow up to 10 seconds before saying, if necessary: Would you like to begin now?]

Candidate B
2 minutes

Interlocutor Thank you.

Select one appropriate response question for Candidate A:

- What do you think?
- Is there anything you would like to add?
- Is there anything you don't agree with?
- How does this differ from your experience?

Candidate A
up to 1 minute

Interlocutor

Address one of the following follow-up questions to both candidates:

- Are most of your friends quiet or loud people?
- Why do people react differently to noise?
- Do you think noise levels in public places should be controlled?

Candidates
1 minute

Interlocutor Thank you. Can I have the booklet please? *Retrieve Part 3 booklet.*

Task 15(b)

When is it preferable to be in a quiet place or a noisy place?

- age
- activity
- time of day

Interlocutor

Now, to finish the test, we're going to talk about 'sound' in general.

Address a selection of the following questions to both candidates:

- Do you find the sounds of nature relaxing? ..... Why (not)?
- What makes a person's voice pleasant or unpleasant?
- Why do you think some people dislike complete silence?
- It is said that some nationalities are louder than others. How true is this?
- "A great film needs a great soundtrack." Do you agree? .... Why (not)?
- Do you think that children are noisier than adults? ..... (In what circumstances?)

up to 4 minutes

Interlocutor Thank you. That is the end of the test.

© UCLES 2005

Appendix B

Candidate Information Sheet

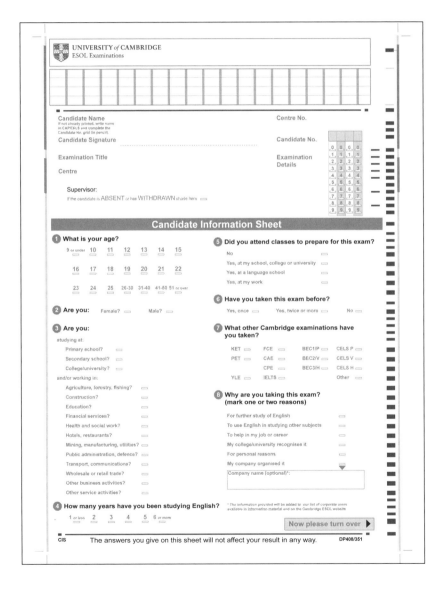

UNIVERSITY *of* CAMBRIDGE
ESOL Examinations

Candidate Name
If not already printed, write name
in CAPITALS and complete the
Candidate No. grid (in pencil).

Candidate Signature

Examination Title

Centre

Supervisor:
If the candidate is ABSENT or has WITHDRAWN shade here

Centre No.

Candidate No.

Examination
Details

Candidate Information Sheet

1 What is your age?

9 or under   10   11   12   13   14   15

16   17   18   19   20   21   22

23   24   25   26-30   31-40   41-50   51 or over

2 Are you: Female?   Male?

3 Are you:

studying at:
Primary school?
Secondary school?
College/university?

and/or working in:
Agriculture, forestry, fishing?
Construction?
Education?
Financial services?
Health and social work?
Hotels, restaurants?
Mining, manufacturing, utilities?
Public administration, defence?
Transport, communications?
Wholesale or retail trade?
Other business activities?
Other service activities?

4 How many years have you been studying English?

1 or less   2   3   4   5   6 or more

5 Did you attend classes to prepare for this exam?

No
Yes, at my school, college or university
Yes, at a language school
Yes, at my work

6 Have you taken this exam before?

Yes, once   Yes, twice or more   No

7 What other Cambridge examinations have you taken?

KET   FCE   BEC1/P   CELS P
PET   CAE   BEC2/V   CELS V
CPE   BEC3/H   CELS H
YLE   IELTS   Other

8 Why are you taking this exam? (mark one or two reasons)

For further study of English
To use English in studying other subjects
To help in my job or career
My college/university recognises it
For personal reasons
My company organised it
Company name (optional)*:

* The information provided will be added to our list of corporate users available in information material and on the Cambridge ESOL website

Now please turn over

CIS   The answers you give on this sheet will not affect your result in any way.   DP408/351

327

9 Where do you come from?
If it is not listed, please complete the box 'other'

001 Afghanistan	075 Guatemala	148 Poland	001 Afrikaans
002 Albania	076 Guinea	149 Portugal	002 Akan
003 Algeria	077 Guinea-Bissau	150 Puerto Rico	003 Albanian
004 American Samoa	078 Guyana	151 Qatar	004 Amharic
005 Andorra	079 Haiti	152 Reunion	005 Arabic
006 Angola	080 Honduras	153 Romania	006 Armenian
007 Antigua	081 Hong Kong	154 Russia	007 Assamese
008 Argentina	082 Hungary	155 Rwanda	008 Aymara
009 Armenia	083 Iceland	156 San Marino	009 Azerbaijani
010 Australia	084 India	157 Sao Tome and Principe	010 Baluchi
011 Austria	085 Indonesia	158 Saudi Arabia	011 Bambara
012 Azerbaijan	086 Iran	159 Senegal	012 Basque
013 Bahamas	087 Iraq	160 Seychelles	013 Bemba
014 Bahrain	088 Ireland	161 Sierra Leone	014 Bengali
015 Bangladesh	089 Israel	162 Singapore	015 Bihari
016 Barbados	090 Italy	163 Slovakia	016 Breton
017 Belarus	091 Ivory Coast	164 Slovenia	017 Bulgarian
018 Belgium	092 Jamaica	165 Solomon Islands	018 Burmese
019 Belize	093 Japan	166 Somalia	019 Byelorussian
020 Benin	094 Jordan	167 South Africa	020 Catalan
021 Bermuda	095 Kampuchea (Cambodia)	168 Spain	021 Chinese
022 Bhutan	096 Kazakhstan	169 Sri Lanka	022 Croatian
023 Bolivia	097 Kenya	170 St.Helena	023 Czech
024 Bosnia-Herzegovina	098 Korea, North	171 St. Kitts-Nevis-Anguilla	024 Danish
025 Botswana	099 Korea, South	172 St.Lucia	025 Dutch
026 Brazil	100 Kuwait	173 St.Pierre and Miquelon	026 Efik
027 British Virgin Islands	101 Laos	174 St.Vincent and the Grenadines	027 Estonian
028 Brunei	102 Latvia	175 Sudan	028 Ewe
029 Bulgaria	103 Lebanon	176 Surinam	029 Faeroese
030 Burkina Faso	104 Lesotho	177 Swaziland	030 Farsi
031 Burundi	105 Liberia	178 Sweden	031 Fijian
032 Cameroon	106 Libya	179 Switzerland	032 Finnish
033 Canada	107 Liechtenstein	180 Syria	033 Flemish
034 Cape Verde	108 Lithuania	181 Tahiti	034 French
035 Cayman Islands	109 Luxembourg	182 Taiwan	035 Fulani
036 Central African Republic	110 Macao	183 Tanzania	036 Ga
037 Chad	111 Madagascar	184 Thailand	037 Georgian
038 Chile	112 Malawi	185 Togo	038 German
039 China (People's Republic)	113 Malaysia	186 Tokelau	039 Gilbertese
040 Colombia	114 Maldives	187 Tonga	040 Greek
041 Comoros	115 Mali	188 Trinidad and Tobago	041 Gujarati
042 Congo	116 Malta	189 Tunisia	042 Haitian Creole
043 Costa Rica	117 Marshall Islands	190 Turkey	043 Hausa
044 Croatia	118 Martinique	191 Turks and Caicos Islands	044 Hebrew
045 Cuba	119 Mauritania	192 Tuvalu	045 Hindi
046 Cyprus	120 Mauritius	193 Uganda	046 Hungarian
047 Czech Republic	121 Mexico	194 United Arab Emirates	047 Ibo/Igbo
048 Denmark	122 Moldova	195 Ukraine	048 Icelandic
049 Djibouti	123 Monaco	196 United Kingdom	049 Igala
050 Dominica	124 Mongolia	197 Uruguay	050 Indonesian
051 Dominican Republic	125 Montserrat	198 US Virgin Islands	051 Italian
052 Ecuador	126 Morocco	199 USA	052 Japanese
053 Egypt	127 Mozambique	200 Uzbekistan	053 Javanese
054 El Salvador	128 Myanmar	201 Vanuatu	054 Kannada
055 Equatorial Guinea	129 Namibia	202 Vatican	055 Kashmiri
056 Estonia	130 Nauru	203 Venezuela	056 Kazakh
057 Ethiopia	131 Nepal	204 Vietnam	057 Khmer
058 Faeroe Islands	132 Netherlands	205 Wallis and Futuna Islands	058 Korean
059 Fiji	133 Netherlands Antilles	206 Western Samoa	059 Lao
060 Finland	134 New Caledonia	207 Yemen, Republic of	060 Latvian
061 France	135 New Zealand	208 Yugoslavia	061 Lithuanian
062 French Guiana	136 Nicaragua	210 Zaire	062 Luba
063 French Polynesia	137 Niger	211 Zambia	063 Luo
064 Gabon	138 Nigeria	212 Zimbabwe	064 Luxemburgish
065 Gambia	139 Niue (Cook Island)		065 Malagasy
066 Georgia	140 Norway	300 Other (please write below)	066 Malay
067 Germany	141 Oman		067 Malayalam
068 Ghana	142 Pakistan		068 Malinka
069 Gibraltar	143 Palestine		069 Maltese
070 Greece	144 Panama		070 Maori
071 Greenland	145 Papua New Guinea		071 Marathi
072 Grenada	146 Paraguay		072 Marshallese
073 Guadaloupe	147 Peru		073 Masai
074 Guam			074 Mende

10 Which is your first language?
(i.e. your mother tongue).
If it is not listed, please complete the box 'other'.

075 Mongolian	
076 Nepali	
077 Norwegian	
078 Oriya	
079 Palauan	
080 Panjabi	
081 Pashto	
082 Polish	
083 Ponapean	
084 Portuguese	
085 Quechua	
086 Rajasthani	
087 Riff	
088 Romanian	
089 Romansch	
090 Russian	
091 Samoan	
092 Serbian	
093 Shona	
094 Sindhi	
095 Singhalese	
096 Slovak	
097 Slovene	
098 Somali	
099 Spanish	
100 Swahili	
101 Swazi	
102 Swedish	
103 Swiss German	
104 Tagalog	
105 Tahitian	
106 Tamil	
107 Tatar	
108 Telugu	
109 Thai	
110 Tibetan	
111 Tigrinya	
112 Tongan	
113 Trukese	
114 Tulu	
115 Tupi/Guarani	
116 Turkish	
117 Uighur	
118 Ukrainian	
119 Ulithan	
120 Urdu	
121 Uzbek	
122 Vietnamese	
123 Wolof	
124 Xhosa	
125 Yao	
126 Yapese	
127 Yiddish	
128 Yoruba	
129 Zulu	
300 Other (please write below)	

This listing of places implies no view regarding questions of sovereignty or status.

denote Print Limited 0121 520 5100

Appendix C
Standard procedures for the production of Speaking test material

Cambridge ESOL employs a set of standardised systems, processes and procedures for designing, developing and delivering all of the examinations offered by the board, Speaking test papers included. This appendix provides a brief description of the standard procedures for the production of Speaking test materials. They are reported in greater detail, though, in the *Work Instructions for Routine Test Production,* a reference document for Assessment Managers, Chairs and Outsourcing Coordinators, and they are included in item writer guidelines as appropriate.

This appendix focuses on the process of question paper production (QPP) and the standard procedures employed during this process. The procedures and processes are certified as meeting the internationally recognised ISO 9001:2000 standard for quality management.

The key objectives of the QPP process are:

- production of valid tests to a defined timescale
- production of items, tasks and test papers that are of a consistently high quality and appropriate difficulty
- ensuring task and item banks contain the appropriate number of test items and tasks
- co-ordinating test production schedules to the appropriate time scales
- keeping an accurate record of items/tasks and test usage.

The production of examination material for any given paper is the responsibility of the assessment manager for that paper, who is a Cambridge ESOL staff member, and the chair of the Item Writing team, who is an external consultant. An assessment group manager, who is also a staff member, has overall responsibility for all the papers in their suite of examinations.

The role of the chair of the Item Writing team is principally concerned with the technical aspects of writing the examination materials and ensuring that the item writers on the team are fully trained and equipped to produce material to the best of their ability. In conjunction with the assessment manager and other members of the team, the chair ensures that tasks for their paper are appropriate in terms of topic, content and level and that they comply fully with the specifications for the paper and item writer guidelines. The assessment manager is responsible for managing the production of the examination material through the various stages, ensuring that sufficient material is produced to the agreed schedule and that test papers are produced to schedule and of appropriate quality. Both the chair and the assessment manager bring expertise to the partnership from their personal experience of teaching and assessment.

Stages in QPP process

There are several stages in the production of an examination paper: commissioning, pre-editing, editing, pretesting/trialling, pretest/trial review, paper construction and exam overview. Below is a brief description of these stages/procedures as they relate to the production of Speaking test materials.

Figure 1 provides a visual representation of the question paper production (QPP) process.

Commissioning

Commissioning of item writers is the first stage of the QPP process and is a task that has been centralised for Cambridge ESOL exams. The aims of centralised commissioning are:

- to co-ordinate the timing of commissions
- to plan well in advance across all Cambridge ESOL examinations
- to co-ordinate and utilise effectively the item writer resource
- to standardise commissioning procedures across examinations.

The assessment manager for each paper, in consultation with the assessment group manager and chair, determines the number of commissions and the amount of material required for the forthcoming year in accordance with current banks of material and future requirements.

Pre-editing

Pre-editing takes place when commissioned tasks are received by Cambridge ESOL for the first time. The pre-editing stage is intended to select material which will progress in the production process and to improve the quality and maximise the quantity of material available for editing. The aims of pre-editing are:

- To suggest appropriate changes to material requiring amendments or re-writing.
- By reference to the item writer guidelines, to reject unsuitable, problematic or weak material.
- To comment on the item writer's proposed exploitation of a topic or a visual prompt and to suggest possible alternatives (where appropriate).

Figure 1 Question paper production process

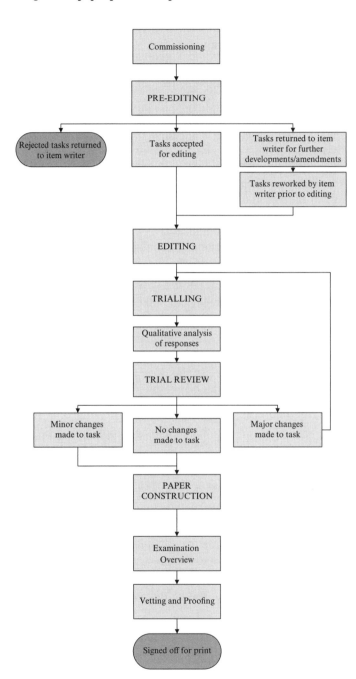

However, it is not intended that material is edited or rewritten by the pre-editing team, as this is not a function of this stage.

- To carry out an initial check on the descriptive system information provided on the Task Description form.
- To speed up the editing process (i.e. item writers will not have to spend time working on unsuitable material).
- To increase the efficiency of editing.

Participants in pre-editing include the chair, the assessment manager, and an experienced item writer who is not currently on the team but has experience of working on the paper or on a similar paper at the same level. The pre-editing meeting attendees consider material, decide on the outcome, and prepare feedback for the item writers. Decisions are made on the basis of the quality of the material and conformity to the item writer guidelines. All decisions are based on or justified by reference to the item writer guidelines. Feedback to item writers is communicated on a form and/or notes on the submitted task at the pre-editing meeting. The following are possible outcomes of the pre-editing stage:

- Material passes straight to the editing stage.
- Material is returned to the item writer for fine-tuning and, if necessary, request for additional visual stimuli.
- Material requiring extensive re-writing may be re-submitted for pre-editing as part of a future commission.
- The material may be rejected. In this case it may be used for item writer training, item writer guidelines or offered to another suitable exam.

Editing

Materials which successfully pass the pre-editing stage are re-submitted for editing. The editing stage ensures that, as far as possible, material is of an acceptable standard for inclusion in trials. The aims of editing are:

- to check or re-check the quality of material against specifications and item writer guidelines
- to make any changes necessary to submitted materials so that they are of an acceptable standard for trialling
- to ensure that rubrics and visual stimuli are appropriate and comprehensive
- to fine tune specifications to artwork that needs to be commissioned from an external agency
- to further develop the skills of item writers in order to improve the quality of materials submitted and the input of item writers to future editing sessions.

Each editing group meeting consists of the chair, the assessment manager and members of the Item Writing team. Before the meeting chairs check the material, as appropriate, to make sure all materials are ready for editing, and these are then sent to each member of the editing team in preparation for the meeting. The expectation at the meeting is that material should require minimal changes only. However, re-writing of material and replacement of visuals will sometimes be necessary, and may be an important part of training. Material is not usually rejected at editing on the grounds that it is of unacceptable quality or does not correspond with current guidelines relating to quantity, length, subject matter, level, etc. These aspects have been dealt with at the pre-editing stage. The final decisions on acceptability of material rest with the assessment manager and chair.

Edited material is entered into the appropriate bank in LIBS (local item banking system), i.e. the edited bank, and visuals stored in the Cambridge ESOL Image Library. Attributes, such as task type, are added to LIBS according to the information on the task description form. The tasks are then sent to the chair, who checks them against the editing meeting copy for both content and typographical errors and makes any necessary amendments.

Trialling

After the editing meeting the edited materials are checked by the chair in readiness for trialling. Trialling is intended to confirm that material is of a suitable quality to be used in a live speaking examination. The aims of trialling are:

- to ensure that tasks are at an appropriate level, and, as far as possible, equivalent in terms of difficulty of the input and output (vocabulary, functions and structures that candidates will need to use)
- to ensure that rubrics and visuals provide sufficient stimulus to encourage the production of language
- to check that visual prompts are clear and accessible (where appropriate)
- to fine-tune rubrics.

Trialling takes place at selected centres/schools around the world.

Trial review

After trialling, a meeting is held to review the performance of materials. It aims at:

- reviewing trialled material in the light of candidate performance and feedback from examiners and candidates, as appropriate

- finalising and ensuring that the material is acceptable for use in test paper construction
- decision making, e.g. whether to bank the material for test paper construction, revise and retrial, or reject
- making essential adjustments to rubrics and visuals so that, as far as possible, no editing will need to take place at the paper construction stage.

The trial review meeting takes place as soon as possible after the trialling session. The chair, the assessment manager, and an item writer who was involved in the trailling participate in the meeting. Systematic feedback to item writers is provided either in writing after trial review or as part of a separate item writer training/feedback day.

Paper construction

Paper construction aims to construct sufficient examination papers to meet ongoing requirements and to ensure that all papers meet required standards in terms of level, coverage, content and comparability. Depending on the nature of the paper concerned, the chair may make a proposal for paper content in advance of the paper construction meeting. In the case of Speaking, this comprises a set of materials from which the examiner can make a selection.

This meeting usually consists of the assessment manager, the chair, an experienced item writer and a validation officer (as required). The chair initially and subsequently the teams at the meeting check that:

- a range of topics/tasks is maintained within the set of Speaking materials, bearing in mind the range of cultural perspectives desirable
- there is no obvious overlap in content either within the set or historically
- the tasks are at the right level
- the rubrics are correct and the visuals are clear and uncontroversial.

The draft materials are circulated to those attending in advance of the paper construction meeting for preliminary consideration of content, and range of tasks. After the meeting, draft papers are amended by the paper administrator, any necessary amendments are made to LIBS keys and the assessment manager checks all the material.

Examination overview

The aims of examination overview are:

- to review content of the entire examination in order to confirm earlier decisions made at paper construction

- to ensure the examination as a whole possesses the required continuity
- to check topics across the examination and historically
- to enable assessment managers to communicate across papers and across examinations and to inform other assessment managers of the content of the examination.

The examination overview meeting includes all assessment managers working on the examination as a whole and the assessment group manager. At a meeting chaired by the assessment group manager, draft question papers are circulated and reviewed. Decisions taken at paper construction or trial review are looked at again, decisions are made on remedial action to be taken (if necessary) and the overall level of the paper is checked.

After the meeting, the assessment group manager checks any remedial action taken by the assessment managers. Final copies of examination papers (including the set of Speaking materials) are passed to the QPP Unit. Papers are sent out by secure post to the appropriate chairs and content vetters for content checking. Following this, assessment managers review papers in the light of the feedback from chairs and content vetters. The papers are given a final check by two proofreaders before being signed off for print.

Appendix D

Administrative setting and management of the Speaking tests

It is well recognised that the circumstances under which an examination takes place can have a significant effect upon candidate performance. The socio-cognitive framework for test validation acknowledges this important dimension of the administrative and environmental conditions under which any test is taken. The model shown in Figure 1.1 (see Chapter 1, p. 28) locates this dimension under the heading of Context validity as part of the Setting for the task. It is important to remember, however, that locating a test's administrative setting as an aspect of Context validity is to some degree an oversimplification for the sake of convenience, since administrative and environmental conditions can also impact on both Cognitive validity (i.e. mental processing) and Scoring validity (i.e. quality of rating), especially where direct speaking assessment is concerned. As far as possible, test taking conditions need to be equivalent across administration sites and occasions; if not, the processing involved in completing test tasks or the judgements involved in rating performance quality may well differ in important respects, potentially leading to invalid or unreliable results.

In light of this, examination boards need to set in place clear procedures to ensure that, as far as is possible, a test is administered in the same way whoever is in charge or wherever it takes place. This means that examination staff need to be provided with precise instructions on what they must do and should be familiar and comfortable with all aspects of the test before administering it; test settings should be of equivalent standards with appropriate facilities (chairs, desks, clock); test equipment, e.g. playback equipment, should be carefully checked for any problems before the test is administered; procedures for dealing with any candidates caught cheating should have been sorted out in advance; all administrative details should have been clearly worked out prior to the exam, in particular ground rules for late arrivals, the giving of test instructions by supervisors or invigilators, procedures for confirming candidates' identity and all other necessary details (see Rose (2010) and Saville (2010, and forthcoming), as well as Wild and Ramaswamy (2008) for a comprehensive discussion of the practical aspects of test management.)

As a large-scale, international examination board, Cambridge ESOL has in place an array of documentation dealing with the general requirements for the standardised administration of its English language examinations:

- *Regulations* for the relevant year (available on www.CambridgeESOL. org) specify, for the benefit of schools and candidates, the terms and conditions under which Cambridge ESOL examinations are offered
- *Centre Registration Booklet* (available on CentreNet, a website restricted to Centre Exams Managers and their support staff) gives an outline of the responsibilities of test centres in regard to the administration of Cambridge ESOL exams, particularly with new applicants in mind
- *Handbook for Centres* provides detailed general information on the running of a centre and guidelines on the administration of the examinations
- *Day Booklets* (EDB), supplementary *Timings and Instructions Booklets* (TIB) and *Speaking Test Instructions* provide detailed instructions and guidelines to supervisors and invigilators on the conduct of each examination.

In addition, there exists a wealth of procedural documentation available concerning the specific management of the Cambridge ESOL Speaking tests, including:

- *Instructions to Speaking Examiners*
- *Team Leader System* document
- *Team Leader Handbook*
- *Guidelines for Speaking Examiner Training and Co-ordination*
- *Speaking Examiner Trainer/Co-ordinator Handbook*
- *Speaking Examiner Support File* [containing advice on examining candidates with special requirements].

All documentation for test centres is regularly updated by the Cambridge ESOL Centre Support Unit and the Assessment and Operations unit. The publications listed above are issued to Centre Exams Managers or examiner trainers and are supplemented by promotional materials for specific examinations, e.g. exam specific handbooks or leaflets (available on www. CambridgeESOL.org).

The administrative elements of the assessment, which may be centralised (i.e. Cambridge ESOL) or local (i.e. centre-based), include: ensuring that the candidates have information on what to expect when they are examined (the experiential dimension discussed in Chapter 2); making all necessary arrangements for the administration of tests under secure, standardised or special conditions (see Chapter 2 also for full discussion of special arrangements); providing the candidates with their results, with the means to interpret them and, if there are grounds, to have their results checked; and – to those candidates who have gained appropriate grades – issuing their certificates (see more on this in Chapter 5). Responsibility for these elements of carrying out assessment is shared between Cambridge ESOL administrative staff based in Cambridge and staff in the test centres where examinations take place (Centre Exams Managers, their supervisors, invigilators and examiners).

For those candidates with special requirements which make it difficult for them to demonstrate their ability in English (e.g. those with a permanent disability or with short-term difficulties), applications can be made to Cambridge ESOL for Special Arrangements to be set in place so that, insofar as possible, they are then able to take the examination on an equal footing with other candidates. The Scheduled Processing Unit (Special Circumstances) at Cambridge is able to give advice on the most appropriate arrangements for any given candidate. There is also a *Special Circumstances Booklet* available on CentreNet to assist test centre staff with any administrative support arrangements, and an *Access Technology Guide* for help involving specialist equipment. Documentation for test centres stresses the importance of ensuring that candidates with genuine needs receive the assistance they require, as to do otherwise would be discriminatory. Special Arrangements fall into two main categories: those involving the provision of modified material (often in conjunction with administrative arrangements), and those involving administrative arrangements only. (See Chapter 2 on test taker characteristics in relation to Special Arrangements made before the candidate sits the examination and during the examination.)

Uniformity of administration

There are some general administrative requirements that relate to the conduct of all examination papers, irrespective of which skill is being tested. These cover aspects such as: timetabling, supervision of candidates, checking IDs, completing the attendance register, late arrival of candidates, irregular conduct, emergency procedures, Special Consideration (for candidates who have been disadvantaged), collation of Speaking mark sheets and secure storage of Speaking test materials. These will be outlined briefly below in the following section.

In addition, detailed instructions for individual papers are provided in the instructions. Every supervisor in each centre is required to follow specific procedures for each of the respective examination papers and those that apply for the Speaking tests are described later in this Appendix.

General examination requirements and arrangements

In Cambridge ESOL examinations the selection of venues must take into account a number of key factors including general ambience, accessibility of location and suitability of rooms. Cambridge ESOL seeks to ensure that any room in which an examination is conducted, whether on centre premises or in an external venue, provides candidates with appropriate conditions in which to take the examination. Matters such as general cleanliness, air temperature, lighting, ventilation and the level of external noise must be taken into careful consideration.

All candidates (except for the YLE tests) are informed that they are required to provide evidence of identity at each separate paper, by passport or national identity card. Ensuring that candidates' identities are checked against photographic evidence – a key responsibility for Centre Exams Managers – provides confidence regarding a candidate's true identity and is especially important for tests which carry high stakes. Methods are currently being explored that would enable photos of test takers on the day of their test to be uploaded for future checking by prospective test score users as part of enhanced security measures.

Cambridge ESOL has clear rulings on examination supervision. The purpose of supervision and invigilation is to ensure that all candidates are under surveillance for every moment of each examination period. Supervision and invigilation arrangements for the examinations are entrusted to the Centre Exams Manager, who ensures that these tasks are carried out by suitably qualified people. Relatives of candidates in the examination room are specifically not eligible to serve as a supervisor or invigilator.

The supervisor is the person appointed at each centre or venue to be responsible for overseeing the general conduct of the examination sessions. The invigilator is the person in the examination room responsible for the conduct of a particular paper.

Centres must ensure that supervisors and invigilators are trained at least once a year, preferably before a major exam session. Training includes: checking IDs, detecting imposters and preventing fraud; being vigilant about the inappropriate use of electronic devices; being familiar with the exam regulations as contained in the *Exam Day Booklets*. Centres must keep brief records of this training, including details of when and how this training was conducted. Supervisors and invigilators are expected to abide by Cambridge ESOL requirements and must preserve the confidentiality and integrity of test materials before and after the examination.

Supervisor and invigilator familiarity with the relevant requirements is assured through the *Speaking Test Instructions* – a copy of which is kept in the venue's administrative area on the day of the exam. Venue supervisors must also be able to quickly access information and support if needed. For example, they should be able to contact their centre for advice, or refer to the *Handbook for Centres*. Centres keep signed records of the invigilation arrangements for each examination paper which are made available to Cambridge ESOL on request.

Cambridge ESOL reserves the right to visit centres unannounced during the period of the examinations to inspect the arrangements made for the security of confidential examination material (see more on this below) and for the conduct of examinations. Inspections are intended to ensure that arrangements are in order, but can also offer an opportunity to capture first-hand knowledge of any problems from the centre's point of view. Centre Exams Managers are expected to point out the security facilities and examination rooms to visiting inspectors. A copy of the inspector's report is left with the centre and any shortcomings identified in the report are rectified. In the case of an adverse report which indicates cause for concern, the Cambridge ESOL centre inspections officer will send the centre an Action Plan to complete, including details of how and when faults will be rectified.

Requirements for Speaking test venues

The face-to-face Cambridge ESOL Speaking tests, which are normally taken during a 'window' (or specified period) of between one and three weeks, have particular administrative and security requirements which are outlined below.

Supervisors and invigilators are required to be aware of the specific venue requirements for the Speaking tests. The basic requirements for the Speaking test are separate rooms with adequate lighting and ventilation, and the room should be checked for temperature and cleanliness. In assessing the suitability of a room and in preparation for holding a Speaking test the following additional points need to be taken into account:

- The room must be able to accommodate 4–5 people (i.e. two examiners and up to three candidates).
- Wherever possible, any examination with younger candidates, such as KET for Schools and PET for Schools, should be held in rooms with interior glass windows or doors, taking care that the test material is not visible to any waiting candidate.
- The whole test area should be situated as far as possible from noise and disturbance.
- The room must be equipped with a suitably sized table and sufficient number of chairs, arranged according to one of the furniture layout diagrams recommended in the *Handbook for Centres*.
- Tests must not be held simultaneously in a shared room.
- Candidates who have already taken their Speaking test must be separated from those who are waiting to take their test. The waiting/marshalling area(s) should be a central administration area where candidates can have their ID checked and can be assigned to Speaking test rooms. This area must be some distance from the test rooms.

- The waiting/marshalling area should ideally contain enough chairs for candidates to sit in reasonable comfort while they wait to take their test. Candidates may be given their personalised mark sheets in this area, with a reminder not to fold or crease them.
- Clear direction signs must be displayed where appropriate to enable candidates to find the test room easily.
- Posters that might be helpful to candidates must not be visible in the test room.
- Provision must be made for the storing of bags, coats and any electronic devices, either outside the test rooms or on a chair/table inside the test room away from the area where the candidates and examiners are seated. Mobile phones may be placed in a metal box to block signals.

The conduct of the Speaking tests

Centres are responsible for the pairing of candidates in advance to suit local requirements; if necessary, i.e. where there is an odd number of candidates, then a group of three candidates can be scheduled for the final session. Candidates are required to arrive at least 30 minutes before the start of their test and to wait in a specially set aside area where they are supervised and marshalled to ensure they are in place and ready to start at the designated time. Supervisors deal with a range of administrative tasks: checking of time-tabling arrangements with examiners; completion of paperwork; checking of identification; instructions and reminders to candidates; adjusting pairings in case of unexpected absence or illness to avoid delays; handing out mark sheets; ensuring separation of candidates who have already been examined from those still awaiting their examination.

Two examiners are always required for the standard (paired) or group test format and both examiners are familiar with the roles and responsibilities of interlocutor and assessor (see more on this approach in Chapters 4 and 5). Roles are exchanged during the course of an examining session (usually a 3-hour period) in order to allow both examiners an equal opportunity to maintain their experience in both roles. Examiners are not asked to examine for more than two 3-hour sessions in any day. Before entering the examination room each candidate will usually be provided with a mark sheet printed with their name and number. At the start of the test, the interlocutor invites the candidates to hand these over and then passes them to the assessor.

The interlocutor manages the interaction in the test and assesses the candidates using the global achievement assessment scales. In order to deliver the Speaking test equally to all candidates, the interlocutor adheres strictly to the interlocutor frame and procedural instructions; keeps to the prescribed timings for all parts of the test; and ensures that all candidates are treated fairly and given an equal opportunity to speak.

The assessor completes the mark sheets and assesses the candidates using the analytical assessment criteria. To do this, the assessor sits a little to one side where they can see the candidates' faces and is therefore able to hear the candidates clearly; listens but takes no active role in the interaction; finalises the analytical scales marks by the end of the test and enters them on the mark sheets; asks the interlocutor for their global marks and enters them on the mark sheets, but not until after the end of the test when the candidates have left the room, repeating the marks to the interlocutor to confirm they have heard correctly. The assessor also enters other details on the marks sheets (i.e. candidates' numbers, date, examiners' numbers, test materials used).

Examiners make their assessments independently using the appropriate scales; they must not discuss the marks or adjust their marks in light of those given by their co-examiner. Only one mark sheet is needed for each candidate, as the marks of both interlocutor and assessor are entered on the same sheet. Completed mark sheets are kept secure during the 3-hour examining session and then handed to the Centre Exams Manager or supervisor for collation and subsequent secure despatch to Cambridge.

Examiners must not examine candidates known to them in a personal capacity and emergency procedures are in place to deal with an unexpected situation in which the examiner encounters a candidate known to them, examined by them within the previous six weeks or taught by them within the previous three years. In such cases, the candidate is redirected to another examiner.

No unauthorised person is permitted to enter the examination room during the Speaking test, though Team Leaders are authorised to sit in during Speaking tests for monitoring purposes. The policy of sending Team Leaders to monitor examiners conducting Speaking tests at some sessions is designed to contribute to the effective co-ordination of Speaking test procedures and marking standards and thus maintain the integrity of Cambridge ESOL examinations. Speaking tests are sometimes recorded for research and validation or for examiner monitoring purposes when the Team Leader can not attend in person.

Cambridge ESOL has in place a Malpractice Procedure to deal with any infringement of regulations. Malpractice is relatively rare in Speaking tests but examiners are asked to be on the lookout for the misuse of mobile phones and electrical devices, or the use of crib notes. Cases of misconduct or dishonesty may lead to a candidate's result being disqualified. All incidents of irregularity or suspected malpractice in connection with an examination are reported to Cambridge ESOL using the Suspected Malpractice form which can be downloaded from CentreNet, and which must be supplemented with a copy of the room plan and a completed Special Consideration form if another candidate appears to have been disadvantaged in any way.

Arrangements for Speaking test examiners

Chapter 5 has already described in some detail the nature of Cambridge ESOL's Team Leader System which is designed to ensure the professional quality of the Speaking tests. The TL System has two main features: i) a team structure, involving several levels of personnel – Professional Support Leaders (PSLs), Regional Team Leaders (RTLs), Team Leaders (TLs), speaking examiner trainer/co-ordinators (SETCs) and speaking examiners (SEs); ii) a set of quality assurance procedures relating to minimum professional requirements at all levels – Registration, Induction, Training, Certification and Performance Feedback.

Overall responsibility for the administrative management and logistical deployment of speaking examiners varies slightly according to whether a test centre is based in the UK or overseas. Within the UK, Cambridge ESOL manages the quality assurance (QA) procedures for speaking examiners. UK centres book their examiners for an upcoming test administration session using the relevant Speaking Test (ST) forms available via CentreNet. Overseas test centres wishing to offer any of the Cambridge Speaking tests are required to have a sufficient number of speaking examiners available locally who have been trained and certificated in line with Cambridge ESOL's formal QA procedures in advance of the relevant test administration sessions. This means that centres should engage suitably qualified and experienced examiners from a range of appropriate local institutions in addition to their own. They must ensure that the examiners are inducted, trained, and certificated, and that their performance is regularly monitored as laid down by Cambridge ESOL. In countries where the TL System is well-established (currently around 100 countries worldwide) Centre Exams Managers work closely with the in-country TLs and PSL/RTL to ensure they have access to sufficient approved speaking examiners who are trained and certificated for the appropriate Speaking tests. The Centre Exams Manager collaborates with one or more TLs to arrange examiner training and certification, and to provide TLs with detailed timetables of all examiner assignments so that on-site monitoring can be carried out. Once examiner monitoring has taken place, the Centre Exams Manager returns all completed monitoring checklists to Cambridge ESOL for processing and analysis. Cambridge ESOL maintains a database of all Speaking test examiners who examine for the Cambridge ESOL Speaking tests. This central database records details of an examiner's quality assurance history, including performance feedback and recommended follow-up actions. Records from this database are made available to centres so they can verify, update and amend them for the examiners attached to that centre.

In countries where the Team Leader System is not yet in place, perhaps because the country concerned is small or remote, or because candidate numbers are still low there, test centres must nominate a speaking examiner trainer/co-ordinator (SETC) who is able to fulfil the training and certification functions of a Team Leader. The centre must also provide facilities for recording practice or live Speaking tests for the purpose of performance feedback.

Centres are required to deploy examiners to ensure that the Speaking tests are conducted according to the *Handbook for Centres* and *Speaking Test Instructions,* and in the best interests of the candidates.

Security

Test security is a high priority if the scores from a test are to maintain their integrity and be useful to stakeholders. Security is especially important in tests used for high-stakes decision making purposes.

Security measures are intended to restrict access to test content and associated materials to those who need to know it for test development, test delivery, test scoring and test validation purposes. If test security is compromised then there is a risk that some candidates will be able to prepare their answers in advance and thus unfairly enhance their performance, potentially gaining scores that are not a valid and reliable indication of their actual ability.

The *Handbook for Centres* notes that, in the light of increasingly compact and sophisticated technology, it is important to be aware of the potential risks to the security of the examinations. Nowadays there exists a number of technological innovations such as digital sound recorders, MP3 players, scanning pens and mobile phones with cameras that would enable candidates to copy examination materials or make sound recordings and take them out of the examination room with the intention of publicising or circulating them. Supervisors, invigilators and speaking examiners are encouraged to be fully aware of such threats and to be watchful for anything unusual. If they have strong suspicions about any candidate's behaviour, they are required to report it to Cambridge ESOL by using a Suspected Malpractice form (see above).

Speaking test materials

The test centre and its staff, especially the Centre Exams Manager and the speaking examiners, are responsible at all times for ensuring the utmost security of examination materials, whether these materials are stored on centre premises or are in transit between venues. Materials must be transported in sealed packets and must never be left unattended during transfer. Any breach of question paper security (before, during or after an examination) is taken extremely seriously and may lead to a centre's authorisation being terminated.

Confidential test materials, both before and after an examination, must be locked away in a place of high security, ideally a strong safe. If a safe is not available or is of insufficient capacity, then a non-portable, lockable, reinforced steel or metal cabinet or other similar container can be used. The safe or container must be in a securely locked room with access ideally restricted to no more than two or three key holders. The room should preferably be windowless and on an upper floor; all windows, whether internal or external, should be fitted with security devices. In addition, the door to the room should be of solid construction (i.e. not hollow), have secure hinges and be fitted with a secure lock. Following their removal from the storage container, materials must be kept under constant and close supervision until they are ready to be used, during use and afterwards until they are returned to storage and subsequently securely destroyed.

Materials for the Cambridge ESOL Speaking tests are despatched twice a year by secure consignment to all its speaking examiners in the UK and to the Centre Exams Managers at its overseas test centres, along with instructions to destroy any old Speaking test materials. At the local level, centres are responsible for distributing the materials to the appropriate speaking examiner before an examination session and then collecting them afterwards for secure storage until the next session. Speaking examiners must be able to familiarise themselves with the content adequately before the start of the live Speaking test period, while still ensuring that the security of the materials is maintained. If materials are taken off the centre premises, examiners are reminded of their confidential nature and the need to maintain security at all times. Each Speaking test pack carries a unique serial number on the back; this allows a logging and signing in/out system to be established which can record each pack by its serial number, thus enabling Speaking test packs to be tracked more easily and ensuring enhanced security.

Copies of the *Instructions to Speaking Examiners* booklets are also made available to all speaking examiners far enough in advance of a Speaking test session to allow adequate preparation. This booklet is a user's manual so examiners need the opportunity to re-familiarise themselves fully with its contents. Speaking examiners keep their copy of this booklet for the duration of a Speaking test session and take it with them on all examining assignments.

If the security of the question papers or confidential ancillary materials is put at risk by fire, theft, loss, damage, unauthorised disclosure, or any other circumstances, Cambridge ESOL must be informed immediately.

Best practice principles and legal matters

As a responsible test provider, Cambridge ESOL is explicitly committed to operating according to ethical testing principles. As well as putting in place the standardised administrative procedures which have been described above, this commitment means adopting policies and practices which take account of data protection, individual privacy and protection, and equal opportunities that are consistent with the latest laws and regulations (e.g. UK Data Protection Act, UK Disability Discrimination Act, UK Child Protection and Safeguarding legislation, international legislation relating to copyright and intellectual property). As key partners in the delivery of Cambridge ESOL examinations, test centres worldwide are expected to adopt similar principles where possible, and to comply with all local laws and regulations.

Within the UK, for example, all speaking examiners for the YLE tests (where only one examiner and one candidate are present) are required to undergo a Criminal Records Bureau (CRB) check in accordance with the UK government's current Vetting and Barring scheme operated nationally by the Independent Safeguarding Authority (ISA) (<http://www.direct.gov.uk/en/campaigns/Vetting/DG_183221>). Speaking examiners for the other Cambridge Speaking tests are not currently required to undergo CRB checks or be ISA-registered since their contact with minors is limited, as defined by the national vetting scheme, and because the examinations are in paired format, i.e. there are two candidates and two examiners present. Overseas test centres are expected to adopt similar principles and to comply with all local laws and regulations relating to child protection and safeguarding matters. The issue of child protection is emphasised to all Cambridge ESOL Speaking examiners and a set of *Guidelines for Adults conducting Speaking Tests with Minors* is included in training materials. This highlights appropriate behaviour for conducting assessments.

Appendix E

ESOL Staff Induction Worksheet on the CEFR

Topic: The Common European Framework of Reference (CEFR)

Time req'd: 45-50 mins approx (accessing, reading, answering inc.)

Materials (all needed):
1. Council of Europe's (CoE) website on the CEFR
2. CEFR, 2001, Council of Europe
3. CoE's Publications List website
4. Materials illustrating the CEFR levels

Where to find materials:
1. http://www.coe.int/t/dg4/linguistic/CADRE_EN.asp
2. http://www.coe.int/t/dg4/linguistic/Source/Framework_EN.pdf
   or the CEFR hard copy ('blue book') in the ESOL library:
   Council of Europe (2001) *Common European Framework of Reference for Languages: Learning, teaching, assessment*, Cambridge: Cambridge University Press
3. http://www.coe.int/t/DG4/linguistic/Publications_EN.asp
4. http://www.coe.int/T/DG4/Portfolio/?L=E&M=/main_pages/illustrationse.html

Aims: - To understand the aims, uses and nature of the CEFR;
- To learn about the CEFR 'toolkit'.

Induction worksheet
CODE: R&V/009/1/11.03.08

The Common European Framework of Reference

Name ....

Unit ....

Location ....

CEFR: Its aims, uses and nature

Please consult the CoE's website on the CEFR [No 1 in the Materials list above] and answer the following questions.

1. In your own words what is the CEFR and what are its main aims?
   ....
   ....

2. To whom and why may the CEFR be of interest?
   ....
   ....

3. How many language versions of the CEFR currently exist?
   ....

Now please read pp. 1-2, 5-8 of the CEFR [2 in the Materials list], and answer the following questions.

4. Name two practical uses of the CEFR.
   ....
   ....

5. Why is the CEFR of interest for an assessment board such as Cambridge ESOL?
   ....
   ....

Please browse through the contents of the CEFR, and answer the following questions.

6. Which chapter of the CEFR discusses assessment issues? What are the main themes/topics in the chapter?
   ....
   ....

7. Two common misconceptions about the CEFR are that it provides a general guide on how to construct good language tests and prescribes a specific approach to test construction. Why do you think these two statements are not true?
   ....
   ....
   ....

UNIVERSITY *of* CAMBRIDGE
ESOL Examinations
English for Speakers of Other Languages

The CEFR 'toolkit'

The CEFR is accompanied by a number of supporting publications and documents.
1. Consult the CoE's Publications List website [3 in the Materials list] and match the following publications with their purpose.

	Publications		Purpose
1.	*Relating Examinations to the Common European Framework of Reference for Languages: A Manual*, January 2009	A.	detailed accounts of the use of the CEFR across Europe for language learning, teaching and assessment purposes
2.	*Illustrations of levels of language proficiency*	B.	a record of the language and cultural skills and experiences of language learners measured against the CEFR levels
3.	*Case studies concerning the use of the Common European Framework of Reference for Languages: Learning, Teaching, Assessment*, 2002	C.	guidelines for examination providers to situate their tests to the CEFR scale in a principled and transparent way
4.	*European Language Portfolio* (ELP)	D.	sample performances exemplifying the CEFR levels

2. Which of these 4 publications has the most relevance for your current job? Why?

3. What are the five stages suggested by the *Manual for Relating Examinations to the CEFR* (2009) for aligning language examinations to the CEFR levels? Consult Chapter 2 (pp. 7-9 & 10-11) of the Manual (or pp. 19-21 & 22-23 in the Adobe Reader Page numbering if you are viewing a pdf version of it). (You can access the Manual from the CoE's website on the CEFR [1 in the Materials list].)

4. Which of the above stages are you engaging in by filling in this induction worksheet?

5. What types of sample performances and materials has Cambridge ESOL published for illustrating the CEFR levels? Look at the 'Illustrations of levels of language proficiency' web page [4 in the Materials list].

Please contact Research & Validation if you have any questions about this worksheet.

References

Abedi, J (2008) Utilizing accommodations in assessment, in Shohamy, E and Hornberger, N (Eds), *Encyclopedia of Language and Education (2nd edition) – Language Testing and Assessment, Volume 7*, New York: Springer Science+Business Media LLC, 331–347.

Abedi, J, Hofstetter, C and Lord, C (2004) Assessment accommodations for English Language Learners: implications for policy-based empirical research, *Review of Educational Research* 74 (1), 1–28.

Adolphs, S and Schmitt, N (2003) Lexical coverage of spoken discourse, *Applied Linguistics* 24 (4), 425–438.

AERA/APA/NCME (1999) *Standards for Educational and Psychological Testing*, Washington, DC: American Educational and Research Association/American Psychological Association/National Council for Measurement in Education.

Aitchison, J (2003) *Words in the Mind,* Oxford: Blackwell, 3rd edn.

Aitchison, J (2008) *The Articulate Mammal,* Abingdon: Routledge, 5th edn.

Alderman, D L and Holland, P W (1981) *Item Performance across Native Language Groups on the Test of English as a Foreign Language,* TOEFL Research Report No. 9, Princeton, NJ: Educational Testing Service.

Alderson, J C (1981) Report of the discussion on Communicative Language Testing, in Alderson, J C and Hughes, A (Eds) *Issues in Language Testing*, *ELT Documents 111*, London: British Council, 55–65.

Alderson, J C (1991) Bands and scores, in Alderson, J C and North, B J (Eds) *Language Testing in the 1990s: The communicative legacy*, London: Modern English Publications and The British Council, 71–86.

Alderson, J C (1995) *Ideas for research into impact, washback and IELTS*, internal paper commissioned by the University of Cambridge Local Examinations Syndicate (UCLES).

Alderson, J C (2000) *Assessing Reading,* Cambridge: Cambridge University Press.

Alderson, J C (2004) Foreword, in Cheng, L, Watanabe, Y and Curtis, A (Eds) *Washback in Language Testing: Research contexts and methods*, London: Lawrence Erlbaum Associates, ix–xii.

Alderson, J and Banerjee, J (1996) *How might impact study instruments be validated?* internal paper commissioned by the University of Cambridge Local Examinations Syndicate (UCLES).

Alderson, J C and Wall, D (1993) Does washback exist? *Applied Linguistics* 14, 115–129.

Alderson, J C and Wall, D (1996) Editorial, *Language Testing* 13 (3), 239–240.

Alderson, J C, Clapham, C and Wall, D (1995) *Language Test Construction and Evaluation*, Cambridge: Cambridge University Press.

American Council for the Teaching of Foreign Languages (ACTFL) (1999) *The ACTFL Proficiency Guidelines: Speaking (revised 1999)*, Yonkers, NY: ACTFL.

Anastasi, A (1988) *Psychological Testing* (6th edition), New York: Macmillan.

Anderson, J R (1983) *The Architecture of Cognition,* Cambridge, MA: Harvard University Press.

Angoff, W H and Sharon, A T (1974) The evaluation of differences in test performances of two or more groups, *Educational & Psychological Measurement* 34, 807–816.

Ashton, K (2006) Can Do self-assessment: investigating cross-language comparability in reading, *Research Notes* 24, Cambridge ESOL, 10–14.

Ashton, M and Khalifa, H (2005) Opening a new door for teachers of English: Cambridge ESOL Teaching Knowledge Test, *Research Notes* 19, Cambridge ESOL, 5–7.

Association of Language Testers in Europe (ALTE) (1994) *Code of Practice*, retrieved 10 March, 2011, from: http://www.alte.org/cop/index.php

Association of Language Testers in Europe (ALTE) (1998) *Multilingual Glossary of Language Testing Terms,* Studies in Language Testing 6, Cambridge: UCLES/Cambridge University Press

Association of Language Testers in Europe (ALTE) Speaking Content Analysis, retrieved 10 March, 2011, from: http://www.alte.org/downloads/index.php

Bachman, L F (1990) *Fundamental Considerations in Language Testing*, Oxford: Oxford University Press.

Bachman, L F (2000) Modern language testing at the turn of the century: assuring that what we count counts, *Language Testing* 17 (1), 1–42.

Bachman, L F (2002) Some reflections on task-based language performance assessment, *Language Testing* 19, 453–476.

Bachman, L F (2004a) *Building and supporting a case for test utilization*, paper presented at LTRC, Temecula, California, March 2004.

Bachman, L F (2004b) *Statistical Analyses for Language Assessment*, Cambridge: Cambridge University Press.

Bachman, L F (2005) Building and supporting a case for test use, *Language Assessment Quarterly* 2 (1), 1–34.

Bachman, L F and Palmer, A S (1996) *Language Testing in Practice,* Oxford: Oxford University Press.

Bachman, L F and Palmer, A S (2010) *Language Assessment in Practice,* Oxford: Oxford University Press.

Bachman, L F, Davidson, F, Ryan, K and Choi, I C (1995) *An Investigation into the Comparability of Two Tests of English as a Foreign Language,* Studies in Language Testing 1, Cambridge: UCLES/Cambridge University Press.

Bae, J and Bachman L F (2010) An investigation of four writing traits and two writing tasks, *Language Testing* 27, 213–234.

Bae, J and Lee, Y S (in press) The validation of parallel test forms: 'mountain' and 'beach' picture series for assessment of language skills, *Language Testing* 28(2), 1–23.

Bailey, K (1996) Working for washback: a review of the washback concept in language testing, *Language Testing* 13 (3), 257–279.

Ball, F (2002a) Developing wordlists for BEC, *Research Notes* 8, Cambridge ESOL, 10–13.

Ball, F (2002b) Investigating the YLE story-telling task, *Research Notes* 10, Cambridge ESOL, 16–18.

Ball, F and Wilson, J (2002) Research projects relating to YLE speaking tests, *Research Notes* 7, Cambridge ESOL, 8–10.

Banerjee, J (1996) *The design of the classroom observation instrument*, internal report for University of Cambridge Local Examinations Syndicate (UCLES).

Banks, C (1999) *An investigation into age bias in PET*, internal Research and Validation Report 22, Cambridge ESOL.

Barker, F (2010) How can corpora be used in language testing? in O'Keeffe, A and McCarthy, M (Eds) *The Routledge Handbook of Corpus Linguistics,* Routledge, 633–645.

Barnet, M A (1989) *More Than Meets the Eye,* Englewood Cliffs, NJ: Prentice Hall Regents.

Barritt, L, Stock, P and Clarke, F (1986) Researching practice: evaluating assessment essays, *College Composition and Communication* 37, 315–327.

Beattie, G (1983) *Talk: An Analysis of Speech and Non-verbal Behaviour in Communication,* Milton Keynes: Open University Press.

Beebe, L M (1980) Sociolinguistic variation in style shifting in second language acquisition, *Language Learning* 30, 433–447.

Bell, C (2009a) FCE Speaking Report 2008, internal Validation Report 1177, Cambridge ESOL.

Bell, C (2009b) CAE Speaking Report, internal Validation Report 1178, Cambridge ESOL.

Bell, C (2009c) CPE Speaking Report, internal Validation Report 1179, Cambridge ESOL.

Bell, C (2009d) PET Speaking Report, internal Validation Report 1180, Cambridge ESOL.

Bell, C (2009e) KET Speaking Report, internal Validation Report 1181, Cambridge ESOL.

Bereiter, C and Scardamalia, M (1987) *The Psychology of Written Composition,* Hillside NJ: Lawrence Erlbaum Associates.

Berry, V (2004) *A Study of the Interaction between Individual Personality Differences and Oral Performance Test Facets,* unpublished PhD Thesis, King's College, The University of London.

Blanchard, J D and Reedy, R (1970) *The Relationship of a Test of English as a Second Language to Measures of Achievement and Self-concept in a Sample of American Indian Students,* Research and Evaluation Report Series No. 58, Bureau of Indian Affairs, US Department of Interior.

Bock, K and Griffin, Z M (2000) Producing words: How mind meets mouth, in Wheeldon, L R (Ed) *Aspects of Language Production,* Hove: Psychology Press, 7–47.

Bonkowski, F (1996) *Instrument for the assessment of teaching materials,* unpublished manuscript, Lancaster University.

Booth, D (2002) Revising the Business English Certificate (BEC) speaking tests, *Research Notes* 8, Cambridge ESOL, 4–7.

Breton, G, LePage, S and North, B (2008) *Cross-language benchmarking seminar to calibrate examples of spoken production in English, French, German, Italian and Spanish with regard to the six levels of the Common European Framework of Reference for Languages (CEFR),* retrievable from http://www.coe.int/T/DG4/Portfolio/?L=E&M=/main_pages/illustrationse.html

Brindley, G (1998) Describing language development? Rating scales and SLA, in Bachman, L F and Cohen, A D (Eds) *Interfaces between Second Language Acquisition and Language Testing Research,* Cambridge: Cambridge University Press, 112–140.

Brooks, L (2003) Converting an observation checklist for use with the IELTS speaking test, *Research Notes* 11, Cambridge ESOL, 20–21.

Brooks, L (2009) Interacting in pairs in a test of oral proficiency: Co-constructing a better performance, *Language Testing* 26 (3), 341–366.

Brown, A (1995) The effect of rater variables in the development of an occupation-specific language performance test, *Language Testing* 12, 1–15.

Brown, A (2000) An investigation of raters' orientation in awarding scores in the IELTS interview, in Tulloh, R (Ed.) *IELTS Research Reports, Volume 3*, Canberra: IDP: IELTS Australia, 30–49.

Brown, A (2003) Interviewer variation and the co-construction of speaking proficiency, *Language Testing* 20 (1), 1–25.

Brown, A (2006) An examination of the rating process in the revised IELTS speaking test, in McGovern, P and Walsh, S (Eds) *IELTS Research Reports, Volume 6*, IELTS Australia and British Council, 41–70.

Brown, A and Hill, K (1998) Interviewer style and candidate performance in the IELTS oral interview, in Woods, S (Ed.) *IELTS Research Reports, Volume 1*, Sydney, 1–19.

Brown, A and Hill, K (1998/2007) Interviewer style and candidate performance in the IELTS oral interview, in Taylor, L and Falvey, P (Eds) *IELTS Collected Papers: Research in speaking and writing assessment*, Studies in Language Testing 19, Cambridge: UCLES/Cambridge University Press, 37–61.

Brown, A and Lumley, T (1997) Interviewer variability in specific-purpose language performance tests, in Huhta, A, Kohonen, V, Kurki-Suonio, L and Luoma, S (Eds) *Current Developments and Alternatives in Language Assessment*, Jyväskyla: Centre for Applied Language Studies, University of Jyväskyla, 137–150.

Brown, A and McNamara, T (2004) The devil is in the detail: Researching gender issues in language assessment, *TESOL Quarterly* 38 (3), 524–538.

Brown, A and Taylor, L (2006) A worldwide survey of examiners' views and experience of the revised IELTS Speaking test, *Research Notes* 26, Cambridge ESOL 14–18.

Brown, G and Yule, G (1983) *Discourse Analysis,* Cambridge: Cambridge University Press.

Brown, G, Anderson, A, Shillcock, R and Yule, G (1984) *Teaching Talk: Strategies for Production and Assessment*, Cambridge: Cambridge University Press.

Brown, J D (1996) *Testing in Language Programs*, Upper Saddle River, NJ: Prentice Hall Regents.

Buck, G (1988) Testing listening comprehension in Japanese university entrance examinations, *JALT Journal* 10 (1), 15–42.

Bybee, J (2000) *Phonology and Language Use*, Cambridge: Cambridge University Press.

Bybee, J and Hopper, P (2001) *Frequency and the Emergence of Linguistic Structure,* Amsterdam: John Benjamins.

Bygate, M (1987) *Speaking*, Oxford: Oxford University Press.

Bygate, M (1999) Quality of language and purpose of task: Patterns of learners' language on two oral communication tasks, *Language Teaching Research* 3 (3), 185–214.

Bygate, M (2001) Effects of task repetition on the structure and control of oral language, in Bygate, M, Skehan, P, and Swain, M (Eds) *Researching Pedagogic Tasks: Second Language Learning, Teaching and Assessment,* Harlow: Longman, 23–48.

Bygate, M, Skehan, P and Swain, M (Eds) (2001) *Researching Pedagogic Tasks: Second Language Learning, Teaching and Assessment,* London: Pearson.

Canagarajah, S (2006) Changing communicative needs, revised assessment objectives: testing English as an international language, *Language Assessment Quarterly* 3, 229–242.

Capel, A (2010) A1–B2 vocabulary: insights and issues arising from the English profile wordlists project, *English Profile Journal* 1 (1), retrieved from <http://journals.cambridge.org/action/display.journal?jid=EPS>.

Carey, M and Mannell, R (2009) The contribution of interlanguage phonology accommodation to inter-examiner variation in the rating of pronunciation in oral proficiency interviews, in Thompson, P (Ed.) *IELTS Research Reports, Volume 9*, British Council and IELTS Australia, 217–236.

Carroll, B J (1980) *Testing Communicative Performance*, Oxford: Pergamon.

Carroll, J B (1968) The psychology of language testing, in Davies, A (Ed.) *Language Testing Symposium: A psycholinguistic approach,* Oxford: Oxford University Press, 46–69.

Chalhoub-Deville, M (2001) Task-based assessments: characteristics and validity evidence, in Bygate, M, Skehan, P and Swain, M (Eds) *Researching pedagogical tasks*, London: Longman, 210–228.

Chalhoub-Deville, M (2009) Standards-based assessment in the US: social and educational impact, in Taylor, L and Weir, C (Eds) *Language Testing Matters: Investigating the wider social and educational impact of assessment – Proceedings of the ALTE Cambridge Conference, April 2008,* Studies in Language Testing 31, Cambridge: UCLES/Cambridge University Press, 281–300.

Chambers, L (2010) *Reviewing the performance of the revised assessment scales for BEC speaking*, internal report for University of Cambridge ESOL Examinations.

Chapelle, C A, Enright, M K and Jamieson, J (2004) *Issues in Developing a TOEFL Validity Argument*, draft paper presented at LTRC, Temecula, California, March 2004.

Chapelle, C A, Enwright, M K and Jamieson, J (2008) *Building a Validity Argument for the Test of English as a Foreign Language*, New York: Routledge.

Charney, D (1984) The validity of using holistic scoring to evaluate writing, *Research in the teaching of English* 18, 65–81.

Cheng, L (2005) *Changing Language Teaching through Language Testing: A washback study*, Studies in Language Testing 21, Cambridge: UCLES/Cambridge University Press.

Cheng, L and Curtis, A (2004) Washback or backwash: a review of the impact of testing on teaching and learning, in Cheng, L, Watanabe, Y and Curtis, A (Eds) (2004) *Washback in Language Testing: Research contexts and methods*: London: Lawrence Erlbaum Associates, 3–17.

Cheng, L, Watanabe, Y and Curtis, A (Eds) (2004) *Washback in Language Testing: Research contexts and methods,* London: Lawrence Erlbaum.

Chun, C (2006) An analysis of a language test for employment: the authenticity of the PhonePass test, *Language Assessment Quarterly* 3 (3) 295–306.

Clapham, C (1996) *The Development of IELTS: A study in the effect of background knowledge on reading comprehension*, Studies in Language Testing 4, Cambridge: Cambridge University Press.

Coates, J (1993) *Women, Men and Language*, London: Longman.

Cohen, A (1994) *Assessing Language Ability in the Classroom*, 2nd Edition, Boston, MA: Heinle and Heinle.

Congdon, P J and McQueen, J (2000) The stability of rater severity in large-scale assessment programs, *Journal of Educational Measurement* 37 (2), 163–178.

Corkhill, D and Robinson, M (2006) Using the global legal community in the development of ILEC, *Research Notes* 25, Cambridge ESOL, 10–11.

Council of Europe (2001) *Common European Framework of Reference for Languages*: *Learning, teaching, assessment*, Cambridge: Cambridge University Press.

Council of Europe (2003a) *Relating Language Examinations to the Common European Framework of Reference for Languages: Learning, Teaching, Assessment (CEF), Manual: Preliminary Pilot Version*, DGIV/EDU/LANG 2003, 5, Strasbourg: Language Policy Division.

Council of Europe (2003b) *Samples of Oral Production Illustrating, for English, the Levels of the Common European Framework of Reference for Languages*, University of Cambridge ESOL Examinations DVD.

Council of Europe (2003c) *Samples of Oral Production Illustrating, for English, the Levels of the Common European Framework of Reference for Languages*, Eurocentres CD-ROM.

Council of Europe (2004) *Reference Supplement to the preliminary pilot version of the manual for Relating Language Examinations to the Common European Framework of Reference for Languages: Learning, teaching, assessment*, Strasbourg: Language Policy Division.

Council of Europe (2005) *Relating Language Examinations to the Common European Framework of Reference for Languages: Learning, teaching, assessment (CEFR). Reading and Listening Items and Tasks: Pilot Samples Illustrating the Common Reference Levels in English, French, German, Italian and Spanish*, CD-ROM.

Council of Europe (2009) *Relating Language Examinations to the Common European Framework of Reference for Languages: Learning, Teaching, Assessment (CEFR). A Manual*, retrieved from: http://www.coe.int/t/dg4/linguistic/Manuel1_EN.asp#TopOfPage

Coxhead, A (2000) A new academic wordlist, *TESOL Quarterly* 34 (2), 213–238.

Crookes, G (1989) Planning and interlanguage variability, *Studies in Second Language Acquisition* 11, 367–83.

Cruttenden, A (1986) *Intonation,* Cambridge: Cambridge University Press.

Dąbrowska, E (2005) *Language, Mind and Brain*, Edinburgh: Edinburgh Press.

Davies, A (2001) The logic of testing languages for specific purposes, *Language Testing* 18 (2), 133–147.

Davies, A (2005) 40 years in Applied Linguistics: an interview with Alan Davies, by Antony Kunnan, *Language Assessment Quarterly* 2 (1), 35–50.

Davies, A (2008) *Assessing Academic English: Testing English Proficiency 1950–1989 – the IELTS solution*, Studies in Language Testing 23, Cambridge: UCLES/Cambridge University Press.

Davies, A, Brown, A, Elder, C, Hill, K, Lumley, T and McNamara, T (1999) *Dictionary of Language Testing*, Studies in Language Testing 7, Cambridge: UCLES/Cambridge University Press.

Davies, A, Hamp-Lyons, L and Kemp, C (2003) Whose norms? International proficiency tests in English, *World Englishes* 22 (4), 571–584.

DeKeyser, R M (2001) Automaticity and automatization, in Robinson, P (Ed.) *Cognition and Second Language Instruction*, Cambridge: Cambridge University Press, 125–151.

DeVelle, S (2008) The revised IELTS pronunciation scale, *Research Notes* 34, Cambridge ESOL, 36–38.

DeVelle, S (2009) Certificating IELTS writing and speaking examiners, *Research Notes* 38, Cambridge ESOL, 26–29.

Douglas, D (2000) *Assessing Languages for Specific Purposes*, Cambridge: Cambridge University Press.

Dudley-Evans, T (1988) A consideration of the meaning of the word 'discuss' in examination questions, in Robinson, P (Ed.) *Academic Writing: Process and Product*, Oxford: Modern English Publications.

Eckes, T (2005) Examining rater effects in Testdaf writing and speaking performance assessments: A many-facet Rasch analysis, *Language Assessment Quarterly* 2 (3), 197–221.

Edgeworth, F Y (1890) The Element of Chance in Competitive Examinations, *Journal of the Royal Statistical Society* 53 (4), 644–663.

Elder, C (2001) Assessing the language proficiency of teachers: are there any border controls? *Language Testing* 18 (2), 149–170.

Elder, C and Davies, A (2006) Assessing English as a lingua franca, in McGroarty, M (Ed) *Annual Review of Applied Linguistics – An official journal of the American Association of Applied Linguistics*, Cambridge: Cambridge University Press, 282–301.

Elder, C and Wigglesworth, G (2006) An investigation of the effectiveness and validity of planning time in Part 2 of the IELTS Speaking Test, in McGovern, P and Walsh, S (Eds) *IELTS Research Reports, Volume 6*, IELTS Australia and British Council, 13–40.

Elder, C, Knoch, U, Barkhuizen, G and von Randow, J (2005) Individual feedback to enhance rater training: Does it work? *Language Assessment Quarterly* 2 (3), 175–196.

Ellis, N C (2003) Constructions, chunking and connectionism, in Doughty, C and Long, M (Eds) *The Handbook of Second Language Acquisition*, Oxford: Blackwell, 63–103.

Ellis, R (2003) *Task-based Language Learning and Teaching,* Oxford: Oxford University Press.

ETS (2001) *TSE and SPEAK score user guide, 2001–2002 edition*, Princeton, NJ: Educational Testing Service.

European Association for Language Testing and Assessment (EALTA) (2006) *Guidelines for Good Practice in Language Testing and Assessment,* retrieved March 10, 2011, from: http://www.ealta.eu.org/guidelines.htm

Fairclough, N (2000) *New Labour: New Language,* London: Routledge.

Feltovich, P J, Prietula, M J and Ericsson, K A, (2006) Studies of expertise from psychological perpectives, in Ericsson, K A, Charness, N, Feltovich, P J and Hoffman, R (Eds) *The Cambridge Handbook of Expertise and Expert Performance*, Cambridge: Cambridge University Press.

ffrench, A (2003a) The change process at the paper level, Paper 5 Speaking, in Weir, C and Milanovic, M (Eds) *Continuity and Innovation: Revising the Cambridge Proficiency in English Examination 1913–2002,* Studies in Language Testing 15, Cambridge: Cambridge University Press, 367–471.

ffrench, A (2003b) The development of a set of assessment criteria for Speaking Tests, *Research Notes* 13, Cambridge ESOL, 1–9.

ffrench, A and Gutch, A (2006) *FCE/CAE Modifications: building the validity argument: application of Weir's socio-cognitive framework to FCE and CAE*, internal report for Cambridge ESOL.

Field, J (2004) *Psycholinguistics: the Key Concepts,* London: Routledge.

Field, J (2008) *Listening in the Language Classroom*, Cambridge: Cambridge University Press.

Fillmore, L W (1979) Individual differences in second language acquisition, in Fillmore, C, Kempler, D and Wang, W Y S (Eds) *Individual Differences in Language Ability and Language Behavior*, New York: Academic Press.

Fishman, P M (1978a) Interaction: The work women do, *Social Problems* 24, 397–406.

Fishman, P M (1978b) What do couples talk about when they're alone? in Butturf, D and Epstein E L (Eds). *Women's Language and Style*, Dept. of English, University of Akron, 11–22.

Foster, P and Skehan, P (1996) The influence of planning on performance in task based learning, *Studies in Second Language Acquisition* 18, 299–324.

Foster, P and Skehan, P (1999) The influence of source of planning and focus of planning on task-based performance, *Language Teaching Research* 3 (3), 215–247.

Fox, J (2004) Biasing for the best in language testing and learning: An interview with Merrill Swain, *Language Assessment Quarterly* 1 (4), 235–251.

Frederiksen, J and Collins, A (1989) A systems approach to educational testing, *Educational Researcher* 18 (9), 27–32.

Fromkin, V A (Ed.) (1973) *Speech Errors as Linguistic Evidence*, The Hague: Mouton.

Fromkin, V A (1988) The grammatical aspects of speech errors, in Newmeyer, F J (Ed) *Linguistics: the Cambridge Survey II,* Cambridge: Cambridge University Press, 117–138.

Fulcher, G (1993) *The Construction and Validation of Rating Scales for Oral Tests in English as a Foreign Language*, unpublished PhD thesis, University of Lancaster, UK.

Fulcher, G (1996) Does thick description lead to smart tests? A rating-scale approach to language test construction, *Language Testing* 13 (2), 208–38.

Fulcher, G (2003) *Testing Second Language Speaking*, Harlow: Longman/ Pearson Education Ltd.

Fulcher, G (2004) Deluded by artifices? The Common European Framework and harmonization, *Language Assessment Quarterly* 1 (4), 253–266.

Fulcher, G and Davidson, F (2007) *Language Testing and Assessment,* London and New York: Routledge.

Fulcher, G and Davidson, F (2009) Test architecture, test retrofit, *Language Testing* 26 (1) 123–144.

Fulcher, G and Reiter, R M (2003) Task difficulty in speaking tests, *Language Testing* 20 (3), 321–344.

Furneaux, C and Rignall, M (2000/2007) The effect of standardisation training of rater judgements for the IELTS Writing Module, in Taylor, L and Falvey, P (Eds) *IELTS Collected Papers: Research in Speaking and Writing Assessment*, Studies in Language Testing 19, Cambridge: UCLES/Cambridge University Press, 422–444.

Galaczi, E D (2003) Interaction in a paired speaking test: the case of the First Certificate in English, *Research Notes* 14, Cambridge ESOL, 19–23.

Galaczi, E D (2005) Upper Main Suite speaking assessment: towards an understanding of assessment criteria and oral examiner behaviour, *Research Notes* 20, Cambridge ESOL, 16–19.

Galaczi, E D (2007a) *Main Suite and BEC assessment scales revision*, internal Validation Report 1083 for Cambridge ESOL.

Galaczi, E D (2007b) *Main Suite and BEC 2008 standardisation videos: multi-facet Rasch analysis*, internal report for Cambridge ESOL.

Galaczi, E D (2008) Peer-peer interaction in a speaking test: the case of the First Certificate in English examination, *Language Assessment Quarterly* 5 (2), 89–119.

Galaczi, E D (2009) *Analysis of PSN standardisation for Main Suite and BEC oral examiners (Oct/Nov 2008)*, internal report for Cambridge ESOL.

Galaczi, E D (2010a) *Reviewing the performance of the revised assessment scales for Main Suite speaking*, internal report for Cambridge ESOL.

Galaczi, E D (2010b) Face-to-face and computer-based assessment of speaking: challenges and opportunities, in Araújo, L (Ed.) *Proceedings of the Computer-based Assessment (CBA) of Foreign Language Speaking Skills*, Brussels, Belgium, European Union, 29–51.

Galaczi, E D and ffrench, A (2007) Developing revised assessment scales for Main Suite and BEC Speaking tests, *Research Notes* 30, Cambridge ESOL, 28–31.

Galaczi, E D and Khalifa, H (2009a) Cambridge ESOL's CEFR DVD of speaking performances: what's the story? *Research Notes* 37, Cambridge ESOL, 23–9.

Galaczi, E D and Khalifa, H (2009b) Project overview: Examples of speaking performances at CEFR levels A2 to C2, retrievable from http://www.cambridgeesol.org/what-we-do/research/speaking-performances.html

Galaczi, E D, ffrench, A, Hubbard, C and Green, A (in press) Developing assessment scales for large-scale speaking tests: a multiple-method approach, *Assessment in Education* 18 (3).

Garrett, M F (1980) The limits of accommodation: arguments for independent sentence processing levels in sentence production, in Fromkin, V A (Ed) *Errors in Linguistic Performance: Slips of the Tongue, Ear, Pen and Hand,* New York: Academic Press, 114–128.

Garrett, M F (1988) Processes in language production, in Newmeyer, F J (Ed.) *Linguistics: the Cambridge Survey III: Psychological and Biological Aspects,* Cambridge: Cambridge University Press, 69–96.

Gates, S (1995) Exploiting washback from standardized tests, in Brown, J and Yamashita, S (Eds) *Language Testing in Japan,* Tokyo: Japan Association for Language Teaching, 101–106.

Geranpayeh, A (2001) *Country bias in FCE listening comprehension*, internal Research and Validation Report for Cambridge ESOL.

Geranpayeh, A and Kunnan, A J (2007) Differential item functioning in terms of age in the Certificate in Advanced English Examination, *Language Assessment Quarterly* 4 (2), 190–222.

Graddol, D (2004) The Future of Language, *Science* 27, 1329, DOI: 10.1126/science1096546.

Graddol, D (2006) *English Next: Why Global English May Mean the End of English as a Foreign Language*, The British Council.

Green, A (1998) *Verbal Protocol Analysis in Language Testing Research: A Handbook*, Studies in Language Testing 5, Cambridge: UCLES/Cambridge University Press.

Green, A (2006a) *Main Suite speaking test modifications questionnaire to oral examiners*, internal report for Cambridge ESOL.

Green, A (2006b) *Marks collection via test parts for main suite speaking tests*, internal report for Cambridge ESOL.

Green, A (2007) *IELTS Washback in Context: Preparation for Academic Writing in Higher Education*, Studies in Language Testing 25, Cambridge: UCLES/Cambridge University Press.

Green, A (2011) *Language Functions Revisited: Theoretical and Empirical Bases for Language Construct Definition across the Ability Range,* Cambridge: UCLES/Cambridge University Press.

Green, A and Hawkey, R (2004) Test washback and impact: what do they mean and why do they matter? *Modern English Teacher* 13, 66–72.

Hale, G A (1988) *The Interaction of Student Major-field Group and Text Content in TOEFL Reading Comprehension*, TOEFL Research Report No. 25, Princeton, NJ: Educational Testing Service.

Hambleton, R and Rodgers, J (1995) Item bias review, *Practical Assessment, Research & Evaluation*, 4 (6).

Hamilton, J, Reddel, S and Spratt, M (2001) Teachers' perceptions of on-line rater training and monitoring, *System* 29, 505–520.

Hamp-Lyons, L (1987) Review of the First Certificate in English exam, in Alderson, C, Krahnke, C and Stansfield, C (Eds) *Review of English Language Proficiency Tests*, Washington DC: TESOL, 18–19.

Hamp-Lyons, L (Ed.) (1991) *Assessing Second Language Writing*, Norwood, NJ: Ablex.

Hamp-Lyons, L (1998) Ethical test preparation practice: the case of the TOEFL, *TESOL Quarterly* 32 (2), 329–337.

Hamp-Lyons, L (2000) Social, professional and individual responsibility testing, *System* 28, 579–591.

Hardcastle, P, Bolton, S and Pelliccia, F (2008) Test comparability and construct compatibility across languages, in Taylor, L and Weir C J (Eds) *Multilingualism and Assessment – Achieving tranparency, assuring quality, sustaining diversity – proceedings of the ALTE Berlin Conference May 2005*, Studies in Language Testing 27, Cambridge: UCLES/Cambridge University Press, 130–146.

Harrison, C (2007a) Teaching Knowledge Test update – adoptions and Courses, *Research Notes* 29, Cambridge ESOL, 30–32.

Harrison, C (2007b) Revising the FCE and CAE Speaking tests, *Research Notes* 30, Cambridge ESOL, 24–28.

Hasselgreen, A (1997) Oral test subskill scores: what they tell us about raters and pupils, in Huhta, A, Kohonen, V, Kurki-Suonio, L and Luoma, S (Eds) *Current Developments and Alternatives in Language Assessment*, Universities of Tampere and Jyväskylä, Tampere, 241–256.

Hasselgreen, A (2005) *Testing the Spoken English of Young Norwegians: A Study of Test Validity and the Role of 'Smallwords' in Contributing to Pupils' Fluency*, Studies in Language Testing 20, New York: UCLES/Cambridge University Press.

Hawkey, R (2002) *The Cambridge ESOL Progetto Lingue 2000 Impact Study*, full report to The Ministry of Education, Italy and Cambridge ESOL.

Hawkey, R (2004a) *A Modular Approach to Testing English Language Skills: The Development of the Certificates in English Language Skills (CELS) Examinations*, Studies in Language Testing 16, Cambridge: UCLES/Cambridge University Press.

Hawkey, R (2004b) *CPE Textbook: Washback Study*, internal report for Cambridge ESOL.

Hawkey, R (2004c) The CPE textbook washback study, *Research Notes* 20, Cambridge ESOL, 19–20.

Hawkey, R (2006) *Impact Theory and Practice: Studies of the IELTS Test and Progetto Lingue 2000*, Studies in Language Testing 24, Cambridge: UCLES/Cambridge University Press.

Hawkey, R (2009) *Examining FCE and CAE: Key Issues and Recurring Themes in Developing the First Certificate in English and Certificate in Advanced*

English Examinations, Studies in Language Testing 28, Cambridge: UCLES/ Cambridge University Press.

Hawkins, J A and Buttery, P (2009) *Criterial features in learner corpora: theory and illustrations*, paper presented at the English Profile Seminar, Cambridge, 5–6 February 2009.

Hawkins, J and Filipovič, L (2011) *Criterial Features in L2 English: Specifying the Reference Levels of the Common European Framework*, Cambridge: UCLES/ Cambridge University Press.

Hazenberg, S and Hulstijn, J H (1996) Defining a minimal receptive second language vocabulary for non-native university students: an empirical investigation, *Applied Linguistics* 17 (2) 145–163.

Herington, R (1996) *Test-takers' background questionnaire design characteristics*, report for UCLES.

Hindmarsh, R (1980) *Cambridge English Lexicon,* Cambridge: Cambridge University Press.

Horak, T (1996) *IELTS Impact Study Project*, unpublished MA assignment, Lancaster University.

Horowitz, D (1986) Essay examination prompts and the teaching of academic writing, *English for Specific Purposes* 5 (2), 107–120.

Hosley, D (1978) Performance differences of foreign students on the TOEFL, *TESOL Quarterly* 12, 99–100.

Hubbard, C, Gilbert, S and Pidcock, J (2006) Assessment processes in speaking tests: a pilot verbal protocol study, *Research Notes* 24, Cambridge ESOL, 14–19.

Hughes, A (2003) *Testing for Language Teachers* (2nd ed), Cambridge: Cambridge University Press.

Hughes, R (2002) *Teaching and Researching Speaking*, London: Longman.

Ingham K and Thighe, D (2006) Issues with developing a test in LSP: the International Certificate in Financial English, *Research Notes* 25, Cambridge ESOL, 5–9.

Ingram, D (1984) *Report on the Formal Trialling of the Australian Second Language Proficiency Ratings (ASLPR)*, Canberra: Australian Government Publishing Service.

Ingram, D E and Wylie, E (1993) Assessing speaking proficiency in the international English language testing system, in Douglas, D and Chapelle, C (Eds) *A New Decade of Language Testing: Selected Papers from the Language Testing Research Colloquium*, Alexandria, VA: TESOL, Inc., 220–234.

International English Language Testing System (IELTS) (2009) *Official IELTS Practice Materials*, The British Council, IDP:IELTS Australia and UCLES.

International Language Testing Association (ILTA) (2000) *Code of Ethics*, retrieved March 10, 2011, from: http://www.iltaonline.com/index. php?option=com_content&task=view&id=57&Itemid=47

International Language Testing Association (ILTA) (2007) *Guidelines for Practice*, retrieved March 10, 2011, from: http://www.iltaonline.com/index. php?option=com_content&view=article&id=122&Itemid=133

Iwashita, N, Brown, A, McNamara, T and O'Hagan, S (2008) Assessed levels of second language speaking proficiency: How distinct? *Applied Linguistics* 29 (1), 24–49.

Iwashita, N, McNamara, T and Elder, C (2001) Can we predict task difficulty in an oral proficiency test? Exploring the potential of an information-processing approach to test design, *Language Learning* 51 (3), 401–436.

Jenkins, J (2006) The spread of English as an international language: a testing time for testers, *ELT Journal* 60, 51–60.

Joint Committee on Testing Practices (2004) *Code of Fair Testing Practices in Education*, Washington, DC: Joint Committee on Testing Practices.

Jones, E E and Gerard H B (1967) *Foundations of Social Psychology*, New York: Wiley.

Jones, N (2000a) Background to the validation of the ALTE Can Do Project and the revised Common European Framework, *Research Notes* 2, Cambridge ESOL, 11–13.

Jones, N (2000b) *IELTS Speaking – validation of new markscheme*, internal EFL Validation Report No 182.

Jones, N (2001) The ALTE Can Do Project and the role of measurement in constructing a proficiency framework, *Research Notes* 5, Cambridge ESOL, 5–8.

Jones, N (2002) Relating the ALTE Framework to the Common European Framework of Reference, in Alderson, J C (Ed.) *Case Studies in the Use of the Common European Framework*, Strasbourg: Council of Europe, 167–183.

Jones, N (2005) Raising the Languages Ladder: constructing a new framework for accrediting foreign language skills, *Research Notes* 19, Cambridge ESOL, 15–19.

Jones, N and Hirtzel, M (2001) The ALTE CAN DO Project, English Version: Articles and Can Do statements produced by the members of ALTE 1992–2002, Appendix D in Council of Europe (2001) *Common European Framework of Reference for Languages*, Cambridge: Cambridge University Press.

Jones, N and Saville, N (2009) European language policy: assessment, learning and the CEFR, *Annual Review of Applied Linguistics* 29, 51–63.

Kane, M T (1992) An argument-based approach to validity, *Psychological Bulletin* 112 (3), 527–535.

Kane, M, Crooks, T and Cohen, A (1999) Validating measures of performance, *Educational Measurement: Issues and Practice* 18 (2), 5–17.

Kellogg, R T (1996) A model of working memory in writing, in Levy, C M and Ransdell, S (Eds) *The Science of Writing*, Mahwah, NJ: Erlbaum, 57–71.

Kempen, G and Hoenkamp, E (1987) An incremental procedural grammar for sentence formulation, *Cognitive Science* 11, 201–258.

Kenworthy, J (1987) *Teaching Pronunciation*, London: Longman.

Kenyon, D and Malabonga, V (2001) Comparing examinee attitudes toward computer-assisted and other proficiency assessments, *Language Learning and Technology* 5 (2), 60–83.

Khalifa, H and ffrench, A (2009) Aligning Cambridge ESOL examinations to the CEFR: issues and practice, *Research Notes* 37, Cambridge ESOL, 10–14.

Khalifa, H and Weir, C J (2009) *Examining Reading: Research and Practice in Assessing Second Language Reading*, Studies in Language Testing 29, Cambridge: UCLES/Cambridge University Press.

Khalifa, H, ffrench, A and Salamoura, A (2010) Maintaining alignment to the CEFR: the FCE case study in Martyniuk, W (Ed.) *Aligning Tests with the CEFR: Reflections on Using the Council of Europe's Draft Manual*, Studies in Language Testing 33, Cambridge: UCLES/Cambridge University Press, 80–101.

Knoch, U (2009) Collaborating with ESP stakeholders in rating scale validation: the case of the ICAO rating scale, *Spaan Fellow Working Papers in Second or Foreign Language Assessment* 7, 21–46.

Knoch, U, Read, J and von Randow, J (2007) Re-training writing raters online: how does it compare with face-to-face training? *Assessing Writing* 12, 26–43.

Kormos, J (1999) Simulating conversations in oral proficiency assessment: a conversation analysis of role plays and non-scripted interviews in language exams, *Language Testing* 16 (2) 163–188.

Kormos, J (2006) *Speech Production and Second Language Acquisition*, New York: Erlbaum.

Kuiper, K (1996) *Smooth Talkers: The Linguistic Performance of Auctioneers and Sportscasters*, Mahwah, NJ: Erlbaum.

Kunnan, A J (1995) *Test Taker Characteristics and Test Performance: A Structural Modelling Approach*, Studies in Language Testing 2, Cambridge: UCLES/Cambridge University Press.

Kunnan, A J (2000) Fairness and justice for all, in Kunnan, A J (Ed.), *Fairness and Validation in Language Assessment, Selected Papers from the 19ᵗʰ LTRC, Orlando, Florida,* Studies in Language Testing 9, Cambridge: UCLES/Cambridge University Press, 1–14.

Kunnan, A (2003) The art of nonconversation by M Johnson, *The Modern Language Journal* 87, 338–340.

Kunnan, A J (2004) Test fairness, in Milanovic, M and Weir, C J (Eds) *European Language Testing in a Global Context*, Studies in Language Testing 18, Cambridge: UCLES/Cambridge University Press, 27–48.

Kunnan, A J (2008) Towards a model of test evaluation: using the Test Fairness and Test Context Frameworks, in Taylor, L and Weir, C J (Eds) *Multilingualism and Assessment: Achieving Transparency, Assuring Quality, Sustaining Diversity – Proceedings of the ALTE Berlin Conference May 2005*, Studies in Language Testing 27, Cambridge: UCLES/Cambridge University Press, 229–251.

Kutas, M, Federmeier, K D and Serreno, M I (1999) Current approaches to mapping language in electromagnetic space, in Brown, C and Hagoort, P (Eds) *Neurocognition of Language*, Oxford: Oxford University Press, 359–392.

Laufer, B (1997) What's in a word that makes it hard or easy? Intralexical factors affecting the difficulty of vocabulary acquisition, in McCarthy, M and Schmitt, N (Eds) *Vocabulary Description Acquisition and Pedagogy*, Cambridge: Cambridge University Press, 140–155.

Laufer, B and Nation, P (1999) A vocabulary-size test of controlled productive ability, *Language Testing* 16 (1), 33–51.

Laver, J (1994) *Principles of Phonetics*, Cambridge: Cambridge University Press.

Lazaraton, A (1992) The structural organization of a language interview: a conversation analytic perspective, *System* 20 (3), 373–386.

Lazaraton, A (1993) *The development of a quality control template based on the analysis of CASE transcriptions,* internal report commissioned for UCLES.

Lazaraton, A (1994) *An analysis of examiner behaviour in CAE paper 5 based on audiotaped transcriptions,* internal report commissioned for UCLES.

Lazaraton, A (1995) *An analysis of examiner behaviour in the KET Speaking component based on audiotaped transcriptions*, internal report commissioned for UCLES.

Lazaraton, A (1996a) *A comparative analysis of examiner behaviour in CAE Paper 5 and the KET Speaking component based on audiotaped transcriptions,* internal report commissioned for UCLES.

Lazaraton, A (1996b) Interlocutor support in oral proficiency interviews: the case of CASE, *Language Testing* 13 (2), 151–172.

Lazaraton, A (1998) *An analysis of differences in linguistic features of candidates at different levels of the IELTS speaking test*, internal report commissioned for UCLES.

Lazaraton, A (2002) *A Qualitative Approach to the Validation of Oral Language Tests,* Studies in Language Testing 14, Cambridge: UCLES/Cambridge University Press.

Lazaraton, A and Frantz, R (1997) *An analysis of the relationship between task features and candidate output for the revised FCE speaking examination,* internal report commissioned for UCLES.

Leet-Pellegrini, H M (1980) Conversational dominance as a function of gender and expertise, in Giles, H, Robinson, W P and Smith, P (Eds) *Language: Social Psychological Perspectives,* Elmsford, NY: Pergamon Press, 97–104.

Lennon, P (1984) Retelling a story in English as a second language, in Dechert, H W, Möhle, D and Raupach, M (Eds) *Second Language Productions,* Tübingen: Günter Narr, 50–68.

Lennon, P (1990) Investigating fluency in EFL: a quantitative approach, *Language Learning* 40, 387–417.

Levelt, W J M (1989) *Speaking,* Cambridge, MA: MIT Press.

Levelt, W J M (1999) Language production: a blueprint of the speaker, in Brown, C and Hagoort, P (Eds) *Neurocognition of Language,* Oxford: Oxford University Press, 83–122.

Linacre, M (1989) *Many-facet Rasch measurement,* Chicago: MESA Press.

Linacre, M (2006) Facets Rasch measurement computer program, Chicago: Winsteps.

Locke, C (1984) *The Influence of the Interviewer on Student Performance in Tests of Foreign Language Oral/Aural Skills,* unpublished MA Project, University of Reading.

Lowe, P (1978) Third rating of FSI interviews, in Clark, J L D (Ed.) *Direct Tests of Speaking Proficiency: Theory and Application,* Princeton, NJ: Educational Testing Service, 159–169.

Lowe, P (1988) The unassimilated history, in Lowe, P and Stansfield, CW (Eds) *Second Language Proficiency Assessment: Current Issues,* Englewood Cliffs, NJ: Prentice Hall Regents, 11–51.

Lowenberg, P (2000) Non-native varieties and issues of fairness in testing English as a world language, in Kunnan A J (Ed.) *Fairness and Validation in Language Assessment – Selected Papers from the 19th Language Testing Research Colloquium, Orlando, Florida,* Studies in Language Testing 9, Cambridge: UCLES/Cambridge University Press, 43–59.

Lu, Y (2003) Insights into the FCE speaking test, *Research Notes* 11, Cambridge ESOL, 15–18.

Lumley, T (2000) *The Process of the Assessment of Writing Performance: The Rater's Perspective,* unpublished PhD dissertation, Department of Linguistics and Applied Linguistics, The University of Melbourne.

Lumley, T and McNamara, T F (1995) Rater characteristics and rater bias: implications for training, *Language Testing* 12 (1), 54–71.

Lumley, T and O'Sullivan, B (2000) *The effect of speaker and topic variables on task-performance in a tape-mediated assessment of speaking,* paper presented at the 2nd Annual Asian Language Assessment Research Forum, The Hong Kong Polytechnic University, January 2000.

Lumley, T and O'Sullivan, B (2005) The effect of test taker gender, audience and topic on task performance in a tape mediated assessment of speaking, *Language Testing* 22 (4), 415–437.

Lunz, M E, Wright, B D and Linacre, J M (1990) Measuring the impact of judge severity on examination scores, *Applied Measurement in Education* 3 (4), 331–345.

Luoma, S (2004) *Assessing Speaking.* Cambridge: Cambridge University Press.

Lynch, B and McNamara, T F(1998) Using g theory and many-facet Rasch measurement in the development of performance assessments of the ESL speaking skills of immigrants, *Language Testing* 15, 158–180.

Martinez, R (2009) *Towards the inclusion of multiword items in vocabulary assessment,* paper presented at the Language Testing Forum, November 2009.

Martyniuk, W (Ed) (2010) *Aligning Tests with the CEFR: Reflections on Using the Council of Europe's Draft Manual,* Studies in Language Testing 33, Cambridge: UCLES/Cambridge University Press.

May, L (2009) Co-constructed in a paired Speaking test: the rater's perspective, *Language Testing* 26 (3), 397–421.

McCrum, R, Cran, W and MacNeil, R (1986) *The Story of English,* New York: Viking.

McNamara, T F (1990) *Assessing the Second Language Proficiency of Health Professionals,* unpublished PhD thesis, University of Melbourne.

McNamara, T F (1996) *Measuring Second Language Performance,* London: Longman.

McNamara, T F (1997a) Interaction in second language performance assessment: Whose performance? *Applied Linguistics* 16 (2), 159–179.

McNamara, T F (1997b) 'Interaction' in second language performance assessment, *Applied Linguistics* 18 (4), 446–65.

McNamara, T F (2000) *Language Testing,* Oxford: Oxford University Press.

McNamara, T F (2006) Validity in language testing: the challenge of Sam Messick's legacy, *Language Assessment Quarterly* 3 (1), 31–51.

McNamara, T and Lumley, T F (1997) The effect of interlocutor and assessment mode variables in overseas assessments of speaking skills in occupational settings, *Language Testing* 14 (2), 140–156.

McNamara, T F and Roever, C (2006) *Language Testing: The Social Dimension,* Malden, MA and Oxford: Blackwell.

Mehnert, U (1998) The effects of different length of time for planning on second language performance, *Studies in Second Language Acquisition* 20, 83–108.

Mehrens, W (1998) Consequences of assessment: what is the evidence? *Evaluation Policy Analysis Archives* 6 (13), 1–30, retrieved 10 March, 2011 from: http:// epaa.asu.edu/ojs/article/view/580/703

Meiron, B and Schick, L (2000) Raters, ratings and test performance: an exploratory study, in Kunnan A J (Ed.) *Fairness and Validation in Language Assessment – Selected Papers from the 19th Language Testing Research Colloquium, Orlando, Florida,* Studies in Language Testing 9, Cambridge: UCLES/Cambridge University Press, 153–176.

Merrylees, B and McDowell, C (1999) An investigation of speaking test reliability with particular reference to examiner attitude to the speaking test format and candidate/examiner discourse produced, in Tulloh, R (Ed.) *IELTS Research Reports, Volume 2,* Sydney: ELICOS Association Ltd, 1–35.

Merrylees, B and McDowell, C (1999/2007) A survey of examiner attitudes and behaviour in the IELTS oral interview, in Taylor, L and Falvey, P (Eds) *IELTS Collected Papers: Research in Speaking and Writing Assessment,* Studies in Language Testing 19, Cambridge: UCLES/Cambridge University Press, 142–182.

Messick, S A (1989) Validity, in Linn, R L (Ed.), *Educational Measurement* (3rd edn), Washington DC: The American Council on Education and the National Council on Measurement in Education, 13–103.

Messick, S (1996) Validity and washback in language testing, *Language Testing* 13 (4), 241–256.

Milanovic, M (2003) Series Editor's note, in Weir, C J and Milanovic, M (Eds) *Continuity and Innovation: Revising the Cambridge Proficiency in English Examination 1913–2002,* Studies in Language Testing 15, Cambridge: UCLES/Cambridge University Press, xv–xx.

Milanovic, M (2009) Cambridge ESOL and the CEFR, *Research Notes* 37, Cambridge ESOL, 2–5.

Milanovic, M and Saville, N (1992a) *Principles of good practice for UCLES examinations,* internal UCLES EFL paper.

Milanovic, M and Saville, N (1992b) UCLES participates in EC examination co-operative, *Research Notes* 1, UCLES EFL, 1–2.

Milanovic, M and Saville, N (1996a) *Considering the impact of Cambridge EFL examinations,* internal UCLES EFL paper.

Milanovic, M and Saville, N (1996b) Introduction, in Milanovic, M and Saville, N (Eds) *Performance Testing, Cognition, and Assessment: Selected Papers from the 15th Language Testing Research Colloquium, Cambridge and Arnhem,* Studies in Language Testing 3, Cambridge: UCLES/Cambridge University Press, 1–17.

Milanovic, M and Weir, C J (2010) Series Editors' note, in Martyniuk, W (Ed.) *Aligning Tests with the CEFR: Reflections on Using the Council of Europe's Draft Manual,* Studies in Language Testing 33, Cambridge: UCLES/ Cambridge University Press, viii–xx.

Milanovic, M, Saville, N and Shuhong, S (1996) A study of the decision-making behaviour of composition markers, in Milanovic, M and Saville, N (Eds) *Performance Testing, Cognition, and Assessment: Selected Papers from the 15th Language Testing Research Colloquium, Cambridge and Arnhem,* Studies in Language Testing 3, Cambridge: UCLES/Cambridge University Press, 92–114.

Milanovic, M, Saville, N, Pollitt, A and Cook, A (1996) Developing rating scales for case: theoretical concerns and analyses, in Cumming, A and Berwick, R (Eds) *Validation in Language Testing,* Clevedon: Multilingual Matters, 15–38.

Miller, G A (1951) *Language and Communication,* New York: McGraw Hill.

Ministry of Education (Italy) *Progetto Lingue in Communicazionedi Servizio,* September 1999 *[www.istruzione.it/argomenti/autonomia/documenti]*

Mislevy, R J (1992) *Linking Educational Assessments: Concepts, Issues, Methods, and Prospects,* Princeton, NJ: Educational Testing Service.

Mislevy, R J, Almond, R G and Lukas, J F (2003) *A Brief Introduction to Evidence-Centred Design,* Research Report RR-03-16, Princeton, NJ: Educational Testing Service.

Mislevy, R J, Steinberg, L S and Almond, R G (2002) Design and analysis in task-based language assessment (TBLA), *Language Testing* 19 (4), 477–496.

Mislevy, R J, Steinberg, L S and Almond, R G (2003) On the structure of educational assessment, *Measurement: Interdisciplinary Research and Perspective* 1 (1), 3–62.

Miyazaki, I (1976) *China's Examination Hell: The Civil Service Examinations of Imperial China,* (translated by Conrad Schirokauer), New York: Weatherhill. (http://www.questia.com/read/85640261)

Moore, T and Morton, J (1999) Authenticity in the IELTS Academic module writing test: a comparative study of Task 2 items and university assignments, in Tulloh, R (Ed.) *IELTS Research Reports, Volume 2,* Sydney: ELICOS Association Ltd, 64–106.

Morrow, K (1979) Communicative language testing: revolution or evolution? in Brumfit, C and Johnson, K (Eds) *The Communicative Approach to Language Teaching*, Oxford: Oxford University Press, 143–159.

Murray, S (2007) Broadening the cultural context of examination materials, *Research Notes* 27, Cambridge ESOL, 19–22.

Myford, C M and Wolfe, E W (2003) Detecting and measuring rater effects using multi-facet Rasch measurement: Part 1, *Journal of Applied Measurement* 4 (4), 386–422.

Myford, C M and Wolfe, E W (2004) Detecting and measuring rater effects using multi-facet Rasch measurement: Part 2, *Journal of Applied Measurement* 5 (2), 189–227.

Nakatsuhara, F (2006) The impact of proficiency-level on conversational styles in paired speaking tests, *Research Notes* 25, Cambridge ESOL, 15–20.

Nakatsuhara, F (2009) *Conversational Styles in Group Oral Tests: How is the Conversation Co-constructed?* unpublished PhD thesis, University of Essex.

Nakatsuhara, F (forthcoming a) The relationship between test-takers' listening proficiency and their performance on the IELTS speaking test, in Taylor, L and Weir, C J (Eds) *IELTS Collected papers 2: Research in Reading and Listening Assessment,* Studies in Language Testing 34, Cambridge: UCLES/ Cambridge University Press.

Nakatsuhara, F (forthcoming b) *The Co-construction of Conversation in Group Oral Tests*, Frankfurt: Peter Lang.

North, B (1995) The development of a common framework scale of descriptors of language proficiency based on a theory of measurement, *System* 23 (4), 445–465.

North, B (2000) *The Development of a Common Framework Scale of Descriptors of Language Proficiency Based on a Theory of Measurement*, PhD thesis, Thames Valley University/New York: Peter Lang.

North, B (2006) *The Common European Framework of Reference: Development, Theoretical and Practical Issues*, paper presented at the symposium 'A New Direction in Foreign Language Education: The Potential of the Common European Framework of Reference for Languages', Osaka University of Foreign Studies, Japan, March 2006.

North, B (2008) The CEFR levels and descriptor scales, in Taylor, L and Weir, C J (Eds) *Multilingualism and Assessment: Achieving Transparency, Assuring Quality, Sustaining Diversity – Proceedings of the ALTE Berlin Conference, May 2005*, Studies in Language Testing 27, Cambridge: Cambridge University Press, 21–66.

North, B (2009) The educational and social impact of the CEFR, in Taylor, L and Weir, C J (Eds) *Language Testing Matters: Investigating the Wider Social and Educational Impact of Assessment – Proceedings of the ALTE Cambridge Conference, April 2008*, Studies in Language Testing 31, Cambridge: Cambridge University Press, 357–377.

North, B and Schneider, G (1998) Scaling descriptors for language proficiency scales, *Language Testing* 15 (2), 217–263.

Norton, B (1997) Language, identity, and the ownership of English, *TESOL Quarterly* 31 (3), 409–429.

Novakovic, N (2006) TKT – a year on, *Research Notes* 24, Cambridge ESOL, 22–24.

Odunze, O J (1982) *Test of English as a Foreign Language and First Year GPA of Nigerian Students*, unpublished PhD dissertation, University of Missouri-Columbia.

Ortega, L (1999) Planning and focus on form in L2 oral performance, *Studies in Second Language Acquisition* 21, 109–148.

O'Keefe, A (2006a) *Certificate in Advanced English – Evaluation of modifications to speaking test*, internal report commissioned for Cambridge ESOL.

O'Keefe, A (2006b) *First Certificate in English - Evaluation of modifications to speaking test*, internal report commissioned for Cambridge ESOL.

O'Loughlin, K (2000) The impact of gender in the IELTS oral interview, in Tulloh, R (Ed.) *IELTS Research Reports, Volume 3*, Canberra: IDP: IELTS Australia and the British Council, 1–28.

O'Loughlin, K (2001) *The Equivalence of Direct and Semi-direct Speaking Tests*, Studies in Language Testing 13, Cambridge: UCLES/Cambridge University Press.

O'Loughlin, K (2002) The impact of gender in oral proficiency testing, *Language Testing* 19 (2) 169–192.

O'Sullivan, B (1995) *Oral Language Testing: Does the Age of the Interlocutor make a Difference?* unpublished MA dissertation, University of Reading.

O'Sullivan, B (2000a) Exploring gender and oral proficiency interview performance, *System* 28 (3): 373–386.

O'Sullivan, B (2000b) *Towards a Model of Performance in Oral Language Tests*, unpublished PhD thesis, University of Reading.

O'Sullivan, B (2002) Learner acquaintanceship and oral proficiency test pair-task performance, *Language Testing* 19 (3), 277–295.

O'Sullivan, B (2005) *A Practical Introduction to Using FACETS in Language Testing Research*, unpublished manuscript, Roehampton University.

O'Sullivan, B (2006) *Issues in Testing Business English: The Revision of the Cambridge Business English Certificates*, Studies in Language Testing 17, Cambridge: UCLES/Cambridge University Press.

O'Sullivan, B (2008) *Modelling Performance in Tests of Spoken Language*, Frankfurt: Peter Lang.

O'Sullivan, B and Lu, Y (2006) The impact on candidate language of examiner deviation from a set interlocutor frame in the IELTS speaking test, in McGovern, P and Walsh, S (Eds) *IELTS Research Reports, Volume 6*, IELTS Australia and British Council, 91–117.

O'Sullivan, B and Rignall, M (2007) Assessing the value of bias analysis feedback to raters for the IELTS Writing Module, in Taylor, L and Falvey, P (Eds) *IELTS Collected Papers: Research in Speaking and Writing Assessment*, Studies in Language Testing 19, Cambridge: UCLES/Cambridge University Press, 446–476.

O'Sullivan, B and Weir, C J (2002) *Research Issues in Testing Spoken Language*, internal report commissioned by Cambridge ESOL.

O'Sullivan, B, Weir, C and Saville, N (2002) Using observation checklists to validate speaking-test tasks, *Language Testing* 19 (1), 33–56.

Papajohn, D (1999) The effect of topic variation in performance testing: the case of the Chemistry TEACH test for international teaching assistants, *Language Testing* 16 (1), 52–81.

Perkins, K (1983) On the use of composition scoring techniques, objective measures, and objective tests to evaluate ESL writing ability, *TESOL Quarterly* 17 (4), 651–671.

Pollitt, A and Murray, N (1996) What raters really pay attention to, in Milanovic, M and Saville, N (Eds) *Performance Testing, Cognition, and Assessment*, Studies in Language Testing 3, Cambridge: UCLES/Cambridge University Press, 74–91.

Porter, D (1991a) Affective factors in language testing, in Alderson, J C and North, B (Eds) *Language Testing in the 1990s,* London: Macmillan and Modern English Publications in association with The British Council, 32–40.

Porter, D (1991b) Affective factors in the assessment of oral interaction: gender and status, in Arnivan, S (Ed.) *Current Developments in Language Testing,* Singapore: SEAMEO Regional Language Centre, Anthology Series 25, 92–102.

Porter, D and Shen Shu Hung (1991) Gender, status and style in the interview, *The Dolphin 21,* Aarhus University Press, 117–128.

Poulisse, N (1993) A theoretical account of lexical communication strategies, in Schreuder, R and Weltens, B (Eds) *The Bilingual Lexicon,* Amsterdam: Benjamins, 633–654.

Qian, D (2009) Comparing direct and semi-direct modes for speaking assessment: affective effects on test takers, *Language Assessment Quarterly* 6 (2), 113–125.

Read, J (2005) Applying lexical statistics to the IELTS speaking test, *Research Notes* 20, Cambridge ESOL, 12–16.

Read, J and Nation, P (2006) An investigation of the lexical dimension of the IELTS Speaking Test, in McGovern, P and Walsh, S (Eds) *IELTS Research Reports, Volume 6,* IELTS Australia and British Council, 207–231.

Roach, J O (1945) *Some Problems of Oral Examinations in Modern Languages: An Experimental Approach Based on the Cambridge Examinations in English for Foreign Students, Being a Report Circulated to Oral Examiners and Local Examiners for Those Examinations,* Cambridge: University of Cambridge Local Examinations Syndicate.

Roberts, B and Kirsner, K (2000) Temporal cycles in speech production, *Language and Cognitive Processes* 15, 129–157.

Robinson, P (2003) Attention and memory during SLA, in Doughty, C J and Long, M H (Eds) *Handbook of Second Language Acquisition,* Oxford: Blackwell, 631–671.

Roelofs, A (1997) The WEAVER model of word-form encoding in speech production, *Cognition* 64, 249–284.

Rose, D (2010) Setting the standard: quality management for language test providers, *Research Notes* 39, Cambridge ESOL, 2–7.

Ross, S and Berwick, R (1992) The discourse of accommodation in oral proficiency interviews, *Studies in Second Language Acquisition* 14 (2), 159–176.

Rubenbauer, F (2009) *Linguistics and Flight Safety: Aspects of Oral English Communication in Aviation,* Aachen: Shaker.

Savignon, S (2005) Communicative language teaching: strategies and goals, in Hinkel, E (Ed.) *Handbook of Research in Second Language Teaching and Learning,* Mahwah, New Jersey: Lawrence Erlbaum Associates, 635–651.

Saville, N (2003) The process of test development and revision within UCLES EFL, in Weir, C J and Milanovic, M (Eds) *Continuity and Innovation: Revising the Cambridge Proficiency in English Examination 1913–2002,* Studies in Language Testing 15, Cambridge: UCLES/Cambridge University Press, 57–120.

Saville, N (2004) *The ESOL Test Development and Validation Strategy,* internal discussion paper for UCLES.

Saville, N (2009) *Developing a Model for Investigating the Impact of Language Assessment within Educational Contexts by a Public Exam Provider,* unpublished PhD thesis, University of Bedfordshire.

Saville, N (2010) Auditing the quality profile: from code of practice to standards, *Research Notes* 39, Cambridge ESOL, 24–28.

Saville, N (forthcoming) Quality management in test production and administration, in Fulcher, G and Davidson, F (Eds) *The Routledge Handbook of Language Testing*, London and New York: Routledge.

Saville, N and Hargreaves, P (1999) Assessing speaking in the revised FCE, *ELT Journal* 53 (1), 42–51.

Saville, N and Hawkey, R (2004) The IELTS Impact Study: investigating washback on teaching materials, in Cheng, L, Watanabe, Y and Curtis, A (Eds), *Washback in Language Testing: Research Contexts and Methods*, London, Lawrence Erlbaum Associates, 73–96.

Saville, N and O'Sullivan, B (2000) Using observation checklists to validate speaking test tasks, *Research Notes* 2, Cambridge ESOL, 16–17.

Schmidt, R (1992) Psychological mechanisms underlying second language fluency, *Studies in Second Language Acquisition* 14, 357–385.

Schmitt, N (2000) *Vocabulary in Language Teaching,* Cambridge: Cambridge University Press.

Schmitt, N (2005) Lexical analysis of input prompts and examinee output of Cambridge ESOL Main Suite writing tests, internal report commissioned by Cambridge ESOL.

Schmitt, N (2009) Lexical analysis of input prompts and examinee output of Cambridge ESOL Main Suite speaking tests, internal report commissioned by Cambridge ESOL.

Schmitt, N, Schmitt, D, and Clapham, C (2001) Developing and exploring the behaviour of two new versions of the Vocabulary Levels Test, *Language Testing* 18 (1), 55–88.

Schneider, W and Schiffrin, R M (1977) Controlled and automatic information processing 1: Detection, search and attention, *Psychological Review* 84, 1–66.

Seedhouse, P and Egbert, M (2006) The interactional organisation of the IELTS Speaking test, in McGovern, P and Walsh, S (Eds) *IELTS Research Reports, Volume 6*, IELTS Australia and British Council, 161–205.

Shaw, S D (2002) IELTS writing: revising assessment criteria and scales (phase 1), *Research Notes* 9, Cambridge ESOL, 16–18.

Shaw, S D and Weir, C J (2007) *Examining Writing: Research and Practice in Assessing Second Language Writing,* Studies in Language Testing 26, Cambridge: UCLES/Cambridge University Press.

Shohamy, E (1990) Discourse analysis in language testing, *Annual Review of Applied Linguistics* 11, 115–31.

Shohamy, E (1994) The validity of direct versus semi-direct oral tests, *Language Testing* 11, 99–123.

Shohamy, E (1996) Competence and performance in language testing, in Brown, G, Malmkjaer, K and Williams, J (Eds) *Performance and Competence in Second Language Acquisition*, Cambridge: Cambridge University Press, 138–151.

Shohamy, E (1997) Testing methods, testing consequences: Are they ethical? Are they fair?, *Language Testing* 14 (3), 340–349.

Shohamy, E (2001) *The Power of Tests: A Critical Perspective on the Uses of Language Tests,* Harlow: Pearson Education.

Shohamy, E (2008) Introduction to Volume 7: Language Testing and Assessment, in Shohamy, E and Hornberger, N (Eds) *Encyclopedia of Language and Education (2nd edition) – Language Testing and Assessment, Volume 7*, New York: Springer Science+Business Media LLC, xiii–xxii.

Shohamy, E, Donitsa-Schmidt S, and Ferman, I (1996) Test impact revisited: washback effect over time, *Language Testing* 13 (3), 298–317.

Sireci, S G, Li, S, and Scarpati, S (2003) The effects of test accommodations on test performance: a review of the literature, *Center for Educational Assessment Research Report No. 485*, Amherst, MA: School of Education, University of Massachusetts Amherst.

Skehan, P (1996) A framework for the implementation of task based instruction, *Applied Linguistics* 17, 38–62.

Skehan, P (1998) *A Cognitive Approach to Language Learning*, Oxford: Oxford University Press.

Skehan, P (2001) Tasks and language performance assessment, in Bygate, M, Skehan, P and Swain, M (Eds) *Researching Pedagogic Tasks*, London: Longman, 167–185.

Skehan, P and Foster, P (1997) The influence of planning and post-task activities on accuracy and complexity in task based learning, *Language Teaching Research* 1 (3), 185–211.

Skehan, P and Foster, P (1999) The influence of task structure and processing conditions on narrative retellings, *Language Learning* 49 (1), 93–120.

Smith, J (1989) Topic and variation in ITA oral proficiency, *English for Specific Purposes* 8, 155–168.

Smith, L E and Nelson, C L (1985) International intelligibility of English: directions and resources, *World Englishes* 4, 333–342.

Spolsky, B (1981) Some ethical questions about language testing, in Klein-Braley, C and Stevenson, D (Eds) *Practice and Problems in Language Testing*, Frankfurt am Main: Verlag Peter D Lang, 5–30.

Spolsky, B (1989) Communicative competence, language proficiency, and beyond, *Applied Linguistics* 10 (2), 138–156.

Spolsky (1990) Oral examinations: an historical note, *Language Testing* 7 (2), 158–173.

Spolsky, B (1995) *Measured Words*, Oxford: Oxford University Press.

Spolsky, B (2008) Introduction – *Language Testing* at 25: Maturity and responsibility? *Language Testing* 25 (3), 297–305.

Spratt, M (2005) Washback and the classroom: the implications for teaching and learning of studies of washback from exams, *Language Teaching Research* 9, 1, 5–29.

Stahl, J A and Lunz, M E (1991) *Judge performance reports: Media and message*, paper presented at the annual meeting of the American Educational Research Association, San Francisco, CA.

Stansfield, C W (1990) An evaluation of simulated oral proficiency interviews as measures of spoken language proficiency, in Alatis, J E (Ed.) *Linguistics, Language Teaching and Language Acquisition: the Interdependence of Theory, Practice and Research*, Washington, DC: Georgetown University Press, 228–34.

Stansfield, C and Kenyon, D (1992) Research on the comparability of the Oral Proficiency Interview and the Simulated Oral Proficiency Interview, *System* 20 (3), 347–364.

Stevens, B (2004) A common solution to a common European challenge, *Research Notes* 17, Cambridge ESOL, 2–6.

SurveyLang (2008) *Inception Report for the European Survey on Language Competence*, submitted to Directorate General Education and Culture of the European Commission.

Suter, R W (1976) Predictors of pronunciation accuracy in second language learning, *Language Learning* 26 (2), 233–253.

Swain, M (2001) Examining dialogue: another approach to content specification and to validating inferences drawn from test scores, *Language Testing* 18 (3), 275–302.

Sweet, H (1899) *The Practical Study of Languages: A Guide for Teachers and Learners*, London: Dent.

Swinton, S S and Powers, D E (1980) *Factor Analysis of the Test of English as a Foreign Language for Several Language Groups,* TOEFL Research Report No. 6, Princeton, NJ: Educational Testing Service.

Tan, S H (1990) The role of prior knowledge and language proficiency as predictors of reading comprehension among undergraduates, in de Jong, J H A L and Stevenson, D K (Eds) *Individualising the Assessment of Language Abilities,* Clevedon PA: Multilingual Matters.

Taylor, L (1999a) *Study of quantitative differences between CPE individual and paired speaking tests*, internal UCLES EFL report.

Taylor, L (1999b) *Constituency matters: responsibilities and relationships in our testing community*, paper delivered to the Language Testing Forum, University of Edinburgh, 19–21 November.

Taylor, L (2000a) Stakeholders in language testing, *Research Notes* 2, Cambridge ESOL, 2–4.

Taylor, L (2000b) Investigating the paired speaking test format, *Research Notes* 2, Cambridge ESOL, 14–15.

Taylor, L (2001a) Revising the IELTS Speaking test, *Research Notes* 4, Cambridge ESOL, 9–12.

Taylor, L (2001b) Revising the IELTS speaking test: developments in test format and task design, *Research Notes* 5, Cambridge ESOL, 2–5.

Taylor, L (2001c) Revising the IELTS speaking test: retraining IELTS examiners worldwide, *Research Notes* 6, Cambridge ESOL, 9–11.

Taylor, L (2003) The Cambridge approach to speaking assessment, *Research Notes* 13, Cambridge ESOL, 2–4.

Taylor, L (2004a) Issues of test comparability, *Research Notes* 15, Cambridge ESOL, 2–5.

Taylor, L (2004b) IELTS, Cambridge ESOL examinations and the Common European Framework, *Research Notes* 18, Cambridge ESOL, 2–3.

Taylor, L (2006) The changing landscape of English: implications for assessment, *ELT Journal* 60 (1), Oxford: Oxford University Press, 51–60.

Taylor, L (2007) Introduction, in Taylor, L and Falvey P (Eds) *IELTS Collected Papers: Research in Speaking and Writing Assessment*, Studies in Language testing 19, Cambridge: UCLES/Cambridge University Press, 1–34.

Taylor, L (2008) Language varieties and their implications for testing and assessment, in Taylor, L and Weir, C J (Eds) *Multilingualism and Assessment: Achieving Transparency, Assuring Quality, Sustaining Diversity – Proceedings of the ALTE Berlin Conference, May 2005*, Studies in Language Testing 27, Cambridge: UCLES/Cambridge University Press, 276–295.

Taylor, L (2009a) Developing assessment literacy, *Annual Review of Applied Linguistics* 29 (1), 21–36.

Taylor, L (2009b) Setting language standards for teaching and assessment: a matter of principle, politics or prejudice? in Taylor, L and Weir, C J (Eds) *Language Testing Matters: Investigating the Wider Social and Educational Impact of Assessment – Proceedings of the ALTE Cambridge Conference, April 2008*, Studies in Language Testing 31, Cambridge: UCLES/Cambridge University Press, 139–157.

Taylor, L and Barker, F (2008) Using corpora for language assessment, in Shohamy, E and Hornberger, N (Eds) *Encyclopedia of Language and*

Education (2nd edition) – Language Testing and Assessment, Volume 7, New York: Springer Science+Business Media LLC, 241–254.

Taylor, L and Falvey, P (Eds) (2007) *IELTS Collected Papers: Research in Speaking and Writing Assessment,* Studies in Language Testing Series 19, Cambridge: UCLES/Cambridge University Press.

Taylor, L and Gutteridge, M (2003) Responding to diversity: providing tests for language learners with disabilities, *Research Notes* 11, Cambridge ESOL, 2–4.

Taylor, L and Jones, N (2006) Cambridge ESOL exams and the Common European Framework of Reference (CEFR), *Research Notes* 24, Cambridge ESOL, 2–5.

Taylor, L and Shaw, S (2002) CELS Speaking: test development and validation activity, *Research Notes* 9, Cambridge ESOL, 13–15.

Taylor, L and Weir (2008) (Eds) *Multilingualism and Assessment: Achieving Transparency, Assuring Quality, Sustaining Diversity – Proceedings of the ALTE Berlin Conference May 2005*, Studies in Language Testing 27, Cambridge University Press.

Taylor, L and Weir (2009) (Eds) *Language Testing Matter Investigating the wider Social and Educational Impact A Assessment – Proceedings of the ALTE Cambridge Conference, April 2008*, Studies in Language Testing 31, Cambridge:UCLES/Cambridge University Press.

Taylor, L and Wigglesworth, G (2009) Are two heads better than one? Pair work in L2 assessment contexts, *Language Testing* 26 (3), 325–339.

Thighe, D (2006) Placing the International Legal English Certificate on the CEFR, *Research Notes* 24, Cambridge ESOL, 5–7.

Thompson, S, Blount, A and Thurlow, M (2002) *A summary of research on the effects of test accommodations: 1999 through 2001 (Technical Report 34).* Minneapolis, MN: University of Minnesota, National Center on Educational Outcomes. Retrieved 12 October, 2005, from http://education.umn.edu/ NCEO/OnlinePubs/Technical34.htm

Tonkyn, A (1998) *IELTS Rating Research Project – Interim Report*, internal report commissioned by UCLES EFL.

Tonkyn, A and Wilson, J (2004) Revising the IELTS speaking test, in Sheldon, L E (Ed.) *Directions for the Future*, Bern: Peter Lang, 191–203.

Toulmin, S E (1958) *The Uses of Argument*, Cambridge: Cambridge University Press.

Toulmin, S E (2003) *The Uses of Argument* (updated edn.), Cambridge: Cambridge University Press.

Towell, R and Hawkins, R (1994) *Approaches to Second Language Acquisition*, Clevedon: Multilingual Matters.

Twist, L and Lewis, K (2005) *An Investigation into the Use of Special Access Arrangements in the End of Key Stage 2 Statutory Assessments for Children with Special Educational and Assessment Needs*, National Council for Educational Research Funded Project.

University of Cambridge ESOL Examinations (2005) *CAE Handbook for Teachers*, Cambridge: University of Cambridge Local Examinations Syndicate (UCLES).

University of Cambridge ESOL Examinations (2006a) *CAE Item Writer Guidelines*, Cambridge: University of Cambridge Local Examinations Syndicate (UCLES).

University of Cambridge ESOL Examinations (2006b) *CPE Item Writer Guidelines,* Cambridge: University of Cambridge Local Examinations Syndicate (UCLES).

University of Cambridge ESOL Examinations (2006c) *FCE Item Writer Guidelines*, Cambridge: University of Cambridge Local Examinations Syndicate (UCLES).

University of Cambridge ESOL Examinations (2006d) *KET Item Writer Guidelines*, Cambridge: University of Cambridge Local Examinations Syndicate (UCLES).

University of Cambridge ESOL Examinations (2006e) *PET Item Writer Guidelines*, Cambridge: University of Cambridge Local Examinations Syndicate (UCLES).

University of Cambridge ESOL Examinations (2007a) *First Certificate in English Handbook for Teachers*, Cambridge: University of Cambridge Local Examinations Syndicate (UCLES).

University of Cambridge ESOL Examinations (2007b) *Preliminary English Test*, Cambridge: University of Cambridge Local Examinations Syndicate (UCLES).

University of Cambridge ESOL Examinations (2008a) *BEC Handbook for Teachers*, Cambridge: University of Cambridge Local Examinations Syndicate (UCLES).

University of Cambridge ESOL Examinations (2008b) *Certificate in Advanced English Handbook for Teachers*, Cambridge: University of Cambridge Local Examinations Syndicate (UCLES).

University of Cambridge ESOL Examinations (2008c) *Certificate of Proficiency in English Handbook for Teachers*, Cambridge: University of Cambridge Local Examinations Syndicate (UCLES).

University of Cambridge ESOL Examinations (2008b/d) *FCE Handbook for Teachers*, Cambridge: University of Cambridge Local Examinations Syndicate (UCLES).

University of Cambridge ESOL Examinations (2008e) *Instructions to Oral Examiners*, Cambridge: University of Cambridge Local Examinations Syndicate (UCLES).

University of Cambridge ESOL Examinations (2008c/f) *Item Writer Guidelines: Upper Main Suite*, Cambridge: University of Cambridge Local Examinations Syndicate (UCLES).

University of Cambridge ESOL Examinations (2008g) *Key English Test Handbook for Teachers*, Cambridge: University of Cambridge Local Examinations Syndicate (UCLES).

University of Cambridge ESOL Examinations (2008h) *Vocabulary List Key English Test (KET)*, Cambridge: Cambridge University Press.

University of Cambridge ESOL Examinations (2008i) *Vocabulary List Preliminary English Test (PET)*, Cambridge: Cambridge University Press.

University of Cambridge ESOL Examinations (2009) *Professional Support Leader Handbook*, Cambridge: University of Cambridge Local Examinations Syndicate (UCLES).

University of Cambridge ESOL Examinations (2010a) *Guidelines for Oral Examiners*, Cambridge: University of Cambridge Local Examinations Syndicate (UCLES).

University of Cambridge ESOL Examinations (2010b) *KET, PET, FCE, CAE and CPE Speaking Tests: Instructions to Speaking Examiners*, Cambridge: University of Cambridge Local Examinations Syndicate (UCLES).

University of Cambridge Local Examinations Syndicate (UCLES) (1933) *Regulations for the Certificate of Proficiency in English*, Cambridge: University of Cambridge Local Examinations Syndicate.

University of Cambridge Local Examinations Syndicate (UCLES) (1943)
Cambridge Examinations in English for Foreign Student Survey for 1943,
Cambridge: University of Cambridge Local Examinations Syndicate.

University of Cambridge Local Examinations Syndicate (UCLES) (1947)
*Regulations for the Certificate of Proficiency in English and the Lower
Certificate in English,* Cambridge: University of Cambridge Local
Examinations Syndicate.

University of Cambridge Local Examinations Syndicate (UCLES) (1958)
Instructions to Oral Examiners, Cambridge: University of Cambridge Local
Examinations Syndicate.

University of Cambridge Local Examinations Syndicate (UCLES) (1973)
Cambridge Examinations in English: Changes of Syllabus in 1975, Cambridge:
University of Cambridge Local Examinations Syndicate.

Upshur, J A and Turner, C E (1995) Constructing rating scales for second
language tests, *ELT Journal* 49, 3–12.

Upshur, J A and Turner, C E (1999) Systematic effects in the rating of second-
language speaking ability: test method and learner discourse, *Language
Testing* 16 (1), 82–111.

Urquhart A H (1984) The effect of rhetorical ordering on readability, in
Alderson, J C and Urquhart, A H (Eds) *Reading in a Foreign Language,*
London: Longman, 160–175.

Vahapassi, A (1982) On the specification of the domain of school writing,
in Purves, A C and Takala, S (Eds) *An International Perspective on the
Evaluation of Written Composition,* Oxford: Pergamon, 265–289.

Van Ek, J and Trim, J (1998a) *Threshold 1990,* Cambridge: Cambridge
University Press.

Van Ek, J and Trim, J (1998b) *Waystage 1990,* Cambridge: Cambridge
University Press.

Van Ek, J and Trim, J (2001) *Vantage,* Cambridge: Cambridge University Press.

Van Hest, E (1996) *Self-repair in L1 and L2 Production,* Tilburg: Tilburg
University Press.

van Lier, L (1989) Reeling, writhing, drawling, stretching and fainting in
coils: oral proficiency interviews as conversations, *TESOL Quarterly* 23,
480–508.

Van Moere, A (2006) Validity evidence in a university group oral test, *Language
Testing* 23 (4), 411–440.

Vidakovic, I and Barker, F (2010) Use of words and multi-word units in Skills for
Life Writing examinations, *Research Notes* 41, Cambridge ESOL, 7–14.

Vidakovic, I and Galaczi, E D (2009) ILEC Speaking: revising assessment criteria
and scales, *Research Notes* 35, Cambridge ESOL, 29–34.

Wall, D (2005) *The Impact of High-stakes Examinations on Classroom Teaching:
A Case Study using Insights from Testing and Innovation Theory,* Studies in
Language Testing 22, Cambridge: UCLES/Cambridge University Press.

Wall, D and Horak, T (2006) *The Impact of Changes in the TOEFL®
Examination on Teaching and Learning in Central and Eastern Europe: Phase
1, The Baseline Study,* RR-06-18 TOEFL-MS-34, Princeton, NJ: Educational
Testing Service.

Wall, D and Horak, T (2008) *The Impact of Changes in the TOEFL Examination
on Teaching and Learning in Central and Eastern Europe: Phase 2. Coping with
Change,* TOEFL iBT Research Series Report No. TOEFL iBT-05, Princeton,
NJ: Educational Testing Service.

Watanabe, Y (2004) Methodology in washback studies, in Cheng, L, Watanabe,

Y and Curtis, A (Eds) *Washback in Language Testing: Research Contexts and Methods,* London, Lawrence Erlbaum Associates, 19–36.

Watts, A (2008) Cambridge Local Examinations 1858–1945, in Raban, S (Ed.) *Examining the World: A History of the University of Cambridge Local Examinations Syndicate*, Cambridge: Cambridge University Press, 36–70.

Weigle, S C (1994a) Effects of training on raters of ESL compositions, *Language Testing* 11 (2), 197–223.

Weigle, S C (1994b) *Using FACETS to model rater training effects*, paper presented at the 16th annual Language Testing Research Colloquium, Washington DC, March.

Weigle, S C (1998) Using facets to model rater training effects, *Language Testing* 15, 263–287.

Weigle, S C (2002) *Assessing Writing,* Cambridge: Cambridge University Press.

Weir, C J (1983) *Identifying the Language Problems of Overseas Students in Tertiary Education in the United Kingdom*, unpublished PhD thesis, University of London.

Weir, C J (1990) *Communicative Language Testing,* New York: Prentice Hall.

Weir, C J (1993) *Understanding and Developing Language Tests,* New York: Prentice Hall.

Weir, C J (2003) A survey of the history of the Certificate of Proficiency in English (CPE) in the twentieth century, in Weir, C J and Milanovic, M (Eds) *Continuity and Innovation: Revising the Cambridge Proficiency in English Examination 1913–2002*, Studies in Language Testing 15, Cambridge: UCLES/Cambridge University Press, 1–56.

Weir, C J (2005a) *Language Testing and Validation: An Evidence-Based Approach*, Basingstoke: Palgrave Macmillan.

Weir, C J (2005b) Limitations of the Council of Europe's Framework of reference (CEFR) in developing comparable examinations and tests, *Language Testing* 22 (3), 281–300.

Weir, C J and Milanovic, M (2003) (Eds) *Continuity and Innovation: Revising the Cambridge Proficiency in English Examination 1913–2002*, Studies in Language Testing 15, Cambridge: UCLES/Cambridge University Press.

Weir C J and O'Sullivan, B (in press) Language testing = validation, in O'Sullivan, B (Ed.) *Language Testing: Theories and Practices,* Basingstoke: Palgrave.

Weir, C J and Vidakovic, I (forthcoming) *Measured Constructs: A history of the constructs underlying English language examinations 1913–2012*, Studies in Language Testing, Cambridge: UCLES/Cambridge University Press.

Weir, C J and Wu, J (2006) Establishing test form and individual task comparability – a case study of a semi-direct speaking test, *Language Testing* 23 (2) 167–97.

Weir, C J, O'Sullivan, B and Horai, T (2006) Exploring difficulty in speaking tasks: an intra-task perspective, in McGovern, P and Walsh, S (Eds) *IELTS Research Reports, Volume 6*, IELTS Australia and British Council, 119–160.

Weir, C J, O'Sullivan, B, Yan J and Bax, S (2007) Does the computer make a difference? The reaction of candidates to a computer-based versus a traditional hand-written form of the IELTS Writing component: effects and impact, in McGovern, P and Walsh, S (Eds) *IELTS Research Reports, Volume 7*, British Council/IELTS Australia, 311–347.

Weir, C J, Hawkey, R, Green, A and Devi, S (2009) The cognitive processes underlying the academic construct as measured by IELTS, in Thompson, P

(Eds) *IELTS Research Reports, Volume 9*, British Council/IELTS Australia, 157–189.

Wheeldon, L R (2000) *Aspects of Language Production*, Hove: Psychology Press.

Widdowson, H (1978) *Teaching Language as Communication*, Oxford: Oxford University Press.

Wigglesworth, G and O'Loughlin, K (1993) An investigation into the comparability of direct and semi-direct versions of an oral interaction test in English, *Melbourne Papers in Language Testing* 2, 56–67.

Wigglesworth, G (1993) Exploring bias analysis as a tool for improving rater consistency in assessing oral interaction, *Language Testing* 10, 305–335.

Wigglesworth, G (1997) An investigation of planning time and proficiency level on oral test discourse, *Language Testing* 14, 85–106.

Wigglesworth, G (2001) Influences on performance in task-based oral assessments, in Bygate, M, Skehan, P and Swain, M (Eds) *Researching Pedagogic Tasks,* Harlow: Longman, 186–209.

Wigglesworth, G and O'Loughlin, K (1993) An investigation into the comparability of direct and semi-direct versions of an oral interaction test in English, *Melbourne Papers in Language Testing* 2, 56–67.

Wild, C L and Ramaswamy, R (2008) (Eds) *Improving Testing. Applying Process Tools and Techniques to Assure Quality*, London and New York: Routledge.

Wilson, K M (1982) *GMAT and GRE Aptitude Test Performance in Relation to Primary Language and Scores on TOEFL*, TOEFL Research Report No. 12, Princeton, NJ: Educational Testing Service.

Winetroube, S (1997) *The design of the teachers' attitude questionnaires*, internal report for UCLES.

Wolf, A (1995) *Competence-Based Assessment*, Bristol: Open University Press.

Wolfson, N (1989) *Perspectives: Sociolinguistics and TESOL,* Boston MA: Heinle and Heinle.

Wray, A (2002) *Formulaic Language and the Lexicon*, Cambridge: Cambridge University Press.

Wright, A (2008) A corpus-informed study of specificity in Financial English: the case of ICFE Reading, *Research Notes* 31, Cambridge ESOL, 16–22.

Wright, A (2010) Testing financial English: specificity and appropriacy of purpose in ICFE, *Research Notes* 42, Cambridge ESOL, 15.

Wyatt, T S and Roach, J O (1947) The examinations in English of the Cambridge University Local Syndicate, *ELT Journal* 1 (5), 125–130.

Young, R (1995) Conversational styles in language proficiency interviews, *Language Learning* 45 (1), 3–42.

Young, S and Milanovic, M (1992) Discourse variation in oral proficiency interviews, *Studies in Second Language Acquisition* 14 (4), 403–24.

Yue, W (1997) *An Investigation of textbook materials designed to prepare students for the IELTS Test: A study of washback*, unpublished Master thesis, Lancaster University.

Zimmerman, D H and West, C (1975) Sex roles, interruptions and silences in conversation, in Thorne, B and Henley, N (Eds) *Language and Sex: Difference and Dominance,* Rowley, MA: Newbury House, 105–129.

Zuengler, J (1993) Explaining NNS interactional behavior: the effect of conversational topic, in Kasper, G and Blum-Kulka, S (Eds) *Interlanguage Pragmatics*, Oxford: Oxford University Press, 184–195.

Zumbo, B (2007) Three generations of DIF analyses: considering where it has been, where it is now, and where it is going, *Language Assessment Quarterly* 4 (2), 223–233.

Author index

Subject index